Research on e-Learning and ICT in Education

Charalampos Karagiannidis • Panagiotis Politis
Ilias Karasavvidis

Editors

Research on e-Learning and ICT in Education

Technological, Pedagogical and Instructional Perspectives

 Springer

Editors
Charalampos Karagiannidis
Department of Special Education
University of Thessaly
Volos, Greece

Panagiotis Politis
Department of Primary Education
University of Thessaly
Volos, Greece

Ilias Karasavvidis
Department of Pre-School Education
University of Thessaly
Volos, Greece

ISBN 978-1-4614-6500-3   ISBN 978-1-4614-6501-0 (eBook)
DOI 10.1007/978-1-4614-6501-0
Springer New York Heidelberg Dordrecht London

Library of Congress Control Number: 2014940942

Research on e-Learning and ICT in Education

Information and Communication Technologies (ICT) have had a huge impact on contemporary society, fundamentally changing the way that we communicate, work, and entertain. Education is one of the fields where ICT applications have been used extensively over the years.

In the early days of computers, educators saw the potential of *digital* material to improve education, at least from a management and economic point of view: digital content can be easily managed and distributed to large groups of learners. With the rapid evolution of computers (with increased processing power, screen displays, and usability) digital learning materials offered additional affordances over "traditional" print materials that can significantly improve the *quality* of education such as multimedia (i.e., multiple representations of the learning material), hypermedia (i.e., non-serial access to the learning material), and interactivity (i.e., active engagement with the learning material). This gave birth to a whole new series of initiatives around the world from ministries, educational organizations, companies, etc., who developed digital learning resources and educational software.

With the advent of the Internet and the web, educators realized the tremendous potential for distributing the digital learning materials and for supporting new forms of web-based learning. This resulted in the development of *e-Learning* systems, which mainly support the sharing of digital learning material and facilitate the communication between learners and educators. At the same time, lifelong learning emerged as a vital necessity since all citizens need to be educated throughout their lives in order to remain competitive in the knowledge-based economy. To meet these needs of supporting access to education and training to anyone, anytime, anyplace, the e-Learning industry has experienced rapid growth over the past decade becoming the second largest industry evolving around the Internet and the web (second only to the e-Health industry).

In this context, the field of ICT in Education and e-Learning in particular has attracted increasing research interest worldwide during the past decades. This research is constantly evolving, especially since technology itself is also evolving at rapid pace and new devices, solutions, and practices are becoming increasingly available. This extensive research interest in the potential of technology to support learning has led to a considerable body of knowledge. Still, many issues remain open such as:

- How can ICT improve learning in preschool and primary education settings?
- How can it improve teaching of programming?
- How can the new Web 2.0 tools support learning in different educational settings?
- How can technology be used to support learning in museums and other cultural institutions?
- How can teachers use ICT to improve teaching and learning practices?

This volume aims to contribute to the literature in ICT in Education and e-Learning by addressing several core issues. The Volume includes 19 chapters which cover a wide variety of topics.

- The first part includes three chapters which attempt to situate ICT in the broader educational context. Underwood questions why digital technology has penetrated our lives so much, but has failed to make an impact in the classroom. *Mikropoulos, Sampson, Nikopoulos,* and *Pintelas* explore the evolution of educational technology through a bibliometric study. *Apostolopoulou, Panagiotakopoulos,* and *Karatrantou* conclude this part through an investigation of the learning theories underlying the development of educational applications for supporting teaching and learning of Mathematics, Physics, and Chemistry in Secondary Education.
- The second part includes three chapters which focus on ICT use in preschool and primary school settings. *Nikolopoulou* investigates how educational software is used in kindergartens. *Zaranis* examines how ICT can facilitate first graders' Geometry concepts. *Halki* and *Politis* investigate how educational software affects the learning outcomes of primary school students in high level skills of critical thinking and programming.
- The third part includes two chapters which address the teaching of programming concepts through ICT. *Malliarakis, Satratzemi,* and *Xinogalos* investigate teaching of programming through educational games. *Misirli* and *Komis* also target programming through robotics in the context of early childhood education.
- The fourth part includes three chapters which investigate how Web 2.0 technologies can affect education. *Eteokleous-Grigoriou* and *Photiou* investigate how blogs can be integrated in primary education. *Altanopoulou, Katsanos,* and *Tselios* investigate the effectiveness of Wikis in undergraduate education. *Kazanidis, Valsamidis, Kontogiannis,* and *Karakos* address the evaluation of courseware at the exams, usage, and content level.
- The fifth part includes two chapters which explore technology-based learning in museums and cultural institutions. *Yiannoutsou* and *Avouris* propose the use of digital games as a means to actively involve museum visitors to participate in the process of culture creation. *Nikonanou* and *Bounia* discuss digital applications created by museums and other cultural institutions.
- The sixth part includes three chapters which investigate how ICT affects Pre- and In-service teachers and their practices. *Karasavvidis* and *Kollias* examine the

ways in-service teachers integrate technology in their designs after an extensive Professional Development Training program. *Khaneboubi* and *Beauné* investigate the effect of ICT in French middle schools involved in a national endowment program on digital textbooks. *Vekiri* investigates the challenges and needs that should be addressed in teacher preparation for educational technology.

* Finally, the seventh part includes three chapters which address specialized topics in ICT in Education. *Tegos, Karakostas*, and *Demetriadis* address conversational pedagogical agents in individual and collaborative learning settings. *Apostolidis* and *Tsiatsos* present a prototype device that measures the anxiety level of a person by collecting bio-signals. *Chatzara, Karagiannidis, Mavropoulou*, and *Stamatis* discuss the potential value of using Digital Storytelling for teaching social skills to children with Autism Spectrum Disorders.

The following sections describe the parts and chapters in detail.

Part I: Situating ICT in Education

Underwood questions why digital technology is a ubiquitous tool outside of the classroom but is less well received within the classroom. She addresses the questions of what happens if we—the educators—fail to embrace technology, and if technology could take education out of the classroom and the hands of educators themselves. The chapter proposes that digital technologies can act as a change agent, a galvanizing force in a way that other previous innovations have failed to do. In doing so, we may need to "merge and evolve," i.e., educators allow ourselves to adapt and respond to the possibilities afforded by the technology and embrace innovation.

Mikropoulos, Sampson, Nikopoulos, and *Pintelas* explore the evolution of educational technology through a bibliometric study. They analyze the 849 papers presented in a specific series of educational technology conferences (HCICTE from 2000 to 2012), in order to study the e-Learning scientific community in Greece, to identify the evolution of salient topics, and the emergence of the trends in the field. Their analysis reveals that there is a wide involvement of researchers in e-Learning innovations at schools and less basic and applied technological research, indicating the need for a more balanced research in both theoretical issues and technological aspects.

Apostolopoulou, Panagiotakopoulos, and *Karatrantou* investigate the learning theories underlying the development of educational applications for supporting teaching and learning of Mathematics, Physics, and Chemistry in Secondary Education. They argue that it is important for teachers to be able to recognize the theories behind these educational applications, in order to utilize them in the most effective way. Their study involved 50 in-service teachers who answered a questionnaire, and 3 teacher trainers who were interviewed. The results showed that there is an increasing tendency towards the utilization of the Theories of Construction of knowledge, and that the perceptions of the in-service teachers are in agreement with the aims of the developers of the applications.

Part II: ICT in Preschool and Primary Education

Nikolopoulou investigates educational software use in kindergartens. She interviews 25 teachers from 17 Greek kindergartens to identify the educational software commonly used by children in the classes, how this software is used, and the main difficulties children face in the use of this educational software. Her analysis reveals that a variety of educational software is used in these classes, most of them being open-ended software aiming to advance language, reading, and writing skills. The main difficulties that children face with the use of this software are related to the requisite motor skills and the language readiness required for their operation.

Zaranis investigates how ICT can improve first grade students' basic geometry achievement, especially regarding circles and triangles. He employs the Realistic Mathematics Education (RME) and the van Hiele models, and compares it against the "traditional" teaching methodology. He experiments with two student groups involving 234 first graders, and concludes that teaching and learning through ICT is an interactive process for students at the first grade level and has a positive effect for learning Geometric concepts when employing RME and the van Hiele model.

Halki and *Politis* investigate the use of ICT for improving critical thinking and programming skills of primary school children. They experiment with two student groups, one using the Scratch educational programming language and the other educational games and experiential learning. They conclude that the two groups presented almost same results in most learning outcomes they examined. The differentiation referred only to debugging skills (which were higher for the group using the Scratch), and to cooperativeness and teamwork skills (which were higher for the group without ICT support).

Part III: ICT and Teaching Programming

Malliarakis, Satratzemi, and *Xinogalos* examine the teaching of programming through educational games. They offer a critical review of the most well-known educational games for teaching programming, which can guide the development of future applications. Their analysis is based on a framework which summarizes the functionality that should be supported by educational games for teaching programming. The proposed framework has been based on an analysis of 70 papers from the related literature.

Misirli and *Komis* address the teaching of programming for early childhood education through robotics. They propose a conceptual framework for designing educational scenarios that integrate programmable toys as a guide to teaching programming concepts. Their framework involves seven phases for designing educational scenarios, including identification of the teaching subject, identification of children's prior knowledge, determination of scenario goals, selection of ICT teaching materials, design of scenario activities, scenario assessment, and scenario documentation. Their framework has been tested and verified by 46 educators on 864 children between the ages of 4–6.

Part IV: Web 2.0 Tools and Learning

Eteokleous-Grigoriou and *Photiou* investigate the integration of Blogs as tools in primary education, and describe the development of a Community of Inquiry (CoI) within a blended learning environment developed through hybrid learning. They analyze the social, cognitive, and teaching presence within a CoI in a specific class, where students use a blog to achieve specific learning objectives. The results of the study reveal the development of a CoI through a blended learning environment and the potential of using blogs as tools to achieve specific learning objectives, and highlight the important role of the educator and lesson's design.

Altanopoulou, *Katsanos*, and *Tselios* investigate the effectiveness of a framed wiki-based learning activity. They report a study which involve 139 first year under-graduates who used Wikis to learn about Web 2.0 and its applications in the context of an introductory course. The study demonstrated significant improvement in learning outcomes, both for students with low and high initial performance. In addition, it was found that students benefited from the activity regardless of their role in the Wiki project. Furthermore, results showed that students with a higher number of logged Wiki actions had a significantly higher learning gain compared to those that were less active.

Kazanidis, *Valsamidis*, *Kontogiannis*, and *Karakos* propose a method which evaluates courseware at the exams, usage, and content level. It defines different measures and metrics for each level, and it uses data mining techniques, such as classification, clustering, association rule mining, and regression analysis, in order to discover possible dependencies of the e-learning data. The proposed method was successfully tested to e-learning data from a Greek University, and the results con-firmed the validity of the approach and showed a relationship among the compo-nents of the proposed three-level schema.

Part V: ICT for Learning in Museums

Yiannoutsou and *Avouris* analyze two different trends that have informed technology for learning in cultural institutions during recent years. The first one supports the information consumption metaphor where museums produce "information" in digital or other form for the visitor to consume, while the second one invites visitors to par-ticipate in the process of culture creation. They then discuss game design as an exam-ple of participatory activity and they identify its learning dimensions. They analyze the role of technology in providing a scaffold that can help museum audience to construct games which can function as "public artifacts" and can be added to the museum's assets, enhancing audience engagement and community building.

Nikonanou and *Bounia* present a qualitative evaluation study of digital applications created by Greek museums and other cultural institutions during the past few years. The study is based on contemporary theoretical approaches in the field of museum education and aims to explore the extent to which these approaches are taken into account when designing a digital application for museum education use. The research highlights that there is a growing interest in developing ICT applications on the part of the museums, but also that there are many possibilities regarding interactivity, active involvement, collaboration, and creative expression that are still open for consideration and exploitation by cultural institutions.

Part VI: ICT and Pre- and In-service Teacher Practices

Karasavvidis and *Kollias* aimed to bridge the knowledge gap of how specific teacher groups respond to in-service Professional Development Training (PDT) on ICT pedagogy. They examined how teachers' backgrounds influence their responses to an extensive PDT program. They report data from a multiple case study involving three in-service teachers who had constructivist teaching philosophies and high academic qualifications. The study inquired whether the teachers integrated technology in ways that supported or transformed their existing practices. The first study finding is that the teachers integrated technology in their designs in ways that supported their existing practices, closely following the dominant science education paradigm in Greece. The second study finding is that the teacher participants were very reluctant to consider other types of technology integration that would lead to more transformative teaching practices. The authors conclude that their results cast serious doubts on the potential of contemporary PDT programs to transform teaching practices through technology and discuss the implications of their work for future conceptualizations of PDT.

Khaneboubi and *Beauné* investigate the effect of ICT in four French middle schools involved in a national endowment program on digital textbooks. The analysis of two datasets collected in 2010 and 2012, involving 89 teachers, provides useful insights into the school dynamics in this context. The use of technologies by teachers in the classrooms seems to be determined by the quality of infrastructure and equipment reliability. Gender and seniority appear as discriminating factors in the perception of technologies' availability. And teachers in charge of pedagogical uses of ICT in each school are almost exclusively sought for technical support.

Vekiri investigates the challenges and needs that should be addressed in teacher preparation for educational technology. She presents a study which analyzed 30 preservice elementary school teachers' lesson plans, representing their first attempts to design a web-based lesson. The analysis focused on the types of activities they had designed, the characteristics of the web resources they had selected, and the scaffolding techniques they had planned to use to support their students. Study findings highlight that, in order to use the Internet productively and creatively, teachers need to develop complex forms of knowledge that require the integration of knowledge about technology, pedagogy, and content.

Part VII: ICT for Specialized Uses

Tegos, *Karakostas*, and *Demetriadis* address conversational pedagogical agents which can guide and scaffold student dialogue using natural language in both individual and collaborative learning settings. They present the results of an experimental collaborative learning activity exploring whether the different agent roles (peer or tutor) may affect the students' perceptions of the agent or their conversational style in their responses to it. The study findings provide valuable insights into how the different agent' appearance and communication styles can have an impact on the degree of formality in students' utterances.

Apostolidis and *Tsiatsos* present a prototype device that measures the anxiety level of a person by collecting bio-signals, namely Galvanic Skin Response and Photoplethysmography. They pilot-tested their device with 13 students, who suggested that the anxiety measurement may be useful to learning activities such as examinations and workshops, that they are willing to reuse these sensors in other academic activities, and that stress level awareness can motivate students to regulate themselves.

Chatzara, *Karagiannidis*, *Mavropoulou*, and *Stamatis* discuss the potential value of using Digital Storytelling for teaching social skills to children with Autism Spectrum Disorders. They present the DiSSA (Digital Structured Storytelling for Autism) tool, a software application for creating digital stories following a structured approach. The system is aimed to cater for the needs of students in the autistic spectrum, taking advantage of structured teaching in the design of the application. It accommodates user's performance data towards the learning outcomes and thereby provides feedback to other users (such as, teachers or parents) about children's progress. DiSSA has been pilot-tested with four pupils (7–11 years) with a formal diagnosis of mild autism, and has demonstrated to be successful in terms of user satisfaction and user task accomplishment.

We would like to express our deepest appreciation to a large number of people who helped us towards the publication of this Volume. First of all to the Hellenic ICT in Education Society who entrusted us with the organization of the HCICTE 2012 Conference and the editing of this volume. We would like to thank all the book contributors for submitting their work and for collaborating closely with us during the course of a very long reviewing and revision process. We extend our gratitude to all the colleagues who have significantly assisted in evaluating and improving the chapters featured in the present volume through their review comments. Finally, many thanks to Melissa James and Joseph Quatela from Springer US for their help and excellent collaboration.

Volos, Greece   Charalampos Karagiannidis
                                                        Panagiotis Politis
                                                        Ilias Karasavvidis

Contents

Contributors

Panagiota Altanopoulou Department of Educational Sciences and Early Childhood Education, University of Patras, Rio, Greece

Hippokratis Apostolidis Department of Informatics, Aristotle University of Thessaloniki, Thessaloniki, Greece

Dimitra Apostolopoulou Department of Primary Education, University of Patras, Rio, Greece

Nikolaos Avouris Department of Electrical and Computer Engineering, University of Patras, Rio, Greece

Aurélie Beauné EDA Université Paris Descartes, Paris, France

Alexandra Bounia Department of Cultural Technology and Communication, University of the Aegean, Lesvos, Greece

Konstantina Chatzara Department of Special Education, University of Thessaly, Volos, Greece

Stavros Demetriadis Department of Informatics, Aristotle University of Thessaloniki, Thessaloniki, Greece

Nikleia Eteokleous-Grigoriou Department of Primary Education, Frederick University, Nicosia, Cyprus

Panagiota Halki Department of Primary Education, University of Ioannina, Ioannina, Greece

Tassos A. Mikropoulos Department of Primary Education, University of Ioannina, Ioannina, Greece

Charalampos Karagiannidis Department of Special Education, University of Thessaly, Volos, Greece

Alexandros Karakos Department of Electrical and Computer Engineering, Democritus University of Thrace, Xanthi, Greece

Anastasios Karakostas Department of Informatics, Aristotle University of Thessaloniki, Thessaloniki, Greece

Ilias Karasavvidis Department of Preschool Education, University of Thessaly, Volos, Greece

Anthi Karatrantou Department of Primary Education, University of Patras, Rio, Greece

Christos Katsanos Hellenic Open University, Patras, Greece

Ioannis Kazanidis Department of Industrial Informatics, Eastern Macedonia and Thrace Institute of Technology, Kavala, Greece

Mehdi Khaneboubi UMR STEF (IFÉ-ENS Cachan), Cachan, France

Vassilis Kollias Department of Primary Education, University of Thessaly, Volos, Greece

Vassilis Komis Department of Educational Sciences and Early Childhood Education, University of Patras, Rio, Greece

Sotirios Kontogiannis Department of Business Administration, Technological Educational Institute of West Macedonia, Ioannina, Greece

Christos Malliarakis Department of Applied Informatics, University of Macedonia, Thessaloniki, Greece

Sofia Mavropoulou Department of Special Education, University of Thessaly, Volos, Greece

Anastasia Misirli Department of Educational Sciences and Early Childhood Education, University of Patras, Rio, Greece

Kleopatra Nikolopoulou Department of Early Childhood Education, National and Kapodistrian University of Athens, Athens, Greece

Niki Nikonanou Department of Preschool Education, University of Thessaly, Volos, Greece

Alexandros Nikopoulos Department of Primary Education, University of Ioannina, Ioannina, Greece

Christos Panagiotakopoulos Department of Primary Education, University of Patras, Rio, Greece

Stella Photiou Department of Primary Education, Frederick University, Nicosia, Cyprus

Panayiotis Pintelas Department of Mathematics, University of Patras, Rio, Greece

Panagiotis Politis Department of Primary Education, University of Thessaly, Volos, Greece

Demetrios G. Sampson Department of Digital Systems, University of Piraeus and CERTH-ITI, Piraeus, Greece

Maya Satratzemi Department of Informatics, University of Macedonia, Thessaloniki, Greece

Demosthenes Stamatis Department of Informatics, Alexander Technological Educational Institute of Thessaloniki, Thessaloniki, Greece

Panagiotis Stylianidis Department of Informatics, Aristotle University of Thessaloniki, Thessaloniki, Greece

Stergios Tegos Department of Informatics, Aristotle University of Thessaloniki, Thessaloniki, Greece

Nikolaos Tselios Department of Educational Sciences and Early Childhood Education, University of Patras, Rio, Greece

Thrasyvoulos Tsiatsos Department of Informatics, Aristotle University of Thessaloniki, Thessaloniki, Greece

Jean Underwood Division of Psychology, Nottingham Trent University, Nottingham, UK

Stavros Valsamidis Department of Industrial Informatics, Eastern Macedonia and Thrace Institute of Technology, Kavala, Greece

Ioanna Vekiri Independent Researcher, Thessaloniki, Greece

Stelios Xinogalos Department of Informatics, University of Macedonia, Thessaloniki, Greece

Nikoleta Yiannoutsou Department of Electrical and Computer Engineering, University of Patras, Rio, Greece

Nicholas Zaranis Department of Primary Education, University of Crete, Rethymnon, Greece

List of Reviewers

Charoula Angeli, University of Cyprus
Tharenos Bratitsis, University of Western Macedonia
Leontios Chatzileontiadis, Aristotle University of Thessaloniki
Anna Chronaki, University of Thessaly
Stavros Dimitriadis, Aristotle University of Thessaloniki
Maria Grigoriadou, National and Kapodistrian University of Athens
Nikos Fachantidis, University of Western Macedonia
Athanasios Jimoyiannis, University of Peloponnese
Achilleas Kameas, Hellenic Open University
Vassilis Kollias, University of Thessaly
Maria Kordaki, University of the Aegean
Dimitrios Koutsogiannis, Aristotle University of Thessaloniki
Panayiotis Michailidis, University of Crete
Anastasios Mikropoulos, University of Ioannina
Christos Panagiotakopoulos, University of Patras
Kyparisia Papanikolaou, School of Pedagogical and Technological Education
Marina Papastergiou, University of Thessaly
Demetrios Sampson, University of Piraeus & CERTH-ITI
Maya Satratzemi, University of Macedonia
Zacharoula Smyrnaiou, National and Kapodistrian University of Athens
Nikolaos Tselios, University of Patras
Trasyvoulos Tsiatsos, Aristotle University of Thessaloniki
Nikolaos Zaranis, University of Crete

Part I
Situating ICT in Education

Digital Technologies: An Effective Educational Change Agent?

Jean Underwood

Naturally Resistant

Although many in education would argue that we are in a constant state of flux the changes, irritating though they may be, are often superficial. As Papert (1993) has argued the education system is highly resistant to change. The proposition explored in this chapter is that digital technologies can act as a change agent, a galvanising force in a way that other previous innovations have failed to do so. This places high expectations on the use of the technology but can it deliver? There are still many who doubt the usefulness of such technologies in the classroom, yet we are very accepting of digital tools in our daily life. Why is this the case? While plotting a timeline of technological development, and even projecting into the future, is a relatively simple task, assessing the impact of those technological developments on teaching and learning is far more problematic. The underlying ambivalence to the educational use of technology makes future projections difficult, and at first sight the prospects are not encouraging.

A Brief History of Digital Technology

Learning technologies are not a recent idea although it is no easy matter to identify their inception; they are as old as written language itself (Westera, 2010). For a long time the slate and the chalkboard were the dominant educational technologies, but the twentieth century proved to be a century of rapid technological advance inside and outside of the classroom. First technologies such as film and radio were added

J. Underwood (✉)
Division of Psychology, Nottingham Trent University, Nottingham NG1 4BU, UK
e-mail: jean.underwood@ntu.ac.uk

C. Karagiannidis et al. (eds.), *Research on e-Learning and ICT*
in Education: Technological, Pedagogical and Instructional Perspectives,
DOI 10.1007/978-1-4614-6501-0_1, © Springer Science+Business Media New York 2014

to the teacher's toolbox, and then, towards the end of the last century, digital technologies first crept and then thrust themselves onto the educational scene. Digital technologies are different from previous technologies in a number of ways not least because they are in a constant state of rapid evolution. This is clearly illustrated by Apple's i-Phone. Just a few years ago Apple released this touchscreen 2G (second generation, that is, digital) mobile phone, which I purchased with pride. It was not just a phone of course; it came with Internet access, a camera, note pad and much more. It was a communication system and mini-office all rolled into one. Four years on and my i-Phone became a poor relation of its 3G cousin the i-Phone 3. As is the way of each new generation of such technologies, the i-Phone 3 was of course faster and had greater memory capacity and enhanced functionalities such video capture and streaming alongside the still image camera. However it too has been superceded by new generations of i-Phones. My first-generation i-Phone is not able to play the cult game "Angry Birds" nor does it allow me to access You-Tube clips or have face-to-face real-time conversations.

That such an iconic object as the original i-Phone became effectively obsolete in less than 4 years, and its successor in even less time than that, graphically illustrates the speed and nature of technology development, which, on the whole, have improved what already exists and also added new functionalities. These new functionalities have resulted in a rapid move towards the personalisation of content, where every user has his or her own custom distribution channel. However, although the technology has become more powerful, that is, it has more on-board memory, a more powerful central processing units (CPU), and most significantly wireless network access, we find activities such as playing "Angry Birds" or sending short video clips absorb all the additional power. This has resulted in a new industry supplying digital storage space in the "clouds". Large clusters of networked servers supply vast processing power and storage capacity at low cost removing the need for large personal data stores for your personal images or music files (Johnson, Levine, & Smith, 2009).

So the technology is faster, more powerful and has greater functionality at a reduced cost, and yet it still disappoints because we want more.

And the Impact of That Technology Is?

As technology has spread through our society new behaviours and new ways of working have emerged; for instance mobile phones have become indispensable to the operation of small independent businesses. This is how we now contact our local plumber or electrician (Crabtree & Roberts, 2003). Further it has become a ubiquitous tool of the young. In the UK over 90 % of all 11–21-year-olds had access to a mobile phone (Haste, 2005), and by 2006 49 % of 8–11-year-olds and 82 % of 12–15-year-olds had their own phones (OfCom, 2006). Moreover, 82 % of 8–11-year-olds and 93 % of 12–15-year-olds spent time texting. Texting has become such a widespread and valued activity among many young learners (c.f., Plester & Wood, 2009).

Typically 16–24-year-olds spend more time on their mobile phones and social networking sites than watching television (OfCom, 2010).

Other changes have been seismic shifts rather than modifications of behaviour. For example, few would have predicted the impact of technology on news reporting, an impact that has led to the rise of the citizen reporter. Armed with a camera phone anyone can be both reporter and editor of current events. What was once hidden is now exposed across the world on You-Tube, often before the official news networks. Such changes necessarily affect the structures of a society. The result is that institutions find themselves unable to handle key changes in the rhythms and patterns of emerging human behaviours, and so new or transformed institutions emerge. Thus the Iranian Government made a huge effort to block images and news reports of the violence following the 2009 elections, but there was still leakage of news (Palser, 2009). However in the USA political structure was transformed post the 2008 presidential elections, which were won and lost in cyberspace. The now US President Obama had three times as many supporters signed up on Facebook than his republican rival John McCain, and 500 million blog posts mentioned Obama compared to 150 mentioning McCain (Aronson, 2012). Obama managed to do what many politicians in the West have failed to, that is, engage a new generation in politics by using their preferred communication tools.

And the Impact on Education Is?

Learners of all ages are exhibiting new behaviours as a result of these ubiquitous high-functioning technologies. Changes may be relatively mundane, such as replacing the school satchel with a memory stick, or profound, as when learners seek out expertise beyond the traditional classroom or move from text to more visual modes of representation. For example we reported on two primary schools, both of which were linked to the same theatre group in order to write a play as part of the web play project (Underwood et al., 2005). While significant, these changes are not necessarily transformational, but it could be argued that given the formal framework of education such transformation may not be possible. Lowendahl (2009) argues that the education system has a history of resistance to change, a resistance born out of disappointment when the "hype cycle" of technology in education fails to deliver. This cycle which starts with a techno-romantic phase often leads to disillusionment when the technology fails to deliver nirvana. There is then a need to pass through to a slope of enlightenment, that is, to make a realistic assessment of what technology can and cannot do, before reaching a plateau of productivity when the technology actually delivers to realistic goals.

Both students and tutors have been shown to underuse many high-level functions such as the communication tools (Sclater, 2010), and teachers often find the more advanced functionalities difficult to customise (Severance, Hardin & Whyte, 2008). Our own research has shown that while there have been significant advances in educational technology they have not always brought about measurable shifts in user behaviour. A study of learning platform use in eight technically savvy English secondary schools (Underwood & Stiller, 2014) showed that while teachers' intentions to use the range of functions available to them on the learning platform varied from extensive to as little as possible, those expressing a desire to use the system creatively found themselves held back by mundane barriers associated with time, personal skills and curriculum demands. Innovative uses of blogs, wikis, and other tools remained aspirational at best even in these schools where technology innovation, at a surface level at least, was actively encouraged.

So while Lowendahl calls for more realism and less hype in technology innovation and acceptance, Westera (2010) argues that the main barrier to effective embedding of technology is a little too much realism. The computer has been used as a sensible teaching aid, quite useful for a specific subset of learning activities, but it has never challenged the educational system as a whole. Resnick (2006) picks up this argument by raising the following question: "Which is the odd one out: the television, the computer or the paintbrush?" He argues that the potential of digital technologies will not be realised until we think of them as modern equivalents of the paintbrush and not as televisions. That is, we need to start seeing computers not simply as information machines but also as a new medium for creative design and expression.

Although those of us who teach see ourselves as innovators, the truth is that change in education is very slow. Seymour Papert (1993) graphically depicted the immovability of education in his story about surgeons and teachers. He argued that a surgeon from a century ago would not recognise a modern operating room but while a teacher might be puzzled by some of the resources in the new classroom, he or she would nevertheless feel at home. Papert posed the question as to why, when so much has changed over the last century, there has not been a comparable change in the way we educate our children. It is not because new tools, the equivalent of the surgeon's heart monitor machine, do not exist. So is it because teachers are inherently resistant to change? While we are cautious professionals we are not Luddites,[1] entrenched opponents of change. The slow pace of change is more to do with need. Medical practice needed to change because people were dying, but traditional methods of teaching do result in children learning, so why are we in such a hurry to change?

So Why Change?

From Aviram and Talmi's (2005) point of view, the centrality of digital technologies in education is both assured and inevitable. That perceived inevitability is built on the assumption of the omnipresence of ICT in our everyday lives and the rise of the generation of digital natives (Prensky, 2001). Indeed Prensky argues that today's students are no longer the people our educational system was designed to teach.

---

[1] Luddites: Workers who violently resisted the introduction of new machinery into the textile industry in nineteenth-century England.

Teachers are told that they have to attract students' interest and attention (Simplicio, 2000), recognising that learners are growing up surrounded by video games, mobile phones and other digital media, all of which are leading to new learner expectations of an acceptable educational environment (Pedró, 2006). However, Watson (2001) queries the automatic link made between the everyday and educational uses of technology, as it does not take into account the fact that technology often fits uncomfortably with teachers' professional judgments. In support of Watson's analysis, the evidence shows that technologies that move teachers outside their comfort zone tend to have a slower take-up and high rejection rates. The conclusion from our own work is that positive impacts are more likely when linked to a teacher's existing pedagogical philosophy, hence the rapid acceptance of interactive whiteboards (IWB) compared to virtual learning (Underwood et al., 2010). Indeed half of the teachers we interviewed identified the IWB as their "must-have" technology. However, some teachers expressed unease with this position, for example stating "IWB and PowerPoint, sadly ....", acknowledging that there were other more exciting ways of using technology although they were not exploiting these opportunities themselves.

The discontinuity between teachers and technology may be more deep-seated than a clash with professional practice though. It may lie in the nature of those who choose to teach. For example, it is not age or sex but membership of the teaching profession that is the defining characteristic of low involvement with video games (Sandford, Uiksak, Facer & Rudd, 2006). Books are the preferred tool of this group as a whole. If teachers, as a group, are inherently low technology users compared to the general population, does this mean that there is a natural resistance to the embedding of technology into the educational processes and practices? While this rather negative portrayal of the teaching profession may be valid in some cases, our evidence of a decade of national research projects presents a more positive picture of a profession that is cautious but constructive in its approach to innovation.

Three Possible Ways Forward

It has long been argued that any good teaching system aligns the teaching method and assessment to the stated learning objectives (Lebrun, 2007). How do we achieve this alignment? There are broadly three strategic responses to the demands to go digital (Underwood & Dillon, 2011).

1. *Minimise the use of technology*: This approach minimises the demands on teachers and maintains the status quo. However, such a strategy raises very real issues of equality. Those learners with access to technology outside of the school will be advantaged, leaving a digital underclass of learners who lack either the economic or the cultural support that would make these technology tools available to them.
2. *Use technology to support current practice*: Accept technology where it fits current educational structures and practices. This approach recognises technology as a useful tool in the right place but removes the role of catalyst for change. So we find that some innovations are more readily assimilated into the classroom than

others; for example digital whiteboards is a case in point. However other ubiquitous technologies such as 3G phones have minimal impact (Wang, Shen, Novak, & Pan, 2009) and are resisted by teacher unions (Robinson, 2010). This way forward feels comfortable and of course is in widespread use. However, there is an inherent risk that such use will lead to learner disaffection and rejection of the educational process, particularly in the case of the digitally savvy learner.

3. *Merge and evolve*: Here, we educators allow ourselves to adapt and respond to the possibilities afforded by the technology and embrace innovation. The approach recognises that digital technologies necessarily require us to reassess how learners learn and teachers teach. From this perspective we need to think about how schools or learning ecologies are organised, including the role of technology, to support meaningful student achievement. Schools will move to be more open educational institutions that "dramatically change their views on knowledge, assessment and the teacher, student and information relationships" (Hernandez & Goodison, 2004, p. xvi). One such example is the emergence of the personal web that will allow learners and teachers to customise the web to their own needs and interests using a range of data management and tracking tools. A second example would be the simulated contexts provided by virtual environments in which participants interact with digital objects and tools, such as historical photographs or virtual microscopes (Clarke-Midura & Dede, 2010).

But Even If We Decide to Merge and Evolve?

The Perils of Joining the Net Generation

In 2009 a comparison of faculty and student responses indicates that students were much more likely than faculty to use Facebook and were significantly more open to the possibility of using Facebook and similar technologies to support classroom work. Faculty members were predisposed to use more "traditional" technologies such as email (Roblyer et al., 2010). However, there are tutors who have joined the Facebook generation, and in doing so they have taken the decision to merge and evolve. However, this brings its own perils. Just as we, the tutors, begin to feel in charge of the technology we are reminded that the potential risks of the digital world are not just for learners but for tutors as well.

A study by Sleigh, Smith, and Laboe (2013) of students' responses to tutors' Facebook pages is illuminating. They examined whether the specific type of self-disclosure on a tutor's profile would affect students' perceptions of the tutor including their expectations of the tutor's classroom practice. Students reported being most interested in professional information on a tutor's Facebook profile, yet they reported being least influenced by that professional profile. They found that tutors who were seen as social individuals had high popularity ratings but the sting in the tail was that, although their profiles were viewed as entertaining, they were judged as inappropriate for a professional. This perception resulted in such tutors being assessed as less skilled professionally. It would appear that students form perceptions about the classroom environment and about their tutors based on the specific details disclosed in tutors' Facebook profiles.

So while tapping into students' interest SNSs may be an effective way for tutors and institutions to communicate and stimulate their students (Junco, 2011), the technology can be revealing and the students' developing perceptions and expectations may not always be what we intended or desired.

And Then There Are MOOCs

Massive open online courses (MOOCs) may seem somewhat tangential to what has gone before in this short piece, but they raise considerable issues for educators and possibly learners too. They are the dream scenario:

> Nothing has more potential to unlock a billion more brains to solve the world's biggest problems. And nothing has more potential to enable us to reimagine higher education than the massive open online course, or MOOC, platforms that are being developed by the likes of Stanford and the Massachusetts Institute of Technology and companies like Coursera and Udacity. (Friedman, 2013, page SR1)

So what are MOOCs, and why are they arousing such interest? MOOCs have been developed to support large-scale, open-access participation that includes varying levels of interaction. While such systems can appear prosaic at first sight, delivering traditional course materials such as videos, readings and exercises through the web, it is the use of interactive user forums designed to build a community of learners and tutors that elevates the MOOC from a delivery system to a new approach to knowledge and learning. Such knowledge, according to Downes (2005), is created by interaction and is not simply a relationship or a distributive pattern between one fact or idea and another. In essence connective knowledge is knowledge of the connection.

For a connectivist dynamic system to exist, Downes (2005) argues that there must be learner autonomy, group diversity, openness and interactivity and connectedness defined as follows:

1. Autonomy—The level of learner autonomy must be high, and the learners must be more than simply managed participants who receive rather than create of knowledge.
2. Diversity—The community will have a diverse membership and not be a self-perpetuating in-group maintaining the status quo and stifling new ideas and connections.
3. Openness—This will support free-flowing communication at various levels of activities with easy access for participants with no clear boundaries between membership and non-membership.
4. Interactivity and connectedness will produce knowledge that is unique within the community. Such knowledge will very likely be complex, representing not simple statements of fact or principle, but rather reflecting a community response to complex phenomena.

However, this utopian dream often falls short even in networks that are open and allow autonomy as only certain perspectives of those of participants occupying the highly connected nodes tend to be circulated to the network as a whole for consideration.

The University of Manitoba delivered an early interpretation of the MOOC principles in the autumn term of 2008. Predicated on this new perception of knowledge and way of learning "connectionism" (Downes, 2005; Siemens, 2004), CCK08 was designed to enable participants to engage with the theory and practice of connectivism. Over 2,000 participants signed up for the course, including Mackness, Mak and Williams (2010) who were keen to explore the Downes's model of learning in practice. They found that all four characteristics of a MOOC, autonomy, diversity, openness and connectedness/interactivity, were present in the MOOC, but that they did not necessarily lead to an effective learning experience. The more autonomous, diverse and open the course, and the more connected the learners, the more the potential for their learning to be limited by the lack of structure, support and moderation normally associated with an online course. These students fell back engaging in traditional groups as opposed to the open network. The finding that there can be too much autonomy has already established in other learning situations (Underwood et al., 2010). These responses constrain the possibility of having the positive experiences of autonomy, diversity, openness and connectedness/interactivity normally expected of an online network. The research suggests that the question of whether a large open online network can be fused with a course has yet to be resolved. Further research studies with larger samples are needed, as is an investigation into the ethical considerations that may need to be taken into account when testing new theory and practice on course participants.

However, the nightmare scenario would see MOOCs as leading to the demise of universities, colleges and even upper secondary or high school education

> I believe that online education will be an important building block of teaching in the future…I see great potential in having the opportunity to learn no matter where you are. You don't need to be in school or in a lecture hall of a university anymore, and therefore I believe that this will dramatically change our lives.
> (Dr. Angela Merkel, Chancellor of the Federal Republic of Germany (https://moocfellowship.org/ 2013, no page)

One cannot deny the size of the MOOC impact on higher education, for example:

> Mitch Duneier, a Princeton sociology professor, wrote an essay in The Chronicle of Higher Education in the fall about his experience teaching a class through Coursera: "A few months ago, just as the campus of Princeton University had grown nearly silent after commencement, 40,000 students from 113 countries arrived here via the Internet to take a free course in introductory sociology. (Friedman, 2013, no page)

Further the first UK-based MOOC platform, Futurelearn, is intended to go live in autumn 2013. It will be populated by MOOC courses designed by its 21 member institutions. It is estimated that it will cost about £30,000 (35,000 euros) to develop a MOOC for this platform (Parr, 2013a). While MOOCs can be linked to other tools such as Facebook such linkage can result in negative consequences. For example,

Kop, Fournier and Mak (2011) found that students had privacy and security concerns about Facebook. It would appear that the level of trust, feelings of confidence and the sense of presence and community are crucial to students engaging with the system, and Facebook leaves them uneasy.

But There Is a Twist in the Tail

Completion rates for MOOC courses, defined by the number of students being awarded some form of certificate, are alarmingly low. The Times Higher Education quotes an average figure of 7 %, that is, 93 % of students failing to complete such courses (Parr, 2013b). There is significant variation in these rates as is shown by the following three courses, all mounted on Coursera (Jordan, 2013). A History of the World course at Princeton University which ran 2012–2013 is recorded as having the poorest completion rate at 0.7 % of students enrolled; that is, 581 of the 83,00 who enrolled were certificated. However the University of Edinburgh had a completion rate of 2.3 % for its Artificial Intelligence Planning in 2013, that is, 660 students out of 28,689 students enrolled on the course. The most successful course in terms of completion rates according to Jordan was a course in Functional Programming Principles from the Ecole Polytechnique Fédérale de Lausanne from 2012-09 to 2012-11. Here 19.2 % completed the course, that is, 9,600 students out of the 50,000 who enrolled.

The headline findings from Jordan's (2013) data are encouraging for those who would hold back the march of online teaching and learning. However, look deeper and you will see that the World History course made assignment completion optional. This suggests that the course was designed with more than one audience in mind. Yes there were students of history seeking qualification, but there were also those who were simply interested in the topic, many of whom I would surmise are learners of the third age, that is, retirees coming back to a subject that interested them in the past but was not seen as providing job skills when younger. How many students are enrolling on these courses as top-up, tasters or as a hobby is yet to be established. The findings from the Edinburgh and Lausanne courses might be of greater concern, as these are not "hobby" subjects for most people. However, even here the numbers passing the course are not insignificant; 9,600 completions in the case of the Lausanne course should not be viewed as an inconsequential with the potential to impact on more traditionally provided courses. That really is cost-effective education.

Where Do You Stand?

Attempts to bed in new technologies necessarily involve some level of disturbance to the educational system. The degree to which these perturbations are tolerated will affect technology acceptance. This raises the question of whether the educational system will allow itself to be transformed or not although the rise of MOOCs may take these decisions out of the hands of educational establishment at least at the university level even if schools are more future proof.

Of course there is always that cynical old "truism". In the UK education circles it has long been the belief that universities will survive all educational revolutions because in the end the middle classes have to send their children somewhere to find suitable husbands and wives. With the advent of social networking and online dating even this role is now under threat.

The equally cynical view of schools as state-provided babysitting services has yet to be questioned although one can see the rise of plugged-in children. In the end if we do not adapt then for some learners the educational system will become increasingly irrelevant and they will carve out a learning environment for themselves, dipping into the formal system only when they see the need. As Prensky (2001) points out we ignore the fundamental fact that in a digital world the students themselves have changed. Will we as educators change with them or will the majority of us become increasingly less relevant?

References

Aronson, E. D. (2012). Cyber-politics: How new media has revolutionized electoral politics in the United States. *Colgate Academic Review*, 9, Article 7. Retrieved from http://commons.colgate.edu/car/vol9/iss1/7

Aviram, A., & Talmi, D. (2005). The impact of information and communication technology on education: The missing discourse between three different paradigms. *E-Learning and Digital Media, 2*, 161–191.

Crabtree, J., & Roberts, S. (2003). *Fat pipes, connected people rethinking broadband Britain*. London: iSociety. Retrieved from http://www.theworkfoundation.com/pdf/fat_pipes.pdf Accessed November 5, 2003.

Clarke-Midura, J., & Dede, C. (2010). Assessment, Technology, and Change. *Journal of Research on Technology in Education, 42*, 309–328.

Downes, S. (2005). *An introduction to connective knowledge*. Retrieved from http://www.downes.ca/post/33034

Friedman, R. L. (2013, January 27). Revolution hits the universities. *New York Times*, page SR1 Retrieved from http://www.nytimes.com/2013/01/27/opinion/sunday/friedman-revolution-hits-the-universities.html?_r=0

Haste, H. (2005). *Joined-Up Texting: The Role of Mobile Phones in Young People's Lives. Report No. 3*. London: Nestlé Social Research Programme.

Hernandez, F., & Goodison, I. F. (2004). *Social geographies of educational change*. Dordrcht, NL: Kluwer Academic.

Johnson, L., Levine, A., & Smith, R. (2009). *The 2009 Horizon Report*. Austin, TX: The New Media Consortium.

Jordan, K. (2013). *MOOC completion rates: The data*. Retrieved from http://www.katyjordan.com/MOOCproject.html

Junco, R. (2011). The relationship between frequency of Facebook use, participation in Facebook activities, and student engagement. *Computers and Education, 58*, 162–171.

Kop, R., Fournier, H., & Mak, J. S. F. (2011). A pedagogy of abundance or a pedagogy to support human beings? Participant support on Massive Open Online Courses. *The International Review of Research in Open and Distance Learning, 12*, 74–93.

Lebrun, M. (2007). Quality towards an expected harmony: Pedagogy and technology speaking together about innovation. *AACE Journal, 15*, 115–130.

Lowendahl, J. -M. et al. (2009). *Hype Cycle for Higher Education, 2008*. Industry Research ID: G00158592) Gartner. Retrieved from http://www.gartner.com/DisplayDocument?id=709014

Mackness, J., Mak, S., & Williams, R. (2010). The ideals and reality of participating in a MOOC. In *Proceedings of the 7th International Conference on Networked Learning 2010* (pp. 266–275). Lancaster: University of Lancaster.

OfCom (2006). Media Literacy Audit: Report on media literacy amongst children, Retrieved from http://stakeholders.ofcom.org.uk/market-data-research/media-literacy/archive/medlitpub/medlitpubrss/children/

OfCom (2010). *UK children's media literacy*. Retrieved from http://stakeholders.ofcom.org.uk/binaries/research/media-literacy/ukchildrensml1.pdf

Papert, S. (1993). *The children's machine: Rethinking school in the age of the computer*. New York, NY: Basic Books.

Palser, B. (2009). Amateur content's star turn. *American Journalism Review, 31*, 42.

Parr, C. (2013a, May 23). Futruelearn reveals big plans to deliver MOOCs on the move. *Times Higher Education*, 9.

Parr, C. (2013b, May 9). How many stay the course? A mere 7 %. *Times Higher Education*, 19.

Pedró, F. (2006). *The new millennium learners: Challenging our views on ICT and learning*. OECD-CERI.

Plester, B., & Wood, C. (2009). Exploring relationships between traditional and new media literacies: British preteen texters at school. *Journal of Computer-Mediated Communication, 14*, 1108–1129. Retrieved from http://www.oecd.org/dataoecd/1/1/38358359.pdf.

Prensky, M. (2001). *Digital game-based learning*. New York, NY: McGraw-Hill.

Resnick, M. (2006). Computer as paintbrush: Technology, play, and the creative society. In D. Singer, R. Golikoff, & K. Hirsh-Pasek (Eds.), *Play = Learning: How play motivates and enhances children's cognitive and social-emotional growth* (pp. 192–208). Oxford: Oxford University Press.

Robinson, H. (2010). *Case prompts mobile crackdown call*. Retrieved from http://news.bbc.co.uk/1/hi/education/10092626.stm

Roblyer, M. D., McDaniel, M., Webb, M., Herman, J., & Witty, J. V. (2010). Findings on Facebook in higher education: A comparison of college faculty and student uses and perceptions of social networking sites. *The Internet and Higher Education, 13*(3), 134–140.

Sandford, R., Uiksak, M., Facer, K., & Rudd, T. (2006). *Teaching with games: Using commercial off-the-shelf computer games in formal education*. Bristol: Nesta Futurelab.

Sclater, N. (2010). eLearning in the cloud. *International Journal of Virtual and Personal Learning Environments, 1*, 10–19.

Severance, C., Hardin, J., & Whyte, A. (2008). The coming functionality mash-up in personal learning environments. *Interactive Learning Environments, 16*, 47–62.

Siemens, G. (2004). *Connectivism: A learning theory for the digital age. Retrieved from elearnspace*. http://www.elearnspace.org/Articles/connectivism.htm

Simplicio, J. S. C. (2000). Teaching classroom educators how to be more effective and creative teachers. *Education, 120*, 675–680.

Sleigh, M. J., Smith, A. W., & Laboe, J. (2013). Professors' facebook content affects students' perceptions and expectations. *Cyberpsychology, Behavior and Social Networking, 16*(7), 489–496. doi:10.1089/cyber.2012.0561.

Underwood, J., Ault, A., Banyard, P., Bird, K. Dillon, G., Hayes, M., Selwood, I., Somekh, B., & Twining, P. (2005). *The impact of broadband in school*. Coventry; Becta. Retrieved from http://dera.ioe.ac.uk/1616/1/becta_2005_impactofbroadband_report_underwood.pdf

Underwood, J., Baguley, T., Banyard, P., Dillon, G., Farrington-Flint, L., Hayes, M., Le Geyt, G., Murphy, J., & Selwood, I. (2010). *Understanding the impact of technology: Learner and school-level factors*. Coventry; Becta. Retrieved from http://research.becta.org.uk/upload-dir/downloads/page_documents/research/understanding_impact_technology_learner_school_level_factors.pdf

Underwood, J., & Dillon, G. (2011). Chasing dreams and recognising realities: Teachers' responses to ICT. *Technology, Pedagogy and Education, 20*, 343–356.

Underwood, J. D. M., & Stiller, J. (2014). Does knowing lead to doing in the case of learning platforms? *Teachers and Teaching, 20*, 229–246.

Wang, M., Shen, R., Novak, D., & Pan, X. (2009). The impact of mobile learning on students' learning behaviours and performance: Report from a large blended classroom. *British Journal of Educational Technology, 40*, 673–695.

Watson, D. M. (2001). Pedagogy before technology: Re-thinking the relationship between ICT and teaching. *Education and Information Technologies, 6*, 251–266.

Westera, W. (2010). Technology-enhanced learning: Review and prospects. *Serdica Journal of Computing, 4*, 159–182.

The Evolution of Educational Technology Based on a Bibliometric Study

Tassos A. Mikropoulos, Demetrios G. Sampson, Alexandros Nikopoulos, and Panayotis Pintelas

Introduction

During the past years, the increased interest for applying technology to improve learning and teaching (Spector, 2012) has led to the evolution of this discipline from educational technology (ET) defined as "the study and ethical practice of facilitating learning and improving performance by creating, using, and managing appropriate technological processes and resources" (Januszewski & Molenda, 2008) to technology-enhanced learning (TeL) referring to a transformative movement in learning and teaching that exploits technological advances for offering learning experiences not possible to be organized in current formal educational settings (Haythornthwaite & Andrews, 2011). Educational technology and TeL are now mature interdisciplinary research areas, and there are already literature studies aiming at the study of scientific communities, the identification and evolution of salient topics, and the emergence of the trends in the field (Cho, Park, Jo, & Suh, 2013; Kinshuk, Huang, Sampson, & Chen, 2013; Masood, 2004; Pham, Derntl, & Klamma, 2012). Such studies are important since they can provide insights into the

T.A. Mikropoulos (✉) • A. Nikopoulos
Department of Primary Education, University of Ioannina,
Ioannina 45110, Greece
e-mail: amikrop@uoi.gr; anikop@cc.uoi.gr

D.G. Sampson
Department of Digital Systems,
University of Piraeus and CERTH-ITI, Piraeus, Greece
e-mail: sampson@iti.gr

P. Pintelas
Department of Mathematics, University of Patras,
University Campus, 26504 Rio, Greece
e-mail: pintelas@math.upatras.gr

C. Karagiannidis et al. (eds.), *Research on e-Learning and ICT*
in Education: Technological, Pedagogical and Instructional Perspectives,
DOI 10.1007/978-1-4614-6501-0_2, © Springer Science+Business Media New York 2014

development of a particular research area. Typically, social network analysis and bibliometric approaches using co-word, performance analysis, and science mapping have been exploited for this purpose (Cobo, López-Herrera, Herrera-Viedma, & Herrera, 2011; Masood, 2004; Muñoz-Leiva, Sánchez-Fernández, Liébana-Cabanillas, & Martínez-Fiestas, 2013).

In educational technology and TeL, there are some efforts to analyze research trends and scientific communities using as sources articles published in journals (Cho et al., 2013; Klein, 1997; LeBaron & McDonough, 2009; Masood, 2004). On the other hand, Randolph, Julnes, Bednarik, and Sutinen have indicated that "there were no practically or statistically significant differences between the articles published in journals and those published in conference proceedings on any of the indicators of methodological quality" (2007). As a result, there have been similar studies where the sources were articles published in international conference such as the IEEE International Conference on Advanced Learning Technologies (ICALT) (Pham et al., 2012; Randolph et al., 2005) and the Artificial Intelligence in Education conference organized by the International Artificial Intelligence in Education (AIED) Society (Rourke, Anerson, Garrison, & Archer, 2001).

In this work, we aim to investigate the evolution of the educational technology field in a European Union member state, namely, Greece, through the analysis of the category of targeted research outcomes and the key topics of interest that have been emerged in all papers presented at the main national scientific conference of this field between 2000 and 2012. More specifically, we analyzed papers presented in the biannual conference of the Hellenic Scientific Association for ICT in Education, a nonprofit scientific association founded in 2000 with the aim to promote research and development in the field of educational technology. Through this analysis, we aim to identify trends between three different categories of targeted research outcomes (theory, technology, practice) and the evolution of different key topics of interest over a period of 12 years. We then discuss these trends in relation to educational technology policies and programs that have stimulated both research and development activities as well as mainstreaming activities aiming to widespread adoption of educational technologies in school education.

Method

Sample

The sample of this study consists of the population, namely, all the articles published in the proceedings of all seven biannual national conferences organized by the Hellenic Scientific Association for ICT in Education between 2000 and 2012. The association is the only scientific, on behalf of membership criteria, body in the field in Greece and represents almost the entire research community in Greece, and its conferences are the biggest in Greece. Thus, it can be considered that a

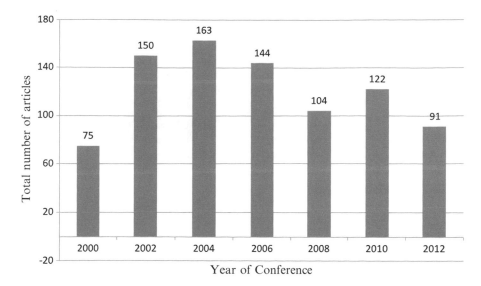

Fig. 1 Population of articles per biannual conference (2000–2012)

bibliometric analysis based on the association's proceedings covers the Greek community of ICT in education in Greece. The number of articles presented and published in both printed and electronic form is 849 which constitutes a significant number of articles from which we can extract meaningful conclusions. Figure 1 shows the distribution of all articles in the seven biannual conferences from 2000 to 2012. It can be seen that there is a reasonably balanced distribution with peaks during 2002–2006 due to the implementation of a large-scale public-funded program for introducing ICT in school education which stimulated interest from both educational practitioners and researchers.

Bibliometric Approach

For the purposes of the present study, the co-word analysis, as a powerful quantitative content analysis technique "in mapping the strength of association between information items in textual data" (Cobo et al., 2011), is applied. Moreover, co-word analysis is used for temporal analysis and "develops a performance analysis of specific themes using a series of basic bibliometric indicators" (Muñoz-Leiva et al., 2013).

The key topics of interest are formed by studying the common keywords from the corpus of the articles. The keywords used are retrieved from the conference index, author's keywords, and their combinations. Moreover, two different coders studied a specific number of articles and found common keywords at a level of 80 % that is usually characterized as standard (Rourke et al., 2001). Based on the common keywords, clusters of keywords are formed, thus creating the key topics of interest.

Results

First, we have identified three different categories of targeted research outcomes, namely, theory, technology, and practice. The first category concerns with theoretical issues of educational technology such as "pedagogy in TeL" and "learning design: theoretical aspects." Thus, we refer to this category as "theory." The second category concerns with a variety of learning technologies, from "authoring tools for educational content and learning designs" and "course management systems" to "wireless, mobile, and ubiquitous technologies" and "Web 2.0 and social computing technologies," and involves articles that emphasize on learning systems based on these technologies. We refer to this category as "technology." The third category concerns with those topics of interest that relate to the practical pedagogical exploitation of ICT in formal and informal learning settings, including ICT in teaching various subject domains, and other implementation issues of ICT in education. Thus, we refer to this category as "practice."

Table 1 presents the categories of targeted research outcomes (level 1) and their corresponding key topics of interest per category of research that have arisen from the co-word analysis (level 2), together with their frequencies (%) and absolute frequencies for the entire 12-year period. It can be noticed that the balance between the three different categories of targeted research (theory—5.18 %, technology—10.95 %, and practice—83.86 %) indicates that the vast majority of conducted research concerns with the practical use of existing theories and technologies in school education.

Figure 2 illustrates how these trends are evolved over time during the 12-year period. It can be noticed that basic research ("theory") tends to be reduced and applied technological research ("technology") has a constant increase (mainly due to the continuing development of new technologies), but still the core bulk of research concerns "practice."

This is consistent with our hypothesis that the community considers that the field of educational technology has matured enough to mainly concern mainstreaming (that is, large-scale implementation of technology-supported educational innovations in formal setting, like schools), rather than basic research or even applied technological research. This is consistent with current European Union policies and trends in TeL.

Figures 3, 4, and 5 illustrate the time evolution of key topics of interest in each category of targeted research outcomes during the 12-year period.

From Fig. 3 it can be noticed that in category "theory" the main topics of interest have been "learning design: theoretical aspects" and "pedagogy in TeL," whereas there are some sporadic contribution in "learning theories in TeL" and "e-assessment: theory and methods." Even so, the topic with a consistent interest over time has been the "pedagogy in TeL," which is reasonable since the implementation of large-scale ICT in school education programs stimulates interest in basic research related with the rethinking of pedagogy in TeL.

Table 1 Key topics of interest in national conferences

Level 1: Category of targeted research outcomes	Level 2: Key topics of interest	Frequencies (%) of level 1 categories over 2000–2012	Absolute frequencies of level 1 categories over 2000–2012 (N=849)	Frequencies (%) of level 2 topics over 2000–2012	Absolute frequencies of level 2 topics over 2000–2012 (N=849)
Theory	Pedagogy in technology-enhanced learning	5.18	44	2.00	17
	Learning theories in technology-enhanced learning			0.35	3
	Learning design: Theoretical aspects			2.71	23
	e-Assessment: Theory and methods			0.12	1
Technology	Authoring tools (educational content, learning design)	10.95	93	2.47	21
	Course management systems			0.59	5
	Virtual environments and worlds			2.00	17
	Digital games			0.24	2
	Educational robotics			0.24	2
	Wireless, mobile, and ubiquitous technologies for learning			0.35	3
	Collaborative technologies			2.00	17
	e-Assessment tools			1.77	15
	Tools for education of people with disabilities			0.47	4
	Web 2.0 and social computing in education			0.24	2
	Hypermedia and multimedia			0.59	5

(continued)

Table 1 (continued)

Level 1: Category of targeted research outcomes	Level 2: Key topics of interest	Frequencies (%) of level 1 categories over 2000–2012	Absolute frequencies of level 1 categories over 2000–2012 (N=849)	Frequencies (%) of level 2 topics over 2000–2012	Absolute frequencies of level 2 topics over 2000–2012 (N=849)
Practice		83.86	712		
	ICT in science education			13.19	112
	ICT in mathematics education			7.54	64
	ICT in language and literature education			7.89	67
	ICT in history education			6.01	51
	ICT in foreign language education			3.42	29
	ICT in computer science education			10.13	86
	e-Assessment: Implementation issues			2.71	23
	Distance learning: Implementation issues			11.90	101
	Digital literacy			8.13	69
	Continuing professional development programs—teachers' training			8.01	68
	Educational management			2.00	17
	Educational policy			1.18	10
	ICT in education of people with disabilities			1.77	15

Fig. 2 Categories of targeted research outcomes over time

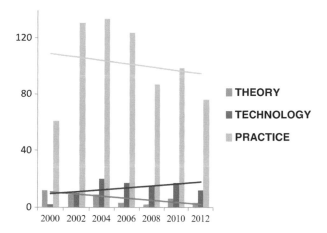

Articles' distribution for theme "theory"

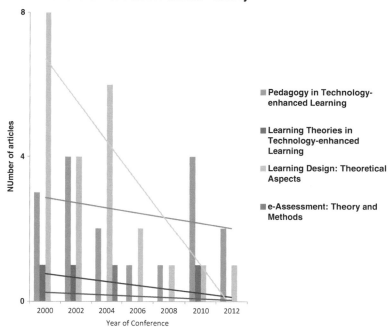

Fig. 3 Time evolution of key topics of interest in "theory"

From Fig. 4 it can be noticed that in category "technology" the main topics of interest have been "authoring tools for educational content and learning designs," "virtual environment and worlds," "collaborative technologies," and "e-assessment tools." It is also interesting to notice that there is a consistent interest on these topics over time. This is reasonable since authoring tools and e-assessment tools are

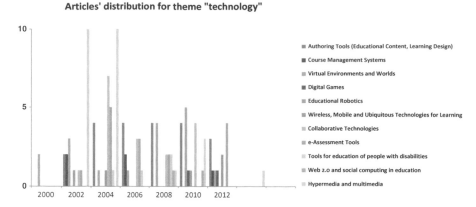

Fig. 4 Time evolution of key topics of interest in "technology"

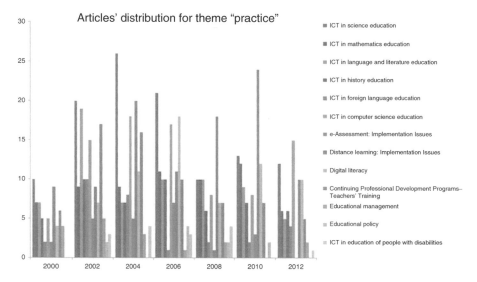

Fig. 5 Time evolution of key topics of interest in "practice"

directly useful in the implementation of large-scale ICT in school education programs, whereas collaborative technologies are attracting practical interest since collaborative learning aspects are considered a major educational innovation that can be supported by technology. On the other hand, applied technological research on topics such as digital games and educational robotics, as well as wireless, mobile, and ubiquitous technologies, appears not to be supported by the Greek research community, mainly due to the lack of national industry that develops such technologies.

From Fig. 5 it can be noticed that in category "practice" the main topics of interest have been "ICT in science education," "ICT in computer science education," and "distance learning: implementation issues." This is reasonable because science, technology, engineering, and mathematics (STEM) are the key school curriculum subject domain topics that can benefit the most from innovative technology-supported teaching and learning strategies (Rocard et al., 2007). This is consistent with finding in other member states of the European Union and all over the world (Rocard et al., 2007).

Conclusions

Educational technology and TeL are now mature interdisciplinary research areas, and there are already literature studies aiming at the study of scientific communities, the identification and evolution of salient topics, and the emergence of the trends in the field. Such studies are important since they can provide insights into the development of a particular research area.

In this work, we investigated the evolution of the educational technology field in a European Union member state, namely, Greece, through the analysis of trends between three different categories of targeted research outcomes (theory, technology, practice) and the corresponding key topics of interest that have been emerged in all 849 papers presented at the main national scientific conference of this field between 2000 and 2012.

Some interesting conclusions can be drawn for the discussion of the obtained results. It appears that the educational technology community, at least in Greece, considers that the field has matured enough to mainly concern mainstreaming (that is, large-scale implementation of technology-supported educational innovations in formal setting, like schools), rather than basic research or even applied technological research. This can be a misleading route which can result to disappointments, since using existing technologies, mainly developed out of the context of learning and education, simply used as a facilitator for implementing incremental innovations in school education has potential risks of failure. In our view, the truly transformative value of educational technologies in formal and informal learning requires disruptive innovations that question the why–what–how–where of learning and teaching in the digital era. To this end, basic and applied technological and pedagogical interdisciplinary research is needed more than any other time in the past.

Acknowledgement Alexandros Nikopoulos' work was partly financially supported by a grant from the Hellenic Scientific Association for ICT in Education.

References

Cho, Y., Park, S., Jo, S. J., & Suh, S. (2013). The landscape of educational technology viewed from the ETR&D journal. *British Journal of Educational Technology, 44*, 677–694.

Cobo, M. J., López-Herrera, A. G., Herrera-Viedma, E., & Herrera, F. (2011). An approach for detecting, quantifying, and visualizing the evolution of a research field: A practical application to the Fuzzy Sets Theory field. *Journal of Informetrics, 5*, 146–166.

Haythornthwaite, C., & Andrews, R. (2011). *E-learning: Theory and practice*. London: Sage.
Januszewski, A., & Molenda, M. (2008). *Educational technology: A definition with commentary*. New York, NY: Lawrence Erlbaum Associates.
Kinshuk, Huang, H.-W., Sampson, D. G., & Chen, N.-S. (2013). Trends in educational technology through the lens of the highly cited articles published in the Journal of Educational Technology and Society. *Educational Technology and Society, 16*(2), 3–20.
Klein, J. D. (1997). ETR&D-Development: An analysis of content and survey of future direction. *Educational Technology Research and Development, 45*(3), 57–62.
LeBaron, J., & McDonough, E. (2009). Research report for GeSCI meta-review of ICT in education. Retrieved January 24, 2013 from http://www.gesci.org/assets/files/Research/meta-research-phase2.pdf
Masood, M. (2004). A ten year analysis: Trends in traditional educational technology literature. *Malaysian Online Journal of Instructional Technology, 1*(2), 73–91.
Muñoz-Leiva, F., Sánchez-Fernández, J., Liébana-Cabanillas, F. J., & Martínez-Fiestas, M. (2013). Detecting salient themes in financial marketing research from 1961 to 2010. *The Service Industries Journal, 9–10*, 925–940.
Pham, M. C., Derntl, M., & Klamma, R. (2012). Development patterns of scientific communities in technology enhanced learning. *Educational Technology and Society, 15*(3), 323–335.
Randolph, J. J., Julnes, G., Bednarik, R., & Sutinen, E. (2007). A comparison of the methodological quality of articles in computer science education journals and conference proceedings. *Computer Science Education, 17*(4), 263–274.
Randolph, J., Bednarik, R., Silander, P., Gonzalez, J., Myller, N., & Sutinen, E. (2005). A critical analysis of the research methodologies reported in the full papers of the proceedings of ICALT 2004. In D. G. Sampson, P. Godyear, Kinshuk, D. J. Yang, & T. Okamoto (Eds.), *Proceedings of the 5th IEEE International Conference on Advanced Learning Technologies (ICALT 2005)* (pp. 10–14). Kaohsiung, Taiwan: IEEE Computer Society.
Rocard, M., Csermely, P., Jorde, D., Lenzen, D., Walberg-Henriksson, H., & Hemmo, V. (2007). *Science education now: A renewed pedagogy for the future of Europe*. Luxembourg: European Commission.
Rourke, L., Anerson, T., Garrison, D. R., & Archer, W. (2001). Methodological issues in the content analysis of computer conference transcripts. *International Journal of Artificial Intelligence in Education, 12*, 8–22.
Spector, J. M. (2012). *Foundations of educational technology*. New York, NY: Routheldge.

Theories of Learning in Math and Science Educational Software

Dimitra Apostolopoulou, Christos Panagiotakopoulos, and Anthi Karatrantou

Introduction

In the history of pedagogical thought and psychology, every definition of learning is supported by an entire world view, a sequence of ontological assumptions concerning nature, man, and the relation between them. In parallel, the phenomenon of learning is approached by distinct disciplines in a different way (Bigge & Shermis, 1999). The variety of Learning Theories has led us to the conclusion that the phenomenon of learning constitutes a complex and composite fact, of various dimensions, since no theory on its own is able to describe and interpret the whole range of learning and its dimensions. The ideological currents and the theories of learning, as well as the methods via which the latter contribute to the shaping of teaching, are various. Among the most widespread schools of thought are those which consider learning as (Ertmer & Newby, 1993; Nagowah & Nagowah, 2009): a change in the observable behavior (*Theories of Behavior—Behaviorism*), an internal mental process of the learner (*Cognitive Theories—Cognitivism*), or an adjustment of mental models to accommodate new experiences (Theories of Construction of Knowledge—*Constructivism*). Teaching with or without the implementation of ICT tools is every time based on certain acceptances regarding what learners have to learn and which way of learning is the best. These arguments are substantially connected directly to a certain learning theory. Thus, the educational software, as well, as a means of learning, is always based on a certain or certain theories of learning, incorporated in it by its creators (Mcleod, 2003; Roblyer, 2006).

D. Apostolopoulou (✉) • C. Panagiotakopoulos • A. Karatrantou
Department of Primary Education, University of Patras,
University Campus, 26504 Rio, Greece
e-mail: apostolopoulou.dimitra@gmail.com; cpanag@upatras.gr; a.karatrantou@eap.gr

C. Karagiannidis et al. (eds.), *Research on e-Learning and ICT
in Education: Technological, Pedagogical and Instructional Perspectives*,
DOI 10.1007/978-1-4614-6501-0_3, © Springer Science+Business Media New York 2014

Today it is commonly accepted that ICT integration in the educational process is able to support educational activities in a rich educational environment in which learners can have multiple representations of complex phenomena and even be individually supported in the construction of knowledge in an authentic learning environment (Cooper & Brna, 2002). Worldwide research, though, has shown that teachers take advantage of capabilities of this kind in a restricted manner, using ICTs mainly for supporting traditional teaching practices and not for designing and implementing educational activities which involve learners actively in the learning process (Sang, Valcke, van Braak, & Tondeur, 2010; Tondeur, van Keer, van Braak, & Valcke, 2008).

In the present research paper an attempt is being made to study teachers' perceptions about applications of educational software which deal with the syllabus of Mathematics, Physics, and Chemistry of Secondary Education regarding the embedded learning theories. *The main research question was to identify which groups of theories of learning are embedded in certain applications, and to what extent, according to in-service teachers' perceptions.* These perceptions were correlated with the ones of experienced teachers in the use of ICT in the classroom and the statements of the developers of the applications under study as they described in the supporting material of each application.

Theories of Learning and Educational Software

Each one of the three groups of learning theories can be used in the educational software (Mcleod, 2003; Roblyer, 2006). Which one precisely and at which point of the software it will be applied depends on the users' background knowledge and their characteristics, as well as the discipline presented via the educational software. A sufficient condition for this to happen is that the design and production team be aware of both the positive and negative elements of each theory, in order for the team to utilize them appropriately (Panagiotakopoulos, Pierrakeas, & Pintelas, 2003).

Theories of Behavior

Learning is defined as a change in learner's behavior arising from experiences, as well as the tasks set by the teacher. Learning occurs through the reinforcement of the desired behavior either through its reward (positive reinforcement) or through punishment (negative reinforcement) (Nagowah & Nagowah, 2009). The teacher plays a central role as a transmitter of knowledge to learners and as a basic factor in the educational process which reinforces the desired behavior.

A learning environment designed in the context of the Theories of Behavior must have specific characteristics concerning the structure of the curriculum in short units, gradual progress of the syllabus according to the learner's learning pace, exposition of the syllabus in increasing order of difficulty, and direct verification of the learner's response (Ertmer & Newby, 1993).

Theories of Behavior constitute the first Learning Theories, which were utilized for the theoretical support of technology application in education. Educational applications integrating the aforementioned theories are mostly of the type of tutorials and drill and practice, and are judged efficient at providing supervisory teaching as well as at consolidating a low level of knowledge and skills (Nagowah & Nagowah, 2009; Panagiotakopoulos, Pierrakeas, & Pintelas, 2003).

Cognitive Theories

Cognitive Learning Theories have ensued from a reaction to Theories of Behavior, since researchers considered that the emphasis laid by the latter theories on the connection of stimulus–response was not efficient enough to interpret human activity during the learning process. They focus on the mental processes put into motion on the basis of the stimuli presented in the human perceptual and cognitive systems. That is, they probe into the functions of the cerebral mechanisms which are related to learning and describe their relations so as for them to be better understood. To the researchers of Cognitive Theories learning is a change in behavior, in thought, in understanding, and in feelings (McLeod, 2003; Porpodas, 2000).

These new models focused on the processes of codification, knowledge representation, on information storage, and on the retrieval and integration of new knowledge into the preceding pieces of information. The aim is still knowledge transfer in the most effective and efficient way. Cognitive Theories have imposed on education metaphors, the analysis of complex concepts into simpler ones and the scrupulous organization of the educational material from the simple to the complicated (McLeod, 2003; Panagiotakopoulos, Pierrakeas, & Pintelas, 2003).

As far as the interaction between the learner and the software is concerned, there is no strictly predetermined sequence in which the learner has to "learn by heart" the subtopics of the syllabus, but he can study any of its subsections and test his knowledge wherever he considers (Anderson, Redder, & Simon, 1998).

Theories of Construction of Knowledge

Learning is a subjective and internal process of concept construction and is deemed to be the result of organizing and adjusting new pieces of information to already existing knowledge. That is, learning demands the rearrangement and reconstruction of the individual's mental structures, so that they adjust to new knowledge, and also "adapt" new knowledge to the subordinate mental structures (Shunk, 2004). A central role is played by the learner, who assumes an active role in the construction of his knowledge, by the preexisting knowledge of the learner, which has to be modified and expanded as a result of learning and by the teacher, who assumes a supportive-consultative role in learners' activity (McLeod, 2003).

The researchers have adopted in their studies several approaches of constructivism, from the view of the theory, which supports that learning is simply the process of adjusting our mental models to accommodate new experiences and involves constructing one's own knowledge from one's own experiences, to sociocultural approach, which emphasizes learning from experience and discourse in authentic learning environments, through collaboration and social interactions (Jonassen, 1999; Mahoney & Granvold, 2005).

A learning environment which is designed to comply with the Theories of Construction of Knowledge, according to Boyle (1997), must have specific features which aim at constructing knowledge, such as providing the learner with experiences, integrating knowledge in a realistic environment directly related to the real world, encouraging the affirmation and expression of perceptions in the learning process, consolidating knowledge via social experience, encouraging the use of multiple forms of knowledge representation, and encouraging self-awareness in the process of constructing knowledge. Educational applications, which are designed to take the aforementioned theories into consideration, should encourage a series of procedures and support the creation of such teaching contexts which would advocate the idea of Knowledge Construction by the learner himself/herself while trying to solve problems and interacting with the environment in this attempt. They should also encourage learners' self-expression and provide authentic learning activities (Edgar, 2012; Jonassen, 1999).

Educational Software for Maths and Science

Until today, there have been many studies about the potential of the educational software to contribute positively to the learning process. These studies have concluded that the use of educational software as an educational tool under certain conditions can be extended to all educational sectors (Bowman, Hodges, Allison, & Wineman, 1999; Vanucci & Colla, 2010).

In the field of mathematics education student's active involvement in their learning has the main role to their engaging with mathematical ideas as it is very important to them to participate in forming and testing hypotheses, trying out models, and developing reasoned solutions to authentic problems. The use of software applications such as dynamic geometry, graphing and data-modeling packages, databases, interactive games, simulations, and programming tools enables students to reach accurate feedback and gain positive motivation (Barzel, Drijvers, Maschietto, & Trouche, 2005). The use of such applications also allows students to focus on strategies and interpretations and not on complex computational calculations. In this way the use of ICT in mathematics education supports constructivist pedagogy and supports students to explore mathematical concepts, relations and procedures, promoting higher order thinking and problem-solving strategies which are in line with the new trends in mathematics education (Ruthven and Hennessy, 2002).

In the field of Science, tools such as the ones used for collecting, processing, and interpreting data, databases and spreadsheets, graphic tools, modeling environments, multimedia software intended for simulating processes and phenomena and for conducting "virtual" experiments, publication and presentation tools and, finally, computer-controlled apparatuses can offer prospects for interactive educational activities (Osborne & Hennessy, 2003).

By utilizing such tools appropriately learners are given the opportunity of working in an environment adapted to specialized educational needs, of comprehending natural phenomena and natural laws by using hypotheses and trial and error methods, and of experimenting in a structured way by exploring a model and discovering the elements of the simulation environment. Furthermore, learners are enabled to use a variety of representations (images, graphs, data tables etc.), which are useful in comprehending concepts and their interrelation. Finally, learners are given the opportunity of expressing concept representation and cognitive models of the surrounding natural world (Osborne & Hennessy, 2003; Velázquez-Marcano, Williamson, Ashkenazi, Tasker, & Williamson, 2004).

Today innovative educational activities, which contribute to the interconnection of concepts and, by extension, highlight the homogeneity of Sciences, are of special interest in the educational process. The contribution of new technologies towards that direction seems to be quite significant, due to the fact that they provide the opportunity to highlight the modern way in which Science and Maths are taught. These technologies also create new prospects in the context of knowledge exploration and collaborative learning as the Theories of Construction of Knowledge prescribe.

Studies have shown that teaching which takes advantage of ICT applications proves to be much more effective, regarding the comprehension of Science-related concepts, processes, and phenomena, than activities designed in a traditional way (Redish, Saul, & Steinberg, 1997), since learners are given the possibility of a direct visualization of natural or/and chemical phenomena (Bowman et al., 1999).

Methodology

For the needs of our research a sample was used which is, to a great extent, a "convenience sample" (Bryman, 1995). To achieve greater reliability and control of internal validity, the collection of data was done by using two research tools: a questionnaire—as the main research tool—and a semi-structured interview (Cohen, Manion, & Morisson, 2007). The questionnaire was addressed to teachers of Science and Maths in Secondary Education, who participated in a national in-service training course. The objective of this course was to educate 28,100 teachers of primary and secondary education, concerning the utilization and application of ICTs in the teaching practice (http://b-epipedo2.cti.gr/en). Participants, after the training course, expressed their perceptions on the educational software applications under investigation, by answering to specific questions related to the Learning Theory or Theories which the applications utilize.

The questionnaire consisted of 50 questions which were divided into two parts, one for collecting demographic data and the other for investigating the main research question. The first part included questions about the teachers' personal profile with special emphasis on their dealing with applications of educational software and on their getting accustomed to using it. The second part (main part) of the questionnaire consisted of 40 questions related to the features of Learning Theories. Fifteen out of the questions posed concerned the Theories of Behavior, seven of them the Cognitive Theories, and eighteen of them the Theories of Construction of Knowledge. The questions lent themselves to two types of answer, the Yes-No type and the 5-grade Likert-type Scale (1 = Never, 2 = Rarely, 3 = Sometimes, 4 = Often, 5 = Always). According to the existing research on the features of learning theories when apply to learning environments, a set of questions was formulated, which fall into the following axes (Anderson, Reder, & Simon, 1998; Atkins, 1993; Edgar, 2012; Ertmer & Newby, 1993; Nagowah & Nagowah, 2009):

- The transparency of the aim and the learning objectives to be achieved
- The existence of a logical distinction and cohesion of the instructional units
- The way in which the syllabus is presented in the software
- The relation between the learner's prior knowledge and the content to be studied
- The cultivating of student's ability to interpret facts and phenomena
- The way a learner can be evaluated/self-evaluated
- Whether the educational activities are able to connect real-life situations based on learners' experiences with representations of the real world and daily life
- Whether they cultivate the use of critical thinking methods allowing for the learner's autonomous course in constructing knowledge
- Whether learners' active participation is promoted and in what way
- Whether the collaborative approach to knowledge and problem-solving is encouraged by cultivating learners' creativity and imagination at the same time

The software applications chosen to be studied are the ones suggested by the Hellenic Ministry of Education and the Pedagogical Institute to be used at schools and which are used at the abovementioned in-service training course (3 closed type and 2 open type ones, 4 regarding Science and 1 regarding Mathematics) out of those most implemented in class.

Thirty-two (32) teachers of Science completed the questionnaire for each one of the four software applications for science, and eighteen (18) teachers of Mathematics completed the questionnaire for the application of mathematics. In order for the data to be processed, the answers to the questionnaires were input to statistical data analysis software. At first, the reliability coefficient α (Chronbach's alpha) of the questionnaire responses, regarding every group of the participants (Science teachers, Mathematics teachers), was estimated. In order for the teachers' descriptive answers to questions to be classified, a content analysis of the responses was conducted (Bogdan & Bilken, 1982).

The interviews conducted with participants who were in key positions in the abovementioned in-service training course (Cohen et al., 2007). Interviewees were three teacher trainers specializing on the utilization and application of ICTs in the teaching practice, who had great training and research experience on issues regarding the utilization of ICTs in the teaching practice. These trainers were educators in the aforementioned in-service teachers' training course. Interviews aimed to provide qualitative data from the view of the trainer-expert, complementary or explanatory to the quantitative data provided by the questionnaires. The interview consisted of 23 questions which were divided into two parts. In the first part demographic data were recorded while in the second part an attempt was made to collect data via open-ended questions related to the research issues. A content analysis to the interviewees' responses was conducted.

Findings and Analysis

The values for the coefficient of internal consistency (Chronbach's alpha) of the questionnaire responses were 0.842 for Science teachers and 0.853 for Mathematics teachers. This fact shows strong reliability of the answers. The sample's characteristics are presented in Table 1.

Twenty-seven (27) of the Science teachers answered that they use general purpose software for the needs of their lesson very often, whereas five (5) of them use it rarely. Twelve (12) of the Mathematics teachers also use general purpose software often, while six (6) of them use it rarely.

The main criteria for the selection of the 3 teacher trainers who participated in the interview were their involvement in the teacher's training courses and their experience in using educational software applications in the classroom. They all had a teaching experience of more than 15 years, great experience in training and research, as well as in using educational software in class.

The following paragraphs present the results of the quantitative (Table 2) as well as the qualitative research of the five (5) characteristic software applications studied. The presentation of the quantitative results is made in relation to the number of questions (related to every Learning Theory), which the teachers estimated that the software fulfills to a "Full" (grade 4 and 5 of the scale) or "Partly" (grade 3 and 2 of the scale) extent.

Table 1 Characteristics of the sample

	Science teachers	Mathematics teachers
Age range:	30–60	32–57
Teaching experience range:	3–31	7–31
Gender (M I F):	22 I 10	11 I 7
Total:	32[a]	18

[a]18 Physics, 6 Chemistry, 5 Biology, and 3 Geology teachers

Table 2 Frequencies of answers per learning theories and software

	Behaviorism (15 criteria)		Cognitivism (7 criteria)		Constructivism (18 criteria)	
Software/learning theory	Full	Partly	Full	Partly	Full	Partly
A wonderful journey in the world of Physics	6	9	3	2	11	5
Interactive Physics	0	0	1	0	7	0
Composite Laboratory Environment—C.L.E.	0	3	2	1	11	4
The Wonderful World of Chemistry	7	8	4	3	9	7
The Geometer's Sketchpad	0	0	1	0	7	0

More specifically:

A Wonderful Journey in the World of Physics

The "A Wonderful Journey in the World of Physics" software fully satisfies six (6) questions about the Theories of Behavior, three (3) questions about the Cognitive Theories and eleven (11) questions about the Theories of Construction of Knowledge. It also partly satisfies nine (9) questions about the Theories of Behavior, two (2) questions about Cognitive Theories, and five (5) questions about the Theories of Construction of Knowledge.

The same findings also emerged from the teacher trainers' interviews, who responded that although the specific software is suitable for being utilized in class through activities aiming at Knowledge Construction by learners, it also includes elements of the Theories of Behavior. More specifically, there seemed to be a distinction between instructional units and a representation of the syllabus in various ways. The examples, simulations and videos provided allow and promote the connection between the learner's prior knowledge and the content to be studied. Thus, the learner's skill to interpret phenomena is cultivated and, simultaneously, a connection is being realized between the learner's experience and the representation of his/her daily life.

Interactive Physics

Regarding the "Interactive Physics" software, due to the fact that it is a type of open software, the teachers who participated in the research chose not to answer to all of the questions in the Likert Scale or in the nominal Yes/No scale, but to answer periphrastically to some of them by making a comment. Based on the questions answered, in the scales, this software fully satisfies seven (7) questions about the Theories of Construction of Knowledge and one (1) question about Cognitive Theories.

In the rest of the questions, it becomes evident from the teachers' comments that this software provides the user-teacher with the ability to design and support educational activities aiming at his/her learners' Construction of Knowledge by planning and utilizing appropriate educational scenarios and worksheets in the classroom.

On the basis of the aforementioned data, the descriptive answers of the participants to the rest of the questions and the teacher trainers' answers in the interviews it could be concluded that this software distinctly applies the Theories of Construction of Knowledge. Teacher trainers agree that, during the utilization of the software, the teacher plays an especially active role. The teacher should, every time, design and create a simulation which provides his/her learners the opportunity to work on powerfully exploratory learning activities via appropriately designed educational scenarios and specific worksheets.

Composite Laboratory Environment (C.L.E.)

The "Composite Laboratory Environment—C.L.E." software fully satisfies eleven (11) questions about the Theories of Construction of Knowledge and two (2) questions about Cognitive Theory. It also partly fulfills three (3) questions about the Theories of Behavior, one (1) question about the Cognitive Theories and four (4) questions about the Theories of Construction of Knowledge. Based on the aforementioned results, it would be concluded that the software orientates towards those which mainly integrate the Theories of Construction of Knowledge.

The interviews lead to the same conclusions, as well. Due to the virtual experiments it provides, this type of software encourages the learner's ability to interpret facts and phenomena. The virtual experiments and the videos included in the software are realistic to a great extent, a fact which facilitates the connection between real-life situations from the learner's experiences and what is being studied through the representation of the real world and everyday life.

The Wonderful World of Chemistry

The "The Wonderful World of Chemistry" software fully satisfies seven (7) questions about the Theories of Behavior, four (4) questions about Cognitive Theories, and nine (9) questions about the Theories of Construction of Knowledge. It also partly satisfies eight (8) questions about the Theories of Behavior, three (3) about Cognitive Theories, and seven (7) questions about the Theories of Construction of Knowledge.

The teacher trainers agree that this type of software is mainly utilized in activities based on the Theories of Construction of Knowledge. However, it includes elements from the Theories of Behavior, as well. The software includes distinct instructional units. The syllabus presentation is carried out through definitions, examples, rules, and simulation examples. The possibility of learner evaluation is provided. The learner is informed on his/her answer correctness through positive or negative feedback. Moreover, via examples, simulations, and videos, the learner's skill to interpret facts and phenomena is cultivated.

The Geometer's Sketchpad

As far as "The Geometer's Sketchpad" is concerned, since it constitutes open software, the teachers participating in the research chose not to answer to all the questions in the Likert Scale or in the nominal Yes/No scale. They also answered periphrastically to some of them by providing a comment. Based on the questions answered in the scales, this type of software fully satisfies seven (7) questions about the Theories of Construction of Knowledge and very much one (1) question about the Cognitive Learning Theories. Thus, this software could be classified as one of the types integrating the Theories of Construction of Knowledge.

On the basis of the aforementioned data, the descriptive answers of the participants to the rest of the questions and the teacher trainer's answers in the interviews it could be concluded that the specific software application is placed among those applications which clearly serves the purpose of the Theories of Construction of Knowledge, since the learner is evidently involved in the construction and structuring of his/her knowledge. It constitutes interactive software, which enables the learner to be actively involved in geometrical design and construction activities, which strongly promote learner autonomy.

All findings are in agreement with the objectives of the developers of the five applications studied, as reported in the supporting material of each application.

Discussion and Conclusions

In the present research paper the dominating Learning Theories were studied in terms of their existence in applications of Educational Software for Science and Mathematics, according to the perceptions of a sample of in-service teachers. These perceptions resulted from the participants' responses on questions concerning the characteristics of five specific educational applications.

According to the sample's perceptions, the results of the five applications presented allow us to conclude that open type applications (Interactive Physics, The Geometer's Sketchpad) serve the Theories of Construction of Knowledge, since through them the teacher is able not only to create new interactional applications according to his/her learners' educational needs, but also to encourage learners in creating by themselves their own simulations and models of interpreting processes and phenomena. These findings are in agreement also with the three expert teachers' responses.

The findings from both the answers of the sample and the three expert teachers interviewed about the close type applications showed that these applications incorporate characteristics of both Theories of Behavior and Theories of Construction of Knowledge. All these findings fall in with the statements of the developers of the five applications studied, as reported in the supporting material of each application. Taking under consideration that the dominating theories of learning are the Theories of Construction of Knowledge, as they can broaden the students' skills better than others (Malabar & Pountney, 2002), it is obvious that the five applications which were studied and are proposed for use in the Greek schools incorporate these theories in whole or in part.

Moreover, it is important for a teacher to be able to recognize specific characteristics of an educational application concerning the embedded learning theories in order to utilize the application in the most proper way in the educational process. Teachers should be supported via suitable training courses towards this direction. However, studies have shown that many factors affect, eventually, the way of integrating ICTs in the educational process. Such factors may be related, except for teacher training, to the technological infrastructure of school units, to both technological and pedagogical support in applying educational activities in class, and to teachers' beliefs about teaching and learning, their attitudes towards ICTs in the field of education, and towards life in general, skills of using ICTs, etc. (Sang et al., 2010). All the aforementioned factors should be studied, taken into account and dealt with in order for ICTs to be fully integrated into school class and practice.

References

Anderson, J. R., Reder, L. M., & Simon, H. A. (1998). Radical constructivism and cognitive psychology. In D. Ravitch (Ed.), *Brookings papers on education policy* (pp. 227–255). Washington, DC: Brookings Institution.

Atkins, M. J. (1993). Theories of learning and multimedia applications: An overview. *Research Papers in Education, 8*(2), 251–271.

Barzel, B., Drijvers, P., Maschietto, M., & Trouche, L. (2005). Tools and technologies in mathematical didactics. *Proceedings of the Fourth Congress of the European Society for Research in Mathematics Education* (pp. 927–938).

Bigge, M. L., & Shermis, S. S. (1999). *Learning theories for teachers*. London: Longman.

Bogdan, R., & Bilken, S. (1982). *Qualitative research for education: An introduction to theory and methods*. Boston: Allyn & Bacon.

Bowman, D., Hodges, L., Allison, D., & Wineman, J. (1999). The educational value of an information–rich virtual environment. *Presence, 8*(3), 317–331.

Boyle, T. (1997). *Designing multimedia*. Columbus, OH: Prentice Hall.

Bryman, A. (1995). *Quantity and quality in social research*. London: Routledge.

Cohen, L., Manion, L., & Morrison, K. (2007). *Research methods in education*. London: Loutledge Falmer.

Cooper, B., & Brna, P. (2002). Supporting high quality interaction and motivation in the classroom using ICT: The social and emotional learning and engagement in the NIMIS project. *Education, Communication and Information, 2*, 113–138.

Edgar, D. W. (2012). Learning theories and historical events affecting instructional design in education: Recitation literacy toward extraction literacy practices. SAGE Open, 1–9. DOI: 10.1177/2158244012462707.

Ertmer, P. A., & Newby, T. J. (1993). Behaviourism, cognitivism, constructivism. Comparing critical features from an instructional design perspective. *Performance Improvement Quarterly,* 6(4), 50–72.

Jonassen, D. H. (1999). Designing constructivist learning environments. In C. M. Reigeluth (Ed.), *Instructional-design theories and models* (A new paradigm of instructional theory, Vol. 2, pp. 215–239). Mahwah, NJ: Lawrence Erlbaum.

Mahoney, M. J., & Granvold, D. K. (2005). Constructivism and psychotherapy. *World Psychiatry,* 4(2), 74–77.

Malabar, I., & Pountney, D. C. (2002). *Using technology to integrate constructivism and visualisation in mathematics education.* Paper presented at the 2nd International Conference on the Teaching of Mathematics. Retrieved October 31, 2013 from http://www.math.uoc.gr/~ictm2/Proceedings/pap227.pdf

McLeod, G. (2003). Learning theory and instructional design. *Learning Matters, 2,* 35–43.

Nagowah, L., & Nagowah, S. (2009). A reflection on the dominant learning theories: Behaviourism, cognitivism and constructivism. *The International Journal of Learning, 16*(2), 279–285.

Osborne, J., & Hennessy, S. (2003). *Literature Review in Science Education and the Role of ICT: Promise, Problems and Future Directions,* Report 6: FuturelabSeries, Futurelab Education.

Panagiotakopoulos, C., Pierrakeas, C., & Pintelas, P. (2003). *The educational software and its evaluation.* Athens: Metaixmio Publishing [in Greek].

Porpodas, K. (2000). *Cognitive psychology.* Athens: Ellinika Grammata [in Greek].

Redish, E. F., Saul, J. M., & Steinberg, R. N. (1997). On the effectiveness of active-engagement microcomputer-based laboratories. *American Journal of Physics, 65,* 45–54.

Roblyer, M. (2006). A tale of two technology integration strategies: Which works best? In M. Roblyer (Ed.), *Integrating educational technology into teaching* (pp. 33–68). Upper Saddle River, NJ: Pearson Education.

Ruthven, K., & Hennessy, S. (2002). A practitioner model of the use of computer-based tools and resources to support mathematics teaching and learning. *Educational Studies in Mathematics, 49*(1), 47–88.

Sang, G., Valcke, M., van Braak, J., & Tondeur, J. (2010). Student teachers' thinking processes and ICT integration: Predictors of prospective teaching behaviors with educational technology. *Computers and Education, 54,* 103–112.

Shunk, H. D. (2004). *Learning theories: An educational perspective* (5th ed.). Boston, MA: Allyn & Bakon.

Tondeur, J., van Keer, H., van Braak, J., & Valcke, M. (2008). ICT integration in the classroom: Challenging the potential of a school policy. *Computers and Education, 51,* 212–223.

Vanucci, M., & Colla, V. (2010). Educational software as a learning tool for primary school students. In S. Soormo (Ed.), *New achievements in technology education and development* (pp. 311–324). Croatia: Intech Publications.

Velázquez-Marcano, A., Williamson, V., Ashkenazi, G., Tasker, R., & Williamson, K. (2004). The use of video demonstrations and particulate animation in general chemistry. *Journal of Science Education and Technology, 13*(3), 315–323.

Part II
ICT in Preschool and Primary Education

Educational Software Use in Kindergarten

Kleopatra Nikolopoulou

Introduction

Although Information and Communication Technology (ICT) use and particularly computer use in early childhood educational settings is under-examined in comparison to other educational levels (e.g., primary and secondary education), the debate is no longer one of should we or should not we use computers in early childhood settings. Electronic culture is already an integral part of early childhood experience for many youngsters (Parette & Blum, 2013). Research studies (Clements & Sarama, 2003; Haugland, 2005; McCarrick & Li, 2007; McKenney & Voogt, 2012; Siraj-Blatchford & Siraj-Blatchford, 2006; Stephen & Plowman, 2003, 2008; Yelland, 2005) reported that computer can be used as a tool to support learning, and assist communication, collaboration, creativity, and language development in young children. Judge, Puckett, and Cabuk (2004) reported that it is increasingly important for early childhood educators to introduce and use computers in their settings, particularly for those children who do not have access at home. They assert that offering access to computers in early childhood settings helps to reduce the digital divide. The essential role of early childhood teachers in the improvement of children's computer/ICT related experiences has also been reported (Stephen & Plowman, 2008). Kindergarten teachers are, for example, responsible for selecting educational software and deciding on the ways of its use. The aim of this research study was to investigate educational software use by young children in kindergarten classes.

For the purpose of this paper, specific terms used are briefly explained. Initially, the term *computers* is used as synonymous and as more preferable to the terms *ICT* (Information and Communication Technology) and *technology*. Apart from computer software, a number of products that incorporate some aspects of ICT are available to

K. Nikolopoulou (✉)
Department of Early Childhood Education, National and Kapodistrian University of Athens, Navarinou 13A, 10680 Athens, Greece
e-mail: klnikolopoulou@ath.forthnet.gr

C. Karagiannidis et al. (eds.), *Research on e-Learning and ICT in Education: Technological, Pedagogical and Instructional Perspectives*, DOI 10.1007/978-1-4614-6501-0_4, © Springer Science+Business Media New York 2014

young children such as electronic-musical keyboards, programmable interactive toys, and digital cameras. However, practitioners define ICT more narrowly as computers and printers and this view is very influential (Stephen & Plowman, 2008) till now. Moreover, this study focuses on computers and software that runs on computers as, for the present, this is the predominant technological device for those kindergarten classrooms in Greece that have access to technology. The term *educational software use* refers to children's computer related activities, as well as the observation of such activities. The term *early childhood settings* is used as synonymous to the terms *kindergartens* and *preschools*. This term refers to kindergarten classrooms (formal educational settings) that attend children above 3 years old.

Theoretical Background

Educational Software Usage in Early Childhood Settings

Regarding educational software usage in kindergarten classes, different software programs/applications have been used such as interactive multimedia environments, games, painting/drawing programs, Word processing, and Logo programming (Chera & Wood, 2003; Clements, 2000; Labbo, Sprague, Montero, & Font, 2000; Sung, Chang, & Lee, 2008). The boundaries between different software applications produced for young children are not necessarily fixed, as different applications are presented in a form of play designed to attract and sustain children's attention. For example, both commercial and educational CD-ROMs incorporate the play component, which should not be seen solely for recreation or fun purposes (Verenikina, Herrington, Peterson, & Mantei, 2010). Early childhood educational software contains activities which quite frequently focus on early development skills such as sorting–classifying, matching, following instructions, and spatial reasoning (Stephen & Plowman, 2003). Regarding its usage in early childhood educational settings, McKenney's and Voogt's study (2010) showed that children 4–7 year old reported playing games, practicing words/maths, and drawing as the most frequently activities done in kindergarten classrooms. Marsh et al. (2005) reported frequent use of painting/drawing packages and rare use of the Internet.

Although there are a variety of educational software programs used by children in kindergarten classes, there is limited empirical evidence on how educational software is used in classrooms. For example, Ljung-Djärf, Åberg-Bengtsson, and Ottosson (2005) reported that computer can be used, among others, as an available option or as an essential activity. Computer use is often something that may be allowed between planned or adult-led activities, which means that it is typically used during the time that is organized as free play (Howard, Miles, & Rees-Davies, 2012; Ljung-Djärf, 2008). In America, the National Association for the Education of Young Children and Fred Rogers Center for early learning and children's media (NAEYC – FRC 2012), in their position statement regarding the role of technology in preschool classrooms, state that (a) technology and interactive media tools must be used appropriately, and (b) technology integration is effective when integrated into the environment, curriculum, and daily routines. When computer use takes place within kindergarten classes, the role of teacher/adult intervention in supporting and extending children's experiences has been emphasized (Nir-Gal & Klein, 2004; Stephen & Plowman, 2003). For example, McKenney and Voogt (2009) found that teacher intervention elicited young children's engagement with literacy concepts and that children were able to work independently with the computer program after a few instruction sessions. Other studies have shown that children are largely left alone at the computer with the teachers seldom to participate in what goes on there (Plowman & Stephen, 2005) and, in particular, when children played computer games there was lack of teacher intervention (Ljung-Djärf et al., 2005; Vangsnes, Økland, & Krumsvik, 2012).

In Greece there are a few empirical studies regarding educational software or Internet usage in kindergarten classes (Chronaki & Stergiou, 2005; Fesakis, Sofroniou, & Mavroudi, 2011). For example, Chronaki and Stergiou (2005) compared computer use in two kindergartens, carrying out interviews with teachers and children. This paper presents research findings regarding educational software use in kindergarten classes in Athens, Greece. Fesakis et al. (2011) carried out an experimental case study of a learning activity meant for teaching preschoolers geometric concepts, via the use of communication tools from the Internet. The results of this study constitute part of a research project regarding ICT use–integration in kindergarten classes in Greece. Thus, some information about ICT in early childhood education in Greece is provided below.

ICT in Early Childhood Education in Greece

The Greek educational system is centrally organized and the main bodies of educational policy and planning are the Ministry of Education (YPEPTH) and the Pedagogical Institute (PI). Until recently, there was a lack of a central plan for the introduction of ICT. The Pedagogical Institute has published a framework for the introduction of ICT in teaching and learning, the so-called "Cross-Thematic Curriculum Framework for ICTs." For early childhood education, it sets directions for programs regarding planning and development of activities in the context of the following subjects: language, mathematics, environmental studies, creation/expression, and computer science (YPEPTH – PI 2003). These programs are not considered as independent subjects, but it is suggested to be taken into account when planning and implementing meaningful and purposeful activities for the children.

Among the essential prerequisites for computer integration in early childhood education are the placement of the computer/ICT in class (i.e., the so called "computer corner") and its inclusion in kindergarten's daily teaching practice (Komis, 2004). In order to successfully implement the curriculum, it is essential for teachers to be provided with the appropriate training and for early childhood classrooms with the appropriate resources. Regarding resources, many kindergartens have lately acquired computers for use by the children. However, those kindergartens with a computer in their classrooms have, more or less, similar technology facilities (i.e., predominantly one or two computers). There are no computer labs in kindergartens. Regarding teachers, they are responsible for translating into practice the expectations/visions of curricula planners. The "Teachers' training on ICT in Education" program (YPEPTH – PI 2009), which is the most widespread in Greece, included the training of early childhood teachers as well. The first phase of the program included training in technical skills and has been attended by the majority of early childhood teachers. The second phase of the program which is dedicated to providing teachers with the pedagogical skills for ICT integration in the classrooms has been attended and is currently being attended by a number of teachers (the actual number is not known yet, as it forms part of internal evaluation of the program which still takes place). This large scale inservice training aims, among others, to familiarize teachers with appropriate educational software and the skills to adopt–integrate ICT in their everyday teaching practices. Within the Greek context, there is currently poor uptake of computers in early childhood settings (Nikolopoulou, 2009).

Method

Objectives of the Study

As stated earlier, the aim of this research study was to investigate the use of educational software in kindergarten classes. Three basic parameters of the study were as follows: (1) the presence of at least one computer in the kindergarten classroom and its use by preschool children, (2) the voluntary participation of kindergarten teachers, and (3) the study to be carried out without artificial intervention by the researcher (i.e., into the "natural" classroom environment). For the purpose of this research, official permission was provided by the research department of the Greek Pedagogical Institute and all kindergarten schools and their participants were treated anonymously. The objectives of this study were:

1. To identify the educational software commonly used by children in kindergarten classes.
2. To investigate how educational software is used in kindergarten classes.
3. To find out possible difficulties children face in the use of educational software.

Sample

Seventeen state kindergartens from Athens, in Greece, participated in this study and their teachers agreed to voluntarily participate in the research project. All kindergarten teachers were women (age range: 26–55), most of whom had attended the first phase of the "Teachers' training on ICT in Education" program (i.e., introductory training in ICT skills). However, none of them had attended the second phase of this program which regards pedagogical training in the use of ICT in classes (this phase has started only recently, see YPEPTH 2012). All schools were committed to the same National Curriculum guidelines. The ages of the children ranged from 4 to 6.5 years. However, over 88 % of the children were aged 5–6.5 years old, as kindergarten attendance in Greece is now obligatory for this age group (i.e., the age group that will attend primary school during the next academic year). Table 1 shows the characteristics of kindergartens, as derived from interviews/discussions with the teachers and observations made in classes. In order to maintain the anonymity, the codes N1–N17 (N1: kindergarten 1, N2: kindergarten 2, etc.) were used. Each kindergarten participated in the research with one or more classes (full-day and/or classic class, as shown in the second column of Table 1). Classes held between 13 and 26 children, except those serving children with special needs. Table 1 also shows the number of teachers interviewed, the total number and ages of children, the number of computers, as well as the frequency and the duration of computer use (per child).

One or two computers were available in 15 (out of the 17) kindergartens and this reflects the typical situation in Greek kindergartens. The computer(s) were located in the classroom, they were set up on a table at the computer corner, while each computer had two kindergarten-sized chairs placed before it: to facilitate collaboration and to provide a place for children to sit and watch their peers if they are waiting to use the computer on their own (according to teachers' explanations). In only one school (N9), the teacher had her desk in the classroom and as a result it was the same computer (located on teacher's desk) being used by both the children and the class teacher (for administrative purposes etc.). Computer use appeared to be an established practice during the last 3 years.

Almost all schools (except N17) were located in central semi-urban areas of the Greek capital, in medium (neither high nor low) socioeconomic areas, without variation in ethnic background. Only the school N17 was located in a working class socioeconomic area, around 17 km away from the city center. Around 90 % of the children of the sample spoke Greek as a first language.

Data Collection Process and Research Instruments

The data were collected between January 2009 and June 2010 and consisted of interviews and informal discussions with the kindergarten teachers, observations and field notes of class activities. All data were collected by the researcher and author of this paper. Qualitative approaches seem practical and valuable for early childhood settings, although they include small samples and are not easily generalizable (Nikolopoulou, 2010). The interviews with the teachers were conducted before the observation sessions, they took place in the classroom (after the preschool day ended) and they were recorded digitally and transcribed. Approximately 8 h of interview recordings was collected and transcribed. The semi-structured interviews were based on specific axes related to the research objectives. The following questions were used: What educational software programs are used by children in the class?

Table 1 The characteristics of kindergartens

Kindergarten	Type of class(es)	No. of teachers	No. of children	Ages of children	No. of computers	Frequency of computer use (per child)	Duration of computer use (min)
N1	Full-day[a]	1	23	4–6	2	2–3 Times/week	10
N2	Full-day	1	25	5–6	1	Once/week	10–15
N3	Classic[b]	2	26	4–6	3	Once/week	30 (max)
N4	Full-day	1	13	4,5–6	1	Once/week	5–15
N5	Classic	1	15	4,5–6,5	2	Every day	10
N6	Full-day	2	21	5–6	1	Once/week	8–15
N7	Classic +, full-day	2	28	5–6	2	Once/week	10
N8	Full-day	2	22	5,5–6	1	Once/month	8
N9	Classic +, full-day	2	43	4,5–6,5	2	Once/week	10
N10	Full-day	1	25	5–6	2	Once/week	10–15
N11	Full-day +, 2 classic	2	57	4–6	1	Every 3 weeks	10–15
N12	Classic +, full-day	2	41	4,5–6,5	2	Weekly –once/month	10–15
N13	2 Full-day	2	49	5–6	3	Once/week	10–20
N14	Classic	1	23	5–6	1	Once/month	10–15
N15	Classic	1	22	5–6	1	Once/week	10–20
N16	Special needs	1	4	4–6	1	Once/week	10–20
N17	Special needs	1	4	4–6	2	Weekly/bi-monthly	10–20

[a]Full-day class: children attend kindergarten from 8:30 a.m. to 4 p.m.
[b]Classic class: children attend kindergarten from 8:30 a.m.to 12.30 p.m.

How are these programs being used? Do children face difficulties when using specific software programs? All teachers were confronted with the same set of core questions, while follow-up questions were formulated in order to offer teachers the opportunity to introduce unexpected ideas and thoughts. The interviews also addressed areas such as demographics and computer availability/access.

In parallel with the interviews, in each kindergarten were conducted two or three observations of computer use (i.e., two or three sessions, each one in a different day), of total duration of 1.6–3 h. All observations took place from January (2009 or 2010) onwards, after negotiation with class teachers. This time period, being 3 months after the commencement of the academic year, was proposed by the teachers because they wanted their children to be initially acquainted to the new kindergarten environment before any research took place. The observations were naturalistic observations of the children's and teachers' activity in the classroom. As the researcher was also an observer, she sat close to the computer corner and she needed to be mindful of her position in the classroom (e.g., as a researcher observing children using computers there was a challenge of supporting their engagement). During the observations, a small number of children (two or three) sat at the computer corner, while the rest of the class was engaged in other free play activities. Children did engage with the computer activities in ways that suggested that they were comfortable with the researcher's presence. The observations involved the writing of detailed field notes (what took place around the computer etc.) during and immediately after the observations. As field notes were reviewed memos were recorded to document emerging thoughts, feelings and questions regarding the observations. Informal discussions with the teachers took place during and mainly immediately after the observations (e.g., for clarifications on various actions).

In order to investigate the first research objective, the data were collected via interviews with the teachers. For the investigation of the second and third objectives, interviews and observations/field notes were used. As a main parameter of the study was to be carried out without an imposed intervention by the researcher (i.e., in the natural environment of the everyday practice), it was the teachers who decided on the timing of the observations, as well as on the software used. There was also negotiation with the teachers with regard to the number of sessions observed (i.e., two or three sessions).

Data Analysis

The qualitative data gathered (from interviews, observations, field notes) were each analyzed using classical content analysis. All the data sources were analyzed to find codes that could be organized into categories. The codes were produced deductively and then included as descriptive information about the data (Lecch & Onwuegbuzie, 2007). Results derived from one source of data were supported by other data sources. Some of the interview statements most strongly supporting the categories are presented.

Ethical Considerations

Regarding ethical considerations, kindergarten teachers were informed about the nature, duration, and the aim of the research study. Ethical issues arise when investigating dependent, vulnerable members of society such as young children in early childhood education settings (Morgan, 2010). Gaining informed consent from research participants is widely regarded as central to ethical research practice and in institutional settings such as schools, access tends to be mediated by teachers, managers, etc. (Heath, Charles, Crow, & Wiles, 2007). Issues of anonymity and confidentiality are also included in ethical considerations, thus the above parameters were assured in this study (i.e., all kindergartens and participants were replaced with codes). Additionally, initial and ongoing consent with teachers was negotiated and participants were informed about research outcomes.

Results and Discussion

This section describes and discusses the results in three subsections, according to the research objectives, with parallel presentation of indicative excerpts from the interviews. This is done because direct quotes from the interviews can help readers to acquire a more complete view of the events and situations (Forman & Hall, 2005). The findings are presented for all schools, descriptively.

Educational Software Commonly Used by Children in Kindergarten Classes

Table 2 shows the educational software/programs most commonly used by young children in classes, as reported by kindergarten teachers: the MS Paint, the commercial series Ram Kid/Kide Pedia (which include many games), followed by the use of

Table 2 Educational programs commonly used in kindergarten classes by children

	No. of times mentioned
MS Paint (and painting/drawing programs such as TuxPaint)	13
Ram Kid, Kide Pedia (commercial series that include many games)	11
Educational CD-ROMs (e.g., "My class")	9
Word processing (MS Word)	8
"Explorer of the computer—Electronic Postman" (educational software distributed to most all-day classes (by the Greek Ministry of Education)	5
Internet	5
Digital games (commercial)	3
MS PowerPoint	2

educational CD-ROMs (e.g., "My class," "Salto and Zelia," "On the road safely") and the MS Word. The programs "MS Paint" and "MS Word" are included in every computer as parts of the Microsoft Office, and thus, there is no extra cost for the kindergartens. Taken into account the limited school budgets, such open ended software is suggested to be embraced in kindergarten classrooms (and as a consequence, it is interesting to investigate examples of good practice and what actually children learn). Additionally, the educational software "Explorer of the computer—Electronic Postman" (contains language and mathematics learning activities) has been distributed recently, during the academic year 2008–2009, by the Greek Ministry of Education in most full-day kindergarten classes without any cost. Some kindergarten teachers use this software in their class and characterized it as particularly interesting. For example, in N4 (full-day class) it is used as a supporting tool for language and mathematics, while the teachers in N7 (classic and full-day classes) use it systematically during the hour of free play activities. However, other teachers (in N1, N2) who have this software in the kindergarten, do not use it in their class because they do not consider it as appropriate for the children. For example, "I do not consider it (the software) appropriate as to its design–placement of specific buttons on screen—because the children can be easily lost" (teacher in N1), or "It has a long introduction and the kids get bored…" (teacher in N2).

Some programs (especially the commercial series Ram Kid/Kide Pedia and the educational CD-ROMs) are frequently brought in classes either by the teachers (e.g., in kindergartens N2, N10, N11, N12, N14) or by the parents (e.g., in N3, N9, N10, N11, N12). Table 2 reveals a limited range of programs used in classes and this may be attributed to the tight school finances. The findings are in some agreement with earlier research. For example, Marsh et al. (2005) reported frequent use of painting/drawing programs and rare use of the Internet, while others (Lee & O'Rourke, 2006) found frequent use of CD-ROMs (e.g., games, talking books). In Greece, Chronaki and Stergiou (2005) found that children carried out educational activities (writing words and numbers, painting), aiming at children's familiarization with the computer. The reasons for using computers with children in kindergarten classes (discussed in another paper) were the development of language and fine motor skills, and the computer's contribution as an incentive in the learning process. In particular, the MS Word was mainly used for the development of language, reading, and writing skills, for emergent literacy skills and in order to support curriculum learning objectives in language—as well as for providing practice in the recognition of the alphabet letters. The Internet (in those kindergartens which had a connection) was reported to be mainly used for downloading/playing games, for carrying out project work and for downloading educational material and photographs.

Independently of the programs used and the tight budgets, the role of the kindergarten teachers was essential because they decided on the program(s) used by their children. An example of an interview excerpt was: "We have some of the Ram Kid series, we intend to buy them with our money. A mother has brought the program 'On the road safely' and when we talk about traffic education we use this very much… We first look at the software, i.e., we see whether the activities included are appropriate for our children. We have found some (programs) that were very nice but they did not correspond to our children's level and interests" (teacher in N11). Different decisions made by the teachers are mentioned in the following sections of the paper. The crucial role of the kindergarten teachers in the computer environment has been reported in literature (Keengwe & Onchwari, 2009; Nir-Gal & Klein, 2004). The essential role of the teachers in this study is also highlighted in the subsequent sections of this paper.

How Educational Software Is Used in Kindergarten Classes

This section discusses how educational software was used in the classes, and it also includes findings regarding when the software was used. Computer use took place, mainly, during the hour of free activities/play at the computer corner. As most teachers stated, one hour every morning or every afternoon is devoted to computer use. These findings are in agreement with the relevant literature which refers to computer use in kindergarten's daily practice so that children can understand its contribution towards teaching and learning (Plowman & Stephen, 2003), and to that computer use took place during the free play activities (Ljung-Djärf, 2008; Ljung-Djärf et al., 2005). In this study, the frequency of computer use, per child, was found to vary between 2 and 3 times per week and once per month (see Table 1). In most kindergartens, teachers reported that every child was entitled to work on the computer (if s/he wanted) once per week with an average time of 10–20 min. In about half of the kindergartens there was a sort of a systematic way for the children to have access to the computer, such as a reference plan. In cases of a lack of a reference plan, children's use of the computer was not recorded, but some teachers said they did remember which children passed from the computer corner. Educational software was often reported to be used in the context of a project in combination with other non-computer based activities (e.g., in N1, N2, N3, N5), or for producing the class' newspaper (in N1). Computer use is suggested to be combined with off-computer classroom activities, as relevant literature has shown that this way can lead to better learning effects (Haugland, 2000; McKenney & Voogt, 2009). Parette and Blum (2013) discussed elements of technology integration and identified key activities in which technologies can be used across preschool settings. Such activities may embrace the use of educational software in order to support and enhance children's leaning.

Class organization in computer environment was found to, mainly, take place in small groups because as two teachers explained: "It works very well as a group because the other child sits next to it and says 'you haven't seen this!' or 'no, we must not do this', i.e., they discuss, they help each other, the child waits his/her turn" (teachers in N11). An exception to group work constituted the kindergarten N17, which serves children with special needs. In this case, each child works with the teacher's help in order to achieve specific objectives: "The autistic child, who can not interact simultaneously with the screen and the teacher, focuses on the screen... It is important for children with special needs to acquire fine motor skills and to understand the cause-effect relationship. There are difficulties depending on the child, for example with the mouse. I do help them… Two objectives can be pursued in parallel, for example, development of fine motor and cognitive skills" (teacher in N17).

Class observations revealed that, in most cases, when children were using different programs there was some type of teacher intervention and guidance. For example, when they were using the program MS Word there was an initial guidance from the teachers and afterwards an intervention-assistance when children did not know specific functions (transition to the next line, error erasing, etc.). The class observations (in kindergartens N1, N3, N4, N6, N7, N9, N10) revealed that children, with the help of their teachers, used successfully different functions of the MS Word such as "delete an error" (button "Backspace"), "transfer to the next line" (button "Enter"), "select a color," "drag and drop," and "save a file." Children were happy to write their name, to select-change a color and to change the size of the letters of their name (as well as of other words). It was also observed that children cooperated and helped each other for the successful outcome of a learning activity. In any case, it was the teacher who knew her children in the class and she decided on the type of intervention needed. For example, an interview excerpt was: "Children sit (on the computer) several times on their own and seek help from other children—they believe they know—rather than from myself… I consider it important to sit next to very young children because when they cannot find something they get bored and leave the computer" (teacher in N7). Teacher's guidance/mediation could be broadly divided into three categories, which were also observed to take place in combination: (a) step-by-step guidance for teaching new concepts/skills, (b) initial explanations (e.g., function of specific buttons) provided by the teachers and then independent work by the children, and (c) teacher guidance/assistance whenever children asked for it. These types of teacher guidance are discussed among the recommendations made by researchers (Plowman & Stephen, 2005; Stephen & Plowman, 2008) for more effective computer integration in early childhood settings. Regarding teacher guidance, the use of computer games (the series Ram Kid, Kide Pedia, etc.) constituted an exception, as children played on their own (without asking for help), they often chose activities they had played before and knew in advance the correct answers (they did not even wait to listen to the instructions), and they never asked for teacher's help. Regarding this point, there is an agreement with other research studies (Ljung-Djärf et al., 2005; Vangsnes et al., 2012) which reported lack of teacher intervention when children played computer games. As evidence-based guidelines for computer use in preschool education are limited (Siraj-Blatchford & Siraj-Blatchford, 2006), it is rather uncertain for teachers on how to achieve the visions-claims reported in literature. The issue of teacher guidance when children use different educational software programs in kindergarten classes is suggested for further investigation.

Teachers reported that children's computer work is often displayed in the classroom. For example, children's drawings made with the program MS Paint alternate as a background on the class computer (in N2), children's printed work is displayed at the end of the year (in N9), while all children's computer work is copied onto a CD for the parents (in N10). For example, "There is a computer folder which is given to parents at the end of the year…it includes all work the child has done on the computer (printouts with names, pictures on Paint etc)" (teacher in N10). In such a way, computer use is considered as an activity carried out in kindergarten's daily practice, an activity like other school activities that may foster the links between school and parents. Additionally, several teachers noted examples of children's evident pleasure during their engagement with ICT (i.e., an aspect of children's preschool experiences that is valued, as promoting a positive disposition towards learning): "After help as to where to click, she was happy to print, a short phrase she wrote using MS Word, independently" (teacher in N4).

The interviews with the teachers also revealed the time period (timing) during which some of the programs are being used in classes. It was shown that computer games are mainly used at the beginning of the academic year, while the word processor is used by the end of the year. Indicative quotes from interviews were: "Computer games are mainly used at the beginning of the year, so that children become acquainted with the use of the mouse, while the word processor is used by the end of the year" (teacher in N3), "Children, especially by the end of the year, recognize the letters of the alphabet, they can make the transfer between lowercase and uppercase letters… thus the word processor is used by the end of the year" (in N7), and "The letters on keyboard are uppercase, while the children in kindergarten learn initially the lowercase letters… the (program) Word is used in spring" (in N9). In another kindergarten where the uppercase letters are being taught first, "Every child who enters the class in the morning is encouraged to sit on the computer to write her/his name on a separate line. They have been taught the uppercase letters and now (month May) we are in the process of teaching the lowercase letters. After March they started to write their name in the Word every morning, as a kind of register –till then they wrote it on a paper" (teacher in N6). It appears that some teachers decide on the learning goals to be achieved in their class before they decide on the type of software, and this decision/sequence is in agreement with earlier research (Haugland, 2005; Lin, 2012). For example, Lin (2012) suggests that teachers can choose the learning objectives and design a series of activities (software use could be among them) in order to accomplish learning goals.

Difficulties Children Face in the Use of Educational Software

The interviews with the teachers in combination with class observations revealed some difficulties children encountered when using the programs MS Paint and MS Word. Interestingly, although the use of MS Paint was most commonly reported (as shown in Table 2), in almost one third of the kindergartens (in N7, N9, N10, N11, and N16) children faced some sort of difficulties. Examples of excerpts from the interviews were: "The children initially preferred games but now they are also using MS Paint with my help, because they have difficulties" (teacher in N10) and "The MS Paint is not used because I find it difficult… in order to get a quality result – painting—it needs time for training" (teacher in N7). One factor that makes the program MS Paint difficult is that some children have not developed the necessary fine motor skills: for example, they have got used to draw a house much easier by hand using traditional materials, rather than by using the Paint program. Drawing with pencils and other traditional materials is an essential traditional activity and the use of the software does not come to replace it but to support and extend children's experiences. Guided interaction (e.g., demonstrating how to use the eraser/paint-brush, or providing feedback so as to encourage the child's efforts) is a way for helping the children overcome some difficulties. Overall, the role of learning in the use of software programs is important and (as a teacher mentioned) time is needed for children's training and practice.

Regarding the use of MS Word, almost in every class where its use was observed, children faced difficulties in identifying specific alphabet letters on the keyboard—because the Greek and the English characters were both present on some buttons. This difficulty could be overcome by placing on the keyboard, stickers with the Greek uppercase letters, a procedure which was successfully followed in kindergarten N6. Furthermore, another difficulty was that children pressed continually one button, with the consequent need to delete several characters (i.e., by using the Backspace button). In order for the MS Word to be used in class, it is suggested for children to have an initial acquaintance with the alphabet letters: this helps children to identify/recognize the relevant letters on the keyboard. Thus, the time period the Word is introduced in class is very important. It has been mentioned that teachers chose to introduce the program in spring, towards the end of the academic year. The role of learning in the use of MS Word is important. For example, as two teachers reported informally, children are sometimes given text to copy and as their skill and accuracy develop, they are expected to type and print short sentences.

Aspects of observations together with the interviews revealed that some children haven't developed the necessary fine motor skills for the use of the software. At the beginning of the academic year some problems appear mainly with those children who do not have a computer at home, but afterwards all children seem to become accustomed to computer use. Difficulties with the mouse seem to be easily overcome, through practice. Examples from interview excerpts were: "Some children need physical guidance to support their development of mouse control. However, after few attempts they get mouse control and become more confident" (teacher in N8), "Children are more familiar with the mouse—because they play games—rather than with the keyboard. They often press continually the keyboard buttons… I've noticed differences in children's fine motor skills due to computer use at home" (teacher in N7), "We found out that some children do not have computer at home and at the beginning they face difficulties. The computer helps in the development of fine motor skills –the mouse helps a lot…In general, when computer games are carefully selected they help a lot" (teacher in N11) and "Gender differences are not intense, the differences appear due to different access to computer at home and due to the frequency of choosing the computer at school…sometimes, children 4 years old handle the mouse much better than older children who rarely choose to use the computer at school" (teacher in N6). Additionally, in a class with children with special needs there were present some initial difficulties, which were then overcome: "We started with the painting program where children struggled a bit because it did not come out—what they wanted—i.e., what comes out with the hand. They faced difficulties with the use of the mouse…Later on, we put children's names on the computer and they were encouraged to write them with different characters" (teacher in N16). The interview excerpts reveal the role of learning/practice as well as the crucial role of the kindergarten teachers in the study. Computers have the potential to support young children's classroom experiences, but for this to happen "it is necessary for teachers to carefully plan for, and articulate to children, suitable classroom tasks" (Kervin & Mantei, 2009, p. 30).

Some of the interview excerpts presented in this paper, as well as others not shown here, revealed issues related (a) to the use of computer by children at home and (b) to children's gender. The already developed children's fine motor skills were often attributed to the use of computer at home. Recent research (McKenney & Voogt, 2010; Plowman, McPake, & Stephen, 2008) reported that young children have access to and use the computer/ICT at home and many children had acquired the basic computer skills already from home (before they entered kindergarten). As there are differences regarding the skills children bring to classroom use of computers, it is suggested for teachers to be aware of these skills (in order, for example, to provide support for those children without previous technological experience). Regarding children's gender, the results appeared contradictory. In some kindergartens (in N9, N10, N12), children's gender appears to be related to the frequency of computer use (is higher for boys) or to children's preferences to different types of software. Some teachers reported that boys were more interested in using the computer because they chose it more frequently during the hours of free activities, while the girls preferred to be engaged in other activities. Two interview excerpts regarding children's preferences were: "Girls prefer activities with puzzles, painting" (in N9) and "Boys prefer action games, games that provide scores" (in N9, N12). However, in other kindergartens (e.g., in N6 and N7) no gender differences were reported, as "When it comes their turn to work on the computer all children want – it did not happen a child not to want (the computer) and to choose another activity" (teacher in N7). In literature, gender differences regarded children's preferences towards interface design (Passig & Levin, 2000) and software's characters (Littleton, Light, Joiner, Messer, & Barnes, 1992). In particular, young boys seem to be attracted by movement, "male" characters and action games, while young girls seem to prefer the colorful buttons of a program and "female" characters. However, other studies did not report on significant gender differences when children use computers in class (Hatzigianni & Margetts, 2012; Shawareb, 2011). As a consequence, the issue of gender can be further investigated.

Concluding Comments and Recommendations for Future Research

The research described in this paper provides some useful insight for researchers and teachers about educational software usage in kindergarten classes. The class observations and the interviews with the teachers revealed some issues difficult to be explored through large-scale quantitative surveys. The data derived from the 17 kindergartens cannot be generalized due to the small sample and its origin from one region. However, taken into account that in Greece (as well as in other countries) there is limited empirical research, this study contributes to our understanding of computer use and classroom practices with young children. Concluding comments are presented below.

The most commonly used programs were painting programs (especially the MS Paint), the commercial series Ram Kid/Kide Pedia (which include many games), educational CD-ROMs and the MS Word, while the use of the Internet was rare. For early childhood settings with tight budgets, the use of software programs that are free, low cost or downloadable seems a good choice. In parallel, researchers have emphasized the issue of using developmentally appropriate software, in appropriate ways (Parette & Blum, 2013). Classroom activities designed using appropriate technologies and NAEYC principles (e.g., the technologies should align with the curriculum, the choice of technology should be based on how it serves classroom learning, see NAEYC – FRC 2012) support the developmental learning needs of young learners. It is the case that not all commercial computer games are developmentally appropriate for use by young children. As a starting point, software/games need to be carefully evaluated by teachers (a process facilitated when teachers have attended appropriate training) before any usage in the classroom.

This study found that computer use took place, mainly, during the hour of free activities at the computer corner. "Playing with the computer" designates a series of qualitatively different activities in which children can, for example, engage in drawing, writing or play (Plowman & Stephen, 2005), and computer use in the hour of free play activities is linked to literacy and pedagogy. For example, the manipulation of symbols and images on computer screen represents a new form of symbolic play, and there is potential in the development of children's higher order thinking (Verenikina et al., 2010; Yelland, 2005). Wohlwend (2009) demonstrated that 5–7-year-old children were accessing new literacies through pretend play—to explore iPods and video games— while Morgan (2010) indicated that teachers value and promote "playful" and interactive technology experiences as vehicles for 3–7-year-old children's learning. Appropriate ways for computer/technology integration could include technology-supported learning experiences during the hour of free activities: for example, instances where children are provided with technology support that help them complete tasks in classroom activities. With regard to the third objective, children encountered some difficulties in using the programs MS Paint and MS Word. Some difficulties with the MS Paint were mainly attributed to children's underdeveloped fine motor skills. The role of learning in the use of such programs is important, because these programs support and extend children's experiences.

The crucial role of early childhood teachers, in the whole process of computer use in kindergarten classes, has emerged. Initially, teachers' participation in this project was voluntary and they suggested the timing for the observations, while later they decided on the program(s) used in their classes and on class organization. The essential role of kindergarten teachers in ICT environments, for supporting and extending children's experiences, has been extensively discussed in relevant literature (Kervin & Mantei, 2009; Stephen & Plowman, 2008). Selwyn (2011) proposed the cultivation of a critical digital literacy approach: for example, the development of creative spaces utilizing digital technologies that bridge formal/informal divide. As young children are entering early childhood settings with dispositions that may not have been part of their repertoire of skills in past decades, early childhood educators need to be aware of this and to develop new learning experiences for young children (Zevenbergen & Logan, 2008). The teachers are the designers and implementers of learning activities for children. The role of the teachers is related to and has implications for teacher training. Teachers' skills, views, and classroom practices have all implications for in-service training in the pedagogical uses of ICT. According to Parette, Quesenberry, and Blum (2010), both preservice education and in-service professional development are important so that early childhood teachers develop and apply skills in integrating and using ICT in classroom settings.

The limitations of this study included the limited amount of time and the limited financial resources. For example, if video recordings were used during class obser-vations, this could have highlighted the interactions between young children and software, as well as the interactions among children (their gestures, dialogues, etc.). It is noted that this study did not investigate the acquisition/development of skills and knowledge through the use of educational software, and this will constitute the focus of another paper.

As there is little empirical evidence on the use of computers in early childhood settings, the following issues are suggested for future research. Investigation of the activities children do on the class computer and the development of specific skills. The research has now moved on from questions about whether ICT can help chil-dren learn (Stephen & Plowman, 2008), with the need to investigate further how and whether it makes a difference in young children's learning and development. For example, Haugland (2000) discussed for developmentally appropriate activities, while Yelland and Kilderry (2010) reported that ICT as a resource is being underutilized and children are being denied access to learning opportunities that promote open-ended applications, problem solving situations/tasks that result in varied learning outcomes. The link between early childhood pedagogy and ICT could also be further explored. It is a fact that software and hardware are constantly changing. Whilst this does not necessarily mean that the pedagogical issues of using ICT in early childhood settings automatically change as well, it cannot be assumed that they remain constant either. There is a need, for example, to identify quality practices and appropriate types of teacher intervention. As Parette and Blum (2013) reported, the key challenge for today's teachers is how to use technologies effec-tively and efficiently in order to support learning experiences for young children in the classroom. Future research could also investigate to what extent the factors "children's use of computer/ICT at home" and "children's gender" impact on chil-dren's use of ICT in early childhood settings. Finally, some other broader fields that might be of interest to educators/researchers include teachers' attitudes and motiva-tions to use ICT in kindergartens. Provided that today's children are surrounded by different technological tools, it is worth investigating how teachers embrace and utilize a broader range of technologies, apart from computers, to support young children's learning in classrooms.

References

Chera, P., & Wood, C. (2003). Animated multimedia 'talking books' can promote phonological awareness in children beginning to read. *Learning and Instruction, 13*(1), 33–52.

Chronaki, A., & Stergiou, E. (2005). The computer in kindergarten class: Children's preferences and access to computers. *Teaching Science: Research and Practice, 13*, 46–54. In Greek.

Clements, D. (2000). From exercises and tasks to problems and projects—unique contributions of computers to innovative mathematics education. *Journal of Mathematical Behaviour, 19*(1), 9–47.

Clements, D., & Sarama, J. (2003). Strip mining for gold: Research and policy in educational technology—A response to 'Fool's Gold'. *Educational Technology Review, 11*(1), 7–69.

Fesakis, G., Sofroniou, C., & Mavroudi, E. (2011). Using the internet for communicative learning activities in kindergarten: The case of the "Shapes Planet". *Early Childhood Education Journal, 38*(5), 385–392.

Forman, G., & Hall, E. (2005). Wondering with children: the importance of observation in early education. *Early Childhood Research and Practice, 7*(2). Retrieved November 18, 2012, from http://ecrp.uiuc.edu/v7n2/forman.html.

Hatzigianni, M., & Margetts, K. (2012). 'I am good at computers': Young children's computer use and their computer self-esteem. *European Early Childhood Education Research Journal, 20*(1), 3–20.

Haugland, S. (2000). *Computers and young children*. Eric Digest, ED438926, 1–2.

Haugland, S. (2005). Selecting or upgrading software and web sites in the classroom. *Early Childhood Education Journal, 32*(5), 329–340.

Heath, S., Charles, V., Crow, G., & Wiles, G. (2007). Informed consent, gatekeepers and go-betweens: Negotiating consent in child- and youth-orientated institutions. *British Educational Research Journal, 33*(3), 403–417.

Howard, J., Miles, G., & Rees-Davies, L. (2012). Computer use within a play-based early years curriculum. *International Journal of Early Years Education, 20*(2), 175–189.

Judge, S., Puckett, K., & Cabuk, B. (2004). Digital equity: New findings from the early childhood longitudinal study. *Journal of Research on Technology in Education, 36*(4), 383–396.

Keengwe, J., & Onchwari, G. (2009). Technology and early childhood education: A technology integration professional development model for practicing teachers. *Early Childhood Education Journal, 37*(3), 209–218.

Kervin, L., & Mantei, J. (2009). Using computers to support children as authors: an examination of three cases. *Technology, Pedagogy and Education, 18*(1), 19–32.

Komis, V. (2004). *Introduction to educational applications of ICT*. Athens: Editions New Technologies. In Greek.

Labbo, L., Sprague, L., Montero, M., & Font, G. (2000). Connecting a computer center to themes, literature and kindergartners' literacy needs. *Reading Online, 4*(1). Retrieved July 8, 2012, from http://www.readingonline.org/electronic/labbo.

Lee, L., & O'Rourke, M. (2006). Information and communication technologies: transforming views of literacies in early childhood settings. *Early Years, 26*(1), 49–62.

Leech, N., & Onwuegbuzie, J. (2007). An array of qualitative data analysis tools: A call for data analysis triangulation. *School Psychology Quarterly, 22*(4), 557–584.

Lin, C.-H. (2012). Application of a model for the integration of technology in kindergarten: An empirical investigation in Taiwan. *Early Childhood Education Journal, 40*(1), 5–17.

Littleton, K., Light, P., Joiner, R., Messer, D., & Barnes, P. (1992). Pairing and gender effects in computer based learning. *Journal of Psychology in Education, 7*(4), 1–14.

Ljung-Djärf, A. (2008). To play or not to play—that is the question: computer use within three Swedish preschools. *Early Childhood and Development, 19*(2), 330–339.

Ljung-Djärf, A., Åberg-Bengtsson, L., & Ottosson, T. (2005). Ways of relating to computer use in preschool activity. *International Journal of Early Years Education, 13*(1), 29–41.

Marsh, J., Brooks, G., Hughes, J., Ritchie, L., Roberts, S., & Wright, K. (2005). *Digital beginnings: Young children's use of popular culture, media and new technologies*. Sheffield: University of Sheffield.

McCarrick, K., & Li, X. (2007). Buried treasure: the impact of computer use on young children's social, cognitive, language development and motivation. *AACE Journal, 15*(1), 73–95.

McKenney, S., & Voogt, J. (2009). Designing technology for emergent literacy: The PictoPal initiative. *Computers & Education, 52*(4), 719–729.

McKenney, S., & Voogt, J. (2010). Technology and young children: How 4–7 year olds perceive their own use of computers. *Computers in Human Behavior, 26*(4), 656–664.

McKenney, S., & Voogt, J. (2012). Teacher design of technology for emergent literacy: An explorative feasibility study. *Australasian Journal of Early Childhood, 37*(1), 4–12.

Morgan, A. (2010). Interactive whiteboards, interactivity and play in the classroom with children aged three to seven years. *European Early Childhood Education Research Journal, 18*(1), 93–104.

NAEYC – FRC (2012). Technology and interactive media as tools in early childhood programs serving children from birth through age 8. Retrieved August 30, 2013, from http://www.naeyc.org/files/naeyc/file/positions/PS_technology_WEB2.pdf

Nikolopoulou, K. (2009). *Information and communication technologies in early childhood education: Integration and use.* Athens: Patakis. In Greek.

Nikolopoulou, K. (2010). Methods for investigating young children's learning and development with information technology. In A. McDougall, J. Murnane, A. Jones, & N. Reynolds (Eds.), *Researching IT in education: Theory, practice and future directions* (pp. 183–191). London: Routledge.

Nir-Gal, O., & Klein, P. (2004). Computers for cognitive development in early childhood—the teachers' role in the computer learning environment. *Information Technology in Childhood Education, 1*(1), 97–119.

Parette, H., & Blum, C. (2013). *Instructional technology in early childhood: Teaching in the digital age.* Baltimore, MD: Brookes.

Parette, H., Quesenberry, A., & Blum, C. (2010). Missing the boat with technology usage in early childhood settings: A 21st century view of developmentally appropriate practice. *Early Childhood Education Journal, 37*(5), 335–343.

Passig, D., & Levin, H. (2000). Gender preferences for multimedia interfaces. *Journal of Computer Assisted Learning, 16*(1), 64–71.

Plowman, L., & Stephen, C. (2003). A 'benign addition'? Research on ICT and pre-school children. *Journal of Computer Assisted Learning, 19*(2), 149–164.

Plowman, L., & Stephen, C. (2005). Children, play and computers in preschool education. *British Journal of Educational Technology, 36*(2), 145–157.

Plowman, L., McPake, J., & Stephen, C. (2008). Just picking it up? Young children learning with technology at home. *Cambridge Journal of Education, 38*(3), 303–319.

Selwyn, N. (2011). *Schools and schooling in the digital age.* London & New York: Routledge.

Shawareb, A. (2011). The effects of computer use on creative thinking among kindergarten children in Jordan. *Journal of Instructional Psychology, 38*(4), 213–220.

Siraj-Blatchford, I., & Siraj-Blatchford, J. (2006). *A guide to developing the ICT curriculum for early childhood education.* UK: Trentham Books.

Stephen, C., & Plowman, L. (2003). Information and communication technologies in pre-school settings: A review of the literature. *International Journal of Early Years Education, 11*(3), 223–234.

Stephen, C., & Plowman, L. (2008). Enhancing learning with information and communication technologies in pre-school. *Early Child Development and Care, 178*(6), 637–654.

Sung, Y., Chang, K., & Lee, M. (2008). Designing multimedia games for young children's taxonomic concept development. *Computers & Education, 50*(3), 1037–1051.

Vangsnes, V., Økland, N., & Krumsvik, R. (2012). Computer games in pre-school settings: Didactical challenges when commercial educational computer games are implemented in kindergartens. *Computers & Education, 58*(4), 1138–1148.

Verenikina, I., Herrington, J., Peterson, R., & Mantei, J. (2010). Computers and play in early childhood: Affordances and limitations. *Journal of Interactive Learning Research, 21*(1), 139–159.

Wohlwend, K. (2009). Early adopters: Playing new literacies and pretending new technologies in print-centric classrooms. *Journal of Early Childhood Literacy, 9*(2), 117–140.

Yelland, N. (2005). Curriculum, pedagogies and practice with ICT in the information age. In N. Yelland (Ed.), *Critical issues in early childhood education* (pp. 224–242). UK: Open University Press.

Yelland, N., & Kilderry, A. (2010). Becoming numerate with information and communications technologies in the twenty-first century. *International Journal of Early Years Education, 18*(2), 91–106.

YPEPTH – PI (2003). *Cross-Thematic Curriculum Framework for nursery school.* Retrieved December 9, 2012 from http://www.pi-schools.gr/programs/depps/index_eng.php

YPEPTH – PI (2009). In-service teacher training in the use of ICT in education. Retrieved December 9, 2012 from http://www.pi-schools.gr/programs/epeaek_b_epipedo

YPEPTH (2012). Programme "In-service teacher training -level B'- in ICT integration and use in teaching process". Retrieved December 9, 2012 from http://b-epipedo2.cti.gr/project-m/about-project-bepipedo-m.html

Zevenbergen, R., & Logan, H. (2008). Computer use by preschool children: Rethinking practice as digital natives come to preschool. *Australian Journal of Early Childhood, 33*(1), 37–44.

Geometry Teaching Through ICT in Primary School

Nicholas Zaranis

Introduction

Nowadays, it is becoming increasingly accepted that various ICT applications are developmentally appropriate technological resources for children of primary and secondary school age (Druin & Fast, 2002; Passey, 2006; Plowman & Stephen, 2003; Zaranis, 2011). It is obvious now that the original "aphorism" and the ignoring of ICT are no longer effective strategies and are gradually replaced by more realistic solutions as influenced by related research (Remtulla, 2010).

Technology, in this enlarged view, acts as a catalyst in their social interaction and moreover provides additional opportunities for a rich learning environment that is consistent with the modern era. International research confirms that the implementation of computers in education can have positive results in different subjects (Chou & Liu, 2005; Finegan & Austin, 2002; Livingstone, 2012). These technologies can therefore play an essential role in achieving the objectives of the primary curriculum in all sectors and subjects if supported by developmentally appropriate software applications embedded in appropriate educational scenarios (Dwyer, 2007; Fisher, Denning, Higgins, & Loveless, 2012; Lee, 2009; Zaranis & Oikonomidis 2009).

ICT and Mathematics

In the most ideal setting, information communication technologies are treated as a tool for teaching and learning (Burnett, 2009; Sife, Lwoga, & Sanga, 2007; Sutherland et al., 2004). They are used as a tool for the students to become more

N. Zaranis (✉)
Department of Primary Education, University of Crete,
Gallos University Campus, 74100 Rethymnon, Greece
e-mail: nzaranis@edc.uoc.gr

C. Karagiannidis et al. (eds.), *Research on e-Learning and ICT
in Education: Technological, Pedagogical and Instructional Perspectives*,
DOI 10.1007/978-1-4614-6501-0_5, © Springer Science+Business Media New York 2014

familiar with new technology and to integrate investigation, communication, and understanding across the full range of the curriculum. Particularly, in the cognitive field of mathematics an evaluation of learning outcomes regarding computer based mathematical teaching in students showed that computer-assisted learning can significantly help in developing proper mathematical skills and the cultivation of deeper conceptual thinking in comparison to the traditional mathematical teaching method (Dimakos & Zaranis 2010; Hardman, 2005; Keong, Horani, & Daniel, 2005).

Researchers suggest that the mathematical difficulties students encounter later are correlated with insufficient development of mathematical thinking in their early years (Bobis et al., 2005; Gersten, Jordan, & Flojo, 2005). Various researches' results relate the appropriate use of computers with the ability of students to more efficiently understand the different mathematical notions (Howie & Blignaut, 2009; Trouche & Drijvers, 2010). Thus, it becomes obvious that in the primary school level a very attractive environment of investigating the computer use in mathematics education emerges. Indeed, a vast number of studies show a positive interrelation between the use of computers and the development of mathematical thinking in school (Clements, 2002; Vale & Leder, 2004). Nonetheless, computer based activities should reflect the theoretical ideas behind them (Clements & Sarama, 2004; Dissanayake, Karunananda, & Lekamge, 2007).

Following this principle, the software designed and the students' activities developed and examined for the purposes of the current study were inspired by the framework of Realistic Mathematics Education (RME) and the van Hiele model. RME was based and developed principally upon Freudenthal's (1968) view of mathematics as a "human activity." According to his perspective, in order for mathematics to be of human value, it has to be taught so as to be useful, it has to be closely related to reality, close to children and relevant to the society (Freudenthal, 1968; Van den Heuvel-Panhuizen & Wijers, 2005). RME is an active and constantly evolving theory of teaching and learning mathematics (Van den Heuvel-Panhuizen, 2001). Indicative of this, the learning and teaching trajectories with intermediate attainment targets were first conducted for the subject of mathematical calculation at the primary school level and extended to the subject of geometry (Van den Heuvel-Panhuizen & Buys, 2008).

In the whole trajectory of the RME teaching theory, five main characteristics of understanding geometry concepts are involved: (a) introducing a problem using a realistic context; (b) identifying the main objects of the problem; (c) using appropriate social interaction and teacher intervention to refine the models of the problem; (d) encouraging the process of reinvention with the development of the problem; and (e) focusing on the connections and aspects of mathematics in general (Van den Heuvel-Panhuizen, 2001). These should be the main focuses of the learning and teaching procedure concerning geometry in primary school.

Moreover, the theory of the van Hiele model deals specifically with geometric thought as it develops through several levels of sophistication under the influence of a school curriculum (Clements & Battista, 1992). The van Hiele model uses five levels, however, for the first grade students only the first two levels were used. In the Visual Level, students were able to identify figures such as circles and triangles as visual gestalts. Conceptualization at this level includes being able to name, reproduce and group similar geometric objects by visual recognition. For instance, they might say that a figure is a rectangle because it looks like a door. In the Descriptive/ Analytic Level, students were able to identify shapes from their properties. Conceptualization at this level includes identifying geometric objects according to their properties. For example, a student sees a rhombus as a figure with four equal sides (Zaranis, 2012). Following the theoretical framework that blends together Realistic Mathematics Education (RME), the van Hiele model of geometric thinking and the use of ICT in primary school, we designed a new model referred to as the First Class Primary Shape Model (FCPSM) which consisted of five levels.

The majority of previous studies aggregately examined the effects of various teaching on the geometric shapes. However, a small number of studies have found that in the first levels of primary school, various shapes are understood differently by students (Walcott et al., 2009; Wong et al., 2007). These studies examined the impact of various teaching interventions on each shape distinctively. Specifically, in the case of circles, only the thickness and size may be varied. Rectangles and triangles may also share differences in characteristics of thickness and size with the addition of other variable characteristics such as length of sides and orientation. Moreover, triangles may vary in the degree of their angles, resulting in a greater variety of shapes. Thus, from the perspective of characteristic features, circles are the simplest. On the contrary, triangles are the most complex, and rectangles are of intermediate difficulty (Satlow & Newcombe, 1998; Wong et al., 2011).

Our study was based on the above mentioned international literature; we set out to investigate the following research question: Is the concept of triangles more difficult to understand than circles for the first grade students?

In addition, based on the previous studies, we set out to investigate the following hypotheses:

1. The students who will be taught circles with educational intervention based on FCPSM will have a significant improvement in comparison to those taught using the traditional teaching method according to the first grade curriculum.
2. The students who will be taught triangles with educational intervention based on FCPSM will have a significant improvement in comparison to those taught using the traditional teaching method according to the first grade curriculum.

The present study makes an important contribution to the literature; we examined and compared the effects of a new model which combines computer and noncomputer activities for teaching circles and triangles separately.

Methodology

Subjects

The study was carried out during the 2011–2012 school year in ten public primary schools located in the cities of Rethymno in Crete (two classes) and Athens (eight classes). It was an experimental research which compared the FCPSM teaching process to traditional teaching based on first grade curriculum. The sample included 234 first graders consisting of 123 girls and 111 boys age 6–7 years old. There were two groups in the study, one control ($n = 121$) and one experimental ($n = 113$). In the control group there was not a computer available for the students' use. The classes in the experimental group, in order to participate, were required to have a laptop computer and a video projector available for use by children as part of the teaching procedure. For the uniformity of the survey, instructions were given to the teachers who taught in the experimental or control groups. Teachers who participated in the study had university degrees in education. The teachers in the experimental group ranged from 40 to 50-year-olds with in-service teaching experience ranging from 18 to 28 years. The teachers in the control group were of ages 38–48 years with in-service teaching experience ranging from 15 to 25 years.

Instructional Intervention

In the second phase the control group taught with traditional teaching according to kindergarten curriculum. Group and individual activities were given to children every day. The experimental group covered the same material at roughly the same time according to the FCPSM teaching. The content of the 4-week syllabus of the FCPSM divided in five levels. It comprised of shapes including a variety of topics concerning fundamental geometry concepts and focus on circles and triangles.

The first level of the teaching intervention was according to the first characteristic of the teaching theory of RME which introduces a problem using a realistic context. In this level a story called "The Family of Shapes" was presented to the students. Various geometrical shapes including circles and triangles are presented in this story in a fictional family setting where each member of the family represents a particular shape. This story was designed using Flash CS3 Professional Edition and presented with the video projector in the classroom. In this story Mrs. Square and Mr. Triangle (Fig. 1-left) had a daughter Miss Circle. Later in the story, Miss Circle met Mr. Rectangle, got married, and had many children that looked like their parents and grandparents.

The second level started with an activity which identifies the main objects of the problem as underlined by the RME theory. According to the first level of the van Hiele model and the second characteristics of the RME theory, the students (a) identified various geometrical shapes by examining objects in their classrooms, (b) drew certain geometrical shapes (Fig. 1-right), and (c) named the shape of a set of various objects presented to them by the teacher.

The third level of the teaching procedure included activities using appropriate social interaction to refine the models of the problem. Firstly, a child had to draw a shape from a bag and to find out the name of the shape without seeing it. Then, the students split into groups and each group had to construct a dog or a man using a set of shapes. The final part of this level involved a computer-based group activity in which the student had to recognize and choose the correct shape among other shapes (Fig. 2-left) as implied by the first van Hiele level.

Fig. 1 Students watched the story "The Family of Shapes" (*left*—first level) and did a drawing activity (*right*—second level)

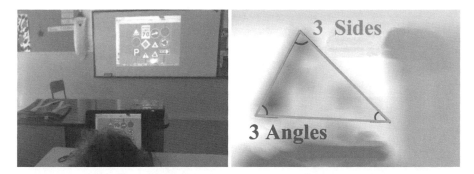

Fig. 2 The student had to recognize shapes (*left*—third level) and students viewed the properties of a triangle on the computer (*right*—fourth level)

In the fourth level of the teaching procedure, according to the second level of the van Hiele model and the RME theory, we implemented a process of reinvention with the development of the shapes in a higher cognitive level where the properties of an object were presented in a software activity (Fig. 2-right). Next, the children were separated into groups and cooperated with one another to make a shape with their bodies on the floor (Fig. 3-left). Then, they divided into groups and each group was assigned a specific shape. Each of these groups was instructed to make fake cookies from plasticine in the form of the groups' assigned shape. At the end of this activity, the students in each group shared their cookies with the other groups.

In the last level of the teaching process, as the second level of van Hiele theory implied, the students played card games with the properties of shapes. The goal of this card game is to focus on the connections and aspects of the properties of circles and triangles as implied by the fifth characteristic of the RME theory. There were two kinds of card games: the white cards with shapes and their properties of sides and the yellow cards with shapes and their properties of angles. The students are separated into groups and each student in a group starts with a number of cards in their hand. Each student takes his/her turn throwing a card on the table.

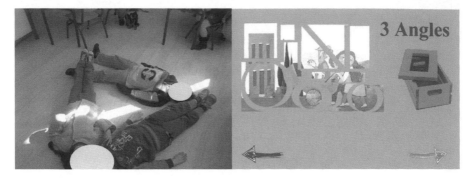

Fig. 3 Students made a shape with their bodies on the floor (*left*—fourth level) and completed a software activity (*right*—fifth level)

The purpose of the game is to match cards with identical properties and to collect those cards. At the end of the game the child who had the majority of cards was the winner. Afterwards, there were computer activities where the children had to recognize the shapes from using only the properties of the shapes. The computer presents a picture as a puzzle. The students then must drag and drop the corresponding shape, based the geometrical property displayed on the screen, into the box (Fig. 3-right).

In the software represented above, once an activity is selected, a problem is announced verbally and directions are given to the user through a recorded message. The feedback users get after following these directions is represented by two different screens, one positive and one negative. This feedback is accompanied with the corresponding audio messages. In the first case, the user receives a "well-done" message and in the second case the user gets a "try it again" message. In both cases, though, an effort was made to keep these messages to be as little emphatic as possible. This way, the children's' interest is focused more on the mathematical procedure of the application rather than their result or the competition.

Educational Measures

The present research was conducted in three phases. In the first phase, the pretest was given to the classes of the experimental and control groups during the beginning of December 2011 to isolate the effects of the treatment by looking for inherent inequities in the geometry achievement potential of the two groups. The pretest was referred to as First Class Primary Shape Test (FCPST) and it contained thirty tasks in total. The first twenty tasks of the FCPST were based on the first level of the Van Hiele model and the last ten were from the test that was used in the research by Clements, Swaminathan, Zeitler-Hannibal, and Sarama (1999) based on the second van Hiele level. Due to the young age of the students, the pretests were administrated in the class with explicit and detailed instructions of the teacher. These were pencil-and-paper tasks in which the children were asked to select shapes including

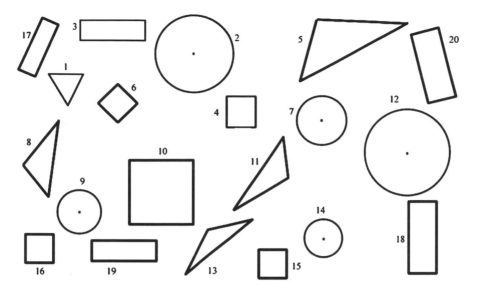

Fig. 4 Student marks circles

rectangles, squares, triangles, and circles on a page with various geometric figures (Fig. 4). Each task had a weighted grade that was computed from the student's answers. Particularly, for each correct answer the student was given one grade and lost one grade for each incorrect. Scores were computed for each of the individual geometrical tasks of the FCPST. Since the numbers of problems varied across tasks, a mean proportion of correct responses for each of the thirty tasks were produced by dividing the number of correct responses by the total number of problems on that task (possible range of standardized scores, 0–1.00). Moreover, for the purposes of the present study, we measured the score of circles and the score of the triangles separately. The scale used to measure the unstandardized scores for circles is based on a scale from 0 to 69. The scale used to measure the unstandardized scores for triangles is based on a scale from 0 to 40.

Similarly, during the third and final phase of the study, after the teaching intervention, the same test (FCPST) was given to all students in both the experimental and control groups as a posttest at the beginning of March 2012 to measure their improvement on circles and triangles separately.

Research Design

The present study was a quasi-experimental design with one experimental and one control groups. Eight first grade classes from Athens and two from Rethymno participated in this study. From the eight classes located in Athens, we randomly assigned four classes to the control group and the remaining four classes were assigned to the experimental group. We then randomly assigned one of the two classes from Rethymno to the control group and the other class to the experimental group. Therefore, five classes were in the control group ($n=121$) and the remaining five classes were in the experimental group ($n=113$).

Results

A set of analyses was conducted to determine the effects of the mathematics intervention on first grade students' geometry knowledge for circles and triangles. The pretest and posttest were taken by 234 students. Analysis of the data was carried out using the SPSS (ver. 19) statistical analysis computer program. The independent variables were the group (experimental group and control group) and the shape (circles or triangles). The dependent variable was the students' FCPST posttest score.

Comparing the Difficulty Between Understanding Circles and Triangles

The first analysis was a paired *t*-test among the students' FCPST pretest scores of circles and triangles in order to examine whether the concept of triangles is more difficult to understand than circles. There was a significant difference in the students' FCPST pretest scores for circles ($M=0.94$, $SD=0.04$) and triangles ($M=0.83$, $SD=0.07$); $t(233)=25.93$, $p<0.001$.

The descriptive statistics for students' scores for circles and triangles are presented in Table 1. Observing the standardized values, students scored higher for circles and triangles after receiving the intervention than before receiving it. Moreover, the score of the students in triangles was lower than those in circles after the teaching intervention (Table 1).

Evaluate the Effectiveness of FCPSM for Circles

Before conducting the analysis of ANCOVA on the students' FCPST posttest scores for circles to evaluate the effectiveness of the intervention, checks were performed to confirm that there were no violations of the assumptions of homogeneity of

Table 1 Descriptive statistics for students' standardized scores of experimental and control groups

	Circles				Triangles			
	Pretest		Posttest		Pretest		Posttest	
Group	M	SD	M	SD	M	SD	M	SD
Control	0.94	0.04	0.95	0.03	0.82	0.05	0.85	0.06
Experimental	0.95	0.04	0.97	0.03	0.83	0.08	0.91	0.06

Table 2 Comparison of student scores for circles in posttest: ANCOVA analysis

Sources	Type III sum of squares	df	Mean squares	F	Sig.	Partial eta squared
Pretest	0.105	1	0.105	155.990	0.000	0.403
Group	0.031	1	0.031	46.513	0.000	0.168
Error	0.156	231	0.001			

Table 3 Comparison of student scores for triangles in posttest: ANCOVA analysis

Sources	Type III sum of squares	df	Mean squares	F	Sig.	Partial eta squared
Pretest	0.197	1	0.197	69.645	0.000	0.232
Group	0.197	1	0.197	69.715	0.000	0.232
Error	0.654	231	0.003			

variances and homogeneity of regression slopes (Pallant, 2001). The result of Levene's test when pretest for circles was included in the model as a covariate was not significant, indicating that the group variances were equal, $F(1, 232)=0.476$, $p=0.491$; hence, the assumption of homogeneity of variance was not been violated.

The value of the covariance by dependent variable interaction (group×score for circles) was not significant, $F(1, 230)=2.042$, $p=0.154$, $\eta^2=0.009$; therefore, the assumption homogeneity of regression slopes was tenable. After adjusting for FCPST scores for circles in the pretest (covariate), the following results were obtained from the analysis of covariance (ANCOVA). A statistically significant main effect was found for type of intervention on the FCPST posttest scores for circles, $F(1, 231)=46.513$, $p<0.001$, $\eta^2=0.168$ (Table 2); thus, the experimental group performed significantly higher in the FCPST posttest for circles than the control group.

Evaluate the Effectiveness of FCPSM for Triangles

Then, the analysis of ANCOVA on the students' FCPST posttest scores for triangles was performed to evaluate the effectiveness of the intervention. The result of Levene's test when pretest for triangles was included in the model as a covariate was not significant, indicating that the group variances were equal, $F(1, 232)=0.044$, $p=0.834$; hence, the assumption of homogeneity of variance was not been violated.

The value of the covariance by dependent variable interaction (group×score for triangles) was not significant, $F(1, 230)=0.214$, $p=0.644$, $\eta^2=0.001$; therefore, the assumption homogeneity of regression slopes was tenable. After adjusting for FCPST scores for triangles in the pretest (covariate), the following results were obtained from the analysis of covariance (ANCOVA). A statistically significant main effect was found for type of intervention on the FCPST posttest scores for triangles, $F(1, 231)=69.715$, $p<0.001$, $\eta^2=0.232$ (Table 3); thus, the experimental group performed significantly higher in the FCPST posttest for triangles than the control group.

Results of this study expand the research on the effects of appropriate software embedded in a computerized environment as a tool for visualization and mathematical reasoning used alongside with specially designed activities (Bobis et al., 2005; Dimakos & Zaranis, 2010; Dissanayake et al., 2007; Gersten et al., 2005; Howie & Blignaut, 2009; Starkey, Klein, & Wakeley, 2004; Trouche & Drijvers, 2010; Wong et al., 2007, 2011; Zaranis, 2012). Also, the outcomes of the present study create a new teaching model with computer and non-computer activities based on the theoretical framework that blends together Realistic Mathematics Education and the van Hiele model of geometric thinking in primary school.

Discussion

The overall purpose of the study was to investigate the impact of instructional intervention using the First Class Primary Shape Model (specially designed mathematics activities and software based on Realistic Mathematics Education and the van Hiele model) for the purpose of teaching the basic geometrical concepts of circles and triangles in regard to the geometry competence of the first grade students of primary school. In this research, we found that it is more difficult for first grade students to understand the concept of triangles than circles. These students carried a relatively great amount of geometric knowledge from kindergarten and as a result, it is possible that the students understand circles and their properties better than triangles because triangles are more complex shapes than circles (Bobis et al., 2005; Clements & Sarama, 2004). Our findings agree with similar researches (Satlow & Newcombe, 1998; Walcott et al., 2009; Wong et al., 2007, 2011) which implied that circles are simpler and triangles are most complex. As a result, the research question answered positively.

Moreover, we found that the students that were taught circles with educational intervention based on FCPSM had a significant improvement compared to those taught using the traditional teaching method according to the first grade curriculum (hypothesis 1). Our results overlap with the results of other analogous studies which indicate the positive effects of a computer based-model of teaching geometry (Bobis et al., 2005; Dissanayake et al., 2007; Wong et al., 2007; Zaranis, 2012). Therefore, the first hypothesis was confirmed.

Also, our findings suggest that the students were taught triangles with educational intervention based on FCPSM had a significant improvement compared to those taught using the traditional teaching method (hypothesis 2). Our outcomes overlie the results of other similar studies which indicate the positive effects of a computer based teaching model for geometric shapes (Dimakos & Zaranis, 2010; Howie & Blignaut, 2009; Starkey et al., 2004; Trouche & Drijvers, 2010; Wong et al., 2011). Thus, the second hypothesis was answered positively. In addition, as it mentioned in the results section, students in both the experimental and the control groups scored higher for shapes of circles or triangles after receiving the teaching intervention than before the teaching process.

Moreover, an important statistical outcome of the present study was that the partial eta squared for triangles ($\eta^2 = 0.232$, Table 3) is higher than it was for circles ($\eta^2 = 0.168$, Table 2). This outcomes supports that, our teaching intervention had a somewhat greater impact in learning triangles than of learning circles for first grade students. Also, the present study demonstrates that our first grade teaching process, the non-computer based mathematics activities and the computer based mathematics activities, may support the learning of both difficult and simple mathematics in the primary school level. Our findings agree with other similar researches supporting the effective role of ICT in education and more specifically in mathematical reasoning (Clements & Sarama, 2004; Dimakos and Zaranis 2010; Furner & Marinas, 2007; Hardman, 2005; Howie & Blignaut, 2009; Keong et al., 2005; Vale & Leder, 2004).

The above discussion should be referenced in light of some of the limitations of this study. The first limitation of the study is that the data collected was from the participants residing the cities of Athens and Rethymno. The second limitation was the generalizability of this study which was limited to participants attending public schools. Therefore, the results from this research can be generalized only to similar groups of students. The results may not adequately describe students from other regions of Greece. However, as the study was of small scale and context specific, any application of the findings should be done with caution.

Furthermore, the undertaken computer assisted educational procedure revealed an extended interest for the tasks involved from the part of the students. It is an ongoing challenge for the reflective teacher to decide how this technology can be best utilized in education; especially in light of the current researches on the effects of such an implementation. This study is one small piece in the puzzle of geometry education in primary schools.

References

Bobis, J., Clarke, B., Clarke, D., Thomas, G., Wright, R., Gould, P., et al. (2005). Supporting teachers in the development of young children's mathematical thinking: Three large scale cases. *Mathematics Education Research Journal, 16*(3), 27–57.

Burnett, C. (2009). Research into literacy and technology in primary classrooms: An exploration of understandings generated by recent studies. *Journal of Research in Reading, 32*(1), 22–37. doi:10.1111/j.1467-9817.2008.01379.x.

Chou, S.-W., & Liu, C.-H. (2005). Learning effectiveness in a Web-based virtual learning environment: a learner control perspective. *Journal of Computer Assisted Learning, 21*, 65–76.

Clements, D. H. (2002). Computers in early childhood mathematics. *Contemporary Issues in Early Childhood, 3*(2), 160–181.

Clements, D. H., & Battista, M. T. (1992). Geometry and spatial reasoning. In D. A. Grouws (Ed.), *Handbook of research on mathematics teaching and learning* (pp. 420–464). New York: Macmillan.

Clements, D. H., & Sarama, J. (2004). Building blocks for early childhood mathematics. *Early Childhood Research Quarterly, 19*, 181–189.

Clements, D. H., Swaminathan, S., Zeitler-Hannibal, M., & Sarama, J. (1999). Reviewed work(s). *Journal for Research in Mathematics Education, 30*(2), 192–212. National Council of Teachers of Mathematics Stable. http://www.jstor.org/stable/749610.

Dimakos, G., & Zaranis, N. (2010). The influence of the Geometer's Sketchpad on the geometry achievement of Greek school students. *The Teaching of Mathematics, 13*(2), 113–124. Retrieved March 29, 2011, from http://elib.mi.sanu.ac.rs/files/journals/tm/25/tm1324.pdf.

Dissanayake, S. N., Karunananda, A. S., & Lekamge, G. D. (2007). Use of computer technology for the teaching of primary school mathematics. *OUSL Journal, 4*, 33–52.

Druin, A., & Fast, K. (2002). The child as learner, critic, inventor, and technology design partner: An analysis of three years of Swedish student journals. *The International Journal for Technology and Design Education, 12*(3), 189–213.

Dwyer, J. (2007). Computer-based Learning in a primary school: Differences between the early and later years of primary schooling. *Asia-Pacific Journal of Teacher Education, 35*(1), 89–103. doi:10.1080/13598660601111307.

Finegan, C., & Austin, J. (2002). Developmentally appropriate technology for young children. *Information Technology in Childhood Education Annual, 1*, 87–102.

Fisher, T., Denning, T., Higgins, C., & Loveless, A. (2012). Teachers' knowing how to use technology: Exploring a conceptual framework for purposeful learning activity. *Curriculum Journal, 23*(3), 307–325. doi:10.1080/09585176.2012.703492.

Freudenthal, H. (1968). Why to teach mathematics so as to be useful? *Educational Studies in Mathematics, 1*, 3–8.

Furner, J. M., & Marinas, C. A. (2007). Geometry sketching software for elementary children: Easy as 1, 2, 3. *Eurasia Journal of Mathematics, Science & Technology Education, 3*(1), 83–91.

Gersten, R., Jordan, N., & Flojo, J. (2005). Early identification and interventions for students with mathematics difficulties. *Journal of Learning Disabilities, 38*(4), 293–304.

Hardman, J. (2005). An exploratory case study of computer use in a primary school mathematics classroom: New technology, new pedagogy? *Perspectives in Education, 23*(4), 99–111.

Howie, S., & Blignaut, A. S. (2009). South Africa's readiness to integrate ICT into mathematics and science pedagogy in secondary schools. *Education Information Technology, 14*, 345–363. doi:10.1007/s10639-009-9105-0.

Keong, C. C., Horani, S., & Daniel, J. (2005). A study on the use of ICT in mathematics teaching. *Malaysian Online Journal of Instructional Technology (MOJIT), 2*(3), 43–51.

Lee, Y. (2009). Pre-K children's interaction with educational software programs: An observation of capabilities and levels of engagement. *Journal of Educational Multimedia and Hypermedia, 18*(3), 289–309.

Livingstone, S. (2012). Critical reflections on the benefits of ICT in education. *Oxford Review of Education, 38*(1), 9–24. doi:10.1080/03054985.2011.577938.

Pallant, J. (2001). *SPSS survival manual*. Buckingham, UK: Open University Press.

Passey, D. (2006). Technology enhancing learning: Analysing uses of information and communication technologies by primary and secondary school pupils with learning frameworks. *Curriculum Journal, 17*(2), 139–166. doi:10.1080/09585170600792761.

Plowman, L., & Stephen, C. (2003). A "benign addition"? Research on ICT and pre-school children. *Journal of Computer Assisted Learning, 19*(2), 149–164.

Remtulla, K. A. (2010). "Media Mediators": Advocating an alternate paradigm for critical adult education ICT policy. *Journal for Critical Education Policy Studies, 7*(3), 300–324.

Satlow, E., & Newcombe, N. (1998). When is a triangle not a triangle? Young children's developing concepts of geometry shape. *Cognitive Development, 13*, 547–559. Ablex Publishing.

Sife, A. S., Lwoga, E. T., & Sanga, C. (2007). New technologies for teaching and learning: Challenges for higher learning institutions in developing countries. *International Journal of Education and Development using Information and Communication Technology (IJEDICT), 3*(2), 57–67.

Starkey, P., Klein, A., & Wakeley, A. (2004). Enhancing young children's mathematical knowledge through a pre-kindergarten mathematics intervention. *Early Childhood Research Quarterly, 19*, 99–120. Elsevier.

Sutherland, R., Armstrong, V., Barnes, S., Brawn, R., Breeze, N., Gall, M., et al. (2004). Transforming teaching and learning: embedding ICT into everyday classroom practices. *Journal of Computer Assisted Learning, 20*(6), 413–425. doi:10.1111/j.1365-27 29.2004.00104.x.

Trouche, L., & Drijvers, P. (2010). Handheld technology for mathematics education: Flashback into the future. *ZDM: The International Journal on Mathematics Education, 42*(7), 667–681. doi:10.1007/s11858-010-0269-2.

Vale, C., & Leder, G. (2004). Student views of computer-based mathematics in the middle years: Does gender make a difference? *Educational Studies in Mathematics, 56,* 287–312.

Van den Heuvel-Panhuizen, M. (2001). Realistic mathematics education as work in progress. In F. L. Lin (Ed.), Common sense in mathematics education, *Proceedings of 2001, the Netherlands and Taiwan Conference on Mathematics Education, Taipei, Taiwan* (pp. 1–40). Retrieved November 19–23, 2001.

Van den Heuvel-Panhuizen, M., & Buys, K. (Eds.). (2008). *Young children learn measurement and geometry. A learning-teaching trajectory with intermediate attainment targets for the lower grades in primary school.* Rotterdam/Tapei: Sense Publishers.

Van den Heuvel-Panhuizen, M., & Wijers, M. (2005). Mathematics standards and curricula in the Netherlands. *Zentralblatt für Didaktik der Mathematik (ZDM), 37*(4), 287–307.

Walcott, C., Mohr, D., & Kastberg, S. (2009). Making sense of shape: An analysis of children's written responses. *The Journal of Mathematical Behavior, 28,* 30–40.

Wong, W. K., et al. (2007). LIM-G: Learner-initiating instruction model based on cognitive knowledge for geometry word problem comprehension. *Computers and Education Journal, 48*(4), 582–601.

Wong, W.-K., et al. (2011). Using computer-assisted multiple representations in learning geometry proofs. *Educational Technology & Society, 14*(3), 43–54.

Zaranis, N. (2011). The influence of ICT on the numeracy achievement of Greek kindergarten children, In A. Moreira, M. J. Loureiro, A. Balula, F. Nogueira, L. Pombo, L. Pedro, P. Almeida, (Eds.), *Proceedings of the 61st International Council for Educational Media and the XIII International Symposium on Computers in Education (ICEM&SIIE'2011) Joint Conference* (pp. 390–399). Portugal: University of Aveiro. Retrieved September 28–30, 2011.

Zaranis, N. (2012). The use of ICT in preschool education for geometry teaching. In R. Pintó, V. López, & C. Simarro (Eds.), *Proceedings of the 10th International Conference on Computer Based Learning in Science, Learning Science in the Society of Computers* (pp. 256–262). Barcelona, Spain: Centre for Research in Science and Mathematics Education (CRECIM). Retrieved June 26–29, 2012.

Zaranis, N., & Oikonomidis, V. (2009). *ICT in preschool education.* Athens: Grigoris Publications. Text in Greek.

Teaching Informatics in Primary School With and Without Educational Software Support

Panagiota Halki and Panagiotis Politis

Introduction

A series of studies suggest that learning programming languages affects the development of critical and structured thinking and the acquiring of higher thinking skills, while at the same time programming languages support learning in other areas (Mikropoulos, 2004). From 1970 and for almost 2 decades Informatics was taught mainly in secondary education and focused mainly on learning some programming language (Komis, 2004). At the same time there has been research on the didactics of programming. It focused on charting the relevant students' initial misconceptions so as to develop standards, both for the teaching materials and for the teaching methods that were in agreement with constructivism (Jimoyiannis, 2005).

The need for constructivist and exploratory approaches in teaching Informatics become even more relevant with the introduction of Programming, as part of the module "Programming the computer" of the Cross-thematic Curriculum Framework (CCF), in the 5th and 6th grades of Primary education in Greece a few years ago, specifically in 2011 (CCF, 2011).

P. Halki (✉)
Department of Primary Education, University of Ioannina,
45110 Ioannina, Greece
e-mail: pahalki@gmail.com

P. Politis
Department of Primary Education, University of Thessaly,
38221 Volos, Greece
e-mail: ppol@uth.gr

C. Karagiannidis et al. (eds.), *Research on e-Learning and ICT
in Education: Technological, Pedagogical and Instructional Perspectives*,
DOI 10.1007/978-1-4614-6501-0_6, © Springer Science+Business Media New York 2014

Research Questions

In order to address the research question, the following points were taking into consideration.

- There are no textbooks available for teaching Programming in the Primary School (Pedagogical Institute, 2013) and the teaching material presently offered is limited and often has not been previously implemented and assessed (Ministry of Education, 2013).
- Results of a series of studies focused on the experiential teaching of computer science without any use of computers show that the experiential learning of programming promotes collaboration and teamwork (Bell, 2000; Bell, Alexander, Freema, & Grimley, 2009; Curzon & McOwan, 2008; Taub, Ben-Ari, & Armoni, 2009).
- In the CCF for ICT teaching in primary education, the initial students' misconceptions have not been taken into account. However, available research points out that students assume that the computer has "anthropomorphic characteristics" and that it has a "hidden intelligence" (Pea, 1986; Taylor, 1990),

Through these three points the parameters of the research question were determined.

The purpose of this study is to assess the learning outcomes of teaching scenarios, designed by our team, for the module "Programming the computer" of the CCF for teaching Informatics in the 5th Grade. These teaching scenarios promoted problem solving and the development of critical thinking and included exploratory, constructive and collaborative activities (CCF, 2011). Moreover, the initial students' misconceptions and students' specific cognitive difficulties related to learning computer programming were taken into account.

The following research questions were addressed:

1. What is the improvement in critical thinking skills (Matsagouras, 2000, 2005, 2007) that is achieved through the teaching of the designed module "Programming the computer" in a programming environment?
2. What is the improvement in critical thinking skills (Matsagouras, 2000, 2005, 2007) that is achieved through the teaching of the designed module "Programming the computer" without computer usage, namely experientially?
3. Does the teaching of the designed module whether in a programming environment or without the use of computer (experientially) promote collaboration, inquiry, critical thinking and development of problem solving skills, in accordance with the general purpose of ICT integration in the Primary School (CCF, 2011)?

Theoretical Framework

Since the design of the module followed the constructivist approach, it took into account the students' initial misconceptions and the cognitive difficulties that they face (Skoumios, 2011). Summarising the studies on the cognitive difficulties and the students' initial misconceptions on Programming leads to the following conclusions:

- Students need to not only understand the syntax and the specific semantics of a programming language, but also to use properly and in a structurally coherent way these programming language tools, which are not related to their prior practical-experiential knowledge (Jimoyiannis, 2005).
- The concept of some terms, already known to the students, such as "equal", "data", found in other cognitive areas (mathematics, science) are not identical to that in the field of Programming. This differentiated concept creates difficulties for students in understanding and writing in a programming environment (Jimoyiannis, 2005).
- In any programming environment, students face difficulties in writing commands following the correct syntax, since this is the first time they come in contact with the syntax and semantics of the specific programming language commands. With no exception, programming languages require a rigorous design in the syntax and structure of their own commands (Jimoyiannis, 2005).
- Students cannot understand the role of the computational machine during the execution of program. Students have difficulty in understanding the data flow in a computer system (Jimoyiannis, 2005). They also have difficulty to develop effective models for the computer and its operation during the execution of a program (Bonar & Soloway, 1985; Rogalski & Vergnaud, 1987). Students perceive hardware as a "black box" and attribute to it several anthropomorphic characteristics as if it is a "mental giant" or has "hidden intelligence" (Pea, 1986; Taylor, 1990). Moreover, students create their own model based on their initial perceptions about computer operation.
- Students face difficulties to learn how to use the available tools of a programming environment, prior to begin learning the main programming concepts of the programming language itself (Du Boulay, 1989).

The main objectives set by the CCF for teaching the module "Programming the computer" are introducing to and familiarising students with:

- The concept of algorithms.
- The use of strict syntax and interpretation of basic commands solving a concrete problem, through their implementation in a visual programming environment.
- The breaking up of problems into simpler ones.
- The composition of a task from individual components.
- The use of debugging techniques (CCF, 2011).
  The computational flow of data directly related to a program's execution is not among the objectives that students have to achieve, nor is the interpretation of a program written in any programming language into the language "understood" by the computer.

As mentioned above, the main purpose of this study is to assess learning outcomes of teaching scenarios that were created on the basis of the CCF guidelines taking into account the students' misconceptions regarding the computational flow

Table 1 Learning levels of critical thinking (Matsagouras 2000, 2005, 2007)

Learning levels	Skills	Learning outcomes

First level
Informational learning (best
  learning outcome is the
  completeness of information)
	Data collection
	1. Observation
	2. Identification
	3. Recall
		Information

Second level
Organisational learning (best
  learning outcome is the
  ability on building concepts)
	Data management
	1. Comparison
	2. Categorisation
	3. Regularisation
	4. Classification
		Concepts, simple
		  correlations

Third level
Analytical learning (best
  learning outcome is the
  ability on formulating
  generalisations)
	Data analysis
	1. Structural elements analysis
	2. Relations differentiation
	3. Pattern differentiation
	4. Distinguishes facts from
	  opinions/estimations
	5. Clarification
		Generalisations—
		  principles-schemes

Fourth level
Productive learning (best
  learning outcome is the
  ability on problem solving)
	Going beyond the data
	1. Explanation
	2. Prediction—Hypothesis
	3. Confirmation—Inference
	4. Organisation
		Problem solving
		Theory/prototype
		  generation of
		  cognitive/cultural
		  products

of data. However, the teaching scenarios had objectives that promoted the development of critical thinking and followed the learning levels of critical thinking delineated by Matsagouras. Matsagouras (2000, 2005, 2007) schema of learning levels of critical thinking was affected by Bloom's taxonomy of learning domains' and was further developed in a more constructivist point of view (Table 1).

Data Collection

This is the recall and reproduction level of information, where students were asked to retrieve knowledge referring to terminology, specific clues, events, etc. (Matsagouras, 2007; Oosterhof, 2010; Sofos, 2012).

Data Management

This is the skills and concepts level, where the main focus is on procedural knowledge specified by differentiation, concepts and rules. With respect to differentiation what matters is that students differentiate or find similarities among individual stimuli received from the environment. With respect to concepts, what matters is that students perceive the characteristics that can be leveraged so that materials, phenomena, situations, etc. can be classified (Sofos, 2012).

Data Analysis

This is the level of generalisation and strategic thinking. This level's main characteristics are the representation of the problem, the classification of the problem, the selection of strategy, the solving method (Sofos, 2012).

Going Beyond the Data

This is the level of extended operation, thought and research, which refers to going beyond the data. The main characteristic of this level is the scientific approach adopted using various points of view, leading to hypotheses formulation, disciplined inquiry, stating of explanations and decisions, extracting conclusions, etc. These skills are based on the types of learning that are relevant to forming composite rules and to problem solving (Sofos, 2012).

Methodology

The sample consisted of 35 5th grade students, of a primary school located in the capital of one of the largest Greek islands. The students were divided into two groups. The first, the experimental group (EG) consisting of 16 people, used the educational programming environment Scratch to elaborate the teaching scenarios. The second, the control group (CG) consisting of 19 people, used no technological support, elaborated the didactic scenarios through playing games and so achieving experiential learning.

Scratch is an educational programming language and multimedia authoring tool allowing users to use event driven programming. Scratch can be used by students for a range of educational constructivist purposes from math and science projects, including simulations and visualisations of experiments.

Description of the Educational Factors

Four teaching scenarios were developed for the research needs of this study. Each scenario comprised some educational activities and each student group elaborated them for approximately 2 teaching hours. The EG accomplished the activities by using Scratch. The necessary feedback provided to the students was coming mainly from the educational programming environment and the teacher acted as an auxiliary partner. In contrast, the CG accomplished the activities in question through the use of play, where experiential learning was taking place, whilst the feedback was provided publicly in the classroom mainly by the teacher, who acted also as an organiser. Titles, objectives and duration of teaching scenarios (Table 2) were identical for both groups of students.

Table 2 Titles and duration of didactic scenarios

Section/issue	Teaching hours (approximately)
1. What language does the computer "speak"?	2
2. I articulate the commands and move the robot	2
3. I build scenarios by using orders	2
4. I execute and correct final scenarios	2

Table 3 Phases and teaching styles/techniques on teaching scenarios

S/n	Teaching phases	Teaching styles/techniques
1	Presentation geared to problematic situations	Discussion among students and between students and teacher Questions–answers, thought disclosure
2	Highlighting and clarifying initial perceptions	Discussion among students and between students and teacher Plan design for the emergence of students' initial perceptions
3	Constructive processing	Practice, discussion among students and between students and teacher Discussion on everyday life similar cases, trial implementation of proposed decisions
4	Application to new situations, feedback	Discussion among students and between students and teacher, role play, practice, challenge, personal support (experimental group), feedback at the class level (control group)
5	Reflection	Discussion among students and between students and teacher
6	Evaluation	Written tests

Fig. 1 Worksheet (on the *left*) that CG students were asked to fill with the help of their classmates (on the *centre*) and the EG students to fill with the help of Scratch (on the *right*)

The phases of the teaching scenarios as well as the types of teaching techniques according Matsagouras (Matsagouras, 2005) used overall in all units are presented in Table 3.

The 1st Section, "What language does the computer 'speak'?" (based on the scenario developed in the context of the web site Computer Science Unplugged: csunplugged.org) dealt with the computer's binary numbering system, i.e. how the data registered by the man in a PC can be converted by the PC in a language that the computer can process (Fig. 1).

In the 2nd Section, teaching focused on the strict syntax of commands. The students took the roles of the computer and the programmer, of robots and their operators so as to conclude that a computer, unlike men, understands only certain and strictly indexed commands (Fig. 2).

Fig. 2 On the *left* shows the CG students who are trying to find the right commands so as to move their classmate–robot to the desired position. On the *right* shows the corresponding setting in Scratch for EG students

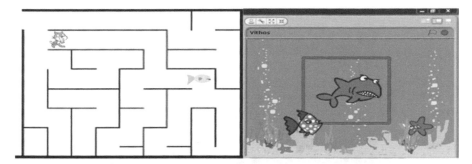

Fig. 3 Tasks: (1) send the cat to eat the fish, (2) make minnow build the cage to protect the starfish from the shark

Fig. 4 Task (on the *left*): a kitty must save her friend whose house is burned and a solution by EG student (on the *centre*) and CG student (on the *right*)

In the 3rd Section, teaching concerned the creation of sequences of a set of commands in order to create a desired image. Students were asked to create sequences that were syntactically and semantically correct (Fig. 3).

The 4th Section dealt with the execution of a sequence of commands that was provided to them and they were asked to analyse its structural elements in order to predict the result of the scenario and debug possible errors inside the code (Fig. 4).

Data Collection and Analysis

The data collection and analysis of the study was based on:

1. Students' answers in Worksheets and Evaluation Sheets that they were given during teaching. Each question in the Worksheets and Evaluation Sheets related to a specific skill according to the levels of critical thinking presented in the theory part of this paper and the analysis was based on counting the frequency of correct answers, indicating the mastering (or not) of the relevant skills (e.g. confirmation, error finding, extract conclusions, etc.).

   An example of evaluation questions is presented below:

   Given the two scenarios of commands below please answer the questions: (1) Write the numbers of the commands that cause movement in the kitty; (skill: recognition). (2) Are commands 7 and 9 the same? Justify your answer; (skill: distinction). (3) What is the difference between the two scenarios shown below? What different would happen if the kitty was performing scenario 3 instead of scenario 2; (skill: comparison). (4) Which set of commands is repeated in Scenario 1; (skill: pattern recognition).

2. The observation sheet. The observation sheet was containing general observations about students' behaviour and attitudes, namely: children's participation in the learning process, their learning interoperability, their tensions, their assistance from other peers or the teacher, etc. Four sheets were complemented in each teaching module, while the final observation sheet was the result of the averaging responses from each individual sheet (low—1, moderate—2, or high—3 level).

Results

Results are classified into four categories according to levels of critical thinking: data collection, organisation, analysis and going beyond. Each figure compares the learning outcomes as produced by the EG and the CG. The experimental group presented slightly better results with regard to data collection and organisation (Figs. 5 and 6). In data analysis, in contrast, the CG has showed slightly better results (Fig. 7) while in going beyond the data the EG displays higher rates in the

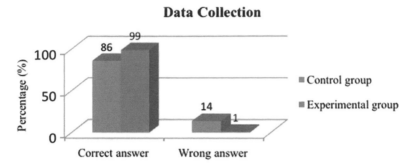

Fig. 5 Learning outcomes and data collection skills

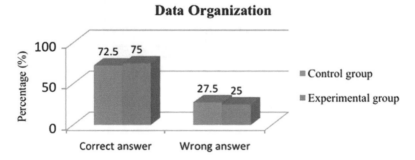

Fig. 6 Learning outcomes and data organisation skills

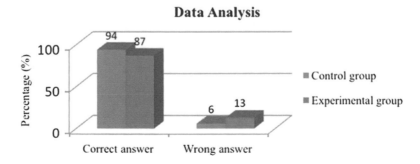

Fig. 7 Learning outcomes and data analysis skills

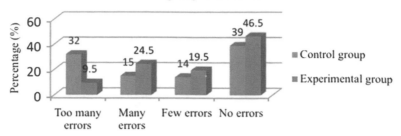

Fig. 8 Learning outcomes and going beyond the data skills

Independent Samples Test

		Levene's Test for Equality of Variances		t-test for Equality of Means						
		F	Sig.	t	df	Sig. (2-tailed)	Mean Differ ence	Std. Error Differen ce	95% Confidence Interval of the Difference	
									Lower	Upper
Problem 1 solution	Equal variances assumed	,001	,979	-1,143	28	,263	-,393	,344	-1,097	,311
	Equal variances not assumed			-1,141	27,319	,264	-,393	,344	-1,099	,313
Problem 1 debugging	Equal variances assumed	1,747	,200	3,412	21	,003	1,545	,453	,603	2,487
	Equal variances not assumed			3,451	20,467	,002	1,545	,448	,613	2,478
Problem 2 solution	Equal variances assumed	,675	,418	-,693	29	,494	-,238	,343	-,938	,463
	Equal variances not assumed			-,690	27,951	,496	-,238	,344	-,942	,467
Problem 2 debugging	Equal variances assumed	2,986	,108	4,798	13	,000	1,833	,382	1,008	2,659
	Equal variances not assumed			5,500	12,075	,000	1,833	,333	1,108	2,559
Problem 3 solution	Equal variances assumed	,079	,781	-,446	32	,659	-,147	,331	-,821	,526
	Equal variances not assumed			-,447	30,597	,658	-,147	,330	-,820	,525
Problem 3 debugging	Equal variances assumed	43,022	,000	3,818	16	,002	1,700	,445	,756	2,644
	Equal variances not assumed			4,295	9,000	,002	1,700	,396	,805	2,595
Code debugging	Equal variances assumed	,458	,503	-,389	32	,700	-,126	,325	-,788	,536
	Equal variances not assumed			-,391	30,919	,698	-,126	,323	-,785	,532

Fig. 9 *T*-Test statistics

responses with fewer errors (Fig. 8). This difference in rates, is mainly due to the error correction skills developed more by the students in the EG because of the immediate and individualised feedback offered by the Scratch, unlike the CG were feedback was neither direct nor individualised, as it was offered at the class level. This is confirmed by the application of the statistical criterion t which shows a statistically significant difference between the two research groups as far as the debugging is concerned. Most likely, there is no such statistically significant difference as far as the problem solution is concerned (Fig. 9).

From the results taken from the observation sheet, students both in the EG and the CG collaborated highly with each other, except that in the CG there was both intra and inter group cooperation. In addition, in the CG students were more enthusiastic in expressing their views. This was in agreement with the teaching method, which in the case of the CG was always collective (solving the exercise, experiential activities, etc.) and was perceived as a play by the students.

Conclusions

Both problem-solving and critical thinking, characteristics that were directly related to the skills that correspond to higher levels of critical thinking (see Table 1), showed equal level in both groups. The two groups were different in that the students without PC usage had a greater difficulty to correct errors than the students with PC usage due to the lack of immediate and individualised feedback. On the other hand, with regard to cooperativeness, the results of our study agree with those of respective investigations which support that teaching without PC enhances the interest and teamwork of students (Bell, 2000; Bell et al., 2009; Curzon & McOwan, 2008; Taub et al., 2009).

The survey results taken from the observation sheet showed that by implementing those specific teaching scenarios, the cooperativity was promoted to a higher degree in CG students. Although the role of the software in developing the "going beyond the data skills" dimension should not be underestimated, the positive results offered by experiential learning relative to the promotion of collaboration and teamwork amongst students are also important.

We are therefore led to the suggestion of devising didactic scenarios that could combine both software and experiential learning process. Such a didactic proposal could be developed with virtual reality software, whose results would be of particular interest.

Moreover, the didactic scenarios that were designed for the section "What language does the computer 'speak'" dealt with the computer's binary numbering system and turned out to be effective in both conditions. The learning results show that students at this age are able to understand this particular section. By applying the same methodology there could be developed didactic scenarios for other modules (e.g. the development of a microworld simulating the computational data flow, the formation of an image on a computer screen etc.) and assessed in the process of curricula teaching transformation for ICT teaching in primary education (Sofos & Kron, 2010).

References

Bell, T. (2000). A low-cost high-impact computer science show for family audiences. *23rd Australasian Computer Science Conference (ACSC 2000)* (pp. 10–16), 31 Jan–3 Feb 2000, Canberra, Australia. Proceedings of ACSC 2000.

Bell, T., Alexander, J., Freema, I., & Grimley, M., (2009). *Computer science unplugged: School students doing real computing without computers*. Retrieved February 2013, from http://swinburne.academia.edu/MickGrimley/Papers/184161/Computer_Science_Unplugged_School_Students_Doing_Real_Computing_Without_Computers.

Bonar, J., & Soloway, E. (1985). Preprogramming knowledge: A major source of misconceptions in novice programmers. *Human-Computer Interaction, 1*, 133–161.

Cross-thematic Curriculum Framework. (2011). *Cross-thematic curriculum framework informatics in primary school*. Athens: Pedagogical Institute, Greek Ministry of Education (in Greek).

Curzon, P., & McOwan, P. (2008). Engaging with computer science through magic shows, *Proceedings of the 13th Annual Conference on Innovation and Technology in Computer Science Education.*

Du Boulay, B. (1989). Some difficulties of learning to program. In E. Soloway & J. C. Spohrer (Eds.), *Studying the novice programmer* (pp. 283–299). Hillsdale, NJ: Lawrence Erlbaum.

Jimoyiannis, A. (2005). Towards a pedagogical framework to teach programming in secondary education. *3rd PanHellenic Conference with International Participation Didactics of Informatics, Corinth* (pp. 99–111). (In Greek)

Komis, V. (2004). *Introduction to ICT educational applications*. Athens: New Technologies Publications (in Greek).

Matsagouras, H. (2000). *Theory and teaching practice – teaching theory: Personal theory as framework of contemplative-critical analysis*. Athens: Gutenberg (in Greek).

Matsagouras, H. (2005). *Theory & teaching strategies. Theory & teaching practice* (Vol. A & B). Athens: Gutenberg (in Greek).

Matsagouras, H. (2007). *Teaching strategies*. Athens: Gutenberg (in Greek).

Mikropoulos, A. (2004). Does Logo have place as cognitive object and holistic model to primary education?, *2nd PanHellenic Conference with International Participation Didactics of Informatics Volos* (pp. 65–72). (In Greek).

Ministry of Education – Greece. (2013). *ICT in primary schools – support team*. Retrieved August 20, 2013, from http://primedu-tpe.sch.gr/index.php/2011-07-25-09-41-30?start=5.

Oosterhof, A. (2010). *Educational evaluation. From theory to practice*. Athens: Ion Publication (in Greek).

Pea, R. D. (1986). Language-independent conceptual "bugs" in the novice programming. *Journal of Educational Computing Research, 2*(1), 25–36.

Pedagogical Institute – Greece. (2013). Educational material for primary school. Retrieved August 20, 2013, from http://www.pi-schools.gr/books/dimotiko/.

Rogalski, J., & Vergnaud, G. (1987). Didactique de l'informatique et acquisitions cognitives en programmation. *Psychologie Française, 32*(2), 267–273.

Skoumios, M. (2011). *The teaching scenario*. Rhodes: University of Aegean (in Greek).

Sofos, A. (2012). *Cognitive skills*. Rhodes: University of Aegean (in Greek).

Sofos, A., & Kron, F. (2010). *Effective teaching using media*. Athens: Grigoris Publications (in Greek).

Taub, R., Ben-Ari, M., & Armoni, M. (2009). The effect of CS unplugged on middle-school students' views of CS. *Proceedings of the 14th Annual SIGCSE Conference on Innovation and Technology in Computer Science Education, Paris, France* (pp. 99–103).

Taylor, J. (1990). Analysing novices analysing Prolog: What stories do novices tell about Prolog. *Instructional Science, 19*, 283–309.

Part III
ICT and Teaching Programming

Educational Games for Teaching Computer Programming

Christos Malliarakis, Maya Satratzemi, and Stelios Xinogalos

Introduction

Students of the twenty-first century have been growing up in a highly digital world, where they learn and react very differently during the learning process in comparison to students not familiarised with technology. This is also due to the fact that computer games invade students' lives from a very early age, making them significantly accustomed to many of the computer's functionalities.

At the same time, students continue to face difficulties in computer science courses such as computer programming, even though their familiarisation with computers would suggest their learning of programming would become easier nowadays. The extended research studies carried out the last two decades state that these difficulties are still present and students seem to be even less interested in programming (Lahtinen, Ala-Mutka, & Jarvinen, 2005).

The hindering of these difficulties is important, as successful teaching and learning of computer programming can be extremely beneficial for twenty-first century generation students. It enables the development of various competences such as critical thinking, by allowing students to create their own programs, and of concept analysis and problem solving, as they are usually required to decipher a given scenario and interpret it into lines of code. Moreover, students learn to work in groups and collaborate with each other in their effort to develop executable programs while exercising in exchanging expertise and communicating ideas. Thus,

C. Malliarakis (✉)
Department of Applied Informatics, University of Macedonia,
156 Egnatia Street, 54006 Thessaloniki, Greece
e-mail: malliarakis@uom.gr

M. Satratzemi • S. Xinogalos
Department of Informatics, University of Macedonia,
156 Egnatia Street, 54006 Thessaloniki, Greece
e-mail: maya@uom.gr; stelios@uom.gr

C. Karagiannidis et al. (eds.), *Research on e-Learning and ICT in Education: Technological, Pedagogical and Instructional Perspectives*, DOI 10.1007/978-1-4614-6501-0_7, © Springer Science+Business Media New York 2014

overall computer programming empowers students to become lifelong learners, a very important benefit for this ever-growing world of knowledge since they can transfer their skills to a number of future work domains (engineering, computer science, etc.) (Law, Lee, & Yu, 2010).

An interesting proposal for alleviating the problems faced is the incorporation of educational games or serious games within computer programming courses. The term educational games is commonly used to describe computer games that are used as educational tools and provide interactive and appealing activities that attract students' interest for learning (Gunter, Kenny, & Vick, 2008). These games reinforce students' intrinsic motivation through the sense of challenge; they pique their curiosity, enforce a sense of security as well as stimulate their imagination (Ho, Chung, & Tsai, 2006). Also, students are able to achieve specific goals and view the success results immediately, not only when they complete the game but also when they pass the game's stages, a process that increases their self-confidence and helps them trust their decision making skills. Hence, there is a need to readjust currently followed learning techniques according to these newly emerged technological trends that can more easily and efficiently pull the new generation of students towards computer programming education.

The main purpose of this paper is to review existing educational games that aim to teach computer programming and correspondingly review how effectively they support students in achieving the educational goals that teachers set in each case. The rest of the paper is organised as follows: the next section provides information regarding the requirements that have been identified in the literature regarding the development of educational games. The following section presents a review and comparative analysis of educational games for teaching computer programming elements, giving emphasis in features that correspond to the requirements identified in the previous section. Finally, the paper concludes with an overview of the work done in the field in terms of how well and to what extend the studied educational games cover the identified requirements and suggests future work.

Educational Games Requirements Specification

Our work was carried out following a rigorous review methodology, where we searched a variety of academic databases (e.g. Web of Science, Scopus, CiteSeer and Google Scholar) for identifying relevant papers. During this search, we used keywords such as: educational games, computer programming, requirements, facilitating tools, etc., in various combinations. Over 70 papers were originally identified and in the end 20 were used for our review after thorough filtering as the most relevant to our scope of interest.

We have studied thoroughly case studies that have proposed and developed frameworks for educational games (Becker, 2010; De Freitas, & Jarvis, 2006; Salen & Zimmerman, 2004; Yusoff, Crowder, Gilbert, & Wills, 2009; Zualkernan, 2006). According to these works, the development of an educational game should be carried out after the examination of a number of aspects, where each aspect determines the features that should be supported in an educational game. All frameworks include similar requirements as concepts that are considered important. In this work, we choose to follow the one suggested by Becker (2010), because its concepts encompass all the ones included in previous frameworks. Thus, we consider it to be a more abstract superset of features that should be supported by all educational games.

Initially, it is suggested that the educational goals should be investigated across two axes by using a different viewpoint, so that their specification will be complete. These axes are:

- *Cognitive axis*, relating to mental competencies (Knowledge). Educational goals should make sure that the information received by the students begin from the first category in the Bloom's taxonomy (Knowledge) and end in the final and most complex category (Evaluation) successfully.
- *Emotional axis*, relating to emotions or emotional areas (Attitude). Educational goals should enable students to handle given situations through the enticement of their emotions. For example, the need and thus the desire to free a prisoner during a game motivates students to solve the assigned task faster and correctly so that they can experience the emotions followed by accomplishing the goal.

Additionally, it is important to select a proper framework that will guide the learning experience with the incorporation of educational games. The construction of a development framework requires the determination of various elements that together structure the framework's components. For example, the processes of the real world that will need to be simulated into the game (which movements will be allowed, how will the virtual world be constructed, how will the players be represented, etc.) need to be clearly identified. This is a very important step as it determines the educational scenarios that can be supported by the game's environment and thus affects the entire learning process.

Following the framework's specification, an architecture will be constructed based on the components identified that will have to be available in an authentic game environment. These components include:

- *The scenario's space*. Students are introduced to the game's storyline once they logon to the environment with a short description of the plot as well as a brief overview of the basic activities they will have to execute.
- *Relevant cases*. Students are provided with a set of pre-solved similar cases from which they can get a better insight of the game's knowledge and skills requirements and thus be better prepared for when it is their turn to solve assigned tasks.
- *Information resources*. Students can access information relevant to the task at hand whenever they are in need of assistance.
- *Facilitating tools*. A set of tools is included that students can use when they are trying to execute a task and that help them build new knowledge. Additionally, the game provides tools that underpin student communication as well as discussion with the teachers regarding any questions, thoughts or reflection on the virtual world.

Also, it is essential to distinguish *information* regarding the student, such as learning goals, learning style (holistic, analytical, etc.) as well cognitive limitations (e.g. behavioural competences that can affect their learning).

Teachers should also be able to set *educational goals* that will have to be accomplished by the students during the game by assigning specific activities for them to participate in. This way, students achieve interim goals by successfully completing tasks that will lead them to absorbing the final learning outcomes set by the teachers.

The above features will underpin the selection of an *authentic scenario* that will provide an attractive story to go along with the game's virtual world. To this end, students should be presented with an interesting and motivating problem that needs solving and it is best if the plot is similar to the ones available in existing computer games. This way, students will be already familiar with the overall concept and the activities they will engage in will seem more like games than teaching exercises. Similarly, the individual *problems* that students will be called to solve during the game should be consistent with the educational goals as well as with any cognitive limitations that may be apparent to the teachers. This is one more reason why both these features are required to be supported in an educational game.

Another important feature is the constant and explanatory *feedback* provided to the students during their navigation through the game's levels. This feedback should be represented in a form of messages that guide students towards understanding what they did right, what they did wrong and how they can achieve their goals, even through the mistakes they have made. This scaffolding technique ensures that students realise why their actions did not lead to successful task execution and thus they will be able to perform better in their next endeavour.

Finally, a number of *generic conditions* need to be taken into consideration while designing and developing an educational game. Such is the location and type of the education to take place (e.g. offline, online, blended learning). For example, if the learning process will be realised entirely online, then the game requires all the educational material to be uploaded within the environment and communication tools should be very well supported and plentiful. Moreover, the course's duration will determine how many hours students will spend on the game and how many scenarios need to be constructed according to the elements that need to be taught in this duration. All of the above require adequate preparation from the teacher and proper configuration of the environment so as to exploit all of the game's benefits and foster knowledge and skills development by the students.

Educational Games for Computer Programming Education

This section presents a series of games that have been developed specifically for computer programming courses. The review of these games was carried out based on the specifications identified and described in the previous section, in the cases where they were explicitly identified by the relevant literature. Moreover, all chosen games have addressed both the cognitive axis and the emotional axis during their development. Thus, in each game students start out by receiving pieces of information, and through their engagement with the game, they move on up the Bloom's taxonomy to the evaluation step by reflecting on their progress and finalising assignments. Also, the emotional axis is addressed via the game scenarios. All scenarios stimulate emotions that motivate students to go through all tasks in order to win.

Two major categories could be distinguished during the research, which sort educational games based on the educational goals they aim to support. The first category includes games that focus on teaching specific computer programming units while the second category represents games that cover multiple educational goals and thus computer programming material. A review for each category is presented in the next two subsections, followed by a comparative analysis presented in Table 1.

Educational Games Focused on Teaching a Specific Unit of Learning

Catacombs. It is a three-dimensional multiplayer game that aims to teach students how to declare variables and use simple and nested if statements and loops. According to the game's scenario, each player represents a wizard that has to rescue two children trapped within catacombs. Towards this goal, the wizards have to answer multiple choice questions trying to solve a given programming code that will help them complete their quests. The answers to the given questions automatically create executable lines of code in a micro-language. If the answers are correct, the wizards progress through the game's levels; otherwise they are given corresponding feedback as to what they answered wrong and are prompted to try again. The game records experience scores for each student and provides explanatory messages as a scaffolding mechanism (Barnes, Chaffin, Powell, & Lipford, 2008; Barnes et al., 2007).

Saving Princess Sera. It is a two-dimensional game that enables students' scaffolding through explanatory messages directed to the player. Each player has to try and save a princess named Sera who has been abducted by a monster named Gargamel, on her sixteenth birthday. Students are required to complete a number of quests in order to progress in the plot of the game. Towards this goal, they complete lines of code that will result to an executable program or they have to correctly map existing lines of code to their proper position or order within a program employing a drag and drop functionality. This way, students learn the quick-sort algorithm along with simple and nested loops with the usage of a micro-language (Barnes et al., 2007; Barnes et al., 2008).

EleMental: The Recurrence. It is a three-dimensional game that aims to teach students how to execute recursion and depth-first search transversal using the C# programming language. The player has to navigate across a virtual binary tree by employing the depth-first transversal and complete three quests by applying recursion. Two avatars named Ele and Cera help students during the game in various ways. For example, once the code is written, Ele crosses the binary tree according to how the written code is deployed, while Cera explains exactly what the code is producing at a specific moment (Chaffin, Doran, Hicks, & Barnes, 2009).

Wu's Castle. It is a two-dimensional role playing game that aims to teach students loops and arrays through interactive activities. Each player is a wizard that can control an army of snowmen. Players recognise logical errors at lines of code written in the C++ programming language. The game allows arrays management through changing the parameters inside the loops and movement of the characters through the execution of nested loops (Eagle & Barnes, 2009).

Robozzle. It is an online puzzle game that provides a series of predefined commands ready for use and does not show any actual code. According to the game's scenario, users have to build functions that will help them achieve each given task in a grid and tiles virtual world. Users can run their functions and see how their hero will move across the world and can therefore easily detect what mistakes they have made and reprogram accordingly (Li & Watson, 2011).

LightBot. LightBot (Piteira & Haddad, 2011) is an online puzzle game similar to Robozzle. It includes a series of predefined commands and no actual code or programming language. Additionally, users have to complete given tasks by building their own functions and moving the hero across a grid and tiles environment and light all the blue tiles. Once a task is completed, the user can move to the next level, which requires the construction of more complex functions.

TALENT. TALENT (Maragos & Grigoriadou, 2011) focuses on teaching if statements and loops in the forms of algorithms by using a micro-language. Each player is an archaeologist that has to navigate across the virtual environment by completing a series of tasks and collect objects that are available at specific locations for their future exhibition at a museum. Towards this goal, students can drag and drop lines of code as well as write them in an editor whenever requested. As a scaffolding mechanism, TALENT provides an agent that acts as a mentor and helps students when needed as well as suggest what their next mission should be.

Educational Games Focused on Teaching Multiple Units of Learning

Robocode. It is a two-dimensional environment that aims to teach computer programming using the Java language. The game comprises of a programming editor, robots and a virtual arena, and students are required to program a robot that will compete against one another in the arena. Students familiarise themselves with the basic commands of structured computer programming and object-oriented programming (e.g. inheritance, polymorphism) while they try to build a robot ready for combat. During its construction, the robot inherits basic methods that can later be extended by students according to the behaviour they want their robots to have inside the arena (O'Kelly & Gibson, 2006).

M.U.P.P.E.T.S. It is a three-dimensional, Web-based and collaborative game that aims to teach object building and in general to familiarise students with the basic concepts of object-oriented programming using the Java language. Students create a robot that has to fight another robot inside a virtual arena, interact with the objects they build and write and compile their lines of code within the embedded development environment that includes a commands console (Phelps, Bierre, & Parks, 2003).

Table 1 Overview of the educational games for computer programming courses

Game	Programming elements	Programming language	Programming activities	Special characteristics
Catacombs	Variables; simple and nested if statements; loops	Micro-language	Multiple choice questions; filling out lines of code	Three dimensional; multiplayer; success scores; scaffolding with explanatory messages from the hero
Saving Sera	If statements; recursion	Micro-language	Filling out lines of code; mapping parts of code in corresponding locations; multiple choice questions	Two dimensional; scaffolding
EleMental	Recursion; depth-first search (DFS) algorithm	C#	Depth-first search algorithm; moving the hero on a fantastical binary tree	Three dimensional; scaffolding
Prog&Play	Structured computer programming, if-statements, loops	Ada, C, Java, OCaml, Scratch, Compalgo	Completing eight missions	Multiplayer; infinite scenarios; available
Wu's Castle	Loops; arrays	C++	Arrays management; movement of the hero; identification of logical mistakes in code	Interaction; role playing
Robozzle	Functions	No code used	Creating functions through the hero's movement	Interactive; available
LightBot	Functions	No code used	Creating functions through the hero's movement	Web based; available
TALENT	If statements; loops	Micro-language	drag and drop lines of code; writing lines of code in an editor	Explanatory messages
Robocode	Structured computer programming; object-oriented programming	Java	Writing lines of code	Every robot stores data of past activities; available
M.U.P.P.E.T.S.	Three-dimensional objects; object-oriented programming	Java	Interaction with the developed objects; writing lines of code; compile	Collaborative; three dimensional; commands panel; embedded development environment
PlayLogo 3D	Basic concepts and commands of structured programming	Logo	Creation of heroes; navigation across the "galaxy" by writing commands	Interaction; multiplayer; three dimensional; available
Gidget	Analysis and design of basic algorithms	Micro-language	Fixing problems and programs; interaction with a personalised robot	Web based; explanatory messages

Prog&Play. It is a library currently integrated in the Web-based, real-time multi-player strategy game Kernel Panic, which enables constant interaction amongst users. Students can program their own heroes and form alliances with each other aiming to prevail in the game. Prog&Play allows students to choose the language in which they prefer to code their programs amongst programming languages such as Ada, C, Java, OCaml, Scratch and Compalgo (Muratet, Torguet, Viallet, & Jessel, 2011).

PlayLogo 3D. It is a three-dimensional, role playing game that allows interaction amongst multiple users and aims to teach basic concepts of structured computer programming. Users are required to program their heroes by writing the corresponding lines of code in the LOGO language, and navigate them across the environment. More specifically, the virtual world consists of the spaceship X-15 located on a constellation of the Andromeda galaxy, where a contest is held each year amongst pilot-robots (Paliokas, Arapidis, & Mpimpitsos, 2011).

Gidget. It is a Web-based game where students can program using a simplified programming language created specifically for the game in order to learn how to design and analyse basic algorithms. A robot named Gidget has problems with a part of his software and thus cannot complete its tasks. Therefore, students are called in to help Gidget by either fixing wrong lines of code, or by completing missing code within given programs. During these processes, students receive constant feedback of their progress (Lee & Ko, 2011).

The above table presents the study with a structured representation of features supported by the most commonly known educational games for computer programming. The programming elements, characteristics as well programming activities identified can be considered as concepts that describe the field. Thus, future researchers and game developers should take them into consideration when designing a new and advanced educational game for computer programming.

Discussion

In this section we provide an overview of the development of existing educational games for computer programming, and their limitations. The results are categorised based on the features identified that should be taken into consideration during the design and development of an educational game for computer programming.

Educational goals. The educational goals seem to cover both the *cognitive* and *emotional axes*. Within the games, these goals are clearly focused in the computer programming concepts that each game aims to teach. This is especially the case in the educational games that cover specific units of learning, and thus the desired learning outcomes are more clearly identified. The emotional goals seem to be accomplished through the numerous attractive scenarios available in each game.

The *problems* students are required to solve are consistent with the set educational goals and their cognitive limitations. In the educational games focused in specific units of learning, students execute and complete quests that teach them knowledge that is relevant to the programming concepts set in the goals. As an example, the simple and nested loops in Catacombs are taught through the completion of lines of code, and their correct syntax allows students to pass to the next level, while the same concepts are taught in Wu's Castle when students move their characters across the world and recognise logical errors. On the other hand, the second category of educational games (e.g. Robocode, M.U.P.P.E.T.S, PlayLogo 3D) employs problems that allow students to interact with each other and execute multiple tasks that will teach them all the basic concepts of computer programming.

Framework. Educational games that focus on specific units of learning seem to have properly defined a framework for their employment in educational contexts. However, games that teach multiple and more complex units of learning, and thus cover multiple educational goals usually set several frameworks. It should be noted that the games Lightbot and Robozzle do not define any framework.

Scenario's space. All educational games present and work based on a *scenario* in order to attract and motivate students. In some cases *introductory information* is provided to the players in regard to the virtual world (e.g. PlayLogo 3D, Wu's Castle).

Information resources. Most educational games provide *explanatory messages*. The games where this feature is more fully supported are Catacombs, Saving Sera, EleMental: The Recurrence and Wu's Castle. Moreover, *scaffolding techniques* are provided through these explanatory messages that appear while students are trying to solve their quests (e.g. Catacombs, Saving Sera, EleMental).

Facilitating tools. Tools where students can write requested lines of code exist in the Catacombs, Saving Sera, EleMental, Robocode and M.U.P.P.E.T.S games. In addition, multiplayer games (e.g. PlayLogo 3D, M.U.P.P.E.T.S., Prog&Play, Catacombs) include features where students can *communicate and interact* with one another.

Generic conditions. The generic conditions have been taken into consideration. This has been carried out more efficiently in the educational games that cover specific units of learning rather than in the ones that teach multiple and complex computer programming concepts. On the other hand, they have not been considered at all during the design of the Robozzle and Lightbot games.

It should be noted that none of the studied games provides *relevant cases* that can prepare students for the activities they will be required to execute. The existence of this feature would significantly increase the quality of the games, since it would provide useful tutorials and guidelines for learners.

We also have to mention that many of the aforementioned information regarding these games derive exclusively from the relevant literature, since they are not available for access. This fact also results in our inability to exploit them in the learning process and actually test them against set educational goals in computer programming courses. Summing up, it seems that all studied games include scenarios that motivate learners, clearly indicate the educational goals that need to be reached and include problems that are set up as specified above. Other features, such as facilitating tools, information resources, one or several frameworks and taking into consideration generic conditions are supported by the majority of the studied games. However, none of the games appear to support relevant cases to prepare learners before engaging with the environments or to act as manuals for when learners require guidance.

Conclusions

The main implications derived from the analysis include that most games have been developed to cover programming concepts (such as variables, simple and nested if statements, loops, arrays, functions) with the exception of M.U.P.P.E.T.S. and Robocode that cover more complex concepts such as object-oriented programming. We do not consider the fact that the games do not tackle all programming concepts as a disadvantage, since they seem to successfully fulfil the educational goals they set regarding the group of concepts they aim to teach.

Also, the study elaborated on the added values of using educational games in computer programming. Our research revealed a number of interesting principles that can help us understand why educational games can improve teaching and learning of computer programming. For example, games seem to have a facilitating role in the learning process during the teaching of specified concepts and could play a small or a big part in the entire course's implementation process, depending on the generic conditions. More specifically, depending on the nature of the course (online, offline, blended), materials, communications, exams, etc. could be supported on different levels by the games' environments. To this end, educational games can provide a number of characteristics, such as storytelling, scaffolding and interactivity, which increase motivation for participation in class as well as attract students to complete their tasks through interesting scenarios.

We examined the educational games in terms of the educational value that they bring, and we derived that they can provide students with:

- Clear educational goals and learning outputs, ensuring that they know what they have to do to achieve the required knowledge and skills.
- A familiar and immersive environment that attracts students' attention facilitates their active participation and increases their motivation.
- Interesting scenarios with comprehensive problems they have to solve, which enable them to learn in a contextual manner (learning specific units of learning periodically).
- Tools that help them communicate and collaborate with their classmates, improving their group work skills and guiding them through the learning process by explaining the possible mistakes they make. These tools can be applied either with chat functionalities or with different types of interactions between the learners and the game while trying to achieve and fulfil common goals.

Furthermore, the study's findings have implications regarding the design of future educational games focused on computer programming, listing and elaborating on the requirements educational game designers and developers should strive to support and thus setting the foundations for future holistic environments.

Educational games can also assist teachers teach programming in their courses by designing the game and setting up its parameters. For example, teachers can use educational games to plan their courses and monitor students' interactions, progress and evaluation through their activities in the game. The establishment of the educational goals, learning outcomes and the setting up of a scenario that will delineate the curriculum into units of learning also enables teachers to be better prepared and have a deeper knowledge of the materials they teach and get more skilled in course planning.

On the other hand, a significant limitation identified in the existing educational games focused on computer programming courses is the ability of the teacher to configure the environment according to the pedagogical goals related to the respective unit of learning. Additionally, the collaboration concept could be reinforced and better supported within multiplayer educational games so that they can teach more complex programming concepts that will be more efficiently understood through team-based learning activities.

The evaluations carried out during the pilots studies, showed that the majority of learners expressed positive attitudes towards the examined environments. Thus, this enables the initial implications of our research to exploit the features considered important by the literature and presented throughout the paper during future design and development of educational games.

Such games will fully support all identified specifications and features and will aim to teach in-depth more complex concepts, such as object-oriented programming.

References

Barnes, T., Chaffin, A., Powell, E., & Lipford, H. (2008). Game2Learn: improving the motivation of CS1 students. *Proceedings of the 3rd International Conference on Game Development in Computer Science Education* (pp. 1–5). Miami, Florida.

Barnes, T., Richter, H., Chaffin, A., Godwin, A., Powell, E., Ralph, T., et al. (2007). The role of feedback in Game2Learn. *CHI, 2007*, 1–5.

Becker, T. (2010). The character of successful trainings with serious games. *International Journal Of Emerging Technologies In Learning (IJET)*, *5*(SI3). Retrieved April 17, 2012, from http://online-journals.org/i-jet/article/view/1498.

Chaffin, A., Doran, K., Hicks, D., & Barnes, T. (2009). Experimental evaluation of teaching recursion in a video game. In S. N. Spencer (Ed.), *Proceedings of the 2009 ACM SIGGRAPH Symposium on Video Games* (New Orleans, Louisiana, August 04–06, 2009). *Sandbox '09* (pp. 79–86). New York, NY: ACM.

De Freitas, S., & Jarvis, S. (2006). A framework for developing serious games to meet learner needs. In *Proceedings Interservice/Industry Training, Simulation, and Education Conference, Florida, USA* (pp. 1–11).

Eagle, M., & Barnes, T. (2009). Experimental evaluation of an educational game for improved learning in introductory computing. *ACM SIGCSE Bulletin, 41*(1), 321–325.

Gunter, G. A., Kenny, R. F., & Vick, E. H. (2008). Taking educational games seriously: using the RETAIN model to design endogenous fantasy into standalone educational games. *Educational Technology Research and Development, 56*(5/6), 511–537.

Ho, P. C., Chung, S.-M., & Tsai, M.-H. (2006). A case study of game design for e-Learning. In Z. Pan et al. (Eds.), *Edutainment* (LNCS, Vol. 3942, pp. 453–462). Berlin Heidelberg: Springer.

Lahtinen, E., Ala-Mutka, K., & Jarvinen, H. (2005). A study of difficulties of novice programmers. *Proceedings of the 10th Annual SIGCSE Conference on Innovation and Technology in Computer Science Education*, June 27–29, 2005, Caparica, Portugal (pp. 14–18).

Law, K. M. Y., Lee, V. C. S., & Yu, Y. T. (2010). Learning motivation in e-Learning facilitated computer programming courses. *Computers & Education, 55*(1), 218–228. doi: http://dx.doi.org/10.1016/j.compedu.2010.01.007.

Lee, M.J., & Ko, A.J. (2011). Personifying programming tool feedback improves novice programmers' learning. *Conference on International Computing Education Research (ICER)* (pp. 109–116), Providence, RI, USA, August 8–9

Li, F.W.B., & Watson, C. (2011). Game-based concept visualization for learning programming. *Proceedings of the 3rd International ACM Workshop on Multimedia Technologies for Distance Learning* (pp. 37–42), Scottsdale, AZ, USA, December 01, 2011

Maragos, K., & Grigoriadou, M. (2011). Exploiting TALENT as a tool for teaching and learning. *The International Journal of Learning, 18*(1), 431–440.

Muratet, M., Torguet, P., Viallet, F., & Jessel, J.-P. (2011). Experimental feedback on Prog & Play: a serious game for programming practice. *Computer Graphics Forum, 30*(1), 61–73.

O'Kelly, J., & Gibson, P. (2006). RoboCode & problem-based learning: a non-prescriptive approach to teaching programming. *ACM SIGCSE Bulletin, 38*(3), 217–221.

Paliokas, I., Arapidis, C., & Mpimpitsos, M. (2011). PlayLOGO 3D: a 3D interactive video game for early programming education: let LOGO be a game. In *Proceedings of Third International Conference on Games and Virtual Worlds for Serious Applications (VS-GAMES)*, 4–6 May 2011 (pp. 24–31).

Phelps, A., Bierre, K., & Parks, D. (2003). MUPPETS: multi-user programming pedagogy for enhancing traditional study. *Proceeding of the 4th Conference on Information Technology Education* (pp. 100–105), Lafayette, IN, USA, October, 2003

Piteira, M., & Haddad, S. (2011). Innovate in your program computer class: an approach based on a serious game. OSDOC: Open Source and Design of Communication Workshop ACM, New York, NY, USA (pp. 49–54).

Salen, K., & Zimmerman, E. (2004). *Rules of play: game design fundamentals* (pp. 56–84). Cambridge: The MIT Press. pp. 304–350.

Yusoff, A., Crowder, R., Gilbert, L., & Wills, G. (2009), A conceptual framework for serious games. *The 9th IEEE International Conference on Advanced Learning Technologies* (pp. 21–23). July 15–17, 2009. doi: 10.1109/ICALT.2009.19.

Zualkernan, I. A. (2006). A framework and a methodology for developing authentic constructivist e-Learning environments. *Educational Technology & Society, 9*(2), 198–212.

Robotics and Programming Concepts in Early Childhood Education: A Conceptual Framework for Designing Educational Scenarios

Anastasia Misirli and Vassilis Komis

Introduction

The term "Educational Robotics" refers to the teaching practice during which the students use the robots to construct knowledge with the help of or for the robots themselves. The term appeared in the 1960s through the educational approach of the Logo programming language. Within this context educational robotics consists of an educational approach which recruits programmable devices to improve the learning process through project-based learning. It is defined by the use of Information and Communication Technologies (ICT) in its own affordances for observation, analysis, modelling and control of various physical procedures (Depover, Karsenti, & Komis, 2007). It concerns an approach which allows the learner to familiarise himself with the Information and Communication Technologies and use them to define a plan, to organise and find a specific solution to the given problem exchanging his opinion with those of others (Denis & Baron, 1993; Leroux, Nonnon, & Ginestié, 2005). The cognitive abilities that develop in early childhood with the use of robotics have been studied since the introduction of the Logo educational approach. A distinct category of educational robotics is the Logo-like programmable toys which are appropriate in early childhood and primary education. These programmable toys are programmable robots which are controlled by the user for the respective movement or path they are ordered to execute. In some cases the connection with the computing environment may be used. The child conceives and defines the commands which are introduced into the robot following the principles of the Logo programming language. This robotics subcategory is inscribed in the

A. Misirli (✉) • V. Komis
Department of Educational Sciences and Early Childhood Education, University of Patras, University campus, 26504 Rio, Greece
e-mail: amisirli@upatras.gr; komis@upatras.gr

C. Karagiannidis et al. (eds.), *Research on e-Learning and ICT in Education: Technological, Pedagogical and Instructional Perspectives*, DOI 10.1007/978-1-4614-6501-0_8, © Springer Science+Business Media New York 2014

psychopedagogical approach of the Logo language, supporting the development of the metacognitive ability, with which the children reflect on the cognitive process adopted, improving the ability of problem-solving and promoting the ability of spatial orientation (Clements & Nastasi, 1999; Clements & Sarama, 2002).

An Overview of Programmable Toys in Early Childhood

The Logo programming language developed in the mid-1960s at the M.I.T. (Massachusetts Institute of Technology). At the same time various types of floor-robots which are programmed with the Logo language make their appearance to aid the implementation of the new programming language in educational contexts after further research activity. Since then a series of robots featuring a common Logo programming language implementation have been used for educational purposes.

A literature review of the integration of robotics in education allows us to distinguish two approaches: (a) the use of educational kits for the construction and function of the robotic system using the appropriate programming language and (b) the use of educational kits with pre-constructed robotic systems using the appropriate programming language.

The first category includes kits like LEGO®-WeDo™ and LEGO®-Mindstorms™. The second category includes the robotic programmable toys such as the Roamer, the Bee-Bot, the Pro-Bot and the Constructa-Bot. The latter require the user to design and compose a program and execute it in order to achieve a goal, thereby solving a problem. Their characteristic is that they are programmed by novice users either through the use of a computer or through the device itself. Most of the programmable toys use the ideas of the initial Logo floor robot—the Logo turtle—and have similar functional and operational characteristics.

Table 1 presents an overview of early childhood and primary education robotic devices (Table 1). It is clear that the majority of the robotic systems refers mainly to pre-constructed robotic devices the so-called "programmable toys" (Hirst, Johnson, Petre, Price, & Richards, 2003). Some have a more attractive appearance and function due to the production of sensory stimuli one of which is the Bee-Bot programmable toy while some others are less complex and are more of a machine such as the PIXIE. In any case, the child designs and defines the total amount of commands which are introduced into the robot following the principles of the Logo programming language. The added value of this specific programming language is the fact that it is appropriate for early childhood development and support abilities such as problem-solving, metacognitive thought as well as skills such as counting, spatial orientation and measurement (Bers, 2008; Highfield, 2010; Highfield & Mulligan, 2008; Highfield, Mulligan, & Hedberg, 2008; Papert, 1980).

Two interesting conclusions can be drawn from this table. First, programmable toys have been under development for the last 40 years within the context of Logo language paradigm. These toys have a Logo-like robust interface and are technological devices using this specific language.

Table 1 Robotic devices for early childhood and primary education

Year of development	Name of Kit	Language	Category	Firmware	Novice users/ Age group	Learning Area	Image
Late 1970s	BIGTRAK (1979)	Logo	Programmable toy	MB	N/A	Maths Literacy Arts	
During 1980s	Tortue Jeulin T2	Logo	Programmable toy, Computer, Pedagogical material	Evreux	N/A	Maths Literacy Arts	
	Tortue Jeulin T3	Logo	Programmable toy, Computer, Pedagogical material		N/A	Maths Literacy Arts	
	Turtle (1985)	Logo	Programmable toy, Programming by computer	Valiant Technology	N/A	Maths Literacy Arts	
During 1990s	Roamer (1999)	Logo	Programmable toy		4–9	Maths Literacy Arts	
	Roamer-Too (2008)	Logo	Programmable toy		4–7	Maths Literacy Arts	
	PIXIE	Logo	Programmable toy, Software	Swallow	5–8	Maths Literacy Arts	
	PIP	Logo	Programmable toy, Software		7–12	Maths Literacy Arts	
	PIPPIN	Logo	Programmable toy, Software		7–12	Maths Literacy Arts	

(continued)

Table 1 (continued)

Year of development	Name of Kit	Language	Category	Firmware	Novice users/ Age group	Learning Area	Image
During 2000s	Lego Mindstorms RCX Brick (1998)	Logo	Construction kit, Software	Lego	>7	STEM	
	Lego Mindstorms NXT (2006)	Logo	Construction kit, Software		>7	STEM	
	Lego WeDo (2009)	Logo	Construction kit Software		>7	STEM	
	Bee-Bot (2005)	Logo	Programmable toy Software, Pedagogical material	TTS	4–7	Maths Literacy Arts	
	Constructa-Bot	Logo	Programmable toy		4–7	Maths Literacy Arts	
	Pro-Bot (2006)	Logo	Programmable toy, Software to transfer programs from the concrete object		7–12	Maths Literacy Arts	

Second they are supported by appropriate educational material and are, apart from the LEGO® robotics kits (LEGO® Mindstorms™ & LEGO® WeDo™), preconstructed systems requiring no construction. Their manipulation focuses on developing the user programming abilities rather than engineering/technology ones. Their educational applications focus on STEM whereas those which are addressed to younger children such as the Bee-Bot may cover other cognitive areas as well (Language, Arts). Most of the recent toys (Bee-Bot and Pro-Bot) have more user friendly (robust) interface and a more playful appearance.

Educational Robotics in Early Childhood Education

The implementation of educational robotics in early childhood education is seen as a way of introducing various concepts and developing different abilities.

Robotics is an interesting cognitive domain because it is a tool through which children have the opportunity to approach mathematical concepts, applying strategies such as problem-solving, inquiry and experimentation (Rogers & Portsmore, 2004). It is worth mentioning that robotics is an educational approach with a variable dimension, which it can be easily integrated in various educational settings (Bers & Horn, 2010). Furthermore, teaching about and through computer programming and robotics using developmentally appropriate approaches increases children's sequencing abilities (Kazakoff, Sullivan, & Bers, 2013). During the planning and constructing procedure of a robotic model children of early childhood put into action cognitive abilities which are under development (Papert, 1980). Programming concepts which may be developed within computing environments are not always developed for children of this age range. There are usually environments which require users to develop the ability of abstract thought.

Hirst et al. (2003) dealt with the review, the description and the presentation of robotic environments which are based on the technology of the LEGO® Mindstorms™ robotics systems. They propose that these specific systems bridge the gap between how the user acts concerning more abstract computing systems and specific conventional tools. They also propose that the creation of a more individualised system of a graphic microworld for novice users must be created so that they are progressively drawn towards a more advanced programming environment.

Therefore, educational robotics in early childhood education uses appropriate cognitive tools, emphasising on tangible use. The use of such tools which is the case of programmable toys is a factor of motivation infusing the interest in children and their actions towards learning. Those tools are developmentally appropriate as they are based on playing and consisting of meaningful action and reaction (Highfield, 2010; Highfield et al., 2008; Highfield & Mulligan, 2008).

Some researchers suggest that learning through interaction with a programmable toy, the construction of more abstract cognitive structures and the development of social skills is reinforced (Bers & Horn, 2010; Yelland, 2007).

However researchers such as Greff (1998, 2001) attempted to reinforce the learning context and developed appropriate teaching materials based on a language of graphic representation of the commands for the approach of algorithmic concepts. A positive aspect of this language was that it offered the user directness because of the appropriateness of its structure and planning during the creation of a program. Thus, algorithms were planned in order to direct the floor-robot to complete a specific path.

Other researchers used the programmable toy floor-robot Roamer in their study. João-Monteiro, Cristóvão-Morgado, Bulas-Cruz, and Morgado (2003) report the results of their teaching intervention within the context of the ICEI programme in preschool settings in Portugal. The floor-robot Roamer was used to support teachers in using the ICT as a cognitive tool. The added value of this particular robot lies in its potential to develop mathematical concepts in children in early childhood.

A look at the studies published in the last decade shows that the use of Logo-like programmable toy Bee-Bot lies in the centre of the scientific interest for this specific age group.

Beraza, Pina, and Demo (2010) in their study presented teacher-orientated robotics activities in order to support teachers in their practice. They claim that the programmable toy Bee-Bot is suitable for early childhood and primary education but provides limited programming opportunities. For this reason and for encouraging teachers in designing suitable educational scenarios with programmable toys robots they proposed the use of the Arduino platform.

In the study by Highfiled (2010) 33 children of early childhood and their teachers chose the Bee-Bots and Pro-Bots from a range of robotic toys. Through a learning process of a combination of robotic toys and engaging tasks mathematical thinking and sustained engagement was promoted.

Pekarova (2008) studied the development of effective teaching practices and attractive activities for children through digital technologies in early childhood education. Her results show the need of an organised context for teaching programming concepts with the use of the Bee-Bot. However, since this procedure is not sufficient enough for activating children's inner motives, the formation and the organisation of appropriate problem-solving tasks as well as the development of teaching materials are required.

Highfield and Mulligan (2008) describe various instances where early childhood and primary school children interacted with the programmable Bee-Bot toys. The desired outcome came through the experimentation with the programmable toy as children applied different strategies in order to discover its functions and features. Especially the experimentation gave children the opportunity to discover the feature of programmable toy to rotate rather than move aside. Similar outcomes have also been stated by Highfield et al. (2008) for the development of mathematical concepts in children of early childhood when using the Bee-Bot programmable toy. This toy facilitates children's learning and in particular the way to approach topics such as measurement and geometrical transformations as opposed to traditional teacher-orientated teaching.

Similar conclusions are drawn by De Michele, Demo, and Siega (2008) where children from primary education used the programmable toy Bee-Bot to program through mathematical concepts of multiplication and addition in typical classroom teaching practices.

Overall, research has shown that there is no systematic and principle-based framework for teaching educational robotics concepts in early childhood settings. What appears to be missing is a developmentally appropriate educational context for developing programming abilities and reinforcing inner motives of children in early childhood. This is important because integration and use of a programmable toy within an appropriate teaching and learning context may infuse cognitive development (Depover et al., 2007) such as mathematical skills and problem-solving abilities in children.

Furthermore, Csink and Farkas (2010) gave emphasis to the use of floor-robot Roamer to teach programming concepts integrated within the curriculum and the additional methodology. They also propose teaching programming that should be in a context with role-playing and 3D games instead of using computer software. The same point of view for integration of programming concepts within the official curriculum is shared by De Michele et al. (2008). Scientific activity in the field of educational robotics and especially in the field of programmable toys seems to influence the curriculum of various countries such as those of England, Australia, Croatia, Estonia and Hungary (Csink & Farkas, 2010) as well as that of Greece in which a clearly distinct thematic approach has been integrated for the teaching of programming. In some cases like England, Australia, Scotland and Greece there is an explicit reference to the use of programmable toys. In England specifically programmable toys have been integrated in the mathematical learning area and children learn to program by designing paths, a procedure through which they develop abilities such as spatial orientation. In Australia the Ministry of Education introduced a teaching guide concerning the integration and use of the Bee-Bot programmable toy in early childhood education (Kopelke, 2007). In Greece a new curriculum proposal announced in 2011 (The Greek Institute of Educational Policy, 2011) is currently being piloted and includes the integration and use of programmable toys in early childhood and primary education. In addition, in Malta since 2011 and Scotland since 2013 educational programmes targeting the use of the Bee-Bot programmable toy have been launched. In these countries, the Bee-Bot programmable toy is being used as a teaching and learning tool in several academic subjects (ICT, Mathematics, Language, Social Studies, and Physical Education).

A Methodology Framework for Educational Scenarios in Programming and Robotics in Early Childhood

As the preceding literature review of educational robotics in early childhood education clearly shows, the relative research is limited in references of implemented teaching activities without systematic educational design or organization. In some cases the researchers have tried to gather students' representations concerning the content of the robot (through the use of a single question) as well as try to record and present students' programming strategies during free experimentation of the children with the Bee-Bot (Pekarova, 2008). In other cases an attempt to trace children's initial representations and their manipulation of the Bee-Bot is recorded. However, there is still lack of systematic observation and recording of children's learning processes (Highfield, 2010; Highfield et al., 2008; Highfield & Mulligan, 2008).

In the above studies we can additionally observe that there is no specific or organised meaningful context. In other words, they lack in presenting a context suitable for teaching programming as well as for problem-solving situations. Especially the more recent studies use the researcher's demonstration of a particular path and the aim is that children reproduce the same path (Highfield et al., 2008; Highfield & Mulligan, 2008). On the contrary it is Pekarova (2008) who claims that the programmable toy has attractive features and functions for children of this age but these elements are not efficient enough. There is a need for a clear and appropriate planning program construction orientated for the reinforcement and the function of teamwork.

Greff (1998) shows that the creation of a pseudo-language through the graphic representation of the commands of the Roamer programmable toy is an appropriate teaching strategy for the visualization of the programming procedure. This procedure provides user with the opportunity to not only visualize a program but also reflect on and correct its content. This visualisation technique was evaluated by other researchers using a different methodology. In the study of João-Monteiro et al. (2003), the users were asked to programme the toy to reach a desired position or goal as it is represented on a coloured patterned command on a card.

It is worth mentioning the fact that most studies which used the Bee-Bot programmable toy were not integrated in typical classroom teaching practices. They appear to be more focused on free experimentation with the tool and orientated towards the implementation form the scientists themselves who act either as facilitators of the research or are supported by the classroom teacher (Highfield et al., 2008; Highfield & Mulligan, 2008; Pekarova, 2008). On the other hand, Greff (1996) reports the implementation of a teaching intervention towards the development of a programming ability while placing the children either in the position of the robot or in the position of the user under real classroom conditions. Moreover, Greff (2001) and João-Monteiro et al. (2003) describe cases of use of the Roamer robot in typical classroom conditions for the development of programming and mathematical concepts.

As far as the cognitive context is concerned, concepts referring to either premature programming structures (the sequence of commands) or belonging to mathematical learning areas (counting, shapes) were approached. João-Monteiro et al. (2003) in their study implemented the cross-curricular approach in order for children to construct programming concepts.

The primary aim of this study is to propose an appropriate educational framework for organising the teaching process, one that emphasises the understanding, design and implementation of robotics and programming concepts. The study is situated in the wider scientific research context of robotics use in early childhood education. It follows the *design based research* mixed research model and uses the method of multiple case studies for collecting qualitative and quantitative developmental data (Kelly, Lesh, & Baek, 2008). This kind of research deals with the design, development and evaluation of educational programmes or constructions as part of the teaching practice in such a way that the most efficient conditions for teaching and learning are assured for the benefit of everyone involved (Depover et al., 2007).

Since there is no existing framework for teaching programming in early childhood the approach proposed below is an innovative, new tool for educators. This framework is based on a conceptualization where methodological and pedagogical issues are suitably integrated to facilitate the teaching and learning process, thereby addressing the deficiencies of former studies identified above. Such deficiencies have resulted in unsystematic and unstructured educational interventions, which failed to address issues related to the teaching of programming, educational practices and pedagogical principles. The teaching of programming includes concepts such as algorithms, programs, memory and debugging. Moreover, a structured and systematic educational intervention should give emphasis on and carefully select the appropriate teaching approaches. Such issues refer to defining an objective and the goals which meet early childhood children's needs, to using additional teaching strategies, to comprising didactic transposition on programming concepts and to developing appropriate teaching material. These teaching practices are based on pedagogical principles such as project-based learning, child-centred learning, collaborative learning, and well-organised learning environments.

The proposed educational and methodological framework includes seven (7) distinct phases (Fig. 1) for designing an educational scenario. The importance of designing an educational scenario is to include issues of programming concepts, educational practices and pedagogical principles to lead the teaching process. Therefore the selection of a specific subject orients teaching to set an objective, as well as the goals for delivering its content through seven (7) distinct phases, which in fact present different instances of the planning and the implementation process. These phases are found in the core part of the whole design are closely interrelated and interact at the same time (Komis, 2010; Komis, Tzavara, Karsenti, Collin, & Simard, 2013).

From an educator's point of view designing an educational scenario is very important as it addresses issues such as the integration of ICT at least in some of the phases using a computer or robotic device during its implementation and application. The structure of current methodology describes the method with which the participants (in our case early childhood educators) are asked to use ICT in a suitable planned and well-organised context. Thus, the educational scenarios used within this study adopt concepts and themes of computer science and mathematics curricula expecting children to construct programming concepts by using the Bee-Bot programmable toy.

Based on the above conceptualization, a teaching model was developed for educational robotics which was structured after appropriate adaptations as those which emerged by analysing former studies. So a conceptual model was created of an educational scenario appropriately structured and adapted to the cognitive early childhood children's needs. Anticipations and adaptations that took place aspired to minimise methodological faults with the aim of maximising the validity of research findings. Pekarova (2008) mentioned that emphasis on teaching programming in early childhood children should be given to plan a well-organised and systematic teaching intervention. Particularly, all the adaptations that were taken into account were divided into two categories concerning different approaches such as (a) methodological and (b) pedagogical.

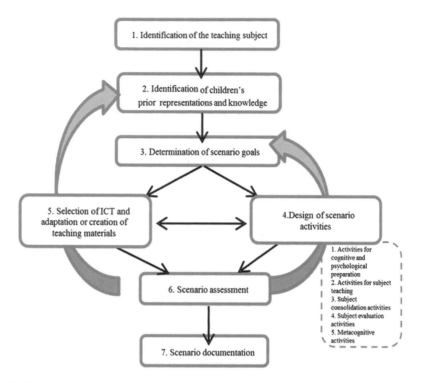

Fig. 1 The phases in designing educational scenarios for robotics

Methodological Approaches

The methodological approaches include: (a) the organisation of the educational scenario, (b) the introduction and the integration of didactic transposition of programming and informatics concepts, (c) the development of instructional design, (d) the integration of inherent teaching strategies in pedagogical and informatics design, (e) the use of explicitly stated teaching contracts and (f) the development of research protocols (instruments gathering data) for each individual.

Educational Scenario

The organisation of the educational scenario (structure and content) followed a spiral developmental procedure, comprising the six (6) following steps: (1) Design, (2) Implementation, (3) Evaluation, (4) Modification, (5) Re-implementation and (6) Re-evaluation with the aim of potentially adapting it in every different educational context or group of children. The interventions which used the programmable toy Bee-Bot do not explicitly mention a systematic implementation to gather data for evaluation and feedback for modification (De Michele et al., 2008; Highfield, 2010;

Highfield et al., 2008; Highfield & Mulligan, 2008; João-Monteiro et al., 2003; Pekarova, 2008). Every educational scenario we designed was pilot tested in a typical classroom setting, before being formally implemented by the in-service teachers.

Didactic Transposition of Programming and Informatics Concept

Moreover, in the published literature there is no illustrated integration of didactic transposition of programming and informatics concepts. All of them are giving more emphasis on the development of abilities concerning mathematical concepts, rather than programming and informatics ones. In our case, the integration of programming and informatics concepts created a more explicit context not only for the children but also for the teachers. For children it is self-evident to deliver the epistemological knowledge under appropriate transposition, while for the teachers it was necessary since they had no previous experience on robotics.

Instructional Design

A development of instructional design underlined the teaching of programming and informatics concepts by increasing the level of cognitive difficulty. This meant that each educational scenario had been designed by increasing the difficulty level in its goals and activities. Researchers, using interventions focused on curricular subjects may have used similar adaptations, however this is not clearly stated (De Michele et al., 2008; João-Monteiro et al., 2003).

Teaching Strategies

Being a more structured and theory-based educational scenario, this has integrated inherent teaching strategies such as problem-solving, cognitive conflict and inquiring. Especially in pedagogical and informatics educational design these strategies provide an ascending engagement and learning process.

Teaching Contract

Furthermore, the use of an explicitly stated teaching contract, customised for each activity was clearly defined, in order to arrange the class' settlement and to motivate the self-regulation of group members, as well as that of the whole class.

Research Protocols

To trace pre and evaluate post-intervention children's ideas, conceptions and representations using Bee-Bot and its functions, research protocols were developed and filled for each individual. Additionally, this process includes children's personal

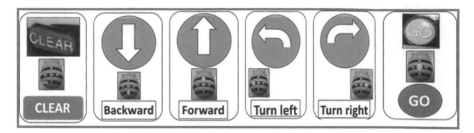

Fig. 2 Graphical representation of Bee-Bot's commands on cards

graphic representations (pre and post drawings) showing their ideas about the Bee-Bot. These two different protocols provide the educator with the opportunity to verify early childhood children's verbal representations, since at this age different approaches are required to facilitate verbal communication.

Pedagogical Approaches

The pedagogical approaches include: (a) the development of a pseudo-language, (b) the development of additional teaching materials, (c) the initiation/organisation of an appropriate learning context and (d) the appropriate adaptation for implementation by in-service teachers in typical classrooms settings, taking the role of facilitators and co-researchers.

Pseudo-Language

The development of a pseudo-language, through a series of graphical representation of commands on cards—based on Greff's study (1998), who had argued that developing such language is developmentally and pedagogical appropriate for the visualization of programming procedures for children in early childhood. This procedure provides the user with the opportunity to not only visualize a program but also reflect on and correct its content. In particular, every command of Bee-Bot's interface has been represented on a card containing three different semiotic systems. Those are: (1) the image or representation of the real object/button, (2) the image of Bee-Bot's interface with the additional button highlighted and (3) the word corresponding to the additional command (Fig. 2).

Every synthesis of card-commands constitutes a full program, which could be executed by the Bee-Bot (Fig. 3). It is also structured according to the program's syntax process (CLEAR–COMMAND OF DIRECTION/ORIENTATION-GO) and placed vertically following of the principles of the Logo language. Each card is 15 cm wide, the same as the Bee-Bot's step length, facilitating children to develop learning strategies for the interrelation between cards, the Bee-Bot's step and the squares of gridded mats.

Fig. 3 Examples of programs developed by a team while working on a teaching activity on orientation concepts

Teaching Materials

Alongside the previous pseudo-language teaching material was developed to support and facilitate the teaching process. Gridded mats of 15 cm each square (the Bee-Bot's step length) on A3 laminated papers were created. This kind of material enabled children to consider the sequence of commands of an algorithm. The child/user is supported and reinforced to find the appropriate commands/cards of orientation and direction, visualizing the program, matching each command/card to a square. Moreover, a series of additional pictures or 3D objects (animals, toys, sticks/ribbons for measuring, adhesive bookmarks), were customised for each educational scenario depending on the learning context they were integrated to.

Learning Context

For each educational scenario an adequate learning context was designed, so as to introduce problem-solving situations as well as to support the educator's teaching practices concerning programming concepts. The so-called learning context initiated an inquiry/problem-solving situation with a developmentally appropriate way, taking into account the children's prior knowledge and experience on programmable toys, as well as programming and mathematical concepts. Through this context open questions (questions stimulating productive activity) were set up for each goal to lead inquiry and problem-solving activities. The learning context takes advantage of the Bee-Bot's animated and playful appearance, enabling children to inquire. In that way the programmable toy is integrated as a member of the team, enabling children to relate to its action and see themselves as co-researchers.

The previous adaptations are based on Papert's ideas about creating a developmentally appropriate constructivist programming environment where concrete material facilitates the construction of abstract ideas and reflection on them (Papert, 1980).

Role of Teachers

Last but not least, an appropriate adaptation for implementation by in-service teachers in typical classrooms, taking the role of facilitators and co-researchers was taken into account. This approach is implied by the broader context of educational robotics thus is the constructionism (Papert, 1980) and the social-constructivism (Vygotsky, 1978). Each teaching activity provided teachers with the knowledge of the learning process they should have, in order for children to construct knowledge. Each activity is comprised of: the learning goal, the question to be explored (inquiry question), one or more teaching strategies, the additional teaching material, the class organisation, the description of the process and finally the conclusion—reference to the prospected learning outcome. Moreover, the scenario documentation (phase 7) comprised of useful references (scientific knowledge) on the children's cognitive development on each teaching subject, additional appropriate vocabulary on programming concepts and guidelines on how to assess and implement the interviews with each child.

Therefore the idea was to divide each educational scenario in two distinct sections. The first section (shared across all scenarios) introduces programming concepts and provides children with basic skills/knowledge to understand the functions and the use of the programmable toy. Within that section a transition from exploration and investigation to more structured activities is applied. Respectively those skills were delivered and extended in the second section where children were engaged in more open-ended activities focused on inquiry and experimentation of mathematical and programming concepts. Mathematical concepts such as spatial awareness are aside to programming concepts due to the Logo-language structure. For example in one educational scenario children applied the robot step as a unit of measure to extend their understanding on length concepts.

The conception and design of educational scenarios of robotics and programming in early childhood education adopt concepts from the cognitive fields of computer science and mathematics. The scientific field of educational robotics concerning the use of the programmable toys is part of the learning theories of constructionism and social constructivism (Bers, 2008; Depover et al., 2007; Papert, 1980; Resnick, 2006). Both these theoretical models lead to the development of abilities of a cognitive style such as inquiry, experimentation, observation, and recording as well as of a social context such as cooperation and discussion with others, reflection on final conclusions and share the results.

An Empirical Investigation of the Framework

Subjects and Setting

The framework outlined above has been implemented for 3 years (2010–2013) through the scientific European project Fibonacci by 46 educators and 864 children between the ages of 4–6. Eventually valuable data was gathered from 38 educators and 674 children. It follows the *design based research* mixed research model and uses the method of multiple case studies for collecting qualitative and quantitative developmental data (Kelly et al., 2008). A concurrent triangulation approach was applied which "provides quantitative statistical results followed by qualitative quotes that support or disconfirm the quantitative results" (Creswell, 2009). The quantitative analysis of the data has not yet been completed; however initial results provide interesting details about the proposed framework.

Measures and Data Collection

Concerning the techniques gathering the quantitative data; different research protocols (instruments) were developed and introduced to the distinct phases of an educational scenario (Fig. 1). All these instruments were tools for educators for recording and evaluating the learning process. A structured interview was introduced at the phase where children's prior representations and knowledge about the programmable toy Bee-Bot were to be identified. It comprised of eleven (11) open-ended questions and was used to assess pre and to evaluate post-intervention children's ideas. These questions formed the categorical variables. The results from the post-intervention interview are embedded in the phase where the scenario activities are designed and particular to the sub-category of subject evaluation process. In the same sub-category three more instruments have been applied. After the first section of teaching activities (function and use of programmable toy), an instrument for assessing every child's prior knowledge on the mathematical concepts was introduced. Another instrument was used to record each child's evaluation on the programming and maths concepts. Its structure provided us with more categorical variables. Moreover, every child was accessed for his reflection on the programmable toy. All these instruments shared the same technique of a structured interview.

Data Analysis

As far as the qualitative analysis is concerned, data from records and videos has been collected but not yet completed. In particular, records are written notes kept by teachers on a daily basis during the implementation of an educational scenario along with notes regarding each child's evaluation on programming and maths.

The data gathered from several case studies (92 children) on the first year of the implementation, indicated that children were having difficulties understanding orientation concepts (Komis & Misirli, 2011). This educational scenario was focused on measurement, enabling children to use the robot step as a unit of measure. The findings indicated the need to engage children with spatial concepts and especially directionality. Therefore an appropriate educational scenario was implemented. In the third year, one more scenario was developed. It was aimed to develop concepts of iteration and sequencing of patterns as those could be initiated through the concept of a program and its structure.

The analysis clearly shows the development of algorithmic thought and programmable abilities as well as the evolution of abilities in diverse mathematical structures. The development and the evolution of these specific cognitive abilities is facilitated through designing and implementing developmentally appropriate educational scenarios which in turn lead to the creation of relative cognitive representations on the function and the use of the Bee-Bot programmable toy (Komis & Misirli, 2011, 2012; Misirli & Komis, 2012).

Data gathered through structured interviews and drawings from ninety two (92) children show a significant shift to more qualitative representations in the post tests. This became apparent by the fact that more explanations was provided (by the children) about the programmable toy's functions and controls (Misirli & Komis, 2012). The interpretation of these preliminary findings attributed to the conception of appropriate teaching activities illustrating and highlighting programmable toy's functions and controls (Greff, 2005).

Concerning the development of algorithmic thought, this was formed through the cognitive process of problem-solving which in our case demanded from each child to plan a spatial path. Thus, a spatial path is sufficiently abstract for this age group, the pseudo-language—a series of card commands—alongside the developed teaching material engaged children in tasks were algorithms were visualised (Komis & Misirli, 2011). The same study showed that a small group of children tried to plan a path mentally without visualizing it. Moreover, gender differences were not significant but differences among different age groups were. The pre and post assessment showed that children aged five and six understand programming concepts more easily.

A very interesting finding is the design and the programming of algorithms by early childhood children (Komis & Misirli, 2013; Misirli & Komis, 2013). During this cognitive construction of an algorithm the children follow two (2) steps: (a) initially they verbalise the abstract conception of the algorithm and (b) they proceed to the syntax of the algorithm by implementing the programming stages respectively. While the syntax procedure takes place, a variance of the amount of commands which are used and rate between three (3) cards-commands and twelve (12) cards-commands for direction and orientation, is observed. On the whole the design of scenario activities (phase 5), were structured and organised to initially familiarise children with the abstract process of conceiving an algorithm. According to Vygotsky (1978) thought is considered as "inner speech" and is the result of language. The "inner speech" was in educational scenario the time when children verbalised (thinking aloud) an algorithm and thus planned their program and consequently organised a strategy to process. This cognitive construction leads children to modelling the solution of a problem as they form it verbally and consequently indicate it by their finger or the programmable toy itself. Moreover, all the activities of a scenario (phase 5) had a teaching contract placed from the very beginning when children were introduced to the activities of cognitive and psychological preparation. It is worth mentioning that all children for the 3 years intervention proceeded to verbalizing an algorithm having the programmable toy as system of reference and not their body as it was proposed from the studies of Greff (1998) and De Michele et al. (2008).

Discussion

The preliminary findings drawn from the present conceptualization and its implementation show that although the programmable toy Bee-Bot has a limited command set (Beraza et al., 2010; Kazakoff et al., 2013) it may be a cognitive tool for children if a systematic, structured, principled and theory-based framework is used. The application of the educational scenarios in typical classrooms in early childhood education, showed that preliminary concepts of programming could be developed through the use of programmable toys. Thus the cognitive potential (Depover et al., 2007) applies not only to the development of mathematical abilities but also to the development of programming abilities and problem-solving situations.

Our proposed framework is validated by quantitative and qualitative data gathered from cases where in-service teachers integrated the educational scenarios in their teaching, without having prior knowledge neither on robotics nor on educational scenarios. This implementation in typical classroom contexts also distinguishes our approach from other researches on programmable toys, which were conducted mostly by researchers and in some cases they have demonstrated to children how to input a program (Beraza et al., 2010; Highfield, 2010; Highfield et al., 2008; Highfield & Mulligan, 2008; Pekarova, 2008). Furthermore, our work demonstrates that the methodological and pedagogical approaches we used to underline this conceptualization, were efficiently addressing the deficiencies of previous studies. Our findings show that although children had no prior experience with programmable toys they finally achieved the cognitive objectives set through inquiry-based activities. They were able to build sequential programs based on graphical representations and transfer them to the programmable toy's tangible interface in a learning context, underlined by appropriate methodological and pedagogical approaches. It seems that the development of programming skills (algorithmic thinking, concept of memory, debugging, structure of sequence, and inputting strategies) requires an appropriate conceptualization to efficiently motivate young children. Based on these preliminary findings, we reach the same conclusion as Highfield et al. (2008): "the Bee-Bot has the potential to enhance children's development of mathematical concepts, particularly ... measurement processes much earlier that traditionally expected." On the top of that we also found spatial orientation (Misirli & Komis, 2013) and sequencing skills.

The present study has drawn conclusions from a specific educational context, but the findings need to be validated in other educational contexts. Several questions such as the role of the teacher in the learning process, the potential differences if the educational scenario is applied it a digital rather than a physical environment, the transfer of programming concepts to other learning areas and metacognitive processes remain open. Our study could be extended and expanded in the future allowing for the above questions to be answered.

In conclusion, the conceptual framework proposed above consists a tool with cognitive potential for early childhood children to develop initial programming concepts via a developmentally appropriate and supportive learning environment. It allows each child to create his/her personal learning "trajectory," one that fulfils his/her own learning needs. There is evidence to suggest that this conceptual model can be integrated into everyday teaching practices and into the everyday processes. In addition, it does not necessarily require educators to be specialized in educational robotics and programming.

Acknowledgements This research was integrated within the context of the European Fibonacci Project. The authors would like to thank the local coordinator Pr. V. Zogza at the Department of Educational Science and Early Childhood Education, University of Patras, participating schools, teachers and children. The authors would like to thank the anonymous reviewers for their constructive comments, which helped us to improve the manuscript.

References

Beraza, I., Pina, A., & Demo, B. (2010). Soft & hard ideas to improve interaction with robots for kids & teachers. *Proceedings of SIMPAR 2010 workshops international conference on simulation, modeling and programming for autonomous robots* (549–555), Darmstadt, Germany, November 15–16, 2010.

Bers, M. (2008). *Blocks to robots: Learning with technology in the early childhood classroom.* New York, NY: Teachers College Press.

Bers, M., & Horn, M. (2010). Tangible programming in early childhood: Revisiting developmental assumptions through new technologies. In I. R. Berson & M. J. Berson (Eds.), *High-tech tots: Childhood in a digital world* (pp. 49–69). Charlotte, NC: Information Age Publishing.

Clements, D. H., & Nastasi, B. K. (1999). Metacognition, learning, and educational computer environments. *Information Technology in Childhood Education Annual, 1,* 3–36.

Clements, D., & Sarama, J. (2002). The role of technology in early childhood learning. *Teaching Children Mathematics, 8*(6), 340–343.

Creswell, W. J. (2009). *Research design: Qualitative, quantitative, and mixed methods approaches.* Thousand Oaks, CA: SAGE Publications.

Csink, L., & Farkas, K. (2010). Lifelong playing instead of lifelong learning teaching robotics without robots and computers. *Proceedings of SIMPAR, workshops international conference on simulation, modeling and programming for autonomous robots* (439–448), Darmstadt, Germany, November 15–16, 2010.

De Michele, S. M., Demo, B. G., & Siega, S. (2008). A Piedmont SchoolNet for a K-12 mini-robots programming project: Experience in primary schools. *In workshop proceedings of SIMPAR 2008 Intl. Conf. on simulation, modeling and programming for autonomous robots* (90–99), Venice, Italy, November 3–4, 2008.

Denis, B., & Baron, G. L. (1993). *Regards sur la robotique pédagogique. Proceedings of the 4th international conference on educational robotics*. Paris: INRP Technologies nouvelles et education.

Depover, C., Karsenti, T., & Komis, V. (2007). *Enseigner avec les technologies: Favoriser les apprentissages, développer des competences*. Montréal, QC: Presses de l'Université du Quebec.

Greff, E. (1996). Les apports du jeu de l'enfant-robot à la didactique de l'informatique. *Actes du 5ème Colloque Francophone de Didactique de l'Informatique Monastir, Tunisie*, Avril, 10–12, 1996 (pp. 67–86).

Greff, E. (1998). Le «jeu de l'enfant-robot»: Une démarche et une réflexion en vue du développement de la pensée algorithmique chez les très jeunes enfants. *Revue Sciences et techniques éducatives, 5*, 47–61.

Greff, E. (2001). Résolution de problèmes en grande section autour des pivotements à l'aide du robot de plancher. *Grand N, 68*, 7–16.

Greff, E. (2005). *Programme cognitive. Proceedings of International Conference «Noter pour penser»*. Paris: Université de Psychologie.

Highfield, K. (2010). Robotic toys as a catalyst for mathematical problem solving. *Australian Primary Mathematics Classroom, 15*(2), 22–27.

Highfield, K., & Mulligan, J. (2008). Young children's engagement with technological tools: The impact on mathematics learning. *Proceedings of international congress in mathematical education 11*, Monterrey, Mexico, July 6–13, 2008.

Highfield, K., Mulligan, J., & Hedberg, J. (2008). Early mathematics learning through exploration with programmable toys. *Proceedings of the joint meeting of PME 32 and PME-NA XXX*, vol. 3 (pp. 169–176), Morelia, México, July 17–21, 2008.

Hirst, A., Johnson, J., Petre, M., Price, B., & Richards, M. (2003). What is the best programming environment/language for teaching robotics using Lego Mindstorms? *Artificial Life Robotics, 7*, 124–131.

João-Monteiro, M., Cristóvão-Morgado, R., Bulas-Cruz, M., & Morgado, L. (2003). A robot in kindergarten. *Proceedings Eurologo'2003 - Re-inventing technology on education*, Porto, Portugal, August 27–30, 2003.

Kazakoff, R. E., Sullivan, A., & Bers, U. M. (2013). The effect of a classroom-based intensive robotics and programming workshop on sequencing ability in early childhood. *Early Childhood Education, 41*, 245–255.

Kelly, E. A., Lesh, A. R., & Baek, Y. J. (2008). *Handbook of design research methods in education*. New York, NY: Routledge.

Komis, V. (2010). *Teaching material for in-service teachers training: Integration and use of ICT to the teaching practice. 2nd Phase of training*. Patras: Institute of Research and Science on Computer Technology.

Komis, V., & Misirli, A. (2011). Robotique pédagogique et concepts préliminaires de la programmation à l'école maternelle: Une étude de cas basée sur le jouet programmable Bee-Bot. In *Proceedings of the 4th conference of "Didactics of Informatics" – DIDAPRO, 24–26 octobre 2011, Université de Patras* (pp. 271–284). Athènes: New Technologies Editions.

Komis, V., & Misirli, A. (2012). L'usage des jouets programmables à l'école maternelle: Concevoir et utiliser des scenarios éducatifs de robotique pédagogique. *Revue Skhôlé, 17*, 143–154.

Komis V., & Misirli A. (2013). *Étude des processus de construction d'algorithmes et de programmes par les petits enfants à l'aide de jouets programmables enfants à l'aide de jouets programmables Dans Sciences et technologies de l'information et de la communication (STIC) en milieu éducatif: Objets et méthodes d'enseignement et d'apprentissage, de la maternelle à l'université*. Clermont-Ferrand, France, October, 28–30, 2013. oai:edutice.archives-ouvertes. fr:edutice-00875628.

Komis, V., Tzavara, A., Karsenti, T., Collin, S., & Simard, S. (2013). Educational scenarios with ICT: An operational design and implementation framework. In R. McBride & M. Searson (Eds.), *Proceedings of society for information technology & teacher education international conference 2013* (pp. 3244–3251). Chesapeake, VA: AACE.

Kopelke, K. (2007). *Making your classroom buzz with Bee-Bots: Ideas and activities for the early phase.*. Sippy Downs, QLD: ICT Learning Innovation Centre – Department of Education, Training and the Arts, Queensland Government.

Leroux, P., Nonnon, P., & Ginestié, J. (2005). *Actes du 8ème colloque francophone de Robotique Pédagogique* (Revue Skhôlé, Ed.). IUFM Aix-Marseille, ISBN: 1263-5898, 135 pages.

Misirli, A., & Komis, V. (2012). Early childhood children's representations regarding the Bee-Bot programmable toy. *Proceedings of the 6th Conference of Didactics of Informatics*, Florina, Greece. April 20–22, 2012, (pp. 331–340).

Misirli, A., & Komis, V. (2013). Construire les notions de l'orientation et de la direction à l'aide des jouets programmables: Une étude de cas dans des écoles maternelles en Grèce. *Actes du 1er Colloque eTIC: Ecole et TICE*, Clermont-Ferrand, France, October 3–4, 2013.

The Greek Institute of Educational Policy. (2011). *New curriculum for early childhood education.* Athens: The Greek Institute of Educational Policy (IEP).

Papert, S. (1980). *Mind-storms, children, computers and powerful ideas.* New York, NY: Basic Books.

Pekarova, J. (2008). Using a programmable toy at preschool age: Why and how? *Proceedings workshop of SIMPAR 2008 international conference on simulation, modeling and programming for autonomous robots* (pp. 112–121), Venice, Italy, November 3–4, 2008.

Resnick, M. (2006). Computer as paintbrush: Technology, play and the creative society. In D. Singer, R. Golikoff, & K. Hirsh-Pasek (Eds.), *Play = learning: How play motivates and enhances children's cognitive and social-emotional growth.* New York, NY: Oxford University Press.

Rogers, C., & Portsmore, M. (2004). Bringing engineering to elementary school. *Journal of STEM Education, 5*, 17–28.

Vygotsky, L. S. (1978). *Mind in society: The development of higher psychological processes.* Cambridge, MA: Harvard University Press.

Yelland, N. (2007). *Shift to the future: Rethinking learning with new technologies in education.* New York, NY: Routledge.

Part IV
Web 2.0 Tools and Learning

Integrating Blogs in Primary Education

Nikleia Eteokleous-Grigoriou and Stella Photiou

Introduction

With the rapid diffusion of the Internet; new approaches to learning were created (Crosta, 2004). As a result, the interest in the development and use of online learning has been steadily increasing (Dabbagh & Kitsantas, 2004) providing "anytime, anywhere learning." More specifically, the technological advancement in information technology and telecommunications resulted in the development of the Web 2.0 and created the appropriate framework for user participation. The traditional one-way communication is transformed into a two-way communication, and process of information. In Web 2.0 users are Contributing, Collaborating, Creating—the 3C's (Ala-Mutka, Punie, & Ferrari, 2009). Various online tools have emerged such as blogs, wikis, discussion forums, online collaborative documents, online sharing of documents, pictures and videos, podcasts, RSS feed, etc. Millions of people use various social and professional networks, such as Facebook, MySpace, Twitter, Delicious, Flickr, LinkedIn, and Live Journal. Nowadays, with the advent of Web 2.0, the Internet has become truly interactive. The aforementioned tools and networks are excellent examples of how definitions, ideas, photographs, videos, and voice can be shared over a powerful Web 2.0 Internet. Technology provides a realistic, visually compelling, and motivating interactive environment for developing the life skills and knowledge needed for today's globalized, hi-tech environment (Goddard, 2002). The Web 2.0 technologies became an essential tool of daily life and a crucial part of students' personal knowledge tools (Lee, Miller, & Newnham, 2008). Consequently, the Web 2.0 tools can be educationally exploited for teaching and learning purposes towards achieving educational objectives, thus transforming social to educational networking.

N. Eteokleous-Grigoriou (✉) • S. Photiou
Department of Primary Education, Frederick University,
7, Y. Frederickou Str., Pallouriotisa, Nicosia 1036, Cyprus
e-mail: n.eteokleous@frederick.ac.cy; stellaphot@hotmail.com

C. Karagiannidis et al. (eds.), *Research on e-Learning and ICT
in Education: Technological, Pedagogical and Instructional Perspectives*,
DOI 10.1007/978-1-4614-6501-0_9, © Springer Science+Business Media New York 2014

Blogs are one of the most popular Web 2.0 tools. In 2009, 133 million blogs were online and two new blogs are created every second! It is supported that blogs have educational value given their characteristics and the opportunities provided to users (Davis, 2005; Eid Neurolearning, 2005; Richardson, 2010). Even though they were around for years, they recently emerged as a popular means of communication, discussion, collaboration, and information sharing. Blogs are Web publishing tools which provide teachers and students an interactive platform where text, images, and links to other blogs, Web pages, are posted mostly focusing on a particular subject. It is supported that blogs have educational value given their characteristics and the opportunities provided to users (Richardson, 2010). Blogs are most popular among students since they are virtual and can be worked at any time and place (Richardson, 2010). It is extremely beneficial to integrate Web 2.0 tools; in this case blogs, as learning-cognitive tools, to add educational value and enhance the teaching and learning process and promote the development of higher-order thinking skills, such as application, synthesis, evaluation, creation (Anderson & Krathwohl, 2001). It can be also suggested that by default blogs facilitate and promote the development of a community. The members of the community are the bloggers, since bloggers share a common interest (a specific subject under "investigation"); connecting to each other by posting comments and discussing. Students extensive use of technology is possible to facilitate the integration of blogs (and technology overall) as tools in the teaching and learning process. Being part of our students' digital world might be more possible to raise their interest, motivate them, transform the classroom environment, and properly prepare them for the rapidly changing information society's needs and demands.

Main Aim of the Study

The current study evaluates blog integration as an educational tool within the teaching and learning process and specifically within the Language and Linguistics course in fifth grade (Subject examined: The time machine) and its role in developing a Community of Inquiry (CoI). The research objectives that guided the current study are the following:

– To investigate the effectiveness and role of blog in achieving specific learning objectives when it is integrated as an educational tool within the teaching and learning process,
– To examine the development of a blended learning environment with the use of blog in relation to in-classroom activity,
– To identify how the role of educator and students differentiate within a blended learning environment,
– To investigate the development of a Community of Inquiry (CoI), by identifying the existence of the three parameters that characterizes a CoI: cognitive, social, and teaching presence.

Theoretical Background

Blogs

Blog is considered an important tool of the Web 2.0 toolbox (Richardson, 2009) and blogging has become one of the most popular Web 2.0 activities. The origins of the blog emerged from the short term of "web log" (Bauer, 2011); an online chronological collection of personal commentary and links that was first used by Barger (1997). A blog is a Web site that is maintained by an individual or a group where readers can comment on blog posts to supply more information and discuss various issues (Allen, 2011). A person that owns a blog and/or posts messages on blogs is called a blogger and the actions within its environment are known as blogging (Hill, 2004). Blogs contain text, graphics, images, videos, and hyperlinks to other Web sites. Bloggers comment on the posts, discuss, argue, and provide their opinions. Blogs create conditions for interaction, reflection, ideas' synthesis, exchange and discussion, self-evaluation, and feedback (Petko, 2011; Sim & Hew, 2010; Zawilinski, 2009).

Blogs and Education

Given the great educational blogging potential, numerous educators have already started using blogs in the classroom. Blogs can be integrated as educational tools across the curriculum, from primary to higher education, achieving collaboration among students and educators even in different schools and countries. Many studies explored the features and educational benefits that blogging offers to students, and discussed the major blog uses in education (Churchill, 2009, Downes, 2004, Richardson, 2009; Richardson, 2010; Siemens, 2005). Specifically, studies integrated blogs into their teaching exploring the learning value of blogging (Chen, Cannon, Gabrio, & Leifer, 2005, Makri & Kynigos, 2007), i.e., for group teaching, collaborative learning, and Web-based collaboration (Grassley & Bartoletti, 2009). Educational blogs provide a practical online platform for discussions that hastens the acquisition of knowledge and learning (Liu & Chang, 2010). Additionally, blogs provide space for the students to reflect and publish their thoughts and understandings, and opportunities for feedback, scaffolding of new ideas, as well as collaborative learning. Blogs also promote the development of higher-order thinking skills such as application, synthesis, evaluation, creation (Anderson & Krathwohl, 2001), and improve flexibility in teaching and learning. Finally, blogs feature hyperlinks, which help students understand the relational and contextual basis of knowledge, knowledge construction, meaning making and experience connective writing (Liu & Chang, 2010; Penrod, 2007; Richardson, 2009). According to Oravec (2002) blogs encourage self-expression and collaboration, which in turn are reflected in enhanced critical thinking skills. A blog offers extended interactivity, increasing students' involvement and motivation (Eteokleous & Pavlou, 2010).

Students can receive instant feedback from the instructor, peers, and other visitors, which enhances learning efficiency (Kaplan, Piskin, & Bol, 2010). Blog participants perform connective writing since they need to read carefully and critically, and develop context that is clear, organized, and convincing. There is a synthesis of ideas, self-evaluation, and reflection. Experiencing blog writing promotes critical, analytical, relational, and creative thinking. It also combines collegiality and social interaction, developing working and social relationships among teachers, educators, and professionals (Davis, 2005; Eid Neurolearning, 2005; Richardson, 2010). Eteokleous (2011) explains the development of student-centered environments and how students become educational content creators, having an increased role in the teaching and learning process when blogs are used as educational tools. Instructor's role in a blog learning environment is extremely important. Glogoff (2005) emphasizes that the instructors should be aware of the delicate balance between the synchronicity of time and place on the one hand and the need to keep discussions focused on the topic. Additionally, Kim (2008) states that the success of the system relies on teachers' capability in providing the appropriate resources. So, it can be suggested that although teaching and reflecting through blogs constitutes an effective medium for teaching, it must be applied in a proper way with the guidance of the instructor in order to foster the best teaching practices (Eteokleous & Nisiforou, 2013a, 2013b; Karaman, 2011).

Blog's pedagogical affordances were examined and reported by various researchers. First of all, it is supported that blogs motivate students to engage positively in the writing process (Barrios, 2003; Cottle, 2009; Shifflet, 2008; Trammel & Ferdig, 2004). Additionally, blogs enhance participation and interactive communication opportunities (Angelaina & Jimoyiannis, 2012) promoting both individualized (Cottle, 2009; Shifflet, 2008) and group reflection on learning experiences. The blog's pedagogical affordances also include the support of authentic learning tasks through peer assessment and formative evaluation of student work (Angelaina & Jimoyiannis, 2012) as well as the promotion of critical thinking and increases learner autonomy (Richardson, 2010). Finally, blog facilitates student collaboration within a community of learners (Nelson & Fernheimer, 2003) and encourages and support blended learning activities by effectively changing formal and informal learning.

Blog as Cognitive-Learning Tool

Blogs serve numerous purposes such as personal, professional, and educational. Focusing on the educational use of blog, four extra categories can be identified: Blog as online course tool, blog as a discussion forum, blog as a research tool, and blog as cognitive-learning tool (Eteokleous & Nisiforou, 2013a, 2013b). For the purposes of the current paper, it is important to better explain the cognitive-learning tool category. Eteokleous and Nisiforou (2013a, 2013b) attempted to define blogs as cognitive-learning tools and examine their role in the teaching and learning process as well their effectiveness in achieving specific learning objectives.

The current paper suggests that blog integration in the teaching and learning practice is defined as the use of blogs by students as a cognitive-learning tool that enhances their learning experience and supports the achievement of specific learning goals. It can be integrated in all educational levels (i.e., pre-primary, primary, and secondary, as well as higher education in numerous departments) and fields and in various subjects (i.e., Mathematics, Literature, Science, etc.). This approach is related to the *learning with* computers or computers as mindtools (Jonassen, 1999b), where computers and overall technology is introduced as students' partners within the teaching and learning process. *Learning with* technology and *effects of* technology use characterizes this trend. *Learning with* requires integrating computers and overall technology as mindtools in the classrooms to support constructive learning. Educators embed or apply technology capacity in the context of ongoing teaching and learning in different school subjects. Based on the above, students learn how to use various technology applications not as an end in themselves, but as tools that help them execute their tasks and promote the balanced development of their mental abilities. As a result they do not learn from technology, but technologies support meaning generated by students (Bielaczyc & Collins, 1999; CTGV, 2003; Jonassen, 1999a, 1999b; Jonassen, 2000).

Blog is integrated within the teaching and learning practice for numerous years; however, the development of a pedagogical framework is extremely important. It will highlight a set of key criteria and parameters for blogs to be integrated as cognitive-learning tools within the teaching and learning process in order to achieve real blogging. Additionally, educator's and students' role should be further examined and clarified. Finally, research on the following needs to be conducted: blog's design, format, content used and uploaded, tools and gadgets employed.

Community of Learning

Communities of learning in schools have been examined by various researchers providing definitions, characteristics, the role as well as the importance of communities of learning. According to Wenger, McDermott, and Snyder (2002) communities of learning "…are groups of people who share a concern, a set of problems, a passion about a topic, and who deepen their knowledge and expertise in this area by interacting on an ongoing basis" (p. 4). Few years later, Wenger (2004) defined communities of learning as "…groups of people who share a passion for something that they know how to do, and who interact regularly in order to learn how to do it better" (p. 2). In the learning environments, the role of a community is to support and facilitate socially constructed knowledge (Job-Sluder & Barab, 2004; Palloff & Pratt, 2005). Finally, Loving, Schroeder, Kang, Shimek, and Herbert (2007) supported that "A learning community is a group of autonomous, independent individuals who are drawn together by shared values, goals, and interests and committed to knowledge construction through intensive dialogues, interaction, and collaboration" (p. 179).

For a learning community to be developed; face-to-face interactions are not necessary. Nevertheless, various online tools can be employed for the development of a learning community. As Loving et al. (2007) suggest, "these virtual learning communities can be built in two forms, synchronous and asynchronous. Blogs are considered one of those tools that can support and promote the development of a learning community, either a fully immersed learning community or either a blended learning community (Oravec, 2003). Consequently, blogs have an important role to play in building an online community of learning.

Community of Inquiry

The current study examines the development of a Community of Inquiry (CoI). C. S. Peirce and John Dewey were the first philosophers to introduce the concept of the community of inquiry. The introductory concept described the nature of knowledge, formation and the process of scientific inquiry. An educational community of inquiry is a group of individuals involved in a process of empirical or conceptual inquiry into problematic situations. Those individuals collaboratively engage in purposeful critical discourse and reflection to construct personal meaning and confirm mutual understanding. The CoI requires intersubjective agreement among those involved in the process of inquiry for legitimacy since it emphasizes that knowledge is necessarily embedded within a social context (Seixas, 1993; Sharp, 2007).

The theoretical framework of the current study focuses on the Community of Inquiry (CoI) model as has been suggested by Shea and Bidjerano (2010) where social, cognitive, and teaching presence are related. The model is based on the work of Garrison, Anderson, and Archer (2000) which introduced the original model of CoI. The CoI model assumes that effective online learning requires the development of a community that supports meaningful inquiry and learning (Shea, 2006). Garrison et al. (2000) developed this model which assumes that deep and meaningful learning results when there are sufficient levels of three components: teaching, social, and cognitive presence. The model outlines the theoretical elements essential to successful knowledge construction in collaborative online environments. The social presence relates to the establishment of a supportive environment such that students feel socially and emotionally connected to each other and to the instructor in a computer-mediated environment. The elements of the social presence are demonstrated through emotional expression, open communication, and group cohesion. The teaching presence involves the design, facilitation, and direction of cognitive and social processes leading to personally meaningful and educationally worthwhile learning outcomes. Elements of the teaching presence include setting curriculum and activities, shaping constructive discourse, and focusing and resolving issues. The cognitive presence is defined as the extent to which learners are able to construct and confirm meaning through continuous suggestion and discussion in a critical community of inquiry. The elements of the cognitive presence include triggering event (sense of puzzlement), exploration (sharing information and ideas), integration (connecting ideas), and resolution (synthesizing and applying new ideas) (Garrison & Arbaugh, 2007; Swan et al., 2008).

Research Methodology

To address the above, a case study approach was employed where qualitative (through in-classroom and blog's observations) and quantitative (through questionnaires) data was collected (Creswell, 2003). The classroom intervention took place within the context of the Language and Linguistic and Art courses during October–December 2011. The unit delivered was "Time Machine" and 20 fifth graders participated at the study. For the purposes of teaching the lessons a blog was developed using *Blogger*. The blog was integrated as an educational tool in the teaching and learning process within six, 40 min lessons (five Language and Linguistics lessons and one Art lesson). A blended learning environment was developed through in-classroom and online activities as well as homework activities. An introductory lesson took place at the computer lab in order to familiarize students with the blog (uses and tools) since it was the very first time used by the educators and the students. Students were given notes regarding the blog use. Regarding the rest of the lessons, both the classroom and the computer lab were used. Additionally, in some cases students were asked to use the blog at home.

Various questions were posted on the blog throughout the five Language and Linguistics lessons. The open questions posted at the blog were related to the subject of the theme delivered ("Time Machine") and they aimed to contribute in achieving the lesson's objectives. The educator constantly reminded students to comment on their classmates' blog—posts, report if they agree/disagree, provide arguments, suggestions, etc. The goal was for a discussion to be conducted, where students' opinions, views, thinking would be revealed at the blog wall. The teaching intervention was designed and developed by the authors in collaboration with two teachers which then delivered the lessons.

The quantitative data collection method conducted using a questionnaire given to students by the completion of the three lessons in the presence of the teacher. Thus, the students had the opportunity to make any clarifying questions about the questionnaire, which was created based on the Community of Inquiry questionnaire (Swan et al., 2008). The questionnaire consisted of two parts: (1) Demographic Data (e.g., gender, country of origin, use and frequency of computer use, use and frequency of Internet use) and (2) Communities of inquiry statements which consists of three main parameters: teaching, social, and cognitive presence. Each parameter consists of several sub-parameters; as a result the questionnaire includes a total of 34 statements. Students were asked to rank the 34 statements using a 5 point Likert scale, where 1 = Strongly Disagree, 2 = Disagree, 3 = Neutral, 4 = Agree, and 5 = Strongly Agree. The statistical package SPSS (Version 19) was employed in order for the quantitative data analysis to be performed. It includes descriptive statistics, namely frequencies, percentages, averages, and standard deviations for all variables of the questionnaire, as well as Cronbach's alpha (α) for internal consistency.

The qualitative method of data collection was conducted by observing in-classroom and blog activity—teacher and students' blog postings. Blog postings were analyzed using an open coding system, attaching labels to blog postings (words or lines of data) and then describing the data at a concrete level, before moving to a more conceptual level (Anfara, Brown, & Mangione, 2002). Firstly, this process was conducted within each blog questions (students' responses) and then across all blog questions (all students' responses). The iterative coding process employed leaded to the identification of themes. It is important to clarify that a blended learning environment was employed where a combination of in-classroom and online activities were performed. Consequently, the students evaluated the development of a CoI based on their experience within the blended learning environment. The data collection process was conducted during October–November 2011.

Results

Demographic Characteristics

Regarding the gender of the students, 55 % was boys and 45 % was girls, while the country of students' origin varies. Specifically, the majority of the students were coming from Cyprus (25 %), followed by Georgia and Ukraine (10 %). The vast majority of the students (85 %) use the computer, of which 25 % use it once per week and 5 % use it daily (mean=2.8; SD=1.11). The majority of the students (70 %) replied that using the Internet, of which 25 % of students answered that rarely uses it, while 15 % use it once per week (mean=2.5; SD=1.19). A 5-point Likert scale was used, where 1=no use and 5=daily.

Communities of Inquiry: Blended Learning Environment

The analysis of the questionnaires revealed some interesting results regarding the development of a Community of Inquiry (CoI) through the use of blog as the main educational tool. Specifically, it can be supported that a CoI was developed through the Lesson Time Machine, where the blog was integrated as an educational tool within a blended learning environment (combination of in-classroom and online blog-based activities).

Generally, it can be suggested that the teacher presence has a vital impact since the mean was 4.80 (SD=0.242; α=0.765). The important role of the educator is highlighted. Specifically, the results suggest that the teacher was properly organized, gave immediate and appropriate instructions, and successfully played the role of the facilitator, so that the students felt comfortable to engage in productive discussions and reflections. The aforementioned mainly took place within the in-classroom activities. On the other hand, the educator did not participate in the blog discussions besides providing questions and clear instructions on students' responsibilities. The educator wanted to grant students the freedom and flexibility needed to express themselves within the blog, without interfering or providing any guidance, help, and/or encouragement, thus not having an active role in the blog. Nevertheless, the educator was observing and following blog activity. The teaching presence within in-classroom and blog activity revealed to be really influential and it played an important role within the teaching and learning process. The educator facilitated and helped students within the teaching and learning process, providing them with clear, direct instructions. Specifically, direct instruction was highly apparent mainly within in-classroom activities than blog activities, since the educator managed to focus discussion on relevant issues, helping students to gain understanding and better realize and comprehend the subjects under investigation. In addition, within in-classroom activities the educator provided constructive feedback to the students. Through the blended learning environment developed the topics and subjects under investigation were clear enough, and the educator provided freedom and flexibility to the students, as well as increased responsibility for their own learning based on their needs, demands, and interests.

The same picture is observed regarding the social presence, though being graded relatively lower scores than the teaching presence. The data supports that it was significantly noticeable ($M=4.42$; $SD=0.51$; $\alpha=0.709$). Students felt to great extent that they belonged to a group in which they could freely express their views, opinions, and thoughts. The interaction developed among students within in-classroom as well as through blog's activities seemed to have strengthened the sense of collaboration. The educator managed to develop a community where the educator and students felt closed and connected to each other, felt part of the course (developed sense of belonging in the course—group cohesion), not only communicating for educational purposes, but interacting socially as well (Affective Expression). Additionally, the participants freely expressed their ideas, views, and opinions through not only the online tools but within in-classroom, vividly participating in the course discussion and frequently interacting with the rest of the participants (Open Communication). Students shared and discussed with their peer views and opinions and in some cases they felt instant connection to other peers. An initial introduction, a welcoming note, and the online ice-breaking activities from the educator helped the students to open up and develop a sense of belonging. Channels of communication were developed among students and the educator through the in-classroom and blog activity showing that the open communication parameter was highly present. Consequently, it can be supported that the social presence has been developed through the use of blogs as educational tools.

Finally, the cognitive presence, had also a really "strong" appearance ($M=4.57$; $S.D.=0.38$; $\alpha=0.801$) within the blended learning environment developed (blog and in-classroom activity), however not as strong as the teaching presence. Specifically, it emerged that the topic of the lesson stimulated in a great degree students' interest, and online postings enabled students to understand the basic concepts of the course. The educator gave various interesting activities, motivated students through questions; however, she did not provide adequate extra academic and scientific information and resources to study. More specifically, the triggering events were greatly apparent attempting to attract and motivate students. The activities developed and performed piqued students curiosity and felt motivated to explore content related questions. It seems that the questions/activities designed and performed increased students' interest regarding the curriculum concepts under investigation and that their interest, motivation, and curiosity were enhanced. Exploration was one of the elements of the cognitive presence that did not get high scores since the educator did not provide adequate academic and scientific information and resources to the students. Additionally, brainstorming, as a process was promoted and implemented through in-classroom and blog discussions, which it helped students come up with answers and solutions. Finally, the total mean for the three presences was 4.59 (SD=0.38). Revealing that the development of Community of Inquiry was achieved in a great degree.

Blog Activity

The blog activity reveals blog role in developing a blended-learning environment where in-classroom and blog-based activities are integrated in achieving the lesson's objectives. Overall nine posts were uploaded by the educator. Specifically, seven of the posts were questions related to the subject under investigation. The very first question posted at the blog was for testing purposes (*"Try to comment on a blog post"*). This question was posted throughout the introductory course conducted in the computer lab in order to give the students the opportunity to experience blogging. Their responses were used by the teacher in order to begin the in-classroom lesson and discussions regarding "Time machine."

The second question posted at the blog was related to a video watched and discussed as an introduction to the lesson "How do you imagine a time machine? Can you describe it? How does it look like externally and internally? What can it do?" Students' replies focused on describing the time machine internally and externally, and what one can do when using a time machine. During the Language and Linguistics course the following question was posted: "Imagine that you are in the time machine ready to travel. Where would you like to travel, into the past or in the future and why? What would you change there?" The current question aimed to trigger their imagination. Analyzing students' responses it is revealed that most of them had special preference to travel into the past, and specifically to find out where their ancestors lived and how they behaved. Additionally, students reported that they would like to travel to the past in order to correct their mistakes, to travel to ancient history eras such as Ancient Greece and the Dinosaurs' Era. Finally, some others chose to travel to the future in order to find out how life would be and to make sure that they will make their dreams come true. The students were requested to begin addressing the questions in class and continue at home.

The next step was to discuss an article included in the Language and Linguistics book. The educator used the students' responses in the previous blog question as an introduction to a book article. In particular, the article was taken from the Focus magazine, entitled "Travelling in time" and uploaded at the blog in order for the discussion to be continued online. After studying and discussing the article in the class, two questions were posted on the blog. The fourth and fifth questions were as follows: "Changing the events in the past and in the future: What would you like to change if you went to the past or the future? What event would you like to change and/or influence?" and "Persons from the past: Which person from the past would you like to represent? What decisions would you change if you were that person?" The students started answering the question at school and continued at home.

By the completion of the Language and Linguistics course the students were requested to visit the blog once more in order to vote in which era they would like to travel using the time machine. It was a multiple question voting system. The choices were the following: Dinosaurs Era, Ice Age, Ancient Greece, their child-hood, the future, the era in which their ancestors lived (parents/grandparents), and other. The students chose to travel to the future and childhood, to the Dinosaurs Era and their ancestors' era. Once more, the educator requested the students to use the blog from home.

Finally, during the Art Lesson, the students were asked to imagine and draw a time machine. Their drawings were scanned and uploaded by the educator to the blog. A blog post accompanied the drawings delineating the following: "Fifth grad-ers draw a time machine! Below you can find your classmates drawings. Each student is requested to write a few words about his/her drawing. You can also comment on your classmates' drawings. We are all waiting to hear your opinions." For this post students showed minimum interest, mainly due to the lack of time.

Discussion

Blog Use

Blog was integrated as a tool at school and at home. There was no extensive use of the blog from home for educational purposes, even though the students reported using the Internet relatively often at home. Even if students did not highly use the blog; its educational potential was revealed, since blog exploitation facilitated the achievement of the lesson's learning objectives. It can be also supported that the blog was integrated as an educational tool on a satisfactory level/degree since it provided a platform for students to interact and discuss issues related to the subject under investigation, activated their imagination and finally helped to significantly achieve the learning goals set by the educator. Overall, the blog was well organized and designed. The effective and successful exploitation use of various blog's tools, functions, and settings by the educator was observed and facilitated the learning process. For example, the posts uploaded by the educator were of different content, text, picture (student drawings) and video. The educator also employed various gadgets such as: voting (in order to perform the eighth post/exercises), calendar (for reminding students when and where the lessons will take place as well as when the exercises were due), blog archives.

Students

Students freely expressed their personal views, thoughts, and opinions; however, they did not comment on their classmates' posts. Unfortunately, the blog was not employed as a tool to promote collaboration and reflection. This result was kind of expected given the novice educator and student experience in blogging and the inexistence of educator's blog role and appearance. Additionally, it is supported that the design of the activities was problematic, since they did not clearly provide instructions and guidelines to students. There was limited discussion, interaction and dialogue among the students at the blog, something that did not happen through in-classroom activities (where the students were lively participated). Students' responses showed that they were able to freely express their personal opinions; however, they did not comment on their classmates' responses. Thus, the blog was not employed as a tool for promoting cooperation and reflective learning. Specifically, the teacher did not create the appropriate environment for students' interaction, dialogue and discussion through the blog. Moreover, not all students had access to computers and Internet at home. Finally, it was the very first time that such as tool (the blog) was used by both students and the teacher for educational purposes.

Educator

Given the above, it is suggested that educator's role is extremely important. Even though educator's overall presence was really influential, managing to develop a blended learning environment; it is important for a number of elements to be taken into consideration when designing and implementing blog-based activities integrated within a blended learning environment. The students needed more guidance, monitoring, assistance (promote interaction, debate, and dialogue) while working in an online environment. In order to effectively and successfully integrate blogs as educational tools within the teaching and learning process a number of factors need to be in place. First of all, the educator should have a greater presence and involvement within blog activity. The educator needs to directly lead and guide the blog activity. Specifically, the educator's participation at the blog for scaffolding, stimulation and motivation purposes considers being extremely important.

Having the same importance; specific and understandable instructions and guidelines regarding blog use and students' responsibilities and expectations is expected to be given to the students. For example, the educators need to make sure that when designing a blog and its posts (exercises), the following parameters are addressed: frequency and consistency of use, initiative to begin discussion, initiative to continue discussion, quality of responses, minimum number of posts and responses to classmates, deadlines, combination of blog and classroom activities; and provide relevant information to the subject under investigation through links and extra readings. The educator's role is important and crucial. His engagement and involvement in blog should be a continuously apparent while playing the role of the facilitator. The educator needs to review students' posts, comment on students' responses, ask questions, make observations, prompt and remind students to respond (Garrison & Arbaugh, 2007). Also, it is important to motivate students, even providing grading related motives.

One more important element is for the educator to highlight the importance of dialogue, discussion, interaction and interactivity, coexistence, and collaboration within a team, and finally the collaborative group result. The educator is responsible in organizing lesson plans and developing activities to achieve the above learning environments. It is also important that the educator organizes and develops well-planned activities which use effectively blog's features, functions, and settings. For example, blog activities are designed to be posted on the blog must have features that promote critical thinking, reflection, collaboration, dialogue, debate, expression of opinions, and interaction (Zawilinski, 2009). Finally, to effectively design blended learning environments; sufficient time for students to use the blog should be given, taking into account other parameters such as possession and use of computers and Internet access at home.

Conclusion

The possibility of incorporating the blog as an educational tool to a greater extent within the primary education is highly evident given the results of the current study. Additionally, the results of the study highlighted the employment of a blog as an educational tool in order to design and develop blended learning environments where Community of Inquiry is achieved. Specifically, the results revealed that both cognitive and social presence as well as teaching presence contributed to knowledge construction (Garrison & Vaughan, 2005). Nevertheless, the use of blog can be characterized as satisfactory given the limited time it was active and its partial use by the students. The current paper highlights the possibility of extensive blog integration as an educational tool in primary education taking into account various factors and suggests the development of a model that incorporates/explains the requirements of effective integration blog in educational practice based on the following parameters: teacher, student, blogs, and content/activities. Through this model, the role and interaction of the four parameters will be reflected and explained.

Finally, it is argued that the model of the blended community of inquiry is considered more suitable for primary education. Future research should focus on adapting the current model of community of inquiry, creating and weighting of a model to the characteristics of primary education.

References

Ala-Mutka, K., Punie, Y., & Ferrari, A. (2009). Review of learning in online networks and communities. In U. Cress, V. Dimitrova, & M. Specht (Eds.), *EC-TEL 2009, LNCS 5794, European communities, 2009* (pp. 350–364). Berlin: Springer.

Allen, A. (2011). "Categorization of social media" Barnes. *Human Relations, 7*, 39–58.

Anderson, L. W., & Krathwohl, D. (Eds.). (2001). *A taxonomy for learning, teaching and assessing: A revision of bloom's taxonomy of educational objectives.* New York, NY: Longman.

Anfara, V. A., Brown, K. M., & Mangione, T. L. (2002). Qualitative analysis on stage: Making the research process more public. *Educational Researcher, 31*(7), 28–38.

Angelaina, S., & Jimoyiannis, A. (2012). Educationalblogging: Developing and investigating a students' community of inquiry. In *Research on e-learning and ICT in education* (pp. 169–182). New York, NY: Springer.

Barger, J. (1997). Robot wisdom weblog for December 1997. Retrieved from http://www.robot-wisdom.com/log1997m12.html

Barrios, B. (2003). The year of the blog: Weblogs in the writing classroom. Computers and composition online. Retrieved from http://www.bgsu.edu/cconline/barrios/blogs/index.html

Bauer, P. (2011). Weblogs and Wikis: Potentials for seminars at university. In T. Bastiaens & M. Ebner (Eds.), *Proceedings of world conference on educational multimedia, hypermedia and telecommunications 2011* (pp. 2360–2365). Chesapeake, VA: AACE.

Bielaczyc, K., & Collins, A. (1999). Learning communities in classrooms: A reconceptualization of educational practice. In C. Reigeluth (Ed.), *Instructional-design theories and models: A new paradigm of instructional theory* (pp. 269–292). Mahwah, NJ: Erlbaum.

Chen, H. L., Cannon, D. M., Gabrio, J., & Leifer, L. (2005, June). Using Wikis and Weblogs to support reflective learning in an introductory engineering design course. Paper presented at the 2005 American Society for Engineering Education annual conference & exposition, Portland, OR, Retrieved from http://riee.stevens.edu/fileadmin/riee/pdf/ASEE2005_Paper_Wikis_and_Weblogs.pdf

Churchill, D. (2009). Educational applications of Web 2.0: Using blogs to support teaching and learning. *British Journal of Educational Technology, 40*(1), 179–183.

Cognition and Technology Group at Vanderbilt. (2003). Connecting learning theory and instructional practices: Leveraging some powerful affordances of technology. In H. O'Neil & P. Perez (Eds.), *Technology application in education: A learning view* (pp. 173–209). Mahwah, NJ: Erlbaum.

Cottle, A. (2009). Integrating 21st century skills in schools using a class blogging project. West Virginia Online Action Research Journal. Retrieved from http://www.wvcpd.org/PLAJournal/ActionResearch-BloggingProject/ActionResearch-BloggingProject/BloggingProject.html

Creswell, J. W. (2003). *Research design: Qualitative, quantitative and mixed methods approaches* (2nd ed.). Thousand Oaks, CA: Sage.

Crosta, L. (2004). Beyond the use of new technologies in adult distance courses: an ethical approach. *The International Journal on E-Learning, 3*(1), 48–61.

Dabbagh, N., & Kitsantas, A. (2004). Supporting self-regulation in student-centered web-based learning environments. *International Journal on E-Learning, 3*(1), 40–48.

Davis, A. (2005). The write weblog: Who says elementary students can't blog? Retrieved from http://itc.blogs.com/thewriteweblog/2004/11/who_says_elemen.html

Downes, S. (2004). Educational blogging: Blogtalk. *Educause Review, 39*, 14–26. Retrieved from http://www.educause.edu/pub/er/erm04/erm0450.asp?bhcp=1.

Eid Neurolearning Blog (2005, March 2). Brain of the blogger. Retrieved from http://eiderneurolearningblog.blogspot/com/2005/03/brain-of-blogger.html

Eteokleous, N. (2011, May 11). Integrating Blogs and Wikis as educational tools to develop student-centered environments: Is it possible? Frederick University Cyprus, BOC Conference Room, Limassol, Cyprus.

Eteokleous, N., & Nisiforou, E. (2013a). Integrating blogs as cognitive learning tools: Designing and evaluating real blogging. In *Proceedings of society for information technology & teacher education international conference 2013* (pp. 3867–3876). Chesapeake, VA: AACE.

Eteokleous, N., & Nisiforou, E. (2013b). Interdiscplinarity achieved through Blogs development. 9th JTEL Workshop, Limassol, Cyprus, 2013.

Eteokleous, N., & Pavlou, V. (2010). Digital natives and technology literate students: Do teachers follow? Published at the Conference proceedings of the *Cyprus Scientific Association of information and communication technologies in education* (pp. 113–124).

Garrison, R., Anderson, T., & Archer, W. (2000). Critical thinking in a text-based environment: Computer conferencing in higher education. *The Internet and Higher Education, 2*(2–3), 87–105.

Garrison, D. R., & Arbaugh, J. B. (2007). Researching the community of inquiry framework: Review, issues, and future directions. *The Internet and Higher Education, 10*(2007), 157–172.

Garrison, D. R., & Vaughan, D. N. (2005). *Blended learning in higher education: Framework, principles, and guidelines.* San Francisco, CA: Joey-Bass.

Glogoff, S. (2005). Instructional blogging: Promoting interactivity, student-centered learning, and peer input. *Journal of Online Education, 1*(5). Retrieved from http://www.innovateonline.info/index.php?view=article&id=126

Goddard, M. (2002). What do we do with these computers? Reflections on technology in the classroom. *Journal of Research on Technology in Education, 35*(1), 19–26.

Grassley, J. S., & Bartoletti, R. (2009). Wikis and blogs: Tools for online interaction. *Nurse Education, 34*, 209–213.

Hill, J. (2004). The voice of the blog: The attitudes and experiences of small business bloggers using blogs as a marketing and communications tool. Unpublished Master's thesis, University of Liverpool, Liverpool.

Job-Sluder, K., & Barab, S. A. (2004). Shared "we" and shared "they" indicators of group in online teacher professional development. In S. A. Barab, R. Kling, & J. H. Gray (Eds.), *Designing for virtual communities in the service of learning.* Cambridge: Cambridge University Press.

Jonassen, D. H. (1999a). *Computer as Mindtools in schools: Engaging critical thinking* (2nd ed.). Columbus, OH: Prentice Hall.

Jonassen, D. H. (1999b). Designing constructivist learning environments. In C. Reigeluth (Ed.), *Instructional design theories and models: A new paradigm of instructional theory* (pp. 215–239). Mahwah, NJ: Erlbaum. Chapter 10.

Jonassen, D. H. (2000). *Computers as Mindtools for schools: Engaging critical thinking* (2nd ed.). Upper Saddle River, NJ: Prentice Hall.

Kaplan, M. D., Piskin, B., & Bol, B. (2010). Educational blogging: Integrating technology into marketing experience. *Journal of Marketing Education, 32*(1), 50–63.

Karaman, T. (2011). Use of blogs in teacher education to reflect on teaching practices, 5th International computer & instructional technologies symposium, September 22–24, 2011, Fırat University, Elazig, Turkey.

Kim, H. N. (2008). The phenomenon of blogs and theoretical model of blog use in educational contexts. *Computers & Education, 51*, 1342–1352.

Lee, M. J. W., Miller, C., & Newnham, L. (2008). RSS and content syndication in higher education: Subscribing to a new model of teaching and learning. *Educational Media International, 45*, 311–322.

Liu, E. Z. F., & Chang, Y. F. (2010). Gender differences in usage, satisfaction, self-efficacy, and performance of blogging. *British Journal of Educational Technology, 41*(3), E39–E43.

Loving, C. C., Schroeder, C., Kang, R., Shimek, C., & Herbert, B. (2007). Blogs: Enhancing links in a professional learning community of science and mathematics teachers. *Contemporary Issues in Technology and Teacher Education, 7*(3), 178–198.

Makri, K., & Kynigos, C. (2007). The role of Blogs in studying the discourse and social practices of mathematics teachers. *Educational Technology & Society, 10*(1), 73–84.

Nelson, T., & Fernheimer, J. (2003). Welcome to the blogosphere: Using weblogs to create classroom community. *Computer Writing and Research Lab, 1*, 1–15.

Oravec, J. A. (2002). Bookmarking the world: Weblog applications in education; weblogs can be used in classrooms to enhance literacy and critical thinking skills. *Journal of Adolescent & Adult Literacy, 45*(5), 616–621.

Oravec, J. A. (2003). Weblogs as an emerging genre in higher education. *Journal of Computing in Higher Education, 14*(2), 21–44.

Palloff, R. M., & Pratt, K. (2005). *Collaborating online: Learning together in community* (Vol. 2). San Francisco, CA: Jossey-Bass.

Penrod, D. (2007). *Using blogs to enhance literacy: The next powerful step in 21st-century learning*. Lanham, MD: Rowman & Littlefield Education. 188 pp. ISBN 1578865662.

Petko, D. (2011). Writing learning journals with weblogs: Didactic principles and technical developments in the www.learninglog.org open source project. In T. Bastiaens & M. Ebner (Eds.), *Proceedings of world conference on educational multimedia, hypermedia and telecommunications, 2011* (pp. 2267–2271). Chesapeake, VA: AACE.

Richardson, W. (2009). Becoming internet wise: Schools can do a far better job of preparing students for their connected futures online. *Educational Leadership, 66*(6), 26–31.

Richardson, W. (2010). *Blogs, Wikis, Podcasts and other powerful Web-tools for classrooms*. Thousand Oaks, CA: Corwin Press.

Seixas, P. (1993). The community of inquiry as a basis for knowledge and learning: The case of history. *American Educational Research Journal, 30*(2), 305–324.

Sharp, A. M. (2007). The classroom community of inquiry as ritual: How we can cultivate wisdom. *Critical and Creative Thinking, 15*(3), 3–14.

Shea, P. (2006). A study of students' sense of learning community in online environments. *Journal of Asynchronous Learning Networks, 10*(1), 35–44.

Shea, P., & Bidjerano, T. (2010). Learning presence: Towards a theory of self-efficacy, self-regulation, and the development of a communities of inquiry in online and blended learning environments. *Computers & Education, 55*(4), 1721–1731.

Shifflet, R. (2008). Instructional use of blogs and wikis for K-12 students. Unpublished doctoral dissertation, Illinois State University, Normal. Retrieved from http://www.scribd.com/doc/7522034/Instructional-Use-of-Blogsand-Wikis-Shifflet

Siemens, G. (2005). Connectivism: A learning theory for the digital age. *International Journal of Instructional Technology and Distance Learning, 2*(1), 3–10.

Sim, J. W. S., & Hew, K. F. (2010). The use of weblogs in higher education: A review of empirical research. *Educational Research Review, 5*(2), 151–163.

Swan, K. P., Richardson, J. C., Ice, P., Garrison, D. R., Cleveland-Innes, M., & Arbaugh, J. B. (2008). Validating a measurement tool of presence in online communities of inquiry. *E-Mentor, 2*(24), 1–12. www.e-mentor.edu.pl/eng.

Trammel, K., & Ferdig, R. (2004, Winter). Pedagogical implications of classroom blogging. Academic Exchange Quarterly. Retrieved from http://findarticles.com/p/articles/mi_hb3325/is_4_8/ai_n29148968/?tag=content;col1

Wenger, E. (2004, January/February). Knowledge management as a doughnut: Shaping your knowledge strategy through communities of practice, *Ivey Business Journal, 68*(3), 1. Ivey Management Services.

Wenger, E., McDermott, C., & Snyder, B. (2002). *Cultivating communities of practice*. Cambridge, MA: Harvard University Press.

Zawilinski, L. (2009). HOT blogging: A framework for blogging to promote higher order thinking. *Reading Teacher, 62*(8), 650–661.

Effectiveness of Wiki-Based Learning in Higher Education

Panagiota Altanopoulou, Christos Katsanos, and Nikolaos Tselios

Introduction

Web 2.0 technologies can be used in education, especially for building project-based learning activities (Duffy & Kirkley, 2004). Among these technologies, wikis seem to offer rich collaboration possibilities (West & West, 2009). A wiki offers the ability to edit a website by adding, modifying, and deleting pages as well as integrating hypermedia.

The open nature of the wiki technology provides opportunities for learning (Mindel & Verma, 2006; Raman, Ryan, & Olfman, 2005; Wheeler & Wheeler, 2009), since all participants should work collaboratively in order to edit and improve the content. Wikis as a collaboration tool can help students to write better (Mak & Coniam, 2008) and can support collaborative knowledge creation (Raman et al., 2005; Wagner, 2004). In addition, wikis can facilitate group learning (Carpenter & Roberts, 2007), foster contribution to peers (West & West, 2009), and improve students' engagement (Molyneaux & Brumley, 2007).

Various skills, such as writing, IT, collaboration, and organizational skills (Lai & Ng, 2011; Wheeler & Wheeler, 2009), can be improved with students' involvement in wiki-based activities. Thus, students' participation in wiki projects can add value

P. Altanopoulou (✉) • N. Tselios
Department of Educational Sciences and Early Childhood Education, University of Patras, University campus, 26504 Rio, Greece
e-mail: galtanopoulou@gmail.com; nitse@ece.upatras.gr

C. Katsanos
Hellenic Open University, Parodos Aristotelous 18, 26335 Patras, Greece
e-mail: ckatsanos@eap.gr

C. Karagiannidis et al. (eds.), *Research on e-Learning and ICT in Education: Technological, Pedagogical and Instructional Perspectives*, DOI 10.1007/978-1-4614-6501-0_10, © Springer Science+Business Media New York 2014

to learning and to their professional success (Frydenberg, 2008). It seems that in well-designed wiki-based activities students are positive towards this technology (Tétard, Patokorpi, & Packalén, 2009). They believe that wikis are useful for sharing knowledge (Elgort, Smith, & Toland, 2008) and a great tool for collaboration (Deters, Cuthrell, & Stapleton, 2010). Unsurprisingly, wikis have been used in various contexts such as developing an online textbook (Ravid, Kalman, & Rafaeli, 2008) and supporting knowledge sharing (Raman et al., 2005). Wikis can also help teachers to manage and mark their students' work (Deters et al., 2010). However, the wiki openness may also be a disadvantage if the context and objectives of the activity are not well determined (Parker & Chao, 2007). As a result, there are examples in which students did not actively participate in creating or editing context (Cole, 2009; Ebner, Kickmeier-Rust, & Holzinger, 2008).

In order to avoid these situations and to provide a rich context and simultaneously a support structure in a wiki environment, West and West (2009) proposed an instructional design process. This process includes the following steps: establish a purpose for the wiki project, define and classify the wiki project's learning goals, design a rich context and problem that support the achievement of the purpose and goals, prepare students for work in the new environment, and promote a collaborative process through which active, social learning can take place (West & West, 2009, p. 22). This approach emphasizes scaffolding. In addition, West and West (2009) used the Bloom's Taxonomy of Learning (Bloom, 1956) to classify the main wiki project's learning domains. From this grouping three wiki project categories emerged: (a) knowledge construction, (b) critical thinking, and (c) contextual application. The wiki activity design was based on the framework proposed by West and West (2009), and its learning domain belongs to the category of knowledge construction. The goal of the designed activity was to learn general information about Web 2.0 and its applications in the frame of a first-year academic course entitled "Introduction to ICT."

The aim of the study presented in this chapter was to investigate the effect of a framed, rigorously designed, wiki-based activity on the learning outcome. In specific, this chapter investigates:

• Students' learning gain after the wiki-based activity
• Whether the students with lower pretest score benefited from the activity at least to the same extent as students with higher pretest score
• Whether students' learning performance was affected by their role while carrying out the activity
• Whether students with more logged wiki edits benefited more than students with less wiki edits

This chapter is organized as follows: Initially, the research methodology, the profile of the participants, and the design of the activity are described. Subsequently, the research results are presented, focusing on learning outcome as assessed by an appropriately designed pre- and posttest questionnaire.

Methodology

Research Method and Materials

A single-group pretest–posttest design was adopted (Cohen, Manion, & Morrison, 2000). A questionnaire with closed questions was the data collection instrument. The pretest questionnaire comprised both demographic (13 questions) and factual knowledge questions (36 questions, each with four possible answers of which only one was correct). The factual knowledge questions were primarily related to general information about Web 2.0 and its applications, whereas the demographic questions were related to personal information regarding ICT, Internet, and wiki usage and adoption. The posttest comprised the same factual knowledge questions. The students were not informed that they would be asked to complete the questionnaire at the beginning or the end of the activity.

The wikispaces service (www.wikispaces.com) was used both for the activity announcement and as the platform provided to the students to construct their wiki. The online questionnaire service SurveyMonkey (www.surveymonkey.com) was used to create and distribute the questionnaires of the study. The obtained data were organized and analyzed using Excel 2007 and SPSS v17.0. The activity presentation, students' presentation of their wikis, and completion of questionnaires took place in the computer lab of the Department.

Procedure and Participants

All in all, 220 first-year university students participated in the study. The students were divided freely into 44 groups comprising 5 members each. In the beginning of the procedure an instruction on the wiki's basic functionality was given to the students. Subsequently, a compulsory assignment was presented to them in the form of a wiki, realized by the researchers. Each team member had a specific role in the group such as collector, organizer, editor, and verifier (West & West, 2009). The responsibilities of each role are delineated in the following.

Eighty-one (81) of the students did not respond to either the pre- or posttest assessment questionnaire and were excluded from the dataset. Analysis was conducted for the data collected by 139 students, 2 male and 137 female, aged 17–37 (mean = 19.3, sd = 3.5). The majority of the participants (127/139) were 17–22 years old. They were attending a compulsory academic course entitled "Introduction to ICT," offered in the first semester in the Department of Education and Early Childhood Education at the University of Patras. Participation in the activity was compulsory and was one of the five required mini-projects given to the students in the context of the laboratory part of the lesson.

Description of the Activity

The design of the activity was based on the framework proposed by West and West (2009). Learning was expected to be achieved by engaging the students into four processes: information seeking and retrieval, argumentation development and refinement to support their thesis, cooperation among members, and their involvement with the wiki-editing process. The assignment was presented to the students through an exemplary wiki, which was constructed by the researchers (available at http://labtpewiki.wikispaces.com).

The exemplary wiki included the purpose and the objectives of the assignment, detailed implementation instructions, expected learning outcome, evaluation criteria, and representative support material. In addition, the topics that students had to cover were outlined and organized into subsections with a short description for each one. Afterwards, the students of each group had to create their own wiki, in which they would develop the topics of the assignment.

The topic of the designed activity was to learn general information about Web 2.0 and its applications. It was selected due to the following reasons: First, the students should be able to understand the impact of Web 2.0 on society in general and on education in particular. In addition, the topic is suitable for covering a variety of educational and technological aspects of Web 2.0, thus giving a fertile ground for argumentation. Finally, it is a notable session of the course's overall outline. The exemplary wiki included nine segment topics: (a) Web 2.0 definitions, (b) characteristics of Web 2.0, (c) YouTube and Slideshare, (d) Twitter, (e) Blogs, (f) Wikis, (g) Skype, (h) description of an educational activity using these technologies, and (i) potential risks of Web 2.0 use.

For this activity wikis were used to promote collaboration with peers and improve their knowledge related to the aforementioned topics (West & West, 2009). The students had to search for information on all of these topics and seek additional material. Furthermore, it was stressed that usage of other's work should follow specific rules since the open nature of Web 2.0 tools could lead to inappropriate use of content from other sources, as reported in Huijser (2008) and West and West (2009). Students were instructed on how to use and cite sources and were also informed that they could only use freely available media or media under a creative commons license.

Each team member was assigned a specific role by the researchers. These roles are delineated by West and West (2009). The first role was that of "collector" who had the responsibility to obtain appropriate material relevant to each subtopic. Two members of each group were "collectors." The second role was that of the "organizer" who was responsible to organize the collected material and to check its consistency and relatedness with the objectives of the project. The "editor" was responsible to check grammar and syntax errors in the content and its compliance with the provided format. The "verifier" was responsible to check the content for its completeness, structure, and compliance with the objectives of the project. However, all students were allowed to participate and contribute in every aspect of the collaboration process.

Finally, the students had to present their work briefly during the laboratory session of the course. Each project was graded by the researchers on a 1–100 scale. The score was multiplied by the number of the group members and was given to the students. Subsequently, the students in each group were asked to discuss and distribute these points fairly according to each member's contribution. As far as the score distribution is concerned, a notable differentiation was observed in only 9 out of the 44 groups. Such grade distribution differentiations possibly indicate a lack of balanced collaboration.

Results

All in all, we analyzed data from 139 first-year university students involved in a wiki-based activity in the context of an introductory ICT course. Table 1 presents participants' demographic-related information in our dataset.

First, a reliability analysis of the provided 36-item knowledge assessment questionnaire was conducted. Reliability refers to the extent to which an instrument, such as a questionnaire, yields the same results under consistent conditions (Nunnally & Bernstein, 1994). It is most commonly measured using Cronbach's alpha, which is a measure of internal consistency. Results showed that the initial 36-item questionnaire used in the study did not have sufficient reliability (alpha = 0.69) to meet the typical minimum standard of 0.70 (Nunnally & Bernstein, 1994). Two questions increased the alpha to 0.70 if they were deleted and thus were excluded from subsequent test score computations.

Next, students' pretest and posttest correct answers in the knowledge assessment questionnaire were converted to a composite test score on a 0–100 scale. In addition, a normalized learning gain score was produced for each participant by using the formula proposed in Nelson et al. (2009) and defined as

$$G = \frac{post_{score} - pre_{score}}{max_{score} - pre_{score}}$$

Table 1 Participants' demographic-related information in our dataset			
Sample size	N	139
Age	Mean	19.3
	SD	3.5
	Range	17–37
Gender	Male	2
	Female	137
School stream	Theoretical	125
	Technological/scientific	14
Web usage frequency [1–5]	Mean	4.2
	SD	1.0
	Range	2–5
Prior wiki usage	Yes	60
	No	79

Table 2 Students' pre- and posttest scores in the knowledge assessment questionnaire and their normalized learning gain

N	Pretest score [0–100] Mean ± 95 % C.I.	Posttest score [0–100] Mean ± 95 % C.I.	Normalized learning gain[a] [%] Mean ± 95 % C.I.
139	43.6 ± 1.9	63.8 ± 2.3	35.1 ± 3.9

[a]Normalized learning gain is measured as (post − pre)/(max score − pre) (Nelson et al., 2009)

This score has the advantage of "normalizing the observed gain (the numerator) against the amount of possible learning that could be achieved (the denominator)" (Nelson et al., 2009, p. 1797). Table 2 presents descriptive statistics of the dependent variables measured in the study.

In all subsequent statistical analyses, we use the correlation coefficient r as an effect size, which is calculated according to the formulas reported in Field (2009).

Did the Wiki-Based Activity Improve Students' Performance?

A dependent t-test was applied to compare students' pretest ($M = 43.6$, $SD = 11.4$) and posttest ($M = 63.8$, $SD = 13.6$) performance, as measured by the provided knowledge assessment questionnaire. The differences between the test scores did not violate the assumption of normality ($D(139) = 0.98$, $p = 0.059$), and thus a parametric test was selected. Results indicated that students achieved significantly higher ($t(138) = 17.74$, $p < 0.001$, $r = 0.83$) test scores after participating in the wiki-mediated learning activity. According to Cohen (1992), this is a very large effect size, which demonstrates the learning effectiveness of a properly designed wiki-mediated learning activity.

Were Students with Lower Pretest Score Benefited at Least to the Same Extent as Students with Higher Pretest Scores?

We recoded our dataset to create two between-subject groups based on students' initial performance: (a) low initial performance ($N = 83$), which included students with pretest score below or equal to the median score of all students, and (b) high initial performance ($N = 56$), in which students with pretest score above the median score of all students were assigned. Table 3 presents descriptive statistics of students' pretest score, posttest score, and normalized learning gain in relation to these groups.

A two-tailed Mann–Whitney U test investigated the effect of students' initial performance on their normalized learning gain. A nonparametric test was selected because the assumption of normality was violated for the high initial performance group ($D(56) = 0.95$, $p < 0.05$), and homogeneity of variance was also violated (Levene's test, $F(1,137) = 9.39$, $p < 0.01$). Results indicated that although students

Table 3 Students' pre- and posttest scores in the knowledge assessment questionnaire and their normalized learning gain grouped by their initial performance

Initial performance group	N	Pretest score [0–100] Mean±95 % C.I.	Posttest score [0–100] Mean±95 % C.I.	Normalized learning gain[a] [%] Mean±95 % C.I.
Low	83	35.8±1.4	59.7±2.8	36.7±4.1
High	56	55.1±1.6	70.0±3.4	32.8±7.8

[a]Normalized learning gain is measured as (post−pre)/(max score−pre) (Nelson et al., 2009)

Table 4 Students' pre- and posttest scores in the knowledge assessment questionnaire and their normalized learning gain grouped by their role in the activity

Role in the wiki activity	N	Pretest score [0–100] Mean±95 % C.I.	Posttest score [0–100] Mean±95 % C.I.	Normalized learning gain[a] [%] Mean±95 % C.I.
Collector	53	42.9±3.0	63.3±4.1	35.4±6.6
Organizer	28	44.0±4.6	61.6±4.3	30.1±7.5
Editor	29	43.4±4.9	69.3±4.5	44.4±7.4
Verifier	29	44.6±3.9	61.6±5.4	30.0±10.6

[a]Normalized learning gain is measured as (post−pre)/(max score−pre) (Nelson et al., 2009)

with low initial performance showed a slightly higher (3.9 %) normalized learning gain compared to those with high initial performance, this difference was not significant ($z=0.14$, $p=0.889$). Also, an insignificant correlation ($r_s=-0.04$, $p=0.668$) between students' pretest score and normalized learning gain was found.

Additional analyses after Bonferroni correction investigated whether the wiki-mediated activity improved students' score for both the low and high initial performance groups. A nonparametric test was selected for the high initial performance group because the distribution of the differences in the dependent variable (test score) between the two related conditions deviated significantly ($D(56)=0.94$, $p<0.01$) from a normal distribution. Results showed that students' test scores were significantly improved in both the low and high initial performance groups: $t(82)=17.16$, $p<0.001$, $r=0.88$ and $z=5.56$, $p<0.001$, $r=0.53$, respectively.

All in all, the above results provide evidence that the wiki-mediated learning activity was beneficial to students with lower initial performance, at least to the same extent as those with higher initial performance.

Did Students' Role in the Wiki-Mediated Activity Affect Their Learning Gain?

Table 4 presents students' performance grouped by their role in the wiki-based activity: collector ($N=53$), organizer ($N=28$), editor ($N=29$), and verifier ($N=29$).

Table 4 shows that the lowest average learning gain (30.0 %) was observed for students with the verifier role, whereas students with the editor role had the highest learning gain (44.4 %) on average. However, a one-way ANOVA did not unveil any

Table 5 Students' pre- and posttest scores in the knowledge assessment questionnaire and their normalized learning gain grouped by their number of wiki edits

Number of logged wiki edits	N	Pretest score [0–100] Mean±95 % C.I.	Posttest score [0–100] Mean±95 % C.I.	Normalized learning gain[a] [%] Mean±95 % C.I.
Low	71	42.4±2.7	59.0±3.1	27.8±5.0
High	68	44.8±2.8	68.9±3.0	42.8±5.7

[a]Normalized learning gain is measured as (post−pre)/(max score−pre) (Nelson et al., 2009)

significant learning gain differences between the four different students' roles ($F(3,135)=2.48, p=0.064$).

Thus, results show that the wiki-mediated learning activity was beneficial to all students, regardless of their specific role in the project.

Were Students with More Wiki Edits Benefited More Than Students with Less Wiki Edits?

We recoded our dataset to create two between-subject groups based on students' logged number of edits in the wiki: (a) low number of wiki edits ($N=71$), which included students with a number of wiki edits below or equal to the median number of wiki edits of all students, and (b) high number of wiki edits ($N=68$), in which students with a number of wiki edits above the median number of wiki edits of all students were assigned. Table 5 presents descriptive statistics of the measured dependent variables in relation to these two groups.

The assumption of normality was violated for the high number of edits group ($D(68)=0.93, p<0.001$); thus a nonparametric test was applied to investigate differences between the two groups. A two-tailed Mann–Whitney U test showed that students with more wiki edits had a significantly higher learning gain ($z=4.32, p<0.001, r=0.37$) compared to students with less wiki edits. In addition, a significant correlation ($r_s=0.41, p<0.01$) was found between students' number of logged wiki edits and normalized learning gain: the more active the students were, the more they improved their performance.

Additional analyses after Bonferroni correction investigated whether the wiki-mediated activity improved students' score for both the students with lower and higher number of wiki edits. Results showed that students' test scores were significantly improved in both groups: $t(70)=10.69, p<0.001, r=0.79$ and $t(67)=15.45, p<0.001, r=0.88$, respectively. As the effect sizes show, this improvement was of higher magnitude for the students who were more active contributors in the wiki.

In sum, it was found that both students with low and high number of logged edits in the wiki improved significantly their performance, but the latter had a significantly higher learning gain.

Conclusions

A study investigating the effectiveness of a wiki-mediated learning activity for ICT education was presented. The evaluation was carried out using a one-group pretest–posttest design. The results showed significant improvement in learning outcomes; the average students' test score improved from 43.6/100 to 63.8/100. In addition, it was found that the wiki-mediated learning activity was equally beneficial to students with lower and higher initial performance. These results suggest that a properly designed, framed wiki-based activity could substantially facilitate students to learn by building content. In a similar vein, there are surveys which indicate that wiki technology can be beneficial to students in various learning domains (Mohammed, 2010), given that a carefully designed activity is introduced to them. Similar findings are reported in Tselios, Altanopoulou, and Katsanos (2011) and Tselios, Altanopoulou, and Komis (2011).

No significant learning gain differences between the four different student's roles (i.e., collector, organizer, editor, verifier) in the wiki activity were identified. This finding is in line with previous research (Strijbos, Martens, Jochems, & Broers, 2004; Tselios, Altanopoulou, & Katsanos, 2011; Tselios, Altanopoulou, & Komis, 2011) which indicates that roles do not affect group members' performance. However, roles can help students who work collaboratively to build knowledge in comparison to students with no distinct roles while collaborating (Schellens, Van Keer, De Wever, & Valcke, 2007).

Furthermore, results showed that students who were more active contributors in the wiki, as measured by their logged number of edits, had a significantly higher learning gain.

However, the reported study is not without limitations. First, it should be noted that our data is gender and age skewed; thus the findings might not be generalizable to male students or older students involved in wiki-mediated learning activities. Furthermore, the results obtained do not explain how the students have benefited from their involvement in the activity. Future research goals constitute the design of additional wiki-based activities in a variety of educational settings as well as investigation of the learners' behavioral intention to use wiki technology using technology acceptance models (Tselios, Daskalakis, & Papadopoulou, 2011). Moreover, the relation between the observed students' activity and the learning outcome will also be examined (Katsanos, Tselios, & Avouris, 2010).

References

Bloom, B. (1956). *Taxonomy of educational objectives, handbook I: The cognitive domain.* New York, NY: David McKay.

Carpenter, P., & Roberts, E. (2007). Going wiki in online technology education courses: Promoting online learning and service learning through wikis. *North Carolina Council on technology Teacher Education Technology Education Journal, 9*, 58–64.

Cohen, J. (1992). A power primer. *Psychological Bulletin, 112*(1), 155–159.

Cohen, M., Manion, L., & Morrison, K. (2000). *Research methods in education* (5th ed.). London: Routledge.

Cole, M. (2009). Using Wiki technology to support student engagement: Lessons from the trenches. *Computers & Education, 52*(1), 141–146.

Deters, F., Cuthrell, K., & Stapleton, J. (2010). Why wikis? Student perceptions of using wikis in online coursework. *Journal of Online Learning and Teaching, 6*(1), 122–134.

Duffy, T., & Kirkley, J. (2004). *Learner-centred theory and practice in distance education cases from higher education*. Mahwah, NJ: Lawrence Erlbaum Associates.

Ebner, M., Kickmeier-Rust, M., & Holzinger, A. (2008). Utilizing wiki-systems in higher education classes: A chance for universal access? *Universal Access in the Information Society, 7*(4), 199–207.

Elgort, I., Smith, A. G., & Toland, J. (2008). Is wiki an effective platform for group course work. *Australasian Journal of Educational Technology, 24*(2), 195–210.

Field, A. P. (2009). *Discovering statistics using SPSS*. Thousand Oaks, CA: Sage.

Frydenberg, M. (2008). Wikis as a tool for collaborative course management. *MERLOT Journal of Online Learning and Teaching, 4*(2), 169–181.

Huijser, H. (2008). Exploring the educational potential of social networking sites: The fine line between exploiting opportunities and unwelcome imposition. *Studies in Learning, Evaluation, Innovation and Development, 5*(3), 45–54.

Katsanos, C., Tselios, N., & Avouris, N. (2010). Evaluating website navigability: Validation of a tool-based approach through two eye-tracking user studies. *New review of Hypermedia and Multimedia, 16*(1–2), 195–214.

Lai, Y. C., & Ng, E. M. (2011). Using wikis to develop student teachers' learning, teaching, and assessment capabilities. *The Internet and Higher Education, 14*(1), 15–26.

Mak, B., & Coniam, D. (2008). Using wikis to enhance and develop writing skills among secondary school students in Hong Kong. *System, 36*(3), 437–455.

Mindel, J. L., & Verma, S. (2006). Wikis for teaching and learning. *Communications of the Association for Information Systems, 18*(1), 1–23.

Mohammed, M. (2010). *Using Wikis to develop writing performance among prospective English as a foreign language teachers*. Retrieved February 19, 2014, from http://www.nauss.edu.sa/acit/PDFs/f1766.pdf

Molyneaux, T., & Brumley, J. (2007, December). The use of wikis as a management tool to facilitate group project work. In *Proceedings AAEE: 18th annual conference of the Australasian association for engineering education* (pp. 1–8), Melbourne, VIC, 9–13 December, 2007.

Nelson, L., Held, C., Pirolli, P., Hong, L., Schiano, D., & Chi, E. H. (2009). With a little help from my friends: Examining the impact of social annotations in sensemaking tasks. In *Proceedings of the SIGCHI conference on human factors in computing systems* (pp. 1795–1798). New York, NY: ACM.

Nunnally, J., & Bernstein, I. (1994). *Psychometric theory*. New York, NY: McGraw-Hill Humanities/Social Sciences/Languages.

Parker, K., & Chao, J. (2007). Wiki as a teaching tool. *Interdisciplinary Journal of e-learning and Learning Objects, 3*(1), 57–72.

Raman, M., Ryan, T., & Olfman, L. (2005). Designing knowledge management systems for teaching and learning with wiki technology. *Journal of Information Systems Education, 16*(3), 311.

Ravid, G., Kalman, Y. M., & Rafaeli, S. (2008). Wikibooks in higher education: Empowerment through online distributed collaboration. *Computers in Human Behavior, 24*(5), 1913–1928.

Schellens, T., Van Keer, H., De Wever, B., & Valcke, M. (2007). Scripting by assigning roles: Does it improve knowledge construction in asynchronous discussion groups? *International Journal of Computer-Supported Collaborative Learning, 2*(2–3), 225–246.

Strijbos, J. W., Martens, R. L., Jochems, W. M., & Broers, N. J. (2004). The effect of functional roles on group efficiency using multilevel modeling and content analysis to investigate computer-supported collaboration in small groups. *Small Group Research, 35*(2), 195–229.

Tétard, F., Patokorpi, E., & Packalén, K. (2009, January). Using wikis to support constructivist learning: A case study in university education settings. In *42nd Hawaii international conference on system sciences* (pp. 1–10), 5–8 January, 2009.

Tselios, N., Altanopoulou, P., & Katsanos, C. (2011). Effectiveness of a framed wiki-based learning activity in the context of HCI education. In *Proceedings of the 15th Pan-Hellenic conference on informatics with international participation* (pp. 368–372). Kastoria, Greece: IEEE CPS.

Tselios, N., Altanopoulou, P., & Komis, V. (2011, October). Don't leave me alone: Effectiveness of a framed wiki-based learning activity. In *WikiSym 2011, international symposium on Wikis and open collaboration* (pp. 49–52), Mountain View, CA, 3–5 October.

Tselios, N. K., Daskalakis, S., & Papadopoulou, M. (2011). Assessing the acceptance of a blended learning university course. *Educational Technology & Society, 14*(2), 224–235.

Wagner, C. (2004). Wiki: A technology for conversational knowledge management and group collaboration. *Communications of the Association for Information Systems, 13*(13), 265–289.

West, J. A., & West, M. L. (2009). *Using Wikis for online collaboration.* San Francisco, CA: Jossey-Bass.

Wheeler, S., & Wheeler, D. (2009). Using wikis to promote quality learning in teacher training. *Learning, Media and Technology, 34*(1), 1–10.

Courseware Evaluation Through Content, Usage and Marking Assessment

Ioannis Kazanidis, Stavros Valsamidis, Sotirios Kontogiannis, and Alexandros Karakos

Introduction

E-learning is a modern learning method, based on information and communication technologies (ICT). Its main characteristics are that it overcomes time and spatial restrictions, since learners can attend the course wherever they are, assuming they have adequate equipment, such as a computer connected to the Internet.

Courseware is a term that combines the words "course" with "software", and was used originally to describe additional educational material for authors and learners apart from the e-learning platform itself. The meaning of the term and usage has expanded and can refer to the entire course and any additional material when used in reference to an online or "computer formatted" classroom. The main objective of constructing courseware is to help authors and developers to carry out the construction/development process of courseware and learning contents automatically. The secondary objective is to promote the reuse/exchange of existing learning resources among different users and systems (Romero & Ventura, 2010).

I. Kazanidis (✉) • S. Valsamidis
Department of Industrial Informatics, Eastern Macedonia and Thrace Institute of Technology, Ag. Loukas, Kavala 65404, Greece
e-mail: kazanidis@teikav.edu.gr; svalsam@teikav.edu.gr

S. Kontogiannis
Department of Business Administration, Technological Educational Institute of West Macedonia, 19 M. Alexandrou Street, Ioannina 45333, Greece
e-mail: skontog@gmail.com

A. Karakos
Department of Electrical and Computer Engineering, Democritus University of Thrace, Panepistimioupoli-Kimmeria, Xanthi 67100, Greece
e-mail: karakos@ee.duth.gr

C. Karagiannidis et al. (eds.), *Research on e-Learning and ICT in Education: Technological, Pedagogical and Instructional Perspectives*, DOI 10.1007/978-1-4614-6501-0_11, © Springer Science+Business Media New York 2014

In any courseware, each course consists of the content, the organisation and the management of the course, the teaching/learning process, the log data, social computing tools, etc. Although the quality of a course does not depend only on its content but also on its structure, organisation, support, delivery, etc., content plays a crucial role for the success of e-learning. In order to ensure this fact, it is necessary to apply processes of continuous evaluation and optimization of the educational material (Kazanidis, Theodosiou, Petasakis, & Valsamidis, 2013). Consequently, it is necessary to provide feedback to a course author, in order to show the means to improve its courseware (Romero, Ventura, & De Bra, 2004). The evaluation of educational material can be made either directly by taking feedback from the learners or through automated data mining techniques applied to the courses log files data (Vialardi, Bravo, & Ortigosa, 2008).

Statistical analysis methods were applied in many cases in order to obtain relevant information from e-learning data. The higher education learner-evaluation data were analysed in Jin, Wu, Liu, and Yan (2009). The number of visits and duration per quarter, top search terms and number of downloads of e-learning resources were described in Grob, Bensberg, and Kaderali (2004). The number of different pages browsed and total time spent browsing different pages was also presented in Hwang, Tsai, Tsai, and Tseng (2008).

Data mining (DM) in education uses computational approaches to analyse educational data in order to analyse upcoming educational issues. According to Romero and Ventura (2010) "the term DM is used in a larger sense than the original/traditional DM definition". Although there is a great deal of research in the field of DM in e-learning that uses typical techniques, such as classification, clustering, association rule mining, sequential mining, etc., there are also a significant number of studies that use techniques belonging to the broader field of DM, such as regression, correlation, etc. The application of data mining (DM) in education is a rapidly growing interdisciplinary area which combines a variety of areas, including individual learning from educational software, computer supported collaborative learning, computer-adaptive testing (and testing more broadly), and the factors that are associated with student failure or non-retention on courses (Baker, 2010). Although data mining (DM) in education uses computational approaches to analyse educational data in order to study educational questions, the methods are often different from standard data mining methods (Baker & Yacef, 2010).

The approach in this paper is twofold. On the one hand, it goes backward to examine whether the usage of the courses by the learners is affected by the educational content exposed by the authors. One the other hand, it examines whether the usage of the courses by the learners on a course is related to the mean performance of the learners on this course. It proposes some new metrics and measures, taking into account several statistics concerning the courses. These include the number of files and their sizes, the number of pages that each course has on the e-learning platform, and statistics concerning the usage of the platform for each course by the learners, such as the number of sessions, the number of visits, the duration of each visit. These measures and metrics aim to help course authors and/or platform administrators review course usage, and find online course weaknesses. Regression analysis is also used for the identification of possible dependencies.

Method

The proposed method adopts a three-level schema for an e-learning platform. It uses six measures and three metrics for both content and usage measurement. Finally, classification, clustering, association rule mining, and regression analysis are applied to the e-learning data. More specifically, the values of the measures and metrics and the mean marks from the corresponding courses are investigated for possible dependencies.

The Three-Level Dependencies

A view of the proposed schema of the approach is depicted in Fig. 1.

In Fig. 1, the Content Level (CL) includes the educational material that is exposed to the learners by the authors. It can be assessed with the use of measures. The Usage Level (UL) includes the usage of the educational material by the learners. Other measures and new metrics are also used to assess the usage. The Exams Level (EL) includes mean marks, the learners performed for each course. The mapping between CL and UL is one to one. Although the values of the measures may change each time (affected by authors' actions and learners' usage), the assessment usually takes place at the end of the semester. The mapping between UL and EL is one to many, since there are n $(n \geq 1)$ opportunities for every learner to participate in the exams.

Measures and Metrics

Some measures are used in the CL and some others in the UL of the courses. With the measures of the Table 1, we quantify the offered educational material to the learners by the authors in terms of input variables on a course.

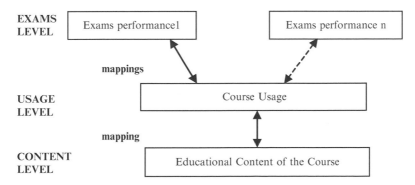

Fig. 1 The 3-level approach

Table 1 Content measures

Measure	Description of the measure
Pages (P)	The total number of pages (modules) existing on the course
Files (F)	The total number of files on the course
Size (S)	The total size of the existing files on the course

Table 2 Usage measures

Measure	Description of the measure
Sessions (E)	The total number of sessions per course viewed by all users
Visits (V)	The total number of visits (page hits) per course by all users
Duration (D)	The duration of (total) visits per course by all users

This category of measures is related to the courses' online educational content of the courses. More specifically, the number of pages, the number of files and their corresponding sizes give an estimation of the content quantity, which is a crucial factor of online educational content. In some e-learning systems instead of the term "page" the term "module" is used. If the number of files and their size are small, this might be due to the weakness of the author to upload enough educational content onto the online platform. If the course has a lot of files with large sizes this could lead learners to face the cognitive overload problem and not study the course effectively.

With the measures of Table 2 (Valsamidis, Kontogiannis, Kazanidis, Theodosiou, & Karakos, 2012), we quantify the usage of the available educational material by the learners in terms of usage variables on a course.

The second category of measures helps researchers to discover learner activity and follow up a course. The number of sessions show how many times learners have logged in. The number of *sessions* and the number of *visits* viewed by all users are counted for the calculation of course activity. Each session reflects when a user logs in to the platform, and after some activity, logs out from the platform. If there is no activity, there is a timeout of 30 s. The number of visits reflects how many pages were viewed by all users. There are some pages of the course which were viewed by many users, but there were also some other pages not so popular. If learners of a specific course visit more pages for a long time, this means that course content is interesting and useful for the learners. This could reflect the course quality. Consequently, a good course in terms of quality may help learners in their study. The number of sessions could be compared with number of visits and duration. The two later variables show if learners find the course useful and like to visit its pages.

The next step is to define some metrics, in order to qualify these quantity metrics. In Table 3, we calculate the quality of the available educational material on a course, in terms of usage by the learners of output variables.

$$VPS = Visits/Sessions\,(V/E) \qquad (1)$$

Metric	Description of the metric
VPS	Visits per session
VPD	Visits per duration
CUP	Course utilisation and user perception

Table 3 Quality metrics

The VPS has a range of between (0, 1]. A low number of VPS outcomes indicates that users stay more time in a page of a course. Since the VPS metric measures the number of visited pages divided by the number of sessions of a course, the higher the number of sessions in the course, the lower is the fraction. On the other hand, the author may update the educational material with more visited pages. So, the fraction has comparable values.

$$VPD = Visits/Duration\,(V/D) \tag{2}$$

The VPD expresses the number of visits per duration. A high number of VPD means that users change pages quickly into the course. This could be an indication that users are experiencing difficulties discovering the desirable content or they already have assimilated most of the course content. Both metrics reflect users' behaviour related to the educational material.

We also define a course quality metric called smooth or distinct Course Utilisation and user Perception metric (CUP). This metric expresses how smooth, or selective, or even randomly visit time of users per course is distributed over the academic semester. That is, from Eq. (3), for n online courses a constant histogram break is used equal to $1/2n$ (break $= 10$ and n expresses weeks ($n = 1\ldots10$)). Then the CUP metric value is calculated as follows:

$$CUP = n \times \left(\max\left(h(x)\right) - \min\left(h(x)\right)\right) \tag{3}$$

where $h(x)$ the histogram density estimate:

$$h(x) = k/n1/w \tag{4}$$

$x =$ cell centred at x with width w that contains k data points and $n \times h(x) = (2/n)k$

if CUP $\to 0$ then we have smooth course utilisation over time, while if CUP $\to 1$ we have only distinct weeks of course utilisation. In cases of CUP > 1 we assume that such courses maintain either a one-time utilisation or abnormal utilisation of very low and very high. We consider such courses as flapping or abandoned courses.

Data Mining

Data mining techniques have been applied to e-learning systems data by many researchers. Apart from the analytical review by Romero and Ventura (2010), there is some more domain specific. Castro, Vellido, Nebot, and Mugica (2007), among others, deal with the assessment of the students' learning performance, provide course adaptation and learning recommendations based on the students' learning behaviour, deal with the evaluation of learning material and educational Web-based courses, provide feedback to both teachers and students of e-learning courses, and detect a typical student's learning behaviour. A survey by Koutri, Avouris, and Daskalaki (2005) provides an overview of the state of the art in research of Web usage mining, while discussing the most relevant criteria for deciding on the suitability of these techniques for building an adaptive web site. One relevant study (Kotsiantis, Pierrakeas, & Pintelas, 2004) predicts the students' performance, as well as to assess the relevance of the attributes involved.

Students are assessed in the final exams of the courses, and they are assigned a mark according to their performance on the course. Having measured the students' activity in the e-learning system according to the measures and metrics, it is possible to investigate whether there is a relationship between student activity in the platform of the e-learning system and the marks of the students in the final exams. A well prepared and implemented online course may help learners in their study and therefore allow them to achieve a better mark. Therefore, it would be useful to check if the previous metrics and measures are related to a learner's mark.

In the classification step, the algorithm 1R (Witten & Frank, 2005) may be applied. It uses the minimum-error attribute for prediction, discretizing numeric attributes (Holte, 1993). The attribute Mark has to be used as class, since it describes the education outcome. In this step the attribute/s which best describe the classification will be discovered.

The clustering step contains course clustering with the use of the SimpleKmeans algorithm (Kaufmann & Rousseeuw, 1990) for unsupervised learning. SimpleKMeans algorithm automatically handles a mixture of categorical and numerical attributes. Furthermore, the algorithm automatically normalises numerical attributes when doing distance computations.

According to Baker (2010) relationship mining is a technique which discovers relationships between variables, in a data set with a large number of variables. There are four types of relationship mining: association rule mining, correlation mining, sequential pattern mining, and causal data mining. In this paper we focus on association rule mining. Association rule mining is one of the most well studied data mining tasks. It discovers relationships among attributes in databases, producing if-then statements concerning attribute-values. An association rule $X \rightarrow Y$ expresses a close correlation among items in a database, in which transactions in the database where X occurs, there is a high probability of having Y as well. In an association rule X and Y are called respectively the antecedent and consequent of the rule. The strength of such a rule is measured by values of its support and confidence. The confidence of the rule is the percentage of transactions with antecedent X in the database that also contain the consequent Y. The support of the rule is the percentage of transactions in the database that contains both the antecedent X and the consequent Y in all transactions in the database. The Weka system has several association rule-discovering algorithms available. The Apriori algorithm will be used for finding association rules over discretized e-learning platform data.

Regression Analysis

Several regression techniques have been used to predict a student's academic performance (using stepwise linear regression) (Golding & Donalson, 2006), to identify variables that could predict success in college courses (using multiple regression), to predict university students' satisfaction (using regression and decision tree analysis), to predict high school students' probabilities of success in university (Mcdonald, 2004), to predict a student's test score (using stepwise regression) (Feng, Heffernan, & Koedinger, 2005) and to predict the probability a student has of giving the correct answer to a problem in an ITS (using a robust ridge regression algorithm) (Cetintas, Si, Xin, & Hord, 2009). Yu, Jannasch-Pennell, Digangi, and Wasson (1999) use a multivariable regression model to predict a learner's performance from log and test scores in Web-based instruction. Multiple linear regression is used for predicting the time to be spent on a learning page (Arnold, Scheines, Beck, & Jerome, 2005). Thomas and Galambos (2004) use regression analysis for predicting university learners' satisfaction.

Linear regression analysis is applied on the CL. The classifier builds linear logistic regression models. In our case, the way the mean mark is affected by the metrics VPS, CUP and VPD of each course is examined. The regression coefficients show the marginal value of input (VPS, CUP and VPD) required measuring Mark.

Results

Study Population and Context

The recording of specific data from the e-learning platform is the first step. The dataset was collected from the Open eClass e-learning platform (GUNet, 2012) which is used at the Kavala Technological Education Institute (TEI). The data are from the Spring semester of 2011 and involve 1,534 students and 34 different courses and are obtained from the server log files.

Case Study

A view of the collected data is shown in Table 4. The values of the measures of Tables 1 and 2, which express measures of UL and CL, are presented. The aforementioned measures contribute to the evaluation of courses content and usage.

Table 4 Tracked data, measures, metrics and marks

CID	Sessions	Visits	Duration	Pages	Files	Size	VPS	VPD	CUP	Mark
AD5104	480	1,567	2,891	6	785	785	3.26	0.542	0.213	5.78
AD5103	477	1,853	3,635	6	3,165	3,165	3.89	0.510	0.16	6.02
AD2104	61	93	116	5	2,065	2,065	1.51	0.802	2.844	4.42
AD2103	3,237	9,756	10,864	6	5,135	5,135	3.01	0.898	0.0462	7.26
AD6102	3,734	6,585	6,571	6	5,696	5,696	1.76	1.002	0.0977	6.2
AD6114	337	938	1,688	6	0	0	2.79	0.556	0.2844	6.48
AD6106	144	271	709	6	0	0	1.89	0.382	0.888	4.49
AD6105	910	2,340	3,586	6	7,198	7,198	2.57	0.653	0.1244	5.88
AD7107	1,115	4,334	6,778	6	42,277	42,277	3.89	0.639	0.0799	6.3
AD4108	378	1,627	3,185	6	100	100	4.30	0.511	0.1777	5.56
AD7105	728	2,184	3,760	6	2,471	2,471	3.00	0.581	0.1244	5.89
AD4101	709	1,501	3,284	6	250	250	2.12	0.457	0.1955	5.65
AD5102	539	921	1,912	6	0	0	1.71	0.482	0.355	6.23
AD5101	414	746	1,731	6	0	0	1.80	0.431	0.444	6.11
AD6112	256	593	1,321	6	410	410	2.31	0.449	1.4222	6.08
AD6111	383	1,352	2,719	6	1,355	1,355	3.53	0.497	0.071	6.34
AD2100	2,063	8,430	15,915	6	358	358	4.09	0.530	0.0319	7.67
AD3107	632	1,713	3,662	6	6,899	6,899	2.71	0.468	0.1777	6.66
AD5106	308	984	1,994	6	121	121	3.20	0.493	0.3555	6.31
AD5105	269	799	1,750	6	0	0	2.97	0.457	0.2844	6.09
AD7101	791	3,206	5,706	6	27	27	4.06	0.562	0.1155	6.05
AD7100	415	1,677	2,724	6	0	0	4.04	0.616	0.2488	6.28
AD6108	2,209	4,565	7,633	9	12,461	12,461	2.07	0.598	0.0888	6.71
AD6107	970	2,088	3,538	10	11,525	11,525	2.15	0.590	0.106	6.53
AD2106	4,793	10,091	14,551	12	5,943	5,943	2.11	0.693	0.0355	7.23
AD2105	5,538	11,832	16,780	13	52,318	52,318	2.14	0.705	0.0266	7.81
AD2107	3,726	10,113	13,824	6	2,206	2,206	2.71	0.732	0.0248	7.19
AD6100	2,697	5,271	8,199	6	29,290	29,290	1.95	0.643	0.053	6.67
AD7102	3,721	7,780	8,846	6	61,213	61,213	2.09	0.879	0.044	6.82
AD3106	706	2,533	5,115	6	108	108	3.59	0.495	0.106	5.98
AD3108	2,759	4,139	5,330	6	4,175	4,175	1.50	0.777	0.106	6.02
AD4100	616	1,401	2,564	6	0	0	2.27	0.546	0.213	6.22
AD3102	490	621	1,515	6	0	0	1.27	0.410	0.3556	4.45
AD4104	252	390	1,147	6	0	0	1.55	0.340	0.444	4.210

First Mapping Dependencies

All the DM techniques were performed using the open source Weka. The data mining methods are applied to the measures of Table 4. The results of the classification based on the OneR algorithm show that the measure Pages is better classified (described) by the measure Sessions as depicted in Fig. 2. For the three bins of the instances (low, mid and high) are described by the low bin of grades. It is easily interpretable, since only one mean mark is greater than 7.66667.

```
=== Classifier model (full training set) ===

Sessions:
        '(-inf-1886.666667]'      -> '(-inf-7.666667]'
        '(1886.666667-3712.333333]'     -> '(-inf-7.666667]'
        '(3712.333333-inf)'       -> '(-inf-7.666667]'
    (30/34 instances correct)
```

Fig. 2 Classification results

Attribute	Full Data (34)	0 (11)	1 (23)
Sessions	'(-inf-1886.666667]'	'(1886.666667-3712.333333]'	'(-inf-1886.666667]'
Visits	'(-inf-4006]'	'(4006-7919]'	'(-inf-4006]'
Duration	'(-inf-5670.666667]'	'(5670.666667-11225.333333]'	'(-inf-5670.666667]'
Pages	6	6	6
Files	'(-inf-27]'	'(-inf-27]'	'(-inf-27]'
Size	'(-inf-20404.333333]'	'(-inf-20404.333333]'	'(-inf-20404.333333]'
AFS	'(-inf-1149.833333]'	'(-inf-1149.833333]'	'(-inf-1149.833333]'
VPS	'(-inf-2.28]'	'(-inf-2.28]'	'(-inf-2.28]'
VPD	'(-inf-0.560667]'	'(0.560667-0.781333]'	'(-inf-0.560667]'
CUP	'(-inf-0.964533]'	'(-inf-0.964533]'	'(-inf-0.964533]'
Mark	'(5.41-6.61]'	'(6.61-inf)'	'(5.41-6.61]'

```
Clustered Instances

0     11 ( 32%)
1     23 ( 68%)
```

Fig. 3 Clustering results

The results of the clustering based on the SimpleKMeans algorithm (Kaufmann & Rousseeuw, 1990) show that there are two clusters which correspond to high Mark (cluster 0) and low Mark (cluster 1), as depicted in Fig. 3. For most attributes of the two clusters there is a high degree of similarity. However, the values of Sessions, Visits, Duration, VPD and Mark are not equal.

The results of the association rule mining based on the Apriori algorithm (Agrawal & Srikant, 1994) show ten rules, as depicted in Table 5.

Table 5 shows how a large number of association rules can be discovered. There are some uninteresting rules, such as rules 8 and 9, since there is obvious dependency between Duration and Visits. Specifically, there is dependency between the low range of Duration (-inf-5670.666667] and the low range of Visits (-inf-4006]. There are also redundant rules, rules with a generalisation of relationships of several rules, like rule 2 with rules 1, and 7, 3 with rules 5 and 9, and 4 with rules 6 and 10. There are some similar rules, rules with the same element in antecedent and consequent, but inter-changed, such as rules 1, 2, 8 and rules 5, 3, 9 respectively. But there are also rules that show relevant information for educational purposes, like those that show con-forming relationships, such as rules 1, 2, 3, 5 and 7. And there are also rules that show interesting relationships, such as rules 4, 6 and 10, which can be very useful for the author in decision making about the activities of their courses. For example, in rule 10, there is a dependency between low range of Visits (-inf-4006] and the low range of Pages (-inf-7.666667]. Similar conclusions can be drawn from the other rules.

Table 5 Apriori algorithm based on confidence metric

Best rules found		
1. Visits = '(-inf-4006]' 23	→	Sessions = '(-inf-1886.666667]' 23 conf:(1)
2. Visits = '(-inf-4006]' Duration = ' (-inf-5670.666667]' 22	→	Sessions = '(-inf-1886.666667]' 22 conf:(1)
3. Sessions = '(-inf-1886.666667]' Duration = ' (-inf-5670.666667]' 22	→	Visits = '(-inf-4006]' 22 conf:(1)
4. Visits = '(-inf-4006]' Pages = '(-inf-7.666667]' 22	→	Sessions = '(-inf-1886.666667]' 22 conf:(1)
5. Sessions = '(-inf-1886.666667]' 24	→	Visits = '(-inf-4006]' 23 conf:(0.96)
6. Sessions = '(-inf-1886.666667]' 24	→	Pages = '(-inf-7.666667]' 23 conf:(0.96)
7. Duration = '(-inf-5670.666667]' 23	→	Sessions = '(-inf-1886.666667]' 22 conf:(0.96)
8. Duration = '(-inf-5670.666667]' 23	→	Visits = '(-inf-4006]' 22 conf:(0.96)
9. Visits = '(-inf-4006]' 23	→	Duration = '(-inf-5670.666667]' 22 conf:(0.96)
10. Visits = '(-inf-4006]' 23	→	Pages = '(-inf-7.666667]' 22 conf:(0.96)

Second Mapping Dependencies

Simple linear regression analysis was applied to the metrics and marks of Table 4. The courses were classified to three classes according to their mean marks.

The first class which corresponds to courses with low marks is described by the equation

$$\text{Mark} = -1.46 + \text{VPS} \times 0.9 + \text{CUP} \times 2.73 \tag{5}$$

The second class which corresponds to courses with mid marks is described by the equation

$$\text{Mark} = 1.21 + \text{VPS} \times 0.55 \tag{6}$$

The third class which corresponds to courses with high marks is described by the equation

$$\text{Mark} = 0.27 + \text{VPS} \times 0.61 - 0.981.21 \times \text{VPD} \tag{7}$$

An increase in the VPS metric leads to higher mean marks for each course. From the formulas (5), (6) and (7), the conclusion is drawn that an increase of one unit to the value of the metric VPS will increase the mean value of the Mark 0.9, 0.55 and 0.61 for the three classes respectively.

Discussion and Conclusions

This study proposes an approach for discovering dependencies based on histories from e-learning data. It tackles the problem of analysing these data at three levels. Initially it examines whether the usage of the courses by the learners is affected by the educational content exposed by the authors. It is proved by the classification results and the dependency between Sessions and Pages (Modules). Then, it examines whether the usage of the courses by the learners on a course is related to the mean performance of the learners on this course. This is proved by regression results and the dependency between VPS and Mark. It proposes some measures, such as the number of files and their sizes, the number of pages that each course has on the e-learning platform, the number of sessions, the number of visits and the duration of each visit. New metrics are also proposed to assess course usage. Three data mining techniques, classification, clustering and association rule mining, were applied to the e-learning data at the first two levels. Furthermore, regression analysis was applied to the same data at the last two levels.

The originality of the study lies in the different use of existing techniques. The study builds on existing work, but also extends it in a different way, encompassing the e-learning field. It has the following advantages: (1) It is independent of a specific e-learning platform, since it is based on the Apache log files and not the e-learning platform itself. Thus, it can be easily implemented for every e-learning platform. (2) It uses measures and metrics, in order to facilitate the evaluation of each course in the e-learning platform and the authors to make proper adjustments to their course educational material. (3) It uses classification, clustering, association rule mining and regression analysis in order discover possible dependencies of the e-learning data.

The results reveal dependencies between content of the course and its usage by the learners. There is a dependency between the number of modules (Pages) of the platform with the number of sessions and the number of visits. The results also confirm the assertion that there is dependency between the students' usage on an e-learning platform with their corresponding performance in the exams.

Feedback about the approach was received by the authors. The authors were informed about the indexing results along with abstract directions on how to improve their courses. Most of authors increased the quality and the quantity of their educational material. They increased the quality by reorganising the educational material in a uniform, hierarchical and structured way. They also improved the quantity by embedding additional educational material. By updating educational material, both quality and quantity were increased. A major outcome through the process of informing the authors about the results is that the ranking of the courses constitutes an important motivation for the authors to try to improve their educational material. Because of their mutual competition, they want their courses to be highly ranked. A few authors complained that their courses organisation does not assist them to have high final scores in the ranking list. They argued that, for example, the measure Pages (Modules) is heavily influenced by the number of web pages used to organise the educational material. Thus, courses that have all their educational material organised in a few pages have a low Pages (Modules) score. They were asked again to reorganise the material for each course in the e-learning platform according to the order taught, in order to facilitate easier use by the students.

The fact that only 34 courses in one platform were investigated is a limitation to the study. Especially for the data mining techniques which demand large datasets. However, this was ineluctable, since the case study department implements this number of online courses. But the proposed approach seems to be quite reliable if the inspection takes place over a long time period.

There are also other limitations to the proposed approach. Although ten parameters were investigated, which are not few, it could be asserted that many more could also be investigated. In addition, the influence of collaboration among the learners could also be investigated, since this plays a crucial role in the educational process. This omission is due to a lack of sufficient enough related logs of the corresponding modules (wikis, chats, forums etc.) of the e-learning platform.

Moreover, there are a number of students who try to read the materials only just before the exams. No one denies that a good site with good material, which is updated frequently, exists, but rarely visited. On the other hand, a bad web site may have frequent visits because student visits are related to their expected mark. So, the frequency and pattern of an individual student accessing an instructor's materials will be an indicator to show such a student's "Laziness" or "Diligence".

The results of this research are remarkable from a pedagogical point of view. On the one hand, this approach contributes to the improvement of courseware content quality, since the proposed measures and metrics, and their correlations to students' marks provide the authors a feedback about their efficiency of their courses. Improvement of course quality provides students the opportunity of asynchronous study of courses with actualized and optimal educational material. On the other hand, since students usage results are correlated with the students' grade, an online platform may provide authors with notifications about their students' online actions. According to our experiment, results usage is closely related to the students' marks. An increased usage leads to better student marks and therefore to an improved educational outcome. For example, a learning platform could record student actions and after the application of specific algorithms classify them into predefined groups according to their estimated performance. Authors could study these groups of students, and try to help and motivate weak students. They could provide the advanced students with more educational content in order to achieve a more in-depth learning programme. Thus, the learning performance of all students could be significantly improved.

References

Agrawal, R., & Srikant, R. (1994). Fast algorithms for mining association rules. *Proceedings of 20th International Conference on Very Large Data Bases* (pp. 487–499).

Arnold, A., Scheines, R., Beck, J. E., & Jerome, B. (2005). Time and attention: Students, sessions, and tasks. In *Proceedings of the AAAI 2005 Workshop Educational Data Mining* (pp. 62–66).

Baker, R. (2010). Data mining for education. In B. McGaw, P. Peterson, & E. Baker (Eds.), *International encyclopedia of education* (3rd ed., Vol. 7, pp. 112–118). Oxford, UK: Elsevier.

Baker, R., & Yacef, K. (2010). The state of educational data mining in 2009: A review and future visions. *Journal of Educational Data Mining, 1*(11), 3–17.

Castro, F., Vellido, A., Nebot, A., & Mugica, F. (2007). Applying data mining techniques to e-learning problems. In L. C. Jain, R. Tedman, & D. Tedman (Eds.), *Evolution of teaching and learning paradigms in intelligent environment* (Studies in computational intelligence, Vol. 62, pp. 183–221). New York, NY: Springer.

Cetintas, A., Si, L., Xin, Y. P., & Hord, C. (2009). Predicting correctness of problem solving from low-level log data in intelligent tutoring systems. *Proceedings of International Conference on Educational Data Mining* (pp. 230–238). Cordoba, Spain.

Feng, M., Heffernan, N., & Koedinger, K. (2005). Looking for sources of error in predicting student's knowledge. *Proceedings of AAAI Workshop on Educational Data Mining* (pp. 1–8).

Golding, P., & Donalson, O. (2006). Predicting academic performance. *Proceedings of Frontiers Educational Conference* (pp. 21–26). San Diego, CA.

Grob, H. L., Bensberg, F., & Kaderali, F. (2004). Controlling open source intermediaries—A web log mining approach. In *Proceedings of ITI '04* (pp. 233–242). Zagreb, Croatia: IEEE Computer Society.

GUNet. (2012). OPEN eClass. Retrieved January 30, 2012, from http://eclass.gunet.gr/

Holte, R. C. (1993). Very simple classification rules perform well on most commonly used datasets. *Machine Learning, 11*, 63–91.

Hwang, G. J., Tsai, P. S., Tsai, C. C., & Tseng, J. C. R. (2008). A novel approach for assisting teachers in analyzing student web-searching behaviors. *Computers and Education, 51*(2), 926–938.

Jin, H., Wu, T., Liu, Z., & Yan, J. (2009). Application of visual data mining in higher-education evaluation system. In *Proceedings of ETCS 2009* (pp. 101–104). Wuhan, China: IEEE Computer Society Press.

Kaufmann, L., & Rousseeuw, P. J. (1990). *Finding groups in data: An introduction to cluster analysis.* New York, NY: John Wiley & Sons.

Kazanidis, I., Theodosiou, T., Petasakis, I., & Valsamidis, S. (2013). Online courses assessment through measuring and archetyping of usage data. *Interactive Learning Environments*. doi:10.1080/10494820.2014.881390.

Kotsiantis, S., Pierrakeas, C., & Pintelas, P. (2004). Predicting students' performance in distance learning using machine learning techniques. *Applied Artificial Intelligence, 18*(5), 411–426.

Koutri, M., Avouris, N., & Daskalaki, S. (2005). A survey on web usage mining techniques for web-based adaptive hypermedia systems. In S. Y. Chen & G. D. Magoulas (Eds.), *Adaptable and adaptive hypermedia systems* (pp. 125–149). Hershey, PA: IRM Press.

Mcdonald, B. (2004). Predicting student success. *Journal for Mathematics Teaching and Learning, 1*, 1–14.

Romero, C., & Ventura, S. (2010). Educational data mining: A review of the state of the art. *IEEE Transactions on Systems, Man, and Cybernetics Part C: Applications and Reviews, 40*(6), 601–618.

Romero, C., Ventura, S., & De Bra, P. (2004). Knowledge discovery with genetic programming for providing feedback to courseware author. User model and user-adapted interaction. *Journal of Personalization Research, 14*(5), 425–464.

Thomas, E. H., & Galambos, N. (2004). What satisfies students? Mining student-opinion data with regression and decision tree analysis. *Research in Higher Education, 45*(3), 251–269.

Valsamidis, S., Kontogiannis, S., Kazanidis, I., Theodosiou, T., & Karakos, A. (2012). A clustering methodology of web log data for Learning Management Systems. *Journal of Educational Technology and Society, 15*(2), 154–167.

Vialardi, C., Bravo, J., & Ortigosa, A. (2008). Improving AEH courses through log analysis. *Journal of Universal Computer Science, 14*(17), 2777–2798.

Witten, I., & Frank, E. (2005). *Data mining practical machine learning tools and techniques.* San Francisco, CA: Morgan Kaufmann.

Yu, C. H., Jannasch-Pennell, A., Digangi, S., & Wasson, B. (1999). Using online interactive statistics for evaluating web-based instruction. *Journal of Educational Media International, 35*, 157–161.

Part V
ICT for Learning in Museums

Game Design as a context for Learning in Cultural Institutions

Nikoleta Yiannoutsou and Nikolaos Avouris

Introduction

This chapter builds on previous work about the use of technologies for learning in cultural institutions (Yiannoutsou, Bounia, Roussou, & Avouris, 2011) where an analysis of selected cases revealed that technology mainly functioned as a medium for information delivery. This use of technology treats culture as something that can be "transferred" from the "knowledge holding" museum to the visitor. In this context museum experience is structured around the consumption metaphor: the museum produces "information" in digital or other form, for the visitor to consume. Studies evaluating this type of cultural experience used the term "museum fatigue" to highlight visitor limited ability to remember, digest and utilise the information offered (Bitgood, 2009). Another line of research, reports decrease in the audience of museums and cultural institutions (Simon, 2010). Taking into account the above observations we could argue that technology has been employed in various ways by museums to support their reconnection with the public where we identify two main trends with respect to the learning experience pursued. The first focuses on refining the information and the way it is delivered to the visitor. The second redefines the role of the visitor and his/her relationship with the museum in the process of culture creation. In this paper we will briefly refer to technologies supporting the information delivery metaphor and we will further expand on how technologies can support a learning experience based on visitor participation in the process of culture creation.

N. Yiannoutsou (✉) • N. Avouris
Department of Electrical and Computer Engineering, University of Patras,
University campus, Rio 26504, Greece
e-mail: nyiannoutsou@upatras.gr; avouris@upatras.gr

C. Karagiannidis et al. (eds.), *Research on e-Learning and ICT*
in Education: Technological, Pedagogical and Instructional Perspectives,
DOI 10.1007/978-1-4614-6501-0_12, © Springer Science+Business Media New York 2014

Personalization and Games: Same Content in New Clothing?

In this section we will discuss the learning implications of two examples which we consider that involve information transfer: personalization and technology-supported games. These two examples represent the current trend in technology development to support and enhance museum experience (see for example the funded EC projects in FP7 and the recent call for digital culture, Cordis, 2012) applied in order to attract more visitors to the museums. Here we will only discuss the rationale underlying in general the learning experience that seems to be supported by these two examples.

Personalization aims at adjusting and transforming cultural experience so as to meet the experiences, interests and knowledge at the level of the individual visitor or the group. To this end, technology suggests the most appropriate content to the user based (i) on visitor profiles, (ii) on the cumulative visitors' history (Bohnert, Zukerman, Berkovsky, Baldwin, & Sonenberg, 2008; de Gemmis, Lops, Semeraro, & Basile, 2008) (iii) on user-generated content (e.g. tags and comments) and on combinations of these methods. The rationale for applying such techniques is that cultural heritage sites have a huge amount of information to present, which must be filtered and personalised in order to enable the individual user to easily access it. Although this approach supports visits adjusted to visitor interests and previous experience, it is underlined by the concept of visitor as consumer of information; more fine grained this time. Thus, personalised interaction eager to bring visitors closer to the museum employs tools and methodologies to accommodate the visitors' interests but at the same time reproduces the initial distance between the visitor and the authority of the museum who owns culture and now also knows what is best for each visitor.

The infusion of new technologies in cultural institutions and more specifically, of mobile technologies have resulted in new ways of experiencing games in cultural institutions (spatial awareness) and have helped in reaching a larger audience (not only children but also adult visitors). We focus on mobile games because they support the cultural experience during the visit of the cultural institutions as opposed to games appearing for example in museum web sites aiming to prepare for the visit or enhance the experience after the visit. Many mobile games however, created for supporting cultural experience with the aim to engage users fail to bring at the centre of the activity the cultural content in playful ways. So there are game and story instances (see for example Akkerman, Admiraal, & Huizenga, 2009; Paay et al., 2008) where players seem to be enjoying the cultural experience but the question remains as to how cultural content is integrated in these games/stories and what game characteristics invoke visitor engagement. Our observation is that quite often visitors engage with cultural content (e.g. explore the historical centre of a city) in the context of following the plot of a mystery story or being engaged in a role playing game. Yet in many cases engagement with cultural content remains at a superficial level as it is not smoothly integrated in the story or the game

(Yiannoutsou & Avouris, 2012). As a result, engagement with the cultural content (e.g. responding to questions, taking pictures) becomes the "price the visitors have to pay" in order for the interesting things and the fun to carry on (e.g. to see what happens next in the mystery story, or who is the murderer, or to continue playing the game). Furthermore, the output of this process is factual information (e.g. visitors end up knowing that there is a convent in the city) leaving outside other aspects of the cultural experience (creativity, finding connections with own experience, gaining ownership over the cultural experience, etc.).

To sum up, in this section we focused on the learning involved when using personalization techniques and games to support cultural experiences. We discussed these two examples due to their wide adoption in cultural institutions during the last years and because they are claimed to result in active visitor engagement with cultural content. Our analysis showed that the mainstream use of these approaches ends up often in consuming or collecting factual information by the visitor where the museum is the entity that holds the knowledge for the visitor to collect it or consume it. This is not to imply that game and personalization technologies can only support the information consumption metaphor. Instead, as we will show in the next section, personalised learning and games can offer rich learning opportunities if they are integrated in a different rationale with respect to the role of the visitor, his/her relationship with the museum and the goal/nature of learning in cultural institutions.

Participation as a Context for Rethinking Technologies that Support Learning in Museums

Participation-based cultural experience is based on the assumption that culture is generated dynamically through the dialectic relationship between the museum and the visitor (Simon, 2010). Proctor (2009) used the metaphor "From Parthenon to Agora" to illustrate the shift from the perception of cultural experience as something that the museum holds and the visitors see but don't touch, to something that can be discussed, shared and negotiated. Apparently, the role of the visitor in this context changes to collaborator and partner (Simon, 2010). Furthermore participatory cultural experiences imply a new relationship between the visitor and the museum which is not restricted to one off or first time visits. Instead, participation aims also at building an enduring relationship with existing audiences and communities (museum friends, volunteers, etc.) related to the museum (Black, 2005). Building an enduring relationship between the visitor and the museum through visitor active participation enhances the cultural experience and enriches the content and the impact of the museum on first time visitors or one off visitors too (ibid).

In the wide spectrum of participatory activities (for a detailed presentation see Simon, 2010) we identified two types of activities relevant to our analysis. The first type of activity reserves for the visitor a role similar to the documentation process performed by the museum. The proliferation of mobile technologies and social media has supported the creation of user generated content using various crowd-sourcing practices. Ridge (2011) has offered a grouping of these practices:

- *Stating preferences*, voting on interesting objects, comments, etc.
- *Tagging*: unstructured text associated with objects, see for example the Steve project http://tagger.steve.museum/ which addresses social tagging as a process that encourages visitor engagement and provides new ways of describing and accessing culture. Twenty-one Institutions participate in the project with 97,041 Objects. In the site appears that 8,346 users have produced 552,105 terms for the above objects.
- *Debunking, criticising*: arguing against other peoples' ideas, tags, etc. (see for example the Freeze Tag project in Brooklyn museum http://www.brooklynmuseum.org/opencollection/freeze_tag/start.php).
- *Recording personal stories*: personal memories associated to museum objects or memorabilia made available to digital collections. See for example Europeana 1914–1918 project in http://www.europeana1914-1918.eu/en.
- *Linking objects or categorising*: grouping of objects or associating them with themes.

The second type of activity aims at resuming or approaching cultural experience through engaging visitors in the creations of "meta-artefacts"—i.e. games or stories based on compositions of elements of cultural content—which are supposed to have a public status. The idea of involving visitors in creating computer-based public artefacts that make use of cultural content is new. It builds on a theoretical background that acknowledges the gap in the communication between the museum and the visitor and calls for active participation of visitors in the dialogue with the museums (Hein, 2006; Simon, 2010).

Three examples are known and presented here: One comes from British Museum which included in the museum activities family workshops on game design. Participants were invited to build their own games inspired by the collections of the British Museum (after visit experience). The new games could be uploaded on the Web to be played at home or shared with friends. The second example comes from Tate Gallery where young visitors (6–12 years) create drawings through game play (Jackson, 2011) and films for pieces of art. The third example is the idea of remixing museum content for the creation of a visitor generated narrative (Fisher & Twiss-Garrity, 2007). This example is grounded on the observation that visitor centric exhibition narratives should not be the objective of the cultural experience, but instead the focus should be cultural activities promoting the construction of narratives by the visitors. Visitor generated narratives build on the transformative connection between the visitor and the exhibit, asserted by Hein (2006). Transformative experiences can occur when the visitor is encountered with challenges to discover connections with the exhibits and is provided with the tools to analyse and manipulate the exhibits in order to transform them into something new, related to his/her experience.

Although both activity types ("crowdsourcing" and "meta-artefacts") reserve an active role for the visitors they have a drawback: visitor generated "products"—content or artefacts—are almost never integrated in the museum's assets because of their low quality (Simon, 2010). This problem is related to the open ended and unstructured participatory activities:

> When it comes to participatory activities, many educators feel that they should deliberately remove scaffolding to allow participants to fully control their creative experience. This creates an open-ended environment that can feel daunting to would-be participants. ... What if I walked up to you on the street and asked you to make a video about your ideas of justice in the next three minutes? Does that sound like a fun and rewarding casual activity to you? (ibid, Chap. 1, p. 13)

What Simon described above draws upon an approach which asserts that learning in museums should focus in triggering visitor creativity and subjective interpretation of cultural content leaving aside the "knowledge of the museum" which prevails in the information consumption metaphor. Simon showed that in participatory activities this perspective has its weaknesses. In the same line comes the idea of "objectified cultural capital" (Bourdieu, 1986) which explains that cultural experience is not just an issue of access (i.e. being able to visit a museum) but it is also an issue of background knowledge that supports the person to appreciate and understand the value of a piece of art. Museums and cultural institutions offer in the process of culture creation not only the objects-exhibits but also the background knowledge necessary to value the exhibits. In our view the key in this process is how background knowledge will become the means to an end (i.e. a tool for the visitor to generate cultural experience) and not the end itself. This means that cultural experience is not diminished into comprehending institutional knowledge instead, the latter needs to come into the visitor's attention as material to be negotiated, discussed, shared and used for the construction of something new. In this context we argue that technology can play a crucial role in supporting the cultural learning experience and we further illustrate this by focusing on the example of game design and its potential in supporting learning in cultural institutions.

Game Design as Learning Activity in Cultural Institutions

Game play is not a new practice for museums. The introduction of digital technologies resulted in revisiting the idea of game play and storytelling in museums. Technologies today play a key role in interaction, interpretation, learning, content creation through crowd-sourcing, outreach, marketing, etc. (for a detailed presentation and overview see Beale, 2011). Whereas there is an extensive analysis on game play, research in cultural heritage sites have not addressed yet the idea of game design as an end user activity.

Interestingly, research in the field of technology enhanced learning has already highlighted the learning potential not only of game play but also of game design and development (Kafai, 2006). Game design activities were identified as having the potential of helping learners to build a new relationship with knowledge, as learners feel ownership over the knowledge and experience deep interaction with the learning concepts to be integrated in the game with a functional role. As Kafai, Franke, Ching, and Shih (1998) observed, learners negotiated with learning concepts in this context, in order for the game to be playable.

Research in the field of game design by non-technical end users—such as students—has focused on the learning activity which has been analysed from two perspectives. The first one focuses on studying learning related to programming or specific skills and concepts (see for example Hoyles, Noss, Adamson, & Lowe 2001) for a discussion on children's causal reasoning and rule understanding during game construction). The second and most recent perspective acknowledges game design as a learning goal in itself (Hayes & Games, 2008). In this trend, researchers have coined the term "Design thinking" to encapsulate the set of learning and meta-cognitive skills involved, such as system based thinking, self-regulation, social, technical, technological, artistic and linguistic skills (Robertson & Howells, 2008; Salen, 2007). The analysis of learning through game design shows that the learning experience is shaped and amplified by the feeling of ownership over the games created by the learners, the participation in communities that share and exchange ideas and the motivation inherent in game play and game design (Rieber, 1996; Robertson & Howells, 2008; Salen, 2007).

Game creation in cultural institutions as participatory learning activity should be integrated in activities that will give the chance to visitors to interact with museum staff and discuss, negotiate and integrate in their games different aspects of cultural content. Game creation can be supported by technological scaffolds (such as game templates) and personalization techniques that present the museum view in order for the audience constructions to meet their standards and become a public artefact that can be used by other visitors, can be shared, revisited, discussed, changed and expanded.

Game Design Platforms and Their Relationship to Learning

When it comes to technology based scaffolds for game design there is a question we need to address: Do we need to design game-creation platforms to support learning in museums or we can use existing solutions such as KODU, storybricks, Game Star Mechanic, Game maker, the Games Factory and many more (for a critical review of technologies for game design see Hayes & Games, 2008). The answer here is that the technologies used for game design are configured to support not only the creation of games but also to facilitate the other objectives related and integrated in game design (e.g. the different types of learning, or in our case the cultural experience). Thus when game design is employed for purposes other than game creation then the design tools consist of elements and support practices related to the purpose for which game design is employed. To make this rationale more explicit we analyse next two examples of games that support end user design of the salient features, rules and content. The first one is a prototype game that is designed to support the learning of spatial concepts and more specifically, issues related to orientation, map alignment, use of systems of reference, etc. The example we selected is designed to facilitate learning in school but it is appropriate for our analysis here because it reveals how the characteristics and affordances of the tool can facilitate specific types of learning.

The "Treasure Hunt" Template

Unlike game design platforms (like KODU) the "Treasure hunt" tool does not lead in designing all sorts of games. Instead, it integrates the idea of game design in what we call game templates. Game templates represent a game genre (in our example treasure hunt) and they can produce different instances of the same genre by manipulating and specifying basic game elements (For a detailed presentation see Yiannoutsou, Sintoris, & Avouris, 2011) like the rules and the content (treasures, hints, etc.). It is thus apparent that game templates are more limited with respect to the spectrum of the produced games but they allow for designing of a learning experience that is oriented towards specific learning objectives (as we will show next). The other advantage of game templates is that while they allow configuration of certain game elements according to the learning objectives, they also provide some ready-made non configurable components which are integrated in the template to guarantee high quality of the games without requiring from the user specialised knowledge and lots of effort (like a 3D terrain for example). In a nutshell, game templates allow for focused learning design and produce high quality games that can meet the quality standards of the users.

In the example we present here, the non configurable game elements of the treasure hunt template are the representations of the terrain. These consist of a 2D and a 3D representation of a neighbourhood which are dynamically linked together. This means that motion of an agent in the 3D space results in a trail on the 2D representation; a treasure and a landmark as soon as they are placed on 2D space they also appear on 3D space (see Fig. 1 below)

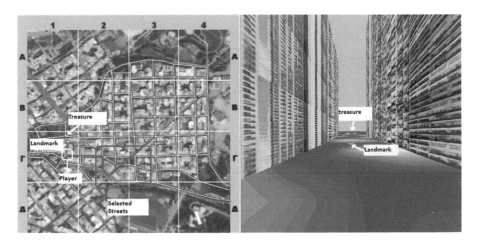

Fig. 1 The terrain of the treasure hunt template

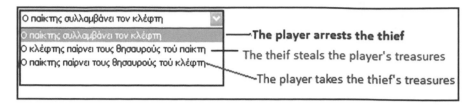

Fig. 2 Refining the rules of the game: defining the player–thief encounter

The dynamic link between the two representations is an important characteristic of the template because game design takes place on the map (2D representation) whereas game play takes place on the 3D space with the option for game designers to make the map available or not (so as to make the game easier).

The configurable elements of the template are the content and the rules. The content involves the number of the treasures and the hints that lead from one treasure to the other. The basic rule of the game remains the same, i.e. in treasure hunt games the player has to collect a set of hints in order to be able to find the treasure. The template however provides some variations around this rule: i.e. instead of having one treasure and a set of hints, there are numbered treasures that lead from the first treasure to the second and so on. Furthermore, the designers can decide if the game will consist of one player who moves in the neighbourhood searching for the treasures or of one player and one thief also searching for treasures. In the latter case the designer has to define what will happen if the player encounters the thief by selecting one of the three options available (see Fig. 2)

Another configurable element of the template is the definition of dangerous streets (see Fig. 1). The designers can designate some streets, normally around treasures, as dangerous areas by clicking on them with the mouse. Next they need to attribute to each area what will happen if the player and the thief step on this street. There are three options here again, losing speed for a specific time period, losing all the treasures collected or losing half of the treasures collected. The next step for the designer is to define the possibilities for the selected events to be activated by moving the cursor on a slider with values from 0 to 100 % (e.g. 60 % possibility for an event to be activated if the player enters the street). To put it briefly, with a set of simple functionalities the treasure hunt template can support non technical designers to construct a rather sophisticated game.

Our concern however in this section was to show the relationship between the characteristics (representations and functionalities) of the game template and the learning pursued. As we mentioned earlier the treasure hunt template was designed to promote spatial thinking and orientation skills. An analysis of data drawn from experimentation of two groups of 14-year-old students first showed that the treasure hunt template did not put any cognitive load to students with respect to technical issues (Yiannoutsou, Sintoris, et al., 2011). Second, student interaction with the template (i.e. what was configurable and what wasn't, functionalities and representations) required that spatial concepts were used as instruments for game construction (ibid). This means that students in order to construct the game negotiated spatial concepts like the difference in the properties of the map and the 3D representation of space—i.e. which one is more appropriate for orientation, what is visible and what is not in each representation—the accuracy of directions, the use of absolute frames of reference, etc. (see the next extract)

S2: *Now the quiz. What should we write for the first treasure?*
S1: *Go south*
S2: *Yeah, but it is not enough. All these are south (shows the streets at the bottom of the map). She said [the Facilitator] that the directions should be precise otherwise the game is not good. They will never find it.*
S1: *Ok then, there is a rectangular here. It is the only south rectangular [he refers to the shapes of the street on the map. (see Fig. 1)]*
S2: *That's good! Let's say "go to the southmost corner of the southmost rectangular"*
S1: *They will find it immediately if you are so precise.*
S2: *Yeah, but they will be on 3D they will not be seeing the map.*

Extract 1: Negotiation of spatial concepts (taken from Yiannoutsou, Sintoris, et al., 2011)

The second configurable game to be analysed is from the field of learning in cultural institutions described by Di Loretto, Divitini, Trimailovas, and Mander (2013) The museum configurable game MagMar is a tool that allows students to create question–answer games. The tool was used in, a study with 18 year old students worked in groups to create multiple choice questions (with an indication for the right answer) for pieces of art of a contemporary museum. The paintings were selected by the teacher and were common for all students. Question construction was created inside the museum and students had at their disposal a small picture of the painting presented in MagMar, access to internet and a guide of the museum. Students were also allowed to go to the room where the painting was located in order to find material for the question construction. Correct answer to a question awarded the group with a raise on their score. From the reported results with respect to the learning experience we highlighted and site here two remarks:

(a) *For the second item students walked around trying to find content for possible answers also in the information exposed in the exhibit (in the specific case, the name of painters contemporary to the one of the focal painting). Though this is clearly not sufficient to draw any general conclusion, it was still interesting to see how the game could actually motivate an exploration of the museum...*
(b) *When they were asked what they remembered from the museum visit, the students answered with the content of the questions they created* (Di Loretto et al., 2013, pp. 527).

Although MagMar doesn't have the characteristics of game templates we described earlier, it shows a rather successful implementation of the idea of visitor participation through the construction of meta-artefacts that can be used during the museum visit. It appears that the learning experience with MagMar proved to be engaging, prompted for exploration and connection finding with other exhibits (remark a) and showed that the process of question construction proved to be more effective—from a learning perspective—than the process of question answering (remark b). Without ignoring that there might be criticism on MagMar related to the emphasis on factual knowledge for example, and to questions about its playful character, it nevertheless shows the learning potential of a participatory activity like the ones we describe here. Apart from that, the idea of question constructin which is central to MagMar is also central to the process of culture generation as it is expressed by J. Landy:

"Artworks are not just fancy ways of delivering messages. One of their most interesting and useful functions is not to provide answers *but to offer questions* we have to answer ourselves. Answering the questions does not involve guessing the artist's intention. Instead, it involves injecting something of ourselves". (J. Landy extract from the video of his course at Stanford that comes under the title: "The art of Living" http://humanexperience.stanford.edu/artofliving#videos). A similar view comes from Simon (2010) who stresses that interesting questions with respect to learning are not those that aim at comprehending the institutional knowledge but those that draw on the visitor's knowledge. These two comments can offer useful insights in refining the design of MagMar so as to move from factual information to more interesting learning objectives.

It becomes apparent then that if we want to employ game design in the cultural experience we need to create a platform that engages users with what is considered crucial for the cultural experience. We attempted to show this with identifying in MagMar an underlying principle which is also important in the process of culture generation. Another suggestion is that game design tools could focus on the connections the visitor can make between the different cultural artefacts and with overarching concepts, beliefs and narratives (Falk & Dierking, 2000; Hein, 2006).

Integration of Participatory Activities in Museum and Visitor Practice

The visitor doesn't have all day to engage in game design. When and how do you expect this to happen? He/she might have a couple of hours to visit the museum and that's all

The above remark—made by one of our colleagues when we first presented the idea of game design—is added here to show the contrast between the technologies that promote a participatory cultural experience and the average visitor practice in a museum which involves one off or first time visits. It also stresses that a new practice—like participation—related to the use of a new technology cannot occur just as a result of the introduction of this technology (Tallon & Walker, 2008). Instead, in order to foster this practice we need to design activities integrating this technology by making the most out of its potential and by describing the roles of the stakeholders (i.e. museum, curators, visitors). As we mentioned at the beginning of this paper, participatory experience assumes a long term relationship between the visitor and the museum and requires structuring in order to result in an output which meets the quality standards of its creator and can become part of the museum assets (Hein, 2006; Simon, 2010). Taking all these into account we envisage learning activities that integrate game design technologies which can have the form of onsite or online workshops taking place regularly and focusing on specific parts of the museum collection each time. In this context we expect that the institutional knowledge about a specific set of exhibits will be discussed, analysed and negotiated between the audience and museum curators in order to be transformed and integrated into visitor constructed games. Social media and platforms that will allow a visitor to present and share his/her game with his/her friends and being able to play it when they visit the museum is an important element of the game construction process.

Concluding Remarks

In this paper we discussed the use of technology as a medium for learning in cultural institutions. Starting with technologies to support learning as information consumption, we moved to more recent approaches that involve visitor participation in the process of culture creation. Our analysis highlighted that participatory activities such as game design when scaffolded by technology and integrated in museum activities can offer rich learning experiences which reserve for the visitor the role of collaborator and partner and entail the creation of an enduring relationship with the museum. We further analysed the idea of cultural experience as participation through the presentation of the idea of game templates and how their characteristics can be related to learning.

Our analysis of two configurable games showed that the design of game templates in order to support a rich and engaging learning experience should be structured around what is considered important to learn when visiting a museum. A final observation involved the design of activities integrating and at the same time demonstrating how the new technology should be used in order to pursue the envisaged participatory learning experience. This rather new approach needs to be further investigated and supported through specific game-design tools and empirical studies.

Acknowledgements The treasure hunt template and research were implemented in the context of project *LeGa* Innovation in Educational Practice—Learning through the Creation of Models and Games, GSRT, R&D Actions in the Information Society, E-learning call, #26/04. Dr Kriton Kyrimis implemented the treasure hunt template and contributed to its design.

References

Akkerman, S., Admiraal, W., & Huizenga, J. (2009). Storification in history education: A mobile game in and about medieval Amsterdam. *Computers & Education, 52*(2), 449–459.
Beale, K. (Ed.). (2011). *Museums at play: Games interaction and learning.* Edinburgh: MuseumsEtc.

Bitgood, S. (2009). Museum fatigue: A critical review. *Visitor Studies, 12*(2), 93–111. doi:10.1080/10645570903203406.

Black, G. (2005). *The engaging museum: Developing museums for visitor involvement*. New York, NY: Routledge.

Bohnert, F., Zukerman, I., Berkovsky, S., Baldwin, T., & Sonenberg, L. (2008). Using interest and transition models to predict visitor locations in museums. *AI Communications, 21*(2–3), 195–202.

Bourdieu, P. (1986). The forms of capital. In J. Richardson (Ed.), *Handbook of theory and research for the sociology of education* (pp. 241–258). New York, NY: Wiley Online Library.

Cordis. (2012). Retrieved August 3, 2012, from http://cordis.europa.eu/fp7/ict/telearn-digicult/digicult-projects-fp7_en.html

de Gemmis, M., Lops, P., Semeraro, G., & Basile, P. (2008). Integrating tags in a semantic content-based recommender. In: P. Pu, et al. (Eds.), *Proc. ACM Conference on Recommender Systems 2008* (pp. 163–170). Lausanne, Switzerland.

Di Loretto, I., Divitini, M., Trimailovas, I., & Mander, M. (2013). Playing in museums by constructing your game. In J. A. Botía, & D. Charitos (Eds.), *Workshop Proceedings of the 9th International Conference on Intelligent Environments: Museums as Intelligent Environments* (Vol. 17, pp. 519–529) doi:10.3233/978-1-61499-286-8-519

Falk, J. H., & Dierking, L. D. (2000). *Learning from museums: Visitor experiences and the making of meaning*. Walnut Creek, CA: Altamira Press.

Fisher, M., & Twiss-Garrity, B. A. (2007). Remixing exhibits: Constructing participatory narratives with on-line tools to augment museum experiences. http://www.museumsandtheweb.com

Hayes, E. R., & Games, I. A. (2008). Making computer games and design thinking: A review of current software and strategies. *Games and Culture, 3*(3–4), 309–332.

Hein, H. S. (2006). *Public art: Thinking museums differently*. Lanham, MD: Altamira Press.

Hoyles, C., Noss, R., Adamson, R., & Lowe, S. (2001). Programming rules: What do children understand? *PME Conference, 3*, 169–176.

Jackson, S. (2011). The Tate kids guide for creating games for Galleries. In K. Beale (Ed.), *Museums at play: Games interaction and learning*. Edinburgh: MuseumsEtc.

Kafai, Y. B. (2006). Playing and making games for learning. *Games and Culture, 1*, 36–40.

Kafai, Y., Franke, M., Ching, C., & Shih, J. (1998). Game design as an interactive learning environment for fostering students' and teachers' mathematical inquiry. *International Journal of Computers for Mathematical Learning, 3*(2), 149–184.

Paay, J., Kjeldskov, J., Christensen, A., Ibsen, A., Jensen, D., Nielsen, G., et al. (2008). Location-based storytelling in the urban environment. *Proceedings of the 20th Australasian Conference on Computer-Human Interaction: Designing for Habitus and Habitat* (pp. 122–129).

Proctor, N. (2009). The Museum as Agora: What is collaboration in museums 2.0., WebWise Conference, Washington DC.

Ridge, M. (2011). Everyone wins: Crowdsourcing games & Museums. In *MuseumNext*. Retrieved January 30, 2014, from http://www.miaridge.com/everyone-wins-crowdsourcing-games-and-museums/

Rieber, L. P. (1996). Seriously considering play: Designing interactive learning environments based on the blending of microworlds, simulations, and games. *Educational Technology Research & Development, 44*(2), 43–58.

Robertson, J., & Howells, C. (2008). Computer game design: Opportunities for successful learning. *Computers & Education, 50*(2), 559–578.

Salen, K. (2007). Gaming literacies: A game design study in action. *Journal of Educational Multimedia and Hypermedia, 16*(3), 301–322.

Simon, N. (2010). *The participatory Museum*. Santa Cruz, CA: Museum 2.0. Retrieved July 15, 2012, from http://www.participatorymuseum.org/read/.

Tallon, L., & Walker, K. (Eds.). (2008). *Digital technologies and the museum experience*. Plymouth: Altamira Press.

Yiannoutsou, N., & Avouris, N. (2012). Mobile games in Museums: From learning through game play to learning through game design. In *ICOM-Education* (Vol. 23, pp. 79–86). Available in http://ceca.icom.museum/node/203

Yiannoutsou, N., Bounia, A., Roussou, M., & Avouris, N. (2011). Technology enhanced learning in sites of cultural heritage: a critical review of selected cases. *Themes in Science and Technology Education*, 4(1). Available from http://earthlab.uoi.gr/thete (in Greek).

Yiannoutsou, N., Sintoris, C., & Avouris, N. (2011). End User configuration of game elements: Game construction as learning activity. In *Proceedings, IS-EUD 2011 Workshop Involving End Users and Domain Experts in Design of Educational Games*, 2011, Torre Canne, Italy.

Digital Applications in Museums: An Analysis from a Museum Education Perspective

Niki Nikonanou and Alexandra Bounia

Introduction

The use of ICT applications for the purpose of museum communication and learning tends to become a main feature of contemporary museum policy. In order to serve their educational goals, different types of museums produce ICT applications that follow the technological developments in the form and shape they take: they range from distribution material in the form of CD and DVD-ROMs to online applications or systems that can be used in terminals inside the museum. The extensive use of these applications in current museum practice has cast the spotlight on a new area of museum education research. The central issue is not anymore whether we should use technology (as it was in the past), but *how* we should use it, in what ways users could become involved in activities and what experiences they could gain from using technology. In this context, an extensive research project took place between 2008 and 2011 in Greece. In the first stage of the project, we conducted a questionnaire-based research in order to record the use of ICT technologies for educational purposes by Greek museums (Bounia, Economou & Pitsiava, 2010). Based on the results of the first phase, in 2010–2011 a systematic qualitative study was carried out on the educational applications that were at the time offered by Greek museums, in order to explore the possibilities inherent in each type of media used, in conjunction with the venues these media are associated with, their target groups, objectives and educational philosophy. In addition we aimed to explore

N. Nikonanou (✉)
Department of Preschool Education, University of Thessaly,
Argonafton & Filellinon, 38221 Volos, Greece
e-mail: niknik@uth.gr

A. Bounia
Department of Cultural Technology and Communication, University of the Aegean,
Administration Building, Mytilene, 81100 Lesvos, Greece
e-mail: abounia@ct.aegean.gr

C. Karagiannidis et al. (eds.), *Research on e-Learning and ICT
in Education: Technological, Pedagogical and Instructional Perspectives*,
DOI 10.1007/978-1-4614-6501-0_13, © Springer Science+Business Media New York 2014

whether and to what extent theoretical perspectives on museum learning, as these have been developed in the relevant literature during the last couple of decades, have been taken into consideration for the creation of such applications.

Theoretical Framework

The last 20 years or so have seen an evolution in understanding what kind of learning happens, or should happen, in museums (Perry, 2012). While in the past theories of learning focused on a "transference model", i.e. one that placed emphasis on information passing from the (museum) educator to the visitor/audience, current museum education theory has embraced different, inclusive and participatory models of learning. Instead of accepting their role as simply passing along information to visitors, museum professionals are involved in attempts to enable visitors to make meaning and actively create knowledge for themselves based on their identities and previous experiences.

The role of constructivism has been crucial in this discussion. According to Hein (1998, 34), "learning requires active participation of the learner in both the way that the mind is employed and in the product of the activity, the knowledge that is required". Learners, in other words, are not just passive recipients of knowledge but active meaning makers, since "knowledge does not exist independently of the learner … it is constructed by the learner" (Hein, 1999, 75). Furthermore, Hein and Alexander (1998) go further to argue that museums are, and should be, constructivist environments, where visitors can construct their own meanings by actively engaging with exhibits, programs, objects and phenomena (Perry, 2012, 13).

According to the interactive model of museum experience, personal context is very important for museum learning, as "learning is a very personal experience, self motivated, emotionally satisfying and very personally rewarding and always constructed from a base of prior knowledge" (Falk & Dierking, 2000, 33). In addition, sociocultural context is equally or sometimes even more important. Museum visitors' research has highlighted the importance of social agenda for museum visiting (Perry, 2012, 11). The social context of a museum visit influences the perspectives and the experiences of every visitor (Falk & Dierking, 1992, 3). In the words of Falk and Dierking (2000, 37) "learning is both an individual and a group experience".

Museum educators have extensively used both these theoretical models in order to argue for a people-oriented (as opposed to object-centred) model of museum learning. Paris and Mercer (2002), summarising museum education research, suggested three models for the relationship between visitors and museum objects. The first is the model of passive reception, i.e. the one where a linear, one-way communication is expected. In this traditional approach, museums are expected to provide information, in a creative and effective way, which is easily understood by the visitors. Despite its shortcomings, this model is still active in many institutions around the world. The second model refers to active construction, and is based on the theories of constructivism, as developed before. The third model is called "transactions" and refers to a highly personalised understanding of learning, where the encounter of the visitor/group of visitors with the exhibits serves to reinforce or develop personal identity and beliefs in a rather idiosyncratic manner.

What all these theories have in common is the understanding that museums are spaces where a special kind of interaction takes place: visitors bearing their personal and/or social agendas encounter museum objects and use this encounter to create meaning, i.e. to learn. Learning within the museum environment is thus understood as a broad process, incorporating many different notions and strategies, ranging from passive reception to active construction and transaction (Perry, 2012, 15).

Within the context of museums, J. Dewey's notion of "experience" and its value in education is also highly relevant. Dewey emphasises active practice, but also the fact that experience in order to be educative has to be organised. In other words, experiences should not be just "hands-on" but also "minds on" in order to be effective (Hein, 1998, 2). Museum education has been historically related to Dewey's "learning by doing" philosophy (König 2002, 34–35), since museums are places where experience is built through the encounter with material objects, but also by the very fact that museum visit is an activity in space and it involves human beings as material entities. It provides multiple opportunities for visitors to experience the world, and consequently it can encourage creative individual thinking and acting—the basis of a democratic society (see also König 2002, 34–35; Sauter, 1994, 171–187).

This experiential approach also relates to the possibilities offered by museums to integrate in the learning process senses other than the sight. Activities during which visitors design, draw, construct and change their environment and themselves are integral parts of museum education programmes (Rottmann, 1998), because "active learning occurs when people … interact with information and experiences at hand" (Tishman, 2009, 2).

An important part of this interaction is the presence of museum exhibits. Museum education has always been concerned with the creation of suitable conditions for visitors' encounters with objects. Learning in museums is different than learning in schools or other similar environments, since it takes place "not in the shadow of objects" (Kerschensteiner 1925, quoted in König 2012, 24) as in the case of schools, where books and words hold the primary position, but through objects. Museum exhibits have a tangible quality and usually aesthetic value. They are "real things", and they can allow for a large number of different narratives to be developed around and through them. Roberts (1997) has highlighted the idea of "narrative" as an educational tool along with the ability of museums in particular to become places *par excellence* for the construction of narrative.

In order to work with museum objects, museum education places special emphasis on how we "ask" objects (Durbin, Morris, & Wilkinson, 1990; Hennigar Shuh, 1999; Hooper-Greenhill, 1994). Museum objects are characterised by a set of values (or qualities) that make them suitable for communication and learning. They are tangible, and they have survived from the past to the present, thus being a unique gateway to that past. They challenge the senses, inspire observation and discussion and provoke creativity. They can support educational processes for the understanding of reality and the past through the senses. They are open to different interpretations, providing opportunities for multiple narratives to be constructed around them and for open-ended learning experiences, meaning making and transaction. Finally, museum objects may serve aesthetic purposes. According to Weschenfelder and Zacharias (1992), the starting point of all museum education design and planning is (and should be) the pedagogical use of the values/qualities that museum objects have.

In the case of ICT applications for museums, the role of museum objects comes at the centre of attention, this time for a different reason. How are possibilities offered by authentic, "real" museum objects altered when they take digital form (see also Doonan & Boyd, 2008)? In this case, issues regarding the quality of digital representation, the advantages of digital copies for enhancing visitors' experience and the enlargement of experiences through new forms of digital mediation are brought to the forefront (also Bayne, Ross & Williamson, 2009, Frost, 2010). Nowadays the borders between real, virtual and illusion, symbolic and abstract and tangible reality and its simulation are more and more fluid (Zacharias, 1995, 72), resulting in a growing loss of the experience of reality through the senses. This fact points out the importance of providing opportunities for the connection of the digital with the real world, for expanding the digital experience into the real world.

On the other hand, information and communication technologies provide increased educational opportunities for interaction, active involvement and personalisation. They provide, or can do so, museum visitors with opportunities to select content and create their own individual routes in their approach to knowledge, as well as opportunities to contribute content and exchange ideas and information with others, thus enhancing the social dimension of their experience. In addition, interactivity and the stimulation of users on an intellectual, emotional and social level are facilitated via the introduction of ICT technologies into museum education (Roussou, 2010; Witcomb, 2006).

The theoretical framework presented above poses a series of issues regarding museum education and the use of ICT applications in museums. The main concern has been whether digital learning environments can support experience and meaning making by the museum visitors, taking into account the values/qualities of museum objects, the knowledge and experiences that users bring with them, the social dimension of the museum experience and the emphasis of museums on creative and experimental learning.

As a result, a series of research questions were developed, which informed the process and the data analysis. We therefore investigated the extent to which ICT applications created and employed by Greek cultural institutions:

- Take into account the previous knowledge and identity of the user and promote meaning-making processes according to the constructivist approach to museum learning
- Take into account the decisive role played by the social dimension of the educational process in the formation of the visitor's experience
- Promote processes that encourage a constructive encounter between visitors and museum exhibits
- Use the educational values/qualities of museum objects

- Promote creative activity on the part of the users
- Offer possibilities of expanding the digital experience into the real world
- Explore the possibilities of interactivity to encourage a more active interpretation of museum material

Research Methodology

For the purposes of this research we collected a total of 25 applications that Greek museums of varying type, size and scope (Table 1) provided to the researchers and explicitly identified as "educational". These were either in the form of a portable medium (CD-ROM/DVD-ROM) or web based; it was important that the institutions themselves considered these applications as "educational" and defined them as such, because this allows us to identify indirectly how institutions feel about education in general. We decided not to include in the research media or applications aiming mainly to museum communication, such as museum websites and social media, since their aims and objectives are not primarily educational (Bounia et al., 2010).

In order to analyse the applications we used qualitative content analysis (Krippendorff, 2004). The tool for this analysis was a form (Table 2) developed by the researchers based on the theoretical approaches and research questions presented above. The aim of the analysis was:

- To investigate the extent to which these applications utilise the aforementioned theories
- To study the opportunities for learning that each of the applications offers to their users

The aim of the study was neither to test the usability of each application nor to evaluate their use by the intended audience. This has been a research performed in order to evaluate the use of museological perspectives in the design of applications aimed to complement museum learning.

After recording the identification parameters of each application (namely institution, title, application form, funding, target group, languages) (see Table 1) the analysis form consisted of the following fields (Table 2):

- Presupposed knowledge/experience of the user
- Significance of collections/objects (authenticity, materiality, aesthetic value, narrative)
- User involvement:

  - Creativity-experimental learning
  - Experience expansion in the real world
  - Social context

Each of these parameters corresponds to a museum learning concern discussed previously.

Table 1 The educational applications studied in this research

Museums/cultural institutions	Educational applications: Title	Funding	Application form	Target group	Languages
Benaki Museum	"Play with a Painting on Your Screen"	EU Operational Programme "Information Society" and National (Greek) Funds (General Secretariat Research and Technology)	Online: http://www.benaki.gr/electronic_game_gr.asp	Children	Greek
Benaki Museum	"The Hidden Treasure of the Benaki Museum"	Benaki Museum and General Secretariat Research and Technology	CD-ROM	School children (6–18 years)	Greek
Benaki Museum	"Greece at the Benaki Museum"	Benaki Museum	DVD ROM	Unspecified	Greek, English
Benaki Museum	"Dedicated to 'Trelantonis'"	Benaki Museum	DVD ROM/multimedia application	Children	Greek
Museum of Traditional Pottery/Centre for the Study of Traditional Pottery	"The Ceramics of Crete in recent years"	EU INTERREG II	CD-ROM	Unspecified	Greek, English
The Network of Mani Museums, Hellenic Ministry of Culture	"Mani: A virtual tour"	Hellenic Ministry of Culture and European Regional Development Fund of the European Union	DVD ROM	Unspecified	Greek, English
Museum of the Macedonian Struggle	"The Struggle for Macedonia: Adventures at the lake"	European Regional Development Fund and national funds	Multimedia game	Unspecified	Greek, English, German
State Museum of Contemporary Art	"Educational CD. Costakis Collection"	EU Operational Programme "Information Society" and national funds	CD-ROM	School children 6–12 years	Greek, English, Russian
Modern Greek Art Museum, Municipality of Rhodes	"Click on Art. Educational Program and Multimedia Game"		CD-ROM	Children	Greek

Institution	Title	Funding	Format/Link	Audience	Language
Numismatic Museum	"Children's website"	Alexandros Onasis Foundation	Online: http://www.nma.gr/kids.coins/	Children	Greek
Mystras (archaeological site)	"The Fortified City of Mystras"	European Regional Development Fund—Regional Operational Programme of the Peloponnese	On-line: http://www.culture.gr/culture/mystras-edu	Children	Greek
Museum of Cycladic Art	"Games"	Nikolaos Goulandris Foundation	Online: http://www.cycladic.gr/frontoffice/portal.asp?cpage=NODE&cnode=135&clang=0	Children	Greek, English
Acropolis Restoration Service, Hellenic Ministry of Culture, first Ephorate of prehistoric and classical Antiquities, National Documentation Centre-National Hellenic Research Foundation	"The Parthenon Frieze"	Operational Programme "Information Society"	Online: http://www.parthenonfrieze.gr/#/home	General public	Greek, English
Acropolis Museum	"Athena, Goodness of the Acropolis"	Acropolis Museum; Bodossakis Foundation; Hellenic Ministry of Culture	Online: http://www.acropolis-athena.gr	Children	Greek, English
Folklife and Ethnological Museum of Macedonia-Thrace	"Mylios on the Road to the Mills"	EU and national funds	DVD ROM	Children 10+ and general public	Greek, English
Historical Museum of Crete	"Nikos Kazantzakis: A traveller to places and ideas"	Historical Museum of Crete and The Society of Cretan Historical Studies	Online: http://www.historical-museum.gr/educational/	Primary school groups 10–13 years and secondary school groups, 14–18 years	Greek

(continued)

Table 1 (continued)

Museums/cultural institutions	Educational applications: Title	Funding	Application form	Target group	Languages
The Athens University Museum	"Collectors of Stories"	EU Operational Programme "Information Society" and National (Greek) Funds	CD-ROM	Young audience	Greek
Museum of the Olive and Greek Olive Oil in Sparta	"Bring out the Oil for Us"	European Regional Development Fund—Regional Operational Programme of the Peloponnese	CD-ROM	Children 7+	Greek
Natural History Museum in Axioupolis, Kilkis	"Electronic games about plants and animals"	EU INTERREG III and national funds	On-site applications	Primary School groups: first to second/third to fourth/fifth to sixth grades	Greek
Museum of Byzantine Culture	"Games"	Archaeological Receipts Fund	Online: http://www.mbp.gr/edu/index.php? option=com_content& view=article&id=62 &Itemid=30&lang=el	Children	Greek
Aiani Archaeological Museum	"Educational Games"	Unspecified	Online: http://www. mouseioaianis.gr/CAME/ GAMEFORSITE/ WebGame.swf	Children	Greek

Museum	Title	Funding	Format	Audience	Language
The Jewish Museum of Greece	"World War II and the Holocaust of Greek Jews, 1941–1944"	Jewish Museum of Greece	DVD ROM	General public, Schools	Greek, English
Historical Archive of the Aegean—Ergani	"Entrepreneurship and Innovation in Northeast Aegean at the end of the nineteenth and the beginning of the twentieth century"	EU Operational Programme "Information Society" and National (Greek) Funds	CD-ROM	General public	Greek, English, French
Herakleidon Museum	"Educational program: Art and Mathematics"	Museum funds	CD-ROM	School groups	Greek
G. Iakovidis Digital Museum	"In the studio of the painter Georgios Iakovidis"	Educational and Cultural Foundation (N.G. Papademetriou)	CD-ROM	Children and School groups	Greek

Table 2 Analysis form

1. General information	Institution, title, application form, founding, target group, languages
2. Contents	Presupposed knowledge/experience of the user
of applications	Significance of collections/objects (authenticity, materiality, aesthetic value, narrative)
3. User involvement	Creativity-experimental learning
	Experience expansion in real world
	Social context

Results

General Characteristics: Target Groups

A wide range of bodies of varying size, legal status and financial strength are actively involved in the production of educational multimedia applications in Greece. The number is growing as well as the interest of museums to acquire a presence in the digital sphere. These bodies seek opportunities to produce such applications either through funding by European programmes or through other kinds of funding, often by private foundations. Of course, there are also a number of self-funded initiatives, which reflect the strong interest and even anxiety of some bodies to acquire a digital "educational voice". While the older applications take the conventional form of a CD/DVD-ROM, the latest ones are Internet based as the importance of easy user access is being increasingly recognised, while at the same time the technological developments providing such possibilities are constantly expanding.

In most cases (23 out of 25) the applications are meant to be used outside the museum; in just two cases they are used on museum premises. In other words, the applications are meant to "accompany" visitors home after their museum visit, so as to consolidate the content of the visit and to reinforce and possibly extend the museum experience. In the case of applications accessible on the Internet, once again these are used at the user's personal space without an actual visit to the relevant museum being necessary. At the same time, it is also possible to see how these applications can motivate users to actually visit the museums that provide them, and so, in this respect, they can claim to have the role of introduction to the respective institutions.

As far as the user groups are concerned, three (3) applications are aimed at the "general public", while seven (7) are targeted specifically at school groups and the educational community. In three cases the school groups are further defined according to their educational level (primary or secondary) such as in the web application of the Historical Museum of Crete. "Children" in general also feature as a target group; more specifically, in these cases it is mainly the lower age limit of the users that is defined (usually ages 7–10). It is evident, therefore, that the applications treat the public, even the children/teenage public, as a unified whole in contrast to museum education activities, which are usually aimed at highly specific age groups.

An exception to this can be found at the Natural History Museum at Axioupolis, where the applications form part of the museum education activities and provide different activities for three different age groups: infants and the first to second grades of primary school, the third to fourth grades of primary school and the fifth to sixth grades of primary school (Economou, Nikonanou, Kasvikis, Economou, & Samaroudi, 2011). It is also worth mentioning that there are no applications in our sample which are intended for special needs groups, despite the fact that digital technologies can provide for different special needs (e.g. enlargements for visually impaired users).

Almost half of the applications (14 out of 25) are offered just in the Greek language. In the case of digital discs (CD-ROMs) there is usually a choice of other languages than Greek, such as in the application for the Costakis Collection, which is also offered in English and Russian, and also in the educational game produced by the Museum of the Macedonian Struggle, which is also offered in English and German, and the application of the Historical Archive of the Aegean—Ergani offered in English and French. Greek and English are offered in eight (8) applications (CD-ROMs and web applications), and the rest is only in Greek (see Table 1). This choice of languages is also relevant to the target audience of the educational provisions of the museums: most of the institutions want to use their applications to cater for tourists as well or for the audience of countries which have a special interest in their collections (as for instance in the case of the Costakis Collection which consists of paintings by Russian artists).

Contents of Applications: The Role of the Object

As far as the contents of the applications are concerned, the analysis examined to what extent the applications presuppose knowledge on the subject by the user. The applications were not found to presuppose any special knowledge on the part of the user, at least no greater level of knowledge than that provided by the applications themselves. In other words, these applications are self-contained packages in which both the provision of knowledge and the suggested activities function as a complete educational unit. They do not refer to the museum environment, and they do not correspond to activities or knowledge that users have had from previous visits or other experiences.

The second parameter that was examined in this section concerns the place that museum objects occupy in each application. Most of the applications (22 out of 25) contain museum exhibits at the centre of their content; in some cases (e.g. "The Parthenon Frieze"), the exhibits are the central feature of the content, while in some others (e.g. "Bring out the Oil for Us") museum exhibits play a minor role (even though they are still there). Applications of the first type can also prepare users for a visit to the museum housing the relevant object, where they will be able to recognise the object in their real encounter with it on the museum premises. In most of the cases where a digital museum object occupies a central place in the application, museum education processes are used in approaching it, such as observation, examination and interpretation (e.g. the Benaki Museum's "Play with a Painting on Your Screen"). More generally, it seems that the role museum objects occupy in the applications depends on their uniqueness or general appreciation, as, for instance, is the case with the frieze from the Athenian Acropolis. In the case objects are considered more "common" or interesting for qualities other than aesthetics and uniqueness, as for instance in the case of the olive pressing machinery, their role in the applications is not that central and the focus goes more to their use or construction technique rather than the objects themselves.

When it comes to the values/qualities of objects, it is clear that those of authenticity, materiality and aesthetics can be used only to a limited extent in a digital environment since they are inseparably bound up with approaching the material substance of real museum objects (Bounia & Nikonanou, 2008). Similarly, despite the fact that in traditional museum educational programmes museum objects are at the centre of the educational process, in the digital applications they are not used in the same way, especially in the narrative.

In order to examine perceptions of materiality and aesthetics, we examined the quality of the digitisation in conjunction with the possibilities for making a visual examination of the object as well as the provision of three-dimensional images (Frost, 2010). The latter has not been used extensively in most of the cases—probably because of the cost of production—except for one case: the application produced by the State Museum of Contemporary Art; in this application technology is used to provide detailed views of art objects.

In order to focus on aesthetics in particular, we also examined the representation of digital spaces. The approach followed in this process is largely based on the conventional aesthetics of children's books, comics or animations or on aesthetic choices oriented towards the aesthetics of the museum objects in each collection (e.g. Costakis Collection). Exception to this is the application of the Numismatic Museum that offers a "screen" with an active "fairytale-like" image and numerous stimuli and prompts encouraging the user to explore and connect to organisations and events "outside the screen". It seems that museums present their objects in similar manners whether in the real or the digital environment: art museums tend to place more emphasis on the aesthetics, uniqueness and materiality of their objects, whereas museums of technology or natural history tend to place more emphasis on the processes and the circumstances connected to their collections and not necessarily on the objects as unique material testimonies.

As for another important value/quality of museum objects, i.e. the possibility to encourage multiple narratives, we realised during the process of analysis that this is very little exploited in the digital applications, although it is not subject to the same limitations of digital space as the three previously mentioned qualities/values. In terms of their narrative content, most of the museum objects presented in the applications have "closed" narratives, based on elements of a factual nature, while users are not encouraged to develop their own individual interpretations of them. Of particular interest in this respect is the application by the Numismatic Museum, which, using the museum exhibits as a starting point, provides users with the opportunity to access further information via web links and make more imaginative connections (such as with not-for-profit environmental groups when discussing coins bearing marine animal symbols).

User Involvement

Learning is not just about content; it is also about processes which concern what the user does and in what kind of context the interaction between learner and content happens (see also Dimaraki, 2008). As a result, it was important to examine whether and how users of the applications were encouraged to interact with museum material, whether and how creativity was promoted and finally whether, and how, the social context of the museum visit was exploited to encourage learning within the museum. Most applications present the user with a variety of activities, which provide different opportunities for interaction.

Most applications draw a distinction between "serious" and "play-based" learning, either providing extensive texts and information as more or less a prerequisite of "play" or offering activities that serve as a "gateway" to knowledge. In the first category belong applications, which require the user to read the information and then to test his/her newly acquired knowledge by filling in crosswords and word search puzzles. Examples of such an approach are those of the "Games" section of the Aiani Archaeological Museum's application or the multiple-choice questions provided in the application of the Historical Museum of Crete.

In the second category belong activities that serve as a "gateway" to knowledge; in these cases, the user receives information concerning the object that he/she is asked to "discover" as a result of the activity and not as a prerequisite for it. This is the case of the puzzles and memory games created by the Museum of Byzantine Culture or the Museum of Cycladic Art. In some other cases of the same category, such as the application of the Benaki Museum entitled "Hidden Treasure" or the games of the Numismatic Museum, the user gets access to information about museum objects, their provenance and so on after choosing them in the context of the activity.

The question regarding these cases is whether, and to what extent, users are motivated to explore the new knowledge provided to them after they have finished with the activity, since this new knowledge is not necessary in order to complete the activity.

Very few applications examined in this research place an emphasis on personal interpretations and the construction of individual meaning along the line of constructivist learning, as this has been discussed above. An exception to this is the creative activities suggested to users in some cases, usually related to art collections and art museums. For instance, the State Museum of Contemporary Art encourages users to employ symbols and elements from the museum artworks in order to create their own works of art and the Iakovidis Digital Museum encourages users to import their own texts. However, this allows for limited personal interpretation and does not take advantage of many other possibilities available through museum objects (Rakhochkine, 2003; Weschenfelder & Zacharias, 1992, 174–88).

Interestingly no attempt is made to link digital to non-digital activities, either creative ones or experimental ones, despite the fact that such an attempt would help towards a more comprehensive use of the materiality of the objects and the involvement of the senses. In the few cases where users can print out their own digital creations, these serve more as a souvenir of their use of the application and less as a stimulus for creative off-screen activities (e.g. "The Fortified City of Mystras"). In other words, there is no attempt to extend the scope of the educational activity beyond the confines of the screen in order to support educational processes that exploit the involvement of the senses.

Finally, as far as the social context of the experience is concerned, we came to realise that all of the applications examined are targeted at the individual user; that is, they do not involve multiple users or collaboration between users, even when they are targeted to school groups. It is evident, therefore, that the social dimension of the users' experience does not lie at the heart of the applications' educational design, despite its importance in the overall experience of museum visitors.

Conclusions

The aim of the research presented in this chapter was to explore whether and to what extent ICT applications created and used by cultural institutions in Greece incorporate the principles of museum education and take advantage of the possibilities offered by new technologies to maximise their effectiveness and appeal. We performed a qualitative content analysis, which highlighted some very interesting and thought-provoking issues.

Greek institutions invest increasingly more in the production of digital applications, thus aiming to enrich their educational provisions and encourage more visitors to take advantage of the museum collections and the knowledge they provide. These applications tend to be web based, so as to be as widely accessible as possible. This is also evident by the fact that the applications aim to address the needs of a wide variety of users and they do not target specific groups or needs.

Unlike real museum experiences though, where encounter with the museum object is at the centre of the educational process, museum digital applications do not take full advantage of the possibilities offered by them. Multiple interpretations, individual meaning making, encouragement of alternative or additional ideas produced by the user/visitor, social interaction, interactivity, creativity and engagement are not encouraged or supported to the extent that they could be. The applications seem to reinforce the model of passive reception, where the museum provides cultural content and the user is expected to accept and internalise the knowledge provided. It is therefore necessary to reconsider the creation of museum educational applications and to design them taking into account museum education theory and the special qualities/values museums and their collections hold. It is important for museum educational applications to encourage a more active involvement of users with museum objects and to provide opportunities for more creative, engaging and enabling activities. At the same time, greater emphasis should be placed on strengthening the social dimension of the overall experience by utilising the possibilities that information and communication technologies offer for user involvement and collaboration and for the exchange of ideas and content.

This research aims to contribute to the discussion regarding digital media use in museum education. We argue that it is time to reconsider the efforts made so far and to promote an interdisciplinary approach that will offer a more personal, rewarding and multi-layered learning experience for all.

Acknowledgements   The authors would like to express their thanks to Nikos Avouris for always being available for collaboration, to Andrew Hendry for his help with the English text as well as to the anonymous reviewers of the second Symposium on Digital Applications for Museum Learning, where this chapter was firstly presented. Of course, all mistakes and shortcomings remain our own.

References

Bayne, S., Ross, J., & Williamson, Z. (2009). Objects, subjects, bits and bytes: Learning from the digital collections of the National Museums. *Museum and Society, 7*(2), 110–124.

Bounia, A., Economou, M., & Pitsiava, E. (2010). The use of new technologies in museum educational programmes: Results from research in Greek museums. In M. Vemi & E. Nakou (Eds.), *Museums and education* (pp. 335–347). Athens: Nesos Publications (in Greek).

Bounia, A., & Nikonanou, N. (2008). Objects and museums: Issues of experience, interpretation and communication. In N. Nikonanou & K. Kasvikis (Eds.), *Educational journeys in time. Experiences and interpretations of the past* (pp. 69–101). Athens: Patakis Publications (in Greek).

Dimaraki, E. (2008). Digital mediation of learning about the past: Designing applications for the orchestration of learning activity. In N. Nikonanou & K. Kasvikis (Eds.), *Educational journeys in time. Experiences and interpretations of the past* (pp. 154–187). Athens: Patakis Publications (in Greek).

Doonan, R., & Boyd, M. (2008). CONTACT: Digital modelling of object and process in artefact teaching. In H. J. Chatterjee (Ed.), *Touch in museums. Policy and practice in objects handling* (pp. 107–120). Oxford, NY: Berg.

Durbin, G., Morris, S., & Wilkinson, S. (1990). *Learning from objects. A teacher's guide.* London: English Heritage.

Economou, M., Nikonanou, N., Kasvikis, K., Economou, D., & Samaroudi, M. (2011). Educational programs and digital applications in the Museum of Natural History Axioupolis: New technologies as a tool before, during and after the museum visit. In I. Gavrilaki (Ed.), *The spring of museums, conference proceedings: Rethymnon: 25th ephorate of prehistoric and classical antiquities* (pp. 243–254). Rethymnon: Association on Historical & Folklore Studies (in Greek).

Falk, J., & Dierking, L. (1992). *The museum experience.* Washington, DC: Whalesback Books.

Falk, J., & Dierking, L. (2000). *Learning from museums. Visitor experiences and the making of meaning.* London: Altamira Press.

Frost, O. C. (2010). When the object is digital: Properties of digital surrogate objects and implications for learning. In R. Parry (Ed.), *Museums in a digital age* (Leicester readers in museum studies, pp. 237–246). London: Routledge.

Hein, G. (1998). *Learning in museum.* London: Routledge.

Hein, G. (1999). The constructivist museum. In E. Hooper-Greenhill (Ed.), *The educational role of the museum* (2nd ed., pp. 73–79). London: Routledge.

Hein, G., & Alexander, M. (1998). *Museums: Places of learning*. Washington, DC: American Association of Museums.

Hennigar Shuh, H.-J. (1999). Teaching yourself to teach with objects. In E. Hooper-Greenhill (Ed.), *The educational role of the museum* (2nd ed., pp. 80–91). London: Routledge.

Hooper-Greenhill, E. (1994). Museum education. In E. Hooper-Greenhill (Ed.), *The educational role of the museum* (pp. 229–257). London: Routledge.

König, G. (2002). *Kinder-und Jugendmuseen. Genese und Entwicklung einer Museumsgattung. Impulse für besucherorientierte Museumskonzepte*. Opladen: Leske & Budrich.

König, G. M. (2012). Das Veto der Dinge. Zur Analyse materieller Kultur. In K. Priem, G. König, & R. Casale (Eds.), *Die Materialität der Erziehung: Kulturelle und soziale Aspekte pädagogischer Objekte, Zeitschrift für Pädagogik 58. Beiheft* (pp. 14–31). Weinheim: Beltz Verlag.

Krippendorff, K. (2004). *Content analysis: An introduction to its methodology* (2nd ed.). London: Sage Publications.

Paris, S. G., & Mercer, M. J. (2002). Finding self in objects: Identity exploration in museums. In G. Leinhardt, K. Crowley, & K. Knutson (Eds.), *Learning conversations in museums* (pp. 401–423). Mahwah, NJ: Lawrence Erlbaum Associates.

Perry, D. L. (2012). *What makes learning fun? Principles for the design of intrinsically motivating museum exhibits*. Lanham, MD: Altamira Press.

Rakhochkine, A. (2003). *Das pädagogische Konzept der Offenheit in internationaler Perspektive*. Münster: Waxmann.

Roberts, L. C. (1997). *From knowledge to narrative. Educators and the changing museum*. Washington, DC: Smithsonian Institution Press.

Rottmann, K. (1998). Eigenes Tun hilft Sehen- Bidnerisch-praktische Vermittlungsarbeit. In P. Noelke & R. Kreidler (Eds.), *Museumspädagogik in Köln* (pp. 75–84). Köln: Museumsdienst Köln.

Roussou, M. (2010). Learning by doing and learning through play: An exploration of interactivity in virtual environments for children. In R. Parry (Ed.), *Museums in a digital age* (Leicester Readers in Museum Studies, pp. 247–265). London: Routledge.

Sauter, B. (1994). *Museum und Bildung*. Hohengehren: Schneider Verlag.

Tishman, Sh. (2009), Learning in museums. Harvard Graduate School of Education, Usable knowledge, Retrieved on 12 October, 2013, from http://www.uknow.gse.harvard.edu/learning/LD2-1.html

Weschenfelder, K., & Zacharias, W. (1992). *Handbuch der Museumspädagogik. Orientierung und Methode*. Düsseldorf: Schwann Verlag.

Witcomb, A. (2006). Interactivity: Thinking beyond. In S. Macdonald (Ed.), *A companion to museum studies* (pp. 353–361). Oxford: Blackwell Publishing.

Zacharias, W. (1995). Orte, Erlebnisse, Effekte der Museumspädagogik. Horizonte des musealen Bildungsauftrags und Spekulationen zur Topografie kultureller Erfahrung. In K. Fast (Ed.), *Handbuch museumspädagogischer Ansätze* (pp. 71–97). Opladen: Leske-Budrich.

Part VI
ICT and Pre- and In-service Teacher Practices

Technology Integration in the Most Favorable Conditions: Findings from a Professional Development Training Program

Ilias Karasavvidis and Vassilis Kollias

Introduction: Technology Uptake

The belief that technology in its various instantiations will transform educational practice is very prevalent and dates back for at least a century. The assumption behind the introduction of technology into educational systems was that it will eventually make them more meaningful, interesting, and relevant for students, thereby drastically improving the quality of learning. However, if there is one consistent finding from the past three decades of research on ICT use in education, it is that technology has failed to transform teaching and learning practices.

There are two interrelated problems with technology use. *First*, research indicates that the *extent of technology use* in classrooms is rather low: teachers do not appear to use technology in their practices to any considerable extent (Hinostroza, Labbé, Brun, & Matamala, 2011; Norris, Sullivan, Poirot, & Soloway, 2003; Ward & Parr, 2010; Webb & Cox, 2004; Wikan & Molster, 2011). *Second, even when teachers do embrace technology, it gets integrated in ways which sustain rather than transform existing practices* (Condie, Munro, Seagraves, & Kenesson, 2007; Cuban, 2001; Cuban, Kirkpatrick, & Peck, 2001; Donnelly, McGarr, & O'Reilly, 2011; Eteokleous, 2008; Hayes, 2007; Hermans, Tondeur, van Braak, & Valcke, 2008; Li, 2007; Norton, McRobbie, & Cooper, 2000; OFSTED, 2004; Player-Koro, 2013; Prestridge, 2012). On an international level, the SITES 2006 study indicated that ICT adoption does not necessarily mean that traditional practices are abolished

I. Karasavvidis (✉)
Department of Preschool Education, University of Thessaly,
Argonafton & Filellinon, 38221 Volos, Greece
e-mail: ikaras@uth.gr

V. Kollias
Department of Primary Education, University of Thessaly,
Argonafton & Filellinon, 38221 Volos, Greece
e-mail: vkollias@uth.gr

C. Karagiannidis et al. (eds.), *Research on e-Learning and ICT*
in Education: Technological, Pedagogical and Instructional Perspectives,
DOI 10.1007/978-1-4614-6501-0_14, © Springer Science+Business Media New York 2014

(Law, 2008). Similar evidence is reported on a national level, e.g., the UK (Selwyn, 2008; Smith, Rudd, & Coghlan, 2008; Yang, 2012) Ireland (McGarr, 2009) and Greece (Vosniadou & Kollias, 2001). The low rate of classroom technology use and the way technology is used to support existing practices are the primary reasons why the vision of transforming education through technology has yet to be realized.

Why has it proven so difficult for teachers to use technologies in their practices? Researchers have sought to determine the reasons behind this technology resistance. More than a decade ago, Becker (2000a) identified four enabling conditions for technology adoption: technology access, training, curriculum compatibility, and constructivist beliefs. Ertmer (1999, 2005) attempted to further systematize technology resistance into obstacles that can be distinguished into first-order and second-order barriers. Typically, first-order barriers are extrinsic to teachers while second-order barriers are teacher related.

First-order barriers are beyond the direct control of the teacher and have to do with what is provided by the local and state authorities in terms of technology infrastructure and support structures such as equipment, training, and support. First, *technology access* is one of the main conditions upon which technology integration depends. Several studies report that one of the strongest predictors of technology use is technology access (Becker, 2000a; Eteokleous, 2008; Granger, Morbey, Lotherington, Owston, & Wideman, 2002; Norris et al., 2003). Second, a certain level of *technological competence* is required if teachers are to use technology. A possible lack of technical skills might potentially undermine technology integration. Several studies report that the greater the personal ICT competence the more likely the teachers were to use ICT in their classrooms (Etcoklcous, 2008; Prestridge, 2012). Moreover, classroom integration of technology has been predicted by computer experience (Mueller, Wood, Willoughby, Ross, & Specht, 2008; Wood, Mueller, Willoughby, Specht, & Deyoung, 2005). Third, *technical support* can also be a hindrance to technology adoption. Several studies report that access to technical support can be a facilitator of technology use (Hayes, 2007; Penuel, Fishman, Yamaguchi, & Gallagher, 2007). Finally, the issue of *leadership* is often stressed as teachers need not only technical but also administrative support. Some studies report that principals and school administrators can play a facilitatory role in terms of technology adoption (Hayes, 2007; Law, 2008).

Technology adoption is clearly contingent on eliminating these first-order barriers. Addressing first-order barriers required lavish funding so as to ensure the availability of resources and training, both technical and pedagogical. Additionally, educational authorities have restructured curricula so as to accommodate technology use and foster technology integration. Progress on all fronts related to first-order barriers has been steadily made over the years (Ertmer, 2005). The underlying assumption that guided much of the thinking was that providing resources and support would somehow naturally lead to greater technology adoption (Ertmer, 1999). It turned out, however, that resources and support were a necessary but not a sufficient condition for technology integration: second-order barriers played a critical role.

Second-order barriers involve teacher beliefs about teaching and learning (Ertmer, 1999). Teacher beliefs about teaching and learning might shape whether and how teachers eventually integrate technology in their classrooms. Therefore, teacher beliefs have been the focus of much attention in the literature (Hermans et al., 2008; van Braak, Tondeur, & Valcke, 2004; see also Baggott la Velle, McFarlane, John, & Brawn, 2004; Ward & Parr, 2010). While addressing first-order barriers was relatively straightforward, addressing second-order barriers proved considerably more challenging (Ertmer, 2005). Generally speaking, second-order barriers have been addressed mainly via professional development training (PDT) programs and activities of many forms.

Professional Development Training on ICT Pedagogy

Ertmer (2005) argued that teachers are likely to think about technology in the same way they think about other educational innovations. Consequently, examining how teachers approach innovations and what makes PDT programs effective might help understand teachers' response to PDT on ICT integration in the classroom. According to the literature on PDT, three properties have been singled out as being critical for its success: form, length, and content. As far as *form* is concerned, many forms of PDT have been found to be effective: workshops (Ertmer, Ottenbreit-Leftwich, & York, 2007; Shriner, Schlee, Hamil, & Libler, 2009), seminars and conferences (Ertmer et al., 2007), independent learning (Gray, Thomas, & Lewis, 2010), school-based professional development by staff (Gray et al., 2010), and personal coaching (Miller & Glover, 2007). When it comes to *length* PDT should be both continuing (Miller & Glover, 2007) and sustained (Garet, Porter, Desimone, Birman, & Yoon, 2001). Finally, with regard to *content*, research suggests that PDT is more likely to be effective if it has a pedagogical rather than a technical orientation (Law, 2008; Law & Chow, 2008b). It is also likely to have an impact if the primary focus is on the academic subject (Garet et al., 2001).

While some essential features of successful PDT have been identified, there are still areas of critical importance which are largely unexplored. More specifically, in addition to form, length, and content, *it has been argued that teachers themselves are one of the most critical determinants of PDT success because their previous experiences might influence the outcomes of any in-service training regardless of its form, length, and content.* The argument is that we need to consider what teachers themselves bring to PDT sessions in terms of former experiences and practices (Penuel et al., 2007). For example, Coburn (2004) has convincingly demonstrated that teachers' responses to innovation appear to be mediated by their preexisting world views and practices. Additionally, teachers' local contexts should also be carefully considered when determining the effectiveness of a PDT program, as the demands posed by the contexts of practice make teachers set specific priorities (Penuel et al., 2007). PDT is bound to be interpreted in terms of the existing policies, schedules, budgets, curricula, hardware, software, technical, and administrative support of teachers' local contexts. For instance, Zhao and Frank (2003) found that the more strongly teachers believed that computers were compatible with their teaching styles, the more often teachers reported using computers in their practices.

Many teacher background variables have been systematically explored as predictors of ICT classroom use (e.g., Hermans et al., 2008; Law & Chow, 2008b; Tondeur, Hermans, van Braak, & Valcke, 2008; van Braak et al., 2004; Ward & Parr, 2010). However, teacher background variables have not been systematically investigated as predictors of PDT success even though their significance has been recognized in the aforementioned literature (Coburn, 2004; Penuel et al., 2007). In particular, when it comes to PDT that is related to ICT integration in the classroom, *researchers have rarely focused on how teachers with specific backgrounds respond to PDT.*

But in what ways can teachers belonging to specific groups be important for understanding the effectiveness of PDT for technology integration? As we argue in this work, this is because examining teachers with specific—and more particularly favorable—background properties is one way of determining the possible upper range of technology integration that we can reasonably expect from PDT programs. Technology integration can vary greatly along the sustain-transform continuum. At one extreme, teachers might make no or limited use of technology. In this case, the impact of technology will range from negligible to small. At the other extreme, teachers might use technology a great deal. In this case, depending on the ways technology gets used, its impact might be far-reaching, ultimately leading to the transformation of teaching and learning practices. As the preceding literature review shows, the majority of teachers do not use technology in their practices and those who actually do tend to domesticate it rather than use it to change their practices. *Examining how the most committed, skilled, qualified, or experienced teachers respond to PDT in ICT use is a possible test of success for current in-service PDT programs since it can be a measure of their maximal effectiveness along the sustain-transform continuum of technology use.* In other words, *if PDT stands any chance of achieving our highest aspirations relevant to transforming current educational practices, then teachers with such qualities are the best possible candidates for proving the case for PDTs.*

To the best of our knowledge, *there are no studies on how teacher background properties such as skills, expertise, or qualifications might influence the effectiveness of a PDT.* Consequently, we draw mainly on studies indicating certain teacher background properties as being either highly conducive to technology adoption or closely related to it. It seems reasonable to assume that *the more properties facilitating technology integration teachers have before attending a PDT program, the less ground these teachers would have to cover in terms of learning while attending the PDT.* Our assumption is that teachers with such properties will show the best and most favorable response to PDT as they would have to make less progress compared to other teachers.

ICT Use as a Function of Teacher Background

Only a handful of studies have closely examined specific teacher groups with respect to technology adoption and use. One group of studies focused on *exemplary technology-using teachers to extract those background properties that make them distinct.*

Exemplary technology-using teachers use technology in their practices in innovative, non conventional ways. In such studies the typical focus is on determining what makes these teachers exemplary technology users, documenting their practices, investigating their beliefs and pedagogical philosophies, and determining factors that either facilitate or hinder their efforts to use technology (Angers & Machtmes, 2005; Becker, 2000b; Becker & Riel, 2000; Ertmer et al., 2007; Hadley & Sheingold, 1990, 1993; Leftwich, 2007; Riel & Becker, 2008). This body of research shows that exemplary technology-using teachers are different from other technology-using teachers and other teachers in general in a number of ways. More specifically, exemplary technology-using teachers actively seek more professional development activities than ordinary teachers, take release time to follow such activities, are more willing to take risks and experiment with technology, and overall have a high level of commitment to improving their students' learning through technology (Angers & Machtmes, 2005; Becker & Riel, 2000; Hadley & Sheingold, 1990; Leftwich, 2007; Riel & Becker, 2008). While the contribution of such studies to our understanding of technology integration is critically important, this line of research has not focused on the processes through which these teachers became exemplary. As a consequence, *the personal learning trajectories of exemplary technology-using teachers are unknown, especially in relation to PDT on ICT pedagogy.* However the aforementioned characteristics of exemplary technology-using teachers can work as rough guidelines in an attempt to locate groups of teachers with background properties that maximize the potential of in-service PDT.

One group of teachers with special background properties which might be important for technology integration are teachers with constructivist beliefs. Several studies have indicated that exemplary technology-using teachers are also highly likely to employ a constructivist, student-centered approach to teaching (Becker & Riel, 2000; Dexter, Anderson, & Becker, 1999; Hermans et al., 2008; Matzen & Edmunds, 2007; van Braak et al., 2004). Overall, a systematic relationship between constructivist approaches to learning and technology use has been reported in the literature: constructivist beliefs are correlated with a higher rate of technology adoption. While the relationship between constructivist teaching philosophies and technology use has been well established in the literature, *how exactly teachers who are very familiar with constructivist teaching and learning in a given subject area or grade level respond to in-service PDT on pedagogical uses of ICT has not been explored.*

Another group of teachers with specific background characteristics that might be important for technology integration are teachers of high academic qualifications. Compared to ordinary teachers, teachers who hold postgraduate degrees have by definition a higher degree of specialization. Riel and Becker (2008) found that a particular area in which professionally engaged teachers are differentiated from other teachers is that they have invested more in their own education and master's degrees were considered to be an indication of such an investment. As Riel and Becker (2008) report, professionally engaged teachers were more likely to (a) have a constructivist teaching philosophy and (b) use ICT more frequently and differently than other teachers (e.g., more tool applications, wider variety of applications). *Although specialization might influence how teachers respond to PDT, how teachers with a high degree of specialization, such as master's or Ph.D. degrees, respond to PDT has not been investigated.*

Focus of the Study

Overall, *there is a knowledge gap in terms of how specific teacher groups respond to in-service PDT on ICT pedagogy*. The present multiple case study aimed to examine how one such group of teachers responded to a PDT program on ICT pedagogy. More specifically, our target was a group of three primary school teachers who participated in an in-service PDT program offered by a University Training Center (hereafter UTC) in Greece. These teachers were selected among the other participants in the PDT program because they deviated maximally from the average teacher in several ways. First, they had a high degree of expertise in the field of science education as they all held relevant Ph.D. degrees. Second, they had a record of academic publications in refereed journals, having authored or coauthored scholarly papers in the area of science education. Third, they were all very experienced, as their teaching experience ranged from 10 to 20 years of service. Fourth, none of them were ICT novices as they all had previously used ICT in their teaching practices. Finally, two of them had participated in national funded research projects which aimed to support science teaching with ICT while the third earned her Ph.D. in a Teacher Education Department in Greece with a reputation for targeting ICT in the teaching of science. For these reasons, *the three teachers had backgrounds which clearly set them apart from the general teacher population*.

Given that these teachers participated in an in-service PDT program, their backgrounds were highly relevant for two main reasons. On the one hand, *their specialization in science education ensured that they were, by definition, among the most theoretically sophisticated teachers in terms of constructivist teaching philosophies and pedagogies*. Based on the literature reviewed above, they were the most likely to respond favorably to technology integration given that constructivist beliefs are related to classroom technology use (Becker & Riel, 2000; Dexter et al., 1999; Hermans et al., 2008; Matzen & Edmunds, 2007; van Braak et al., 2004). On the other hand, *the fact that the three teachers held not only master's but also Ph.D. degrees indicates a very high level of specialization*. Thus, based on the findings of Riel and Becker (2008), this specialization would greatly facilitate in-service PDT training on ICT pedagogy. Therefore, *we assumed that from the whole teacher population these three participants were the most likely to respond favorably to PDT not just on a superficial but also on a substantial level*. In fact, we would go as far as to argue that teachers of such backgrounds represent the ideal audience for seeding technology innovation concepts.

Given that the three teachers who participated in the PDT held constructivist teaching philosophies and had high academic qualifications, this multiple case study examined how they integrated technology in their practices along the sustain-transform continuum.

Given the design challenge of creating instructional scenarios, implementing them in their classrooms, reflecting on them in the context of the PDT, and then revising their initial instructional scenarios the following research questions were addressed:

1. *How did the teachers integrate technology in their designs?*
2. *Where is technology integration situated on the sustain-transform continuum?*

3. *What were teachers' reflections on their designs?*
4. *How did the teachers revise their initial designs?*

The first question aims to provide an account of technology integration in the context of their practicum so as to map out how the different technologies were prescribed to be used. The second question explored whether technology integration supported established practices or transformed them into new directions. The final two questions mapped out the teachers' responses by way of reflection or redesigning to the design challenge, its implementation, and the feedback they received in the UTC.

Method

Participants and Setting

Following the general European Union (EU) policy guidelines, the Greek authorities have adopted a two-level PDT program for primary and secondary teachers. In 2000 the Greek Ministry of Education (MoE) initiated a large EU-funded PDT program of teacher in ICT (see Demetriadis et al., 2003; Jimoyiannis & Komis, 2007, for a comprehensive account of this program). The program had an explicit technological literacy orientation and aimed to develop teachers' ICT skills and competences. It had a total duration of 50 h and was conducted at special school-training centers (STC). Thousands of teachers participated in this ICT training that continued through most of the decade.

In 2007 the MoE established EU-funded UTCs in academic institutions around the country (Jimoyiannis, 2010, provides a detailed account of this program). The objective of these UTCs was to provide high-quality in-service PDT in the area of pedagogical technology integration across the curriculum. The PDT curriculum involved pedagogical issues regarding technology integration in all academic subjects and grade levels. Each PDT program lasted for 350 h and spanned a period of 6 months. All primary and secondary teachers who had successfully completed the former training program were eligible for participation and could apply for a position. After completing the UTC in-service training programs, the participants could take a centralized exam and, if successful, become official ICT mentors in their respective academic subjects. Following the cascade model which was adopted for this PDT program, these teacher mentors would then provide pedagogical ICT training for their fellow teachers in local STCs (see Fig. 1).

Starting in late 2007, three main in-service training programs were offered at the UTC of the University of Thessaly, the authors' host institution. The present work draws on data collected from the third in-service training program (2011–2012). This program followed the general guidelines for successful PDT in terms of form (lectures, seminars and workshops, independent learning, and personal coaching through mentors), *length* (it was extensive covering 350 h and spanned a period of 6 months), and *curriculum* (clear pedagogical rather than technical orientation).

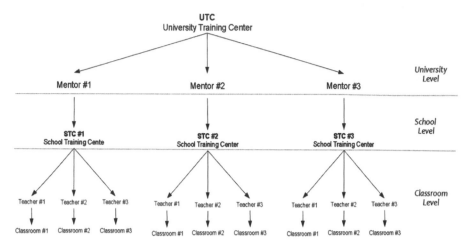

Fig. 1 A cascade model of PDT

A total of eight primary teachers signed up for the third in-service training program. In this work we focus on three of these eight teachers because they naturally formed a group of teachers with very special backgrounds.

PDT Curriculum

The in-service PDT program offered at the UTC in the University of Thessaly comprised a general part and a subject-and-grade-level specific part. The former had a broad, introductory goal and addressed issues related to educational policy in the EU and Greece, history of educational technology, learning theories, and how they relate to educational software, taxonomies of educational software, technical and administration issues related to the school ICT laboratories, and adult education. This general part lasted for 160 h and provided the foundation upon which the second, subject-specific part could build. The second part which lasted for 190 h focused on how to specifically integrate technology in the teaching of various academic subjects and grade levels. Both subject-specific and general-purpose software tools were introduced. Particular emphasis was given to technology integration according to the research literature for each academic subject. To this end, a number of experts specializing in the teaching of academic subjects were contracted as teachers. Following the MoE mandates to ensure the highest possible quality of training, only university staff or Ph.D. holders of various specializations were eligible to teach at the UTCs. In addition to the theory (i.e., general and subject-specific part), the training program also included a short 30-h practicum section. As part of the requirements of the practicum section, the participants had to implement two of their instructional scenarios (a) in their own classrooms and (b) in collaborating STCs. Four teacher ICT mentors who had already successfully completed previous versions of the University of Thessaly UTC in-service PDT program were also contracted to mentor the planning and reflection components of the practicum section.

Design, Procedures, and Data Collection

Following the rationale of qualitative methodology (Lincoln & Guba, 2000), the present study was conducted as a multiple case study (Yin, 2009). The study was designed as a case study in an attempt to understand how teachers of constructivist philosophies and high academic qualifications responded to an in-service PDT program on ICT pedagogy. In this multiple case study design, each teacher was treated as a separate case in order to determine common underlying patterns through replication.

The overall procedure followed is depicted in Fig. 2. The teachers attended the 350-h in-service PDT program which involved both theory and practical applications of ICT across the curriculum. The *theory* section was concluded with the design of ICT-based instructional scenarios. These instructional scenarios were put to practice in the *practicum section*. Each teacher selected two of the instructional scenarios designed in the course of the training and implemented them in their classrooms. The practicum section was followed by a feedback session where the teachers shared their experiences with the group and received feedback and suggestions from their fellow teachers, the teacher ICT mentors, and the authors. In the *reflection* session which followed, the teachers were asked to revise their instructional scenarios in light of their experiences and the feedback received.

Due to the nature and focus of the study, many different types of data were collected in the course of the PDT. For the purposes of the work reported in this chapter, we draw on the following data sources:

(a) *Instructional scenarios.* As artifacts, instructional scenarios were of primary interest as they embodied a teaching plan. The participating teachers developed several instructional scenarios, following a detailed template that was provided as part of the requirements of the training program. The teachers had the freedom to create any instructional scenario, in any subject, using any of the ICT tools available, in any way they saw fit. Following the theory and practice guidelines of the PDT, the main requirement was that the integration of technology in their designs would have to have high added value.

(b) *Group discussions.* Whole-group discussions were also of primary interest as it is during these that the teachers provided explicit accounts of their instructional scenarios, thereby disclosing the rationale behind their designs. Group discussions were held during the feedback session and took place at the UTC with the authors and the ICT-mentor teachers. These group discussions were tape-recorded, and large portions were transcribed verbatim for further analysis.

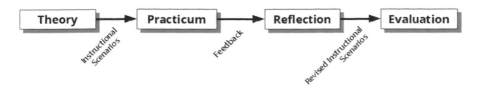

Fig. 2 Overview of the procedure

(c) *Revised instructional scenarios.* Revised instructional scenarios were meant to embody teachers' reflections following the implementation of instructional scenarios in their classrooms and the feedback session that followed. By reflecting on the elements the teachers perceived as problematic, revised instructional scenarios helped pinpoint the "corrective" measures needed. The revised instructional scenarios were also formally required for evaluation purposes.

(d) *Participant observations and field notes.* In the course of the practicum and reflection sections, the authors took various notes of informal communications with the participants (e.g., personal e-mails, informal discussions), questions posed in the practicum section, and problems which surfaced in planning and teaching. All such observations and notes were then combined with the rest of the data to facilitate the analysis.

Data Analysis

Instructional scenarios and revised instructional scenarios were the data sources through which we addressed the first two research questions. They were analyzed following established qualitative data analysis procedures. For each teacher case, this involved data reduction, data display, conclusion drawing, and verifications (Miles & Huberman, 1994). Each instructional scenario comprised several activities, and for the purposes of this work we used the instructional activity as our main unit of analysis. Following a qualitative content analysis approach, we initially used rough descriptive categories to classify technology use in each instructional activity, arriving at general profiles of ICT use per instructional scenario. Subsequent passes led to successive generalizations and mutual agreement between the researchers on the main categories of technology use in the teacher designs. The categories used are described next. These categories were used as indicators of constructivist theoretical underpinnings for the teachers and as a means of assessing which constructivist principles found their way to the instructional scenarios.

1. T*echnology tools.* This category included the various types of software tools used such as stand-alone software or network applications (e.g., web browser). This category assessed the presence of a constructivists' preference for a multitude of information sources so as to address students with different proclivities and intensify the social embeddedness of the information provided. Although a stand-alone software may indeed be specially designed in addressing particular disciplinary needs, the current availability of easily accessible learning resources through the Web makes them natural candidates for lessons addressed to digital natives.

2. *Information modality.* This category addressed the types of content that the technology made available and included text, images, video, and audio. This category assessed the importance of providing information of different modalities so as to supply multiple different representations of information.

3. *Information context*. This category described the nature of the information sources used, distinguishing between educational and authentic sources. It assessed the extent to which authentic information resources and real-time data possibly of local and personal interest were employed in the instructional scenarios. Although including information in the context of school necessitates distancing from the official sources by learned communities, the bulk of information available on the web by varying sources of expertise makes it practically feasible to assess authentic information sources.

4. Students' role in *technology use*. This category referred to who used technology (student vs. teacher), whether technology was used as a tool to process information (yes/no), the locus of choice of technology tools and sources (student vs. teacher), the locus of choice relative to how technology tools were used (critical decisions regarding technology use were made by the students vs. the teacher), and the mode of technology use (individual vs. group use). This category assessed various indicators of constructivist concerns for promoting student agency in the learning process. From a constructivist learning viewpoint, (a) students rather than teachers are expected to be the main users of technology, (b) students are expected to use technology as a tool to process information rather than simply consume information, and (c) students are supported in making the choices regarding technology use.

5. *Technology function*. This category examined the specific role technology played in terms of learning for every instructional activity. Technology was used for providing information, providing representations (without manipulation by the students), and providing opportunity for limited simulation (manipulation demands were minimal). This category assessed the constructivist tendency to harness the potential created by the access to rich information sources and to strong tools for data exploration (e.g., to assess rich information sources, to synthesize information from various—often divergent—sources, to use real-time data to draw conclusions) and to use the visualization affordances of the technology (e.g., to conceptually facilitate the transition from abstract to the concrete, to use multiple representations perhaps in parallel to student manipulation). Finally, since all instructional scenarios were related to science education, it also assessed the presence of technology uses that are in sync with current constructivist learning environments in science education which capitalize (a) explorations of a physical phenomenon in ways impossible in real life, (b) experimentation (hypothesis formation and testing), and (c) developing science process skills.

Each instructional scenario activity was assessed with respect to the categories mentioned above. All six instructional scenarios we analyzed were related to science education, four belonged to earth science, one to physics, and one to environmental studies. The analysis of the transcriptions of the group discussions and the participant observations and field notes focused on themes pertinent to the third research question, i.e., *how the teachers reflected on the design challenge and its implementation*. On the one hand we examined if teachers thought that their designs reflected significant departures from their current practices. On the other hand, we looked at whether they experienced the design of instructional scenarios as a challenging activity. These data were triangulated with the teachers' assessment comments about the implementation of their instructional scenarios that were included in their instructional scenario reports.

Results

Technology Integration

The first question focuses on how the teachers integrated technology in their designs. The instructional scenarios were the main data sources used to answer in this part of the analysis. In order to identify patterns, each instructional scenario for every teacher was treated as a separate case. Despite differentiations, the analysis of the instructional scenarios revealed similar patterns of technology integration. Due to space limitations, one instructional scenario per teacher was randomly selected and is presented here.

Tables 1, 2, and 3 present the results of the analysis of one lesson that each teacher planned and carried out in the practicum section with respect to the categories of technology tools, information modality, information context, and technology func-

Table 1 Teacher A: Grade: 6; academic subject: science; unit: physics, analysis, and synthesis of light

Technology tool	Information modality	Information context	Technology function
Web browser	Text, image	Educational	Information provider
Web browser	Video	Educational	Information provider
			Representation provider
Web browser	Text, image	Authentic	Information provider
Web browser	Animation	Educational	Limited simulation
Web browser	Text, image, video, animation	Educational	Information provider
			Representation provider
			Limited simulation
Web browser	Video	Authentic	Information provider

Table 2 Teacher B: Grade: 4, academic subject: environmental studies, unit: the weather

Technology tool	Information modality	Information context	Technology function
Web browser	Text, image, tables, charts	Authentic	Information provider
Web browser	Text, images, tables, charts	Authentic	Information provider
Web browser	Text, image	Educational	Information provider
Stand-alone software	Text, image, animation	Educational	Information provider
			Representation provider

Table 3 Teacher C: Grade: 6, academic subject: geography, unit: day–night cycle

Technology	Information modality	Information context	Technology function
Stand-alone software	Animation	Educational	Limited simulation
Stand-alone software	Image	Educational	Representation provider
Stand-alone software	Animation	Educational	Information provider
			Limited simulation

tion. Each lesson was actualized within two periods, which is approximately 90 min. Each table row represents the different instructional activities in each lesson.

As can be seen in Tables 1, 2, and 3, technology use involved (a) digital learning resources and (b) interactive software applications. More specifically, taking into consideration all of the designs, technology use was characterized by the use of both general-purpose tools (such as a web browser) and the use of special-purpose educational software. The browser was primarily used for accessing information on the World Wide Web and, to a lesser extent, for running web-based simulations and animations. Although Web 2.0 sources (blog, wiki) were used in two cases by teacher A, they were employed as information sources and the students were not involved with the more constructive functionalities of these tools. The other type of technology use involved stand-alone educational software. It should be noted however that the stand-alone software that was used was the result of research work aiming towards addressing student misconceptions in the relevant natural science domains. Overall, the browser reigned as the main software tool as it was dominant in designs of two out of the three teachers.

In terms of modality, Tables 1, 2, and 3 show the presence of not only the textual mode but also visual modes. Visual modes included realistic videos, simulations, realistic videos that were annotated, realistic images, and charts. This variety is in accordance to the professed constructivism of the teachers. On the other hand auditory modes have attracted less attention.

In terms of authenticity, only some of the information sources used were authentic ones. The majority of the sources were educational, i.e., were tailor-made for educational purposes. Moreover even the authentic sources that were used were authoritative in nature, thus coming as close as possible to univocal educational sources. However the sources were appropriately selected so as to suit the targeted students' age range.

Finally, with respect to the category of students' role in technology use, the results do not show much variation. In all of the designs, technology was exclusively used by the students who collaborated in small groups to complete the assignments. However, technology tools and sources were explicitly selected by the teachers. Moreover, the ways both the technology tools and the information sources were to be used by the students were highly prescribed by the teachers through worksheets. The worksheet was the main tool through which the teachers tried to balance some freedom of choice for the students with a detailed specification of the technology use. Finally, technology tools were mainly used as a gateway to information, not as tools to process data and information or otherwise transform it.

On the whole, the designs of the instructional scenarios were influenced by constructivist principles. The students were the main users of various information sources and simulations in ways that facilitated the expression of their alternative conceptions and a reality check of these conceptions. Nonetheless, two constraining factors characterize most of the categories:

(a) Limitations of openness: Capitalizing on Web 2.0 functionalities, accessing conflicting information sources, and accessing people outside the walls of classroom are all nonexistent in the teacher designs.
(b) Limitations of students' agency: How and for what purpose technology is used are prescribed by the teacher, and any source of challenge (like conflictual information) is avoided.

Technology Integration Along the Sustain-Transform Continuum

The second research question focused on the technology leverage for implementing science education instructional scenarios that were clearly going past current practices in Greece. The initial instructional scenarios and the revised ones were the main data sources for this analysis. Teachers' reflections were also used as a secondary data source but are reported in detail in part c of this section. The main functions of technology can be seen in the rightmost column of Tables 1, 2, and 3. More specifically, when situating the function that technology performs in the context of the instructional scenarios we arrived at two main categories that express the leverage of technology: *accessibility* and *visualization*. The first refers to making accessible content which would be inaccessible without technology. The second refers to the visualization of physical phenomena and models in the context of providing 2D/3D static or dynamic representations as well as other forms of representation.

The first main function that technology played in the designs involved making inaccessible information easily tangible. For example teacher B used a meteorological site run by a state agency to make accessible to students real-time data on the current weather in different sites in Greece and Europe. Undoubtedly, using technology to access information which would be inaccessible through other means utilizes the potential of technology to add currency, relevance, authenticity, multimodality, and interest to one's teaching. Overall, the teachers used the information resources to enrich the curriculum content which had to be delivered. *On the other hand technology was not used to support engagement with students'* own concerns and questions. Moreover, once the information was accessed no further demands of creative craftsmanship either in processing the information or in interpreting the information were put on the students. The absence of conflictual or difficult-to-interpret information was further minimizing opportunities for this craftsmanship to be needed.

The second main technology function involved visualization. Instructional scenarios, worksheets, presentations of the instructional scenarios, and reflections on the instructional scenarios all centered on some form of presentation to the students.

As the analysis of the instructional scenarios suggests, although technology was used by the students themselves, *technology was largely used for demonstration purposes* in order to "show" something as clearly as possible, so that (a) student misconceptions are eradicated through cognitive conflict and (b) students are provided with crucial external representations that facilitate the understanding of the intended concept or process. For example, in the course of an instructional activity teacher C asked the students to stop a simulation showing coordinated representations of the Earth and its position relative to the Sun at specific time intervals. After each simulation freeze, the students had to answer specific questions which were given in the worksheet. Undoubtedly, supporting visualization *is one of the main strengths of technology*, and it is understandable why the teachers made such an extensive use of technology-enabled visualizations. On the whole, the teachers did take into consideration students' alternative conceptions and constructed sequences of predefined experiences alternating raw production of students' ideas with *the "corrective" experience of superb visualization afforded by technology*.

When considering the whole corpus of the instructional scenarios the following common patterns emerged. First, simulations appeared in the teachers' designs, but their use was extremely limited. For example, in the case of the coordinated representations time was the only variable that could change. Moreover the directions in the student worksheets specified the specific values of the time variable where the students were instructed to freeze the simulation. Consequently, while on the surface the students appear to be actively controlling the simulation, from a learning point of view nothing much would have been different had the teachers used a video projector for a whole-class display of the simulation and had they posed similar questions to the whole class.

Second, technology use by students for constructing hypotheses or transforming and representing knowledge or managing the tasks was extremely sparse. There is only one exception to this pattern, teacher C, who on one occasion used GoogleEarth to create limited opportunities of manipulation and provided students with a genuine inquiry question. However the conditions were unfavorable (time allowed, place of the activity in the overall design) and rendered such an inquiry practically impossible.

Third, technology-enabled visualizations seemed to compete with physical artifact-enabled visualizations as if the two were struggling to occupy the same slot in the script of the didactical sequence. There are several manifestations of this. On the one hand, simulations were used sequentially and not in parallel with more traditional "experiments." For instance, teacher A introduced a simulation quite some time after a relevant experiment. On the other hand, teachers underplayed the visualizing and representational affordances of hands-on artifacts (such as the globe, construction, and manipulation of 3D artifacts). The teachers did not use the opportunity to combine digital simulations with the use of hands-on artifacts; instead, they showed an extreme faith on the efficiency of digital visualization as a learning tool. Finally, technology was often used (especially by teachers B and C) to stage a guided presentation of the features of the visualized physical model and to compare these features with selected and heavily transformed pseudo-authentic digital materials. In this final case digital reality took the place of physical reality both in terms of the experimental means and of the observations.

Teachers' Reflection on the Design Challenge and its Implementation

The third research question centered on teachers' reflections on the whole PDT experience and specifically looked at the teachers' perceptions of the design challenge and its implementation.

Technology integration as a challenge

Overall, the teachers did not experience the designs in the practicum section of the PDT as a real challenge. This is not surprising given their high level of expertise. As teacher A noted in the discussion of the reflection session:

> I have been using ICT in my teaching before this [PDT] program. I was certainly using ICT in Science Education which is a subject I know really well. So, it's not that I learned something new that I've just started using in my teaching…That doesn't mean I did not profit somehow from attending the PDT. It [ICT] was more useful for other [academic] subjects. But here [science education], since I taught in a domain that I know well, I feel that I would have still delivered even if I had not attended the PDT (Teacher-A)

Here the teacher clearly delineates what she thought of the PDT, stressing that she did not find it informative enough in her domain of expertise. Overall, the teachers who participated in this study were very confident with their theoretical underpinnings in science education and often cited relevant sources in their reflections. For example, in the following excerpt, teacher A explains the theoretical guidelines that guided their designs:

> From the point of view of current approaches to Instruction in the Natural science, learning is not just acquiring information but a continuous process of resolving of inner cognitive conflicts. Those conflicts are created and resolved through active participation, communication and interaction between the student and the learning and social environment in the classroom (Teacher-A)

This statement clearly reflects the constructivist convictions of the teacher, reflecting both the nature of science learning and an instructional approach to science teaching.

In another occasion teacher C articulated his own stance about when the use of ICT may be productive, largely corroborating our conclusions (section on "Technology Integration Along the Sustain-Transform Continuum" above) about the added value that teachers attributed to technology

> … my conclusion regarding the use of ICT or what we call "digital resources" etc. is that you aim to use ICT whenever you have no particular or no other ways of representation, alternative ways of representation, presentation of a new concept or phenomenon and the second way [of ICT use] is to use ICT in conjunction with the experiment etc. what we call multiple representations, that is as an complementary medium, as a supplementary tool to promote better understanding (Teacher-B)

Teachers' openness to change

Given that the main functions of technology involved information access and visualization, in the group discussion session the authors suggested other ways of technology integration, linking back to the theory and practices of the PDT program. It was pointed out to the teachers that technology might have been well integrated in their designs, but this integration was limited with respect to the potential of technology to support new forms of teaching and learning. Teachers' responses to our proposals were completely unexpected. Not only did they defend their designs but also claimed that both their designs and the ways technology was integrated in these designs were nothing short of exceptional. From our point of view, it was puzzling that the teachers did not seem to be open to suggestions and refused to even consider other proposals for contemplating new ways of technology integration which would have resulted in a more substantial level of technology use, a level that would have entailed a change in the teaching practices. *In an effort to ground the discussion in a concrete way and since visualization was a pivotal point in all of their designs,* each participant was asked to explicitly describe the function of visualization in terms of learning for his/her design. While the UTC training program provided a broad conceptual framework for understanding technology use across the curriculum, *the teachers approached visualization ad hoc in their designs; that is, they neither examined visualization in terms of a learning theory or a specific conceptualization of learning nor did they consider the special mediating role visualization was to play in their students' learning.* It was as if visualizations themselves would somehow provide most of the support needed by the students leaving teachers with the task of selecting and pacing the appropriate technological tools to supply the visualizations in a "just-in-time" fashion. Therefore, *there appeared to be dissociation between the concepts presented in the training curriculum and the concepts the teachers invoked to explain why exactly they chose to use technology in the ways they did.* Essentially, they conceived technology as a gateway to information, fitting a slot in the science education teaching script that they had mastered as opposed to addressing the technology's learning functions and the role of technology in mediating the learning of science content.

Teachers' Revised Instructional Scenarios

In addition to designing instructional scenarios, the PDT also involved implementing these scenarios in real-world settings and the teachers tried them out in their classes in the practicum section of the program. Due to the PDT design, the teachers were asked to reflect on their experiences and to describe in detail how they would change their designs based on their experiences with (a) the actual technology use in their classes and (b) the feedback they received in the reflection session. More specifically, they were asked to revise their instructional scenarios as they see fit so as to achieve the maximum level of technology added value for the same learning objectives. The resulting accounts of technology use would be idealized, free from any sorts of constraints (time, curricular, infrastructure, student background knowledge, etc.). *The analysis of these "idealized" instructional scenarios indicated that the teachers stood by their original designs. The only changes made were minor ones and were unrelated to technology use or function per se.* Consequently, information access and visualization remained the main technology functions in the revised instructional scenarios.

Discussion

The last century has been characterized by recurrent visions of transforming education through various technologies. The high hopes that technology integration into teaching practices would lead to their transformation have not been validated (Condie et al., 2007; Cuban, 2001; Cuban et al., 2001; Donnelly et al., 2011; Eteokleous, 2008; Hayes, 2007; Hermans et al., 2008; Li, 2007; Norton et al., 2000; OFSTED, 2004; Player-Koro, 2013; Prestridge, 2012). Teachers either resist using technology or use technology to sustain rather than transform their practices (Donnelly et al., 2011; Law & Chow, 2008a; Player-Koro, 2013). This failure to transform education through technology has been attributed to first- and second-order barriers (Ertmer, 1999, 2005). As research shows, first-order barriers are a necessary but not a sufficient condition for technology integration. Therefore second-order barriers need to be addressed, and one of the main tools to address them has been teacher training, both preservice and in-service. While there is a substantial body of research on what makes professional development effective, the importance of factors related to teachers' backgrounds has not been thoroughly explored yet (Coburn, 2004; Penuel et al., 2007). The present work contributes to this knowledge gap by examining how a group of teachers who had constructivist teaching philosophies and high academic qualifications responded to an extensive in-service PDT program on ICT pedagogy. The special characteristics of the teacher participants provide a measure of the limits of PDTs as a means to promote technology integration in educational practices in transformative ways.

Due to both the teachers' characteristics and the design of the PDT they participated in, there were no first-order barriers hampering technology integration. With regard to second-order barriers, *these teachers were science education experts and science education is a field where constructivism is championed more than any other educational field* (Duit & Treagust, 1998). It should also be noted that in Greece most Ph.D. dissertations in science education adopt some version of the constructivist paradigm. As the literature shows, teachers who have constructivist beliefs are more likely than other teachers to use technology and also tend to use it in more student-centered ways (Becker & Riel, 2000; Dexter et al., 1999; Hermans et al., 2008; Matzen & Edmunds, 2007; van Braak et al., 2004). On the other hand, one of the potential barriers to technology integration is the time and effort required by teachers to adopt an innovation (Hayes, 2007; Penuel et al., 2007; Sandholtz & Reilly, 2004; Tyack & Tobin, 1994). Teachers are often reluctant to embrace an innovation because there is a lot of work involved in adopting it. In our case, however, the teachers were already accomplished, i.e., had a sound theoretical foundation which in principle should require minimal work and effort on their part regarding technology integration. Overall, because the teachers did not have much theoretical ground to cover, we expected that their responses to PDT would be very positive in two principal ways. First, in terms of technology integration, we expected that *technology would be instrumental in the success of a lesson.* Second, we expected that *technology would not be a mere add-on to current teaching practices but it would leverage them leading to transformations.*

The *former* was fully corroborated by our findings as *the teachers integrated technology in their lessons in a fitting way, closely following the general principles of constructivist learning.* Firstly, the students themselves were the main users of technology. That did not mean the use of technology for drill and practice purposes as is common for novice teachers to do. A wide assortment of digital learning resources was used in the instructional scenarios, giving them currency and relevance. These means were effective in promoting student engagement and facilitated the students' recall of relevant prior knowledge. Secondly, collaborative work and learning were promoted as the students worked in small groups to complete the assignments. Students were indeed prompted to discuss the information and visualizations provided by technology, and certainly some questions could be solved through the joint effort of the students. Thirdly, technology was instrumental for the actualization of these designs and served the teachers' goal of achieving conceptual change in the science topics targeted in each lesson. The teachers themselves reported positive results through assessments they had embedded in the instructional scenarios and realized during the implementation of their designs. Based on teachers' backgrounds and expertise, such high levels of technology integration were hardly surprising and, as corroborated by their own comments, were to a certain degree mastered before following the current PDT program.

The latter, however, was *not supported by our findings. The analysis of the instructional scenarios and in particular the specific technology functions the teachers used indicate that technology was assimilated into their current practices.* To illustrate the nature of this assimilation, we will consider in some detail the dominant instructional paradigm of current science education practices in Greece. More specifically, this paradigm is an adaptation of the model of the "inquiry-scaffolding teaching method" (Schmidkunz & Lindemann, 1992, as reported in Apostolakis et al., 2006). The science education teacher books for grades 5 and 6 elaborate on this didactical model and provide the general guidelines for its use. According to the rationale covered in the teacher books, each lesson follows a specific sequence because

> students' participation in inquiry is not unguided, but follows specific stages and is guided through specific actions, so as to be practically realizable. At every point the teacher can follow how students learn (Apostolakis et al., 2006, p. 32).

This sequence includes a first stage where the teacher transforms the subject he/she has to teach into an initial question or problem. Relevant prior knowledge is brought forth, and students are supported in proposing their ideas ("hypotheses") about the solution to the problem. Student misconceptions surface at this stage. Then the students perform one or more experiments that the teacher has selected for them. As the teacher book suggests, during this phase the teacher should not be too intrusive, allowing students to "really engage in inquiry." However, the time constraints of the implementation indicate that the authors of the teacher guide consider the experiments so well chosen that the students are either expected to arrive themselves at the intended conclusions or that they will be easily convinced by the arguments provided by the teacher. In the next stage, the teacher book proposes to hold a discussion through which the class arrives at the intended interpretation of the experiment and gradually towards answering the initial problem. There is no providence for the cases where students might propose new ideas that could be tested through alterations to the experiments or through new experiments. While the experiments do address students' misconceptions, they do not leave much space for student initiative and creativity in the unfolding of the inquiry. During the closing part of the lesson the teacher guide recommends that students compare their final answers with the ones they gave initially. In the final stage proposed by the teacher book, students should work on teacher-assigned exercises that are expected to lead to a deeper understanding of the science material covered.

As outlined in the teacher guide above, the dominant science education paradigm in Greece is strongly concerned about the pacing of the instruction, trying to balance its constructivist theoretical underpinnings and the appropriation of conceptual change literature with constraints that are inherent in the Greek educational system. Therefore it does not take into account students' own needs and the scaffolding demands placed on the teachers should they choose to support these needs. Out of the four main ICT affordances that Webb (2005) outlined in her review of science learning with ICT-rich environments, this dominant paradigm is compatible only with the following two: (a) promoting cognitive development and (b) relating science to students' own experiences and data in the broader real world. The other two affordances namely

> increasing students' self-management and enabling them to track their progress so that teachers' time is freed to focus on supporting and enabling students learning; and facilitating data collection and presentation of data that helps students to understand and interpret the data, and additionally frees students' time so that they have more time to focus on developing conceptual understanding (Webb, 2005)

are not compatible with the concern about teacher control expressed in the above model. This view is in line with other literature proposals for using ICT in science education. For example, Chang (2013) argued that addressing student needs is probably a main factor in successful scaffolding of science learning through simulations. On the other hand, Osborne and Hennessy (2003) noted the critical role ICT can play for introducing students to scientific inquiry, for developing hypothesis formation and testing, for advancing science process skills, and for solving open-ended problems through various technological tools.

The examination of instructional scenarios against this backdrop leads to the conclusion that the teachers incorporated technology in their existing practices. There are two main indications of this. *First, the way that information was used in the instructional scenarios expressed a strong concern for efficiency in time management: all the information aimed to direct students towards the intended "correct" interpretation.* Even in the cases where authentic sources were used, they were as "school like" as possible: they were used in ways that would not demand judgment and evaluation, only the selection of bits and pieces of relevant information (for an alternative way of using information sources see Bell, 2000). Real-time, detailed, complex, and authentic data sources were utilized in ways that looked more like a guided tour. Finally, Web 2.0 resources were only used to access authoritative information indicating an entrenched practice that avoids introducing real-life conflict in the classroom. *Second, technology was exclusively used in order to provide authoritative information.* There is a striking similarity here between this technology role and the role "experiments" play in the "inquiry-scaffolding teaching method" (as adapted in the teacher guide).

Overall, *the ways teachers integrated technology in their instructional scenarios do not show any significant departure from established science education practices in Greece.* Considering teachers' backgrounds this was not expected as the conditions for transformation were very favorable. Zhao, Pugh, Sheldon, and Byers (2002) reported that one of the factors that might affect classroom technology innovations is the distance from existing practice. In our case this distance was relatively short given the teachers' starting point. Consequently, the teachers did not have much ground to cover in order to integrate technology in a transformative manner, i.e., along the lines proposed by Osborne and Hennessy (2003).

Interestingly enough, not only was technology merely assimilated into existing practices, but *the teachers also refused to question their teaching practices and were not open to suggestions along this direction, that is, despite* the persistent efforts from the authors to explicitly point out the limitations in the ways they had integrated technology in their teaching in the practicum section. In retrospect, there are several possible explanations for this type of resistance. *First*, as the participants in our study were already accomplished teachers and researchers, *they probably did not come to the PDT thinking that they would need to radically transform their teaching practices*, much less of course in science education which was their domain of expertise. In all likelihood, they considered that such radical transformations of their teaching conceptions and practices had already taken place in the course of their professional histories. *Second*, resistance might be due to the fact that the teachers felt that the level of ICT integration they had already achieved was part of the roadmap that other teachers (that they soon would be mentoring) would have to pass through in order to achieve more highbrow goals. In this sense, they were probably excusing themselves from putting cognitive resources in the direction of further pedagogical experimentation. *Third*, it could well be that we have experienced a ceiling effect as *the teachers were already accomplished and there was no room for progress*. Unlike other PDT studies (e.g., Dwyer, Ringstaff, & Sandholtz, 1990; Levin & Wadmany, 2005: Prestridge, 2012) in which the entry level of teachers who participated was that of an "average," "traditional" teacher, in our study the three teacher participants could not be considered "average" or "traditional" by any measure. *Finally*, it could be that the constructivist practices teachers had adopted might have been producing better results in validated tests than the practices of the average Greek teacher who still strives to meet the guidelines of current teacher guides. This means that they did not have many reasons to feel "pedagogical discontentment" (Southerland, Sowell,

Blanchard, & Granger, 2011) with the teaching model they were following. It is likely that neither their former practices nor the PDT program succeeded in generating the "pedagogical discontent" needed for energizing the teachers' search for ICT integration of higher quality.

In terms of the sustain-transform technology integration continuum, we argue that *the responses of the teachers to the in-service PDT marks the upper limit of the possible range of technology integration*, at least in the context of Greece. Our findings suggest that *the teachers in our study who were very advanced theory-wise and already using fully compatible teaching practices could not go past a certain degree of technology use, that of sustaining existing practices.* Although there were no first- or second-order barriers, the *highest level of integration reached was to use technology as a gateway to information and supplying visual representations.* When considering this against the dominant science educational paradigm in Greek education we see that neither of these uses suggests a transformation of teaching practices. Interestingly enough, the teachers did not significantly modify their initial designs, even after (a) trying them out in their classroom and (b) receiving feedback from the authors which highlighted several limitations and missed opportunities for adopting new technology-based practices. This suggests that their vision of technology integration did not go past the ways they were integrating technology in their practices before attending the PDT. As our findings indicate, a more substantial level of technology integration, namely one that would go past information accessibility and visualization and move towards new teaching practices, is probably not very likely even in the most favorable conditions, i.e., with teachers who have constructivist teaching philosophies and very high qualifications.

Implications

The findings of the present study have important implications for in-service PDT on ICT pedagogy. If accomplished teachers can only go so far after attending an extensive in-service PDT program such as the one described in this study, then one can only wonder how far average teachers might go in terms of technology integration so as to achieve the much desired transformation. Not only did the participants not move past a given level of integration, but they also refused to consider other types of technology use. If this is the upper limit obtainable by teachers who hold constructivist philosophies and are highly qualified, how realistic is it to expect any further transformation of teaching practices through technology? That is, *if technology integration does not lead to teaching practice transformation in the most favorable conditions, as the ones described in this study, then perhaps the time has come to rethink PDT programs in ICT integration.*

PDT has come to the spotlight because of the importance of second-order barriers for technology integration. As second-order barriers are considered to be intrinsic to teachers, the focus that much of PDT literature puts on teachers is understandable. In the end, the teacher is broadly acknowledged as the most critical mediating factor for classroom technology use (Ertmer, 2005). The present study clearly indicates potential limitations of current PDT programs if our objective is the transformation of educational practices through ICT. We argue that to address these limitations we will need to reconceptualize the way we approach in-service PDT programs on ICT pedagogy. As we see it, there are three issues pertinent to this reconceptualization.

First, we *need to redefine what technology integration really means*. We need to be very explicit about the range of integration as well as its nature. For example, if the objective is simply to integrate technology so as to enrich the curriculum, then the ways the teachers in our study integrated technology in their lessons are exemplary. From this point of view, current implementations of PDT programs can be very effective. However, if the objective is to integrate technology so as to change current teaching practices in specific directions (such as to foster student-centered learning, meaningful learning, problem-based learning), then the ways our participants integrated technology in their teaching practices are quite limited. It is imperative to define clearly what this direction actually is. In this sense, technology integration would have to be explicitly described not only in terms of teaching practices but also in terms of student learning and the crucial mediating role technology can play in order to achieve this learning. Recently, other researchers have also called for a reconceptualization of what it means to teach with technology and stressed the importance of sketching out such a vision (e.g., Ertmer & Ottenbreit-Leftwich, 2010).

Second, *we need to address other possible background variables that could influence the effectiveness of PDTs*. For example, the presence of pedagogical discontent (Southerland et al., 2011) that was mentioned above is such a variable that might make a difference. Such variables need not be strictly personal. They may be constructs that are strongly determined by the context of teachers' practices. For example even teachers with constructivist beliefs may not have the opportunity in terms of time or available assessment instruments to test the limits of their current designs and thus to experience pedagogical discontent. Or they may not feel psychologically safe to try innovations because they do not have the administrative support to try out very innovative designs in order to conceptualize and desire new goals for their students.

Finally, while a focus on the individual teacher is indispensable, we need to *broaden this focus to take into consideration not just the teachers themselves but also the contexts in which they function*. Ultimately, the "grammar of schooling" (Tyack & Tobin, 1994) is very important as it is these contexts that shape teacher beliefs and attitudes. Take for example the ACOT report conclusion, in which Dwyer et al. (1990) argue:

> Although the direction of change in ACOT classrooms is promising, the pace of change is slow, for even when innovative teachers alter their practices and beliefs, the cultural norms continue to support lecture-based instruction, subject-centered curriculum, and measurement-driven accountability. (p. 2).

This clearly delineates the power current norms have in shaping teacher thinking and consequently to teacher responses to ICT integration—even for innovative teachers. The importance of the context of an innovation has been stressed (Penuel et al., 2007; Starkey, 2010). Therefore, regardless of technology familiarity and constructivist beliefs about learning, the material conditions of actual practice (i.e., curriculum, legislation, high stakes testing, working conditions, resources) exert significant pressures on how teachers eventually come to view innovations in general and technology in particular. As it has been demonstrated, all these influences might eventually shape an object of activity for teachers that is markedly different to the one envisaged by educators, reformers, researchers, parents, politicians, and other stakeholders (Karasavvidis, 2009). For the most part, PDT research has failed to employ theoretical frameworks that take into consideration not only the teacher—as the alleviation of second-order barriers clearly demands—but also other contextual factors that have the power to shape teacher thoughts and practices. Future studies need to draw on theoretical frameworks that help conceptualize PDT programs in systemic terms so that the individual teacher no longer remains the focal point of attention and the sole unit of analysis.

Conclusion

The current research addressed a gap in the current literature with respect to the way teacher background properties such as expertise and qualifications might influence the effectiveness of PDT programs. The first main study finding is that even after attending an extensive in-service PDT program, three teachers with constructivist teaching philosophies and high academic qualifications integrated technology in ways that sustained rather than transformed their existing practices. The second study finding is that the teacher participants found it very challenging to consider other types of technology integration that would be more on the transform end of the sustain-transform continuum. As teachers who hold constructivist beliefs and have high levels of qualification are expected to exhibit the most favorable response to PDT programs, this work raises serious concerns with respect to how far contemporary PDT programs can go in the direction of transforming teaching practices through technology. Despite its main limitation, namely the small number of teachers who participated, we think that the present study contributes to delineating the upper limit of technology integration that could be realistically expected from mainstream PDT programs. Further research in this direction should take the "grammar of schooling" into consideration and carefully examine the shaping influences of context on teacher beliefs and, consequently, on their responses to PDT.

References

Angers, J., & Machtmes, K. (2005). An ethnographic-case study of beliefs, context factors, and practices of teachers integrating technology. *The Qualitative Report, 10*(4), 771–794. Retrieved from http://www.nova.edu/ssss/QR/QR10-4/angers.pdf.

Apostolakis, E., Panagopoulou, E., Savvas, S., Tsagliotis, N., Pantazis, G., Sotiriou, S., Tolias, B., Tsagogeorga, A., & Kalkanis, G. (2006). Science: Teacher guide – 5th grade [In Greek]. Athens.

Baggott la Velle, L. M., McFarlane, A., John, P., & Brawn, R. (2004). According to the promises: The subculture of school science, teachers' pedagogic identity and the challenge of ICT. *Education, Communication & Information, 4*, 109–129.

Becker, H. J. (2000a). Findings from the teaching, learning, and computing survey: Is Larry Cuban right? *Education Policy Analysis Archives, 8*(51), n51.

Becker, H. J. (2000b). How exemplary computer-using teachers differ from other teachers: Implications for realizing the potential of computers in schools. *Contemporary Issues in Technology and Teacher Education [Online Serial], 1*(2), 274–293.

Becker, H. J., & Riel, M. M. (2000). *Teacher professional engagement and constructivist-compatible computer use.* (Tech. Rep. No. 7). CRITO, University of California at Irvine, CA.

Bell, P. (2000). Scientific arguments as learning artifacts: Designing for learning from the web with KIE. *International Journal of Science Education, 22*(8), 797–817.

Chang, H. Y. (2013). Teacher guidance to mediate student inquiry through interactive dynamic visualizations. *Instructional Science, 41*(5), 895–920.

Coburn, C. E. (2004). Beyond decoupling: Rethinking the relationship between the institutional environment and the classroom. *Sociology of Education, 77*(3), 211–244.

Condie, R., Munro, B., Seagraves, L., & Kenesson, S. (2007). *The impact of ICT in schools – A landscape review.* Coventry: Becta. Retrieved from http://publications.becta.org.uk/download.cfm?resID=28221.

Cuban, L. (2001). *Oversold and underused. Computers in the classroom.* Cambridge: Harvard University Press.

Cuban, L., Kirkpatrick, H., & Peck, C. (2001). High access and low use of technologies in high school classrooms: Explaining an apparent paradox. *American Educational Research Journal, 38*(4), 813–834.

Demetriadis, S., Barbas, A., Molohides, A., Palaigeorgiou, G., Psillos, D., Vlahavas, I., et al. (2003). "Cultures in negotiation": Teachers' acceptance/resistance attitudes considering the infusion of technology into schools. *Computers & Education, 41*(1), 19–37.

Dexter, S., Anderson, R. E., & Becker, H. J. (1999). Teachers' views of computers as catalysts for changes in their teaching practice. *Journal of Research on Computing in Education, 31*(3), 221–239.

Donnelly, D., McGarr, O., & O'Reilly, J. (2011). A framework for teachers' integration of ICT into their classroom practice. *Computers & Education, 57*, 1469–1483.

Duit, R., & Treagust, D. (1998). Learning in science - From behaviourism towards social constructivism and beyond. In B. Fraser & K. Tobin (Eds.), *International handbook of science education* (pp. 3–26). Dordrecht, The Netherlands: Kluwer Academic Publishers.

Dwyer, D. C., Ringstaff, C., & Sandholtz, J. H. (1990). *Teacher beliefs and practices Part I: Patterns of change. The evolution of teachers' instructional beliefs and practices in high-access-to-technology classrooms. First-fourth year findings.* ACOT Report #8. Retrieved from ftp://www.grsc.k12.ar.us/ISTESTUFF/New%20stuff/ACOT%20Report.pdf

Ertmer, P. (1999). Addressing first- and second-order barriers to change: Strategies for technology implementation. *Educational Technology Research and Development, 47*(4), 47–61.

Ertmer, P. A. (2005). Teacher pedagogical beliefs: The final frontier in our quest for technology integration? *Educational Technology Research and Development, 53*(4), 25–39.

Ertmer, P. A., & Ottenbreit-Leftwich, A. T. (2010). Teacher technology change: How knowledge, confidence, beliefs, and culture intersect. *Journal of Research on Technology in Education, 42*(3), 255–284.

Ertmer, P., Ottenbreit-Leftwich, A., & York, C. (2007). Exemplary technology use: Teachers' perceptions of critical factors. *Journal of Computing in Teacher Education, 23*(2), 55–61.

Eteokleous, N. (2008). Evaluating computer technology integration in a centralized school system. *Computers & Education, 51*(2), 669 686.

Garet, M. S., Porter, A. C., Desimone, L., Birman, B. F., & Yoon, K. S. (2001). What makes professional development effective? Results from a national sample of teachers. *American Educational Research Journal, 38*(4), 915–945.

Granger, C. A., Morbey, M. L., Lotherington, H., Owston, R. D., & Wideman, H. H. (2002). Factors contributing to teachers' successful implementation of ICT. *Journal of Computer Assisted Learning, 18*, 480–488.

Gray, L., Thomas, N., & Lewis, L. (2010). *Teachers' Use of Educational Technology in US Public Schools: 2009.* First Look. NCES 2010-040. National Center for Education Statistics.

Hadley, M., & Sheingold, K. (1990). *Accomplished teachers: Integrating computers into classroom practice.* New York, NY: Bank Street College of Education Center for Children and Technology.

Hadley, M., & Sheingold, K. (1993). Commonalities and distinctive patterns in teachers' integration of computers. *American Journal of Education, 101*(3), 261–315.

Hayes, D. (2007). ICT and learning: Lessons from Australian classrooms. *Computers & Education, 49*(2), 385–395.

Hermans, R., Tondeur, J., van Braak, J., & Valcke, M. (2008). The impact of primary school teachers' educational beliefs on the classroom use of computers. *Computers & Education, 51*(4), 1499–1509.

Hinostroza, J. E., Labbé, C., Brun, M., & Matamala, C. (2011). Teaching and learning activities in Chilean classrooms: Is ICT making a difference? *Computers & Education, 57*, 1358–1367.

Jimoyiannis, A. (2010). Designing and implementing an integrated technological pedagogical science knowledge framework for science teachers professional development. *Computers & Education, 55*(3), 1259–1269.

Jimoyiannis, A., & Komis, V. (2007). Examining teachers' beliefs about ICT in education: Implications of a teacher preparation. programme. *Teacher Development, 11*(2), 181–204.

Karasavvidis, I. (2009). Activity Theory as a conceptual framework for understanding teacher approaches to Information and Communication Technologies. *Computers & Education, 53*(2), 436–444.

Law, N. (2008). Summary and reflections. In N. Law, W. J. Pelgrum, & T. Plomp (Eds.), *Pedagogy and ICT use in schools around the world: Findings from the IEA SITES 2006 study* (pp. 263–277). Dordrecht: Springer.

Law, N., & Chow, A. (2008a). Pedagogical orientations in mathematics and science and the use of ICT. In N. Law, W. J. Pelgrum, & T. Plomp (Eds.), *Pedagogy and ICT use in schools around the world: Findings from the IEA SITES 2006 study* (pp. 121–179). Dordrecht: Springer.

Law, N., & Chow, A. (2008b). Teacher characteristics, contextual factors, and how these affect the pedagogical use of ICT. In N. Law, W. J. Pelgrum, & T. Plomp (Eds.), *Pedagogy and ICT use in schools around the world: Findings from the IEA SITES 2006 study* (pp. 181–219). Dordrecht: Springer.

Leftwich, A. T. O. (2007). *Expert technology-using teachers: Visions, strategies, and development.* Ann Arbor, MI: ProQuest.

Levin, T., & Wadmany, R. (2005). Changes in educational beliefs and classroom practices of teachers and students in rich technology-based classrooms. *Technology, Pedagogy and Education, 14*(3), 281–308.

Li, Q. (2007). Student and teacher views about technology: A tale of two cities? *Journal of Research on Technology in Education, 39*(4), 377–397.

Lincoln, Y. S., & Guba, E. G. (2000). Paradigmatic controversies, contradictions and emerging confluences. In N. K. Denzin & Y. S. Lincoln (Eds.), *Handbook of qualitative research* (2nd ed., pp. 163–188). Thousand Oaks: Sage.

Matzen, N. J., & Edmunds, J. A. (2007). Technology as a catalyst for change: The role of professional development. *Journal of Research on Technology in Education, 39*(4), 417.

McGarr, O. (2009). The development of ICT across the curriculum in Irish schools: A historical perspective. *British Journal of Educational Technology, 40*(6), 1094–1108.

Miles, M. B., & Huberman, A. M. (1994). *Qualitative data analysis: An expanded sourcebook.* Thousand Oaks, CA: Sage.

Miller, D., & Glover, D. (2007). Into the unknown: The professional development induction experience of secondary mathematics teachers using interactive whiteboard technology. *Learning, Media and Technology, 32*(3), 319–331.

Mueller, J., Wood, E., Willoughby, T., Ross, C., & Specht, J. (2008). Identifying discriminating variables between teachers who fully integrate computers and teachers with limited integration. *Computers & Education, 51*, 1523–1537.

Norris, C., Sullivan, T., Poirot, J., & Soloway, E. (2003). No access, no use, no impact: Snapshot surveys of educational technology in K-12. *Journal of Research on Technology in Education, 36*, 15–27.

Norton, S., McRobbie, C. J., & Cooper, T. J. (2000). Exploring secondary mathematics teachers' reasons for not using computers in their teaching: Five case studies. *Journal of Educational Computing Research, 33*(1), 87–109.

OFSTED. (2004). *Report: ICT in schools: The impact of government initiatives five years on.* London: OFSTED. Retrieved from http://www.ofsted.gov.uk/publications/index.cfm?fuseaction= pubs.displayfile&id=3652&type=pdf.

Osborne, J., & Hennessy, S. (2003). Literature review in science education and the role of ICT: Promise, problems and future directions. Retrieved from http://telearn.archives-ouvertes.fr/ docs/00/19/04/41/PDF/osborne-j-2003-r6.pdf

Penuel, W., Fishman, B., Yamaguchi, R., & Gallagher, L. (2007). What makes professional development effective? Strategies that foster curriculum implementation. *American Educational Research Journal, 44*(4), 921–958.

Player-Koro, C. (2013). Hype, hope and ICT in teacher education: A Bernsteinian perspective. *Learning, Media and Technology, 38*(1), 26–40.

Prestridge, S. (2012). The beliefs behind the teacher that influences their ICT practices. *Computers & Education, 58*, 449–458.

Riel, M., & Becker, H. J. (2008). Characteristics of teacher leaders for information and communication technology. In J. Voogt & G. Knezek (Eds.), *International handbook of information technology in primary and secondary education* (Vol. 20, pp. 397–417). New York, NY: Springer.

Sandholtz, J. H., & Reilly, B. (2004). Teachers, not technicians: Rethinking technical expectations for teachers. *Teachers College Record, 106*(3), 487–512.

Schmidkunz, H., & Lindemann, H. (1992). *Das forschend-entwickelnde unterrichtsverfahren problemlösen im naturwissen-schaftlichen unterricht.* Essen: Westarp Wissenschaften.

Selwyn, N. (2008). Realising the potential of new technology? Assessing the legacy of New Labour's ICT agenda 1997–2007. *Oxford Review of Education, 34*(6), 701–712.

Shriner, M., Schlee, B., Hamil, M., & Libler, R. (2009). Creating teachers' perceptual, behavioral, and attitudinal change using professional development workshops. *Teacher Development: An International Journal of Teachers' Professional Development, 13*(2), 125–134.

Smith, P., Rudd, P., & Coghlan, M. (2008). *Harnessing technology schools survey 2008: Report 2: Data.* Coventry: BECTA.

Southerland, S. A., Sowell, S., Blanchard, M., & Granger, E. M. (2011). Exploring the construct of pedagogical discontentment: A tool to understand science teachers' openness to reform. *Research in Science Education, 41*(3), 299–317.

Starkey, L. (2010). Supporting the digitally able beginning teacher. *Teaching and Teacher Education, 26*, 1429–1438.

Tondeur, J., Hermans, R., van Braak, J., & Valcke, M. (2008). Exploring the link between teachers' educational belief profiles and different types of computer use in the classroom. *Computers in Human Behavior, 24*, 2541–2553.

Tyack, D., & Tobin, W. (1994). The "grammar" of schooling: Why has it been so hard to change? *American Educational Research Journal, 31*(3), 453–479.

van Braak, J., Tondeur, J., & Valcke, M. (2004). Explaining different types of computer use among primary school teachers. *European Journal of Psychology of Education, 19*, 407–422.

Vosniadou, S., & Kollias, V. (2001). Information and communication technology and the problem of teacher training: Myths, dreams, and the harsh reality. *Themes in Education, 2*(4), 341–365.

Ward, L., & Parr, J. M. (2010). Revisiting and reframing use: Implications for the integration of ICT. *Computers & Education, 54*, 113–122.

Webb, M. E. (2005). Affordances of ICT in science learning: Implications for an integrated pedagogy. *International Journal of Science Education, 27*(6), 705–735.

Webb, M., & Cox, M. (2004). A review of pedagogy related to information and communications technology. *Technology, Pedagogy and Education, 13*(3), 235–286.

Wikan, G., & Molster, T. (2011). Norwegian secondary school teachers and ICT. *European Journal of Teacher Education, 34*(2), 209–218.

Wood, E., Mueller, J., Willoughby, T., Specht, J., & Deyoung, T. (2005). Teachers' perceptions: Barriers and supports to using technology in the classroom. *Education, Communication & Information, 5*(2), 183–206.

Yang, H. (2012). ICT in English schools: Transforming education? *Technology, Pedagogy and Education, 21*(1), 101–118.

Yin, R. K. (2009). *Case study research: design & methods* (4th ed.). Thousand Oaks, CA: Sage.

Zhao, Y., & Frank, K. A. (2003). Factors affecting technology uses in schools: An ecological perspective. *American Educational Research Journal, 40*(4), 807–840.

Zhao, Y., Pugh, K., Sheldon, S., & Byers, J. (2002). Conditions for classroom technology innovations. *Teachers College Record, 104*(3), 482–515.

ICT Use in Secondary Education: Schooling Necessities and Needs for Human Resources

Mehdi Khaneboubi and Aurélie Beauné

Introduction

Among various programs of technological equipment in schools, one-to-one programs (1:1) are those that neutralize the access factors. Massive computer endowments are considered by administrators, educators, families, and politics as a part of any major change in a school. However, the relative failure of One Laptop Per Child (OLPC) program (Warschauer & Ames, 2010) shows that personal computers have no pedagogical or didactical added value without other basic plans such as teacher training, reasonable number of students per teacher, resources, and electricity. In a conservative competitive system, like in Western countries, computer uses in classrooms are not raising learning outcomes more than ordinary technology. For the Maine (USA) project, Silvernail (2005) argues that students' results are not affected by computers because the ability to search and find knowledge is not part of the institutional assessment which is based on learning by heart.

However, the way teachers rule the classroom is affected by technology. Windschitl and Sahl (2002) claim that some teachers tend to create a more constructivist pedagogy which is close to the evidence reported by Bebell and Kay (2010). If the teaching modification mechanism is not clearly identified, we suggest that ICT implementations may be a way of affirming a pedagogy overhaul. For example, Karsenti and Colin (2011) report that in Canada, at the Eastern Township School Board, technologies were part of an institutional renewal strategy in a similar way to

M. Khaneboubi (✉)
UMR STEF (IFÉ-ENS Cachan),
61, avenue du Président Wilson, 94235 Cachan Cedex, France
e-mail: mehdi.khaneboubi@ens-cachan.fr

A. Beauné
EDA Université Paris Descartes (EA 4071),
45 rue des Saints-Pères, 75270 Paris Cedex 06, France
e-mail: aureliebeaune@hotmail.com

C. Karagiannidis et al. (eds.), *Research on e-Learning and ICT*
in Education: Technological, Pedagogical and Instructional Perspectives,
DOI 10.1007/978-1-4614-6501-0_15, © Springer Science+Business Media New York 2014

the Grimes and Warschauer (2008) studies on a one-to-one laptop program in California. An example of this phenomenon is the emblematic adjudicate youth program realized with Seymour Papert (Cavallo, Papert, & Stager, 2004) or the Apple Classrooms of Tomorrow project (Dwyer, Ringstaff, Haymore, & Sandholtz, 1994).

In this perspective, achievement of ICT, as reported by Zucker and Light (2009), can be seen not only by direct effects of ICT on cognitive activities but also through a general pedagogical and didactical improvement, where computers constitute the visible part of the iceberg. Beyond schools saturated with technology, teachers' testimonies in regular lower secondary schools are central for understanding what are the key features of a sustainable and an efficient use. In the Norwegian context, Wikan and Molster (2011) report that almost two-thirds of their sample were using ICT once a month, similar to France (Khaneboubi, 2007). In Sweden, on the basis of a focus group methodology, Erixon (2010) claims that insufficient access to computers is one of the most important reasons for not using ICT during classroom.

The most frequent uses of ICT by teachers in secondary schools are for sustaining motivation and search, as pointed by Wikan and Molster (2011). Drent and Meelissen (2008) in the Netherlands claim that early adopters are the "anchor point for stimulating the innovative use of ICT in education." In particular, those teachers are well socialized and technically skilled in regard to their pedagogical needs. Jimoyiannis and Komis (2007), in a quantitative study with Greek teachers, report that personal factors such as subject matter, teaching experience, or gender are associated with their perceptions about ICT in education. In England, Hennessy, Ruthven, and Brindley (2005) report that commitment in ICT activities is tempered by the influence of external constraints.

In France, after active national policies supporting the training of teachers for integrating technologies into their school practices, an approach of new artifacts has been developed, conceiving them as tools (Baron & Bruillard, 1996). Since the 1980s, this approach still dominates. Technology endowment programs in the French schools continue to be accumulated without necessarily being accompanied by national plans for teacher education. Furthermore, mandatory uses of ICT in the curricula are very sparse and decisions about curricula tend to reserve computing into specialized courses. The French one-to-one programs (Jaillet, 2004; Khaneboubi, 2010; Rinaudo, Turban, Delalande, & Ohana, 2008) show a weak state support in regard to the local authorities' implication.

In this chapter, we report a study conducted in 2012 following a first work made in 2010, in four lower secondary schools where teachers and students have a relatively better access to technology and digital resources than in other French schools. Three of them were involved in a national state program on digital textbooks; they had been endowed in 2010 by a local state authority called "académie." Consequently, they were also involved in a series of programs that aim at identifying the conditions and limitations of ICT implementation. The disciplines mostly concerned were mathematics, social studies, literature, and technology and, occasionally, foreign languages and biology. We seek to understand dynamic and evolutions by taking "pictures" at two different times and, according to the actors, trying to retrace what happened.

The purpose of our survey, partially funded by the local state authority, was to get a better understanding of the evolution of ICT uses in the everyday teachers' professional running pattern in order to identify propitious and obstacle factors. To what extent computers are a significant tool in the classrooms to achieve a teaching task? Do teachers have an equal access to equipment? What is the influence of organizational factors on teachers' utilizations of technologies?

Data Collection Methods

The investigation method has been guided by the framework made by Fulton, Glenn, and Valdez (2003, 2004), who draw a list of necessary elements propitious for teaching with ICT. This framework has been adapted to the French context; seven factors were defined as follows:

– The role of the leadership in the school management: Is there a team for piloting ICT projects in the school? What is the importance of ICT in the general school project?
– The roles assumed by teacher(s) responsible for ICT in the school: In each secondary school one or several teachers are discharged for a part of their teaching duty to help and conduct pedagogical use of ICT among his or her colleagues. Very often, this function is allocated to early adopter as described by Drent and Meelissen (2008).
– The manner in which the support and maintenance are performed: In the French context, the national state is responsible for teaching contents and human resources, while authorities on buildings, equipment, and maintenance are devolved to local administrations such as territorial councils and city councils.
– Financing from local communities, state local authority, ministry ….
– State policy on ICT as well as local policies.
– Different support settings for teachers of different disciplines in their use of ICT: Training, guidance, meeting ….
– School position in the environment and links with parents and with local associations.

In the next section, we describe a preliminary study that has nurtured and served the construction of the study conducted in 2012. They are both based on Kathleen Fulton's framework.

The 2010 Pre-study

In 2010, we sought to get a better understanding according to the methodological elements explained in the previous section by performing 30 interviews with innovative teachers and management teams (Bruillard et al., 2011), following an ethnographic perspective as documented by Woods (1996). For each middle school, we have conducted interviews with:

– The management team
– Teachers responsible for ICT
– Teachers-librarians
– Teachers who use digital textbooks or any kind of ICT

The interviews focused on the school characteristics, teaching experience of the teachers responsible for ICT and how they managed these responsibilities, organization of the endowment program in digital textbooks, and changes in teachers' practices related to these new means as well as those occurring due to other technologies available. We did not meet all the teachers, and only ICT users.

Interviews showed disparities in the access to the computer room, and the Internet weaknesses were not perceived in the same way by all teachers. Furthermore, it was often suggested that all teachers were not equal in front of technical and educational assistance.

Literature teachers in particular (often women) seemed unaware of the existence of some equipment. Teachers responsible for ICT said that they did not have time to perform maintenance on all computers. For this reason, there was a high probability that computers used by teachers less close to the management team or in conflict with it did not get the same comfort of use as other teachers. Therefore, it seemed fruitful to test the hypothesis that all teachers do not have the same possibilities in front of infrastructure and equipment deficiencies and that technical assistance is not distributed equiprobably: patterns according to gender, age, or subject taught were potentially observable.

The 2012 Study

Since the 2010 study focused on innovative teachers in a qualitative way, in 2012 we sought to reach a greater number of teachers with a questionnaire in order to get a clearer outline of the dynamics at work in the schools and the possible new (declared) practices in the classroom and for preparation. Therefore, in 2012, interviews were conducted in three middle schools with eight teachers and managers and a questionnaire was filled by 89 teachers in four schools (Beauné, Khaneboubi, Tort, & Bruillard, 2013). This amount of exploitable questionnaires represents approximately 45 % of the teacher target population. Among the five schools participating in the first survey, one school was left out because of the difficulties encountered during the initial investigation.

Schools A, B, C, and E are located in suburban areas near Paris. School D is part of a rural area. Establishments A, B, and C are located in high-poverty area. However, these schools have a relatively large equipment and are known for their significant use of ICT in teaching and learning activities. Each one hosts approximately 500 students and 50 teachers and has more than 100 computers distributed in computer labs, libraries, technology classrooms, etc. There are at least one computer lab and two sets of laptop per school. All the classrooms of the sixth and seventh grades are equipped with a computer and a projector in most cases. In three schools, all rooms are equipped with a computer. However, Internet and network access are not reliable in most places. The stability of the teaching staff such as managers' departures, teachers responsible for ICTs' departures, or major changes in the teams of teachers is not accomplished. In two institutions, an important and frequent turnover has been reported.

In short, in 2012 a quantitative and a qualitative study was made to complete a 2010 work. The first round of interviews made in 2010 was the foundation of our quantitative survey of 2012. Interviews were conducted with administrators and teachers responsible for ICT in three schools (A, D, and C); observations and informal interviews were conducted in the staff room for two schools (A and E). The interviews focused on the changes that occurred between 2010 and 2012. A particular issue was to establish a balance after 2 years of using digital textbooks. We seek to document the changes in the practices that have been observed between the two periods of data collection. When it was possible, interviews were conducted with managers and teachers responsible for ICT as in 2010. We have managed to conduct interviews with the same people or with those who occupy the same function in our school sample.

In those schools which get significatively more equipment than average schools, new equipment is not so frequent. No major changes in the equipment have been reported. Between 2010 and 2012, the main technology that entered the French school was interactive tablet. Less than 20 were endowed in one college of our sample. The weakness of the Internet access has not evolved. Analysis of speeches from managers and teachers responsible for ICT permits a comparison of evolution, a description of the inertia in the teachers' team involvement, and the dynamics at work in the schools.

Teachers' Questionnaire

The questionnaire fulfilled in 2012 is a part of a longer term project. We have sought to build a database during several years in order to make comparative studies and report experiences of teachers while there are technological developments. We also aim at sharing our raw database. For now it is possible to present how the various factors that can be found in the literature are combined in our context.

Based on the interview analysis of the 2010 study, a first draft of the questionnaire was tested in one middle school and one high school in another region. An anonymous four-page questionnaire (shown below in Appendix) was stabilized, with about 60 questions grouped into six themes linked to ICT practices:

– Personal and professional information (status, discipline, experience background ...)
– Mode of the course preparation (frequency uses of software, Internet, digital textbook, etc.)
– Classroom activities (frequency uses of equipment in and out of the classroom, student activities with ICT ...)

– Student assessment activities (where, how, what …)
– Classroom preparation activities (communication with administrators, colleagues, parents …)
– Usage at home (personal equipment, social network uses…)

A total of 89 questionnaires were collected. We stayed in the teacher room in four schools (A, C, D, and E) for 2 days on average, and we proposed to every teacher we met to fill the questionnaire. In the French context, the participation of volunteers is unavoidable to sample our target population, and other sampling method is not possible in lower secondary schools. The sample is not as important as we expected, but the collection rate is similar to other studies using the same method (Khaneboubi, 2007, 2010). We collected between 19 and 25 questionnaires in each school among teachers who agreed to answer. Three half-days were required for school A, two full days in school C, and one half-day in school E. In school D, questionnaires were given to the teacher responsible for ICT who assured the distribution and the collection of questionnaires. In the four schools considered, a total of 89 questionnaires were collected which represents approximately 45 % of our target population.

How to estimate the characteristics of individuals who have not responded to the questionnaire? First, the sampling of volunteers excluded teachers who were not favorable to ICT. Frequently, surveys on technologies tend to "attract" users or teachers favorable to ICT and to "scare" the teachers less comfortable with technology. Then, for three schools, only teachers who attended the staff room were likely to respond to the questionnaire. Teachers who have a disciplinary room where they spend break times are excluded. The disappearance of smoking rooms has also excluded smokers from the sample.

Survey analysis has been made by performing univariate summaries and chi square test. Main ideas expressed during the interviews were crossed with questionnaire data. A regression logistics has been computed to describe three variable interactions. Open questions have been recoded in categories. On this basis, occurrences of the category have been graphically represented in barplot with a package implemented in the software named *R* (R Development Core Team, 2011). Translation has been made for Figs. 3 and 4 by searching for the best analogy between French and English.

Sampling Presentation

The questionnaire required 20 min to be completed. This is a relatively long time that demands concentration and, like all surveys of this type, a form of intrusion into the professional privacy of respondents. Non-responses are more frequent toward the end of the questionnaire than at the beginning. They are also more frequent for open questions and tables. Finally, the format of the open questions includes impassable ambiguities. For example, if teachers distinguish *Word* and *Excel*, they do not distinguish *Writer* from *Calc* and only declare "*Open Office*" or "*Libre Office*."

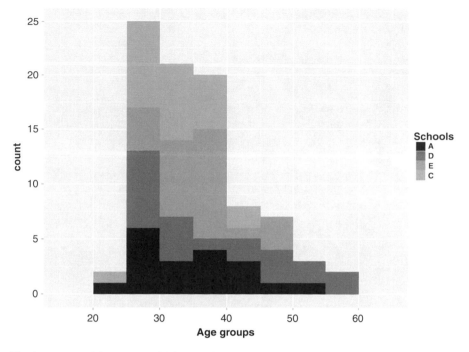

Fig. 1 Age repartition among middle schools

Those 89 usable questionnaires were filled by 57 % of women and 43 % of men. Three-quarters of the sample had a class of sixth grade and 80 % of ninth grade.

As shown in Fig. 1, teachers aged over 40 years are significantly fewer than the age group 25–40 years. More than half of the sample is made up of teachers between 25 and 40 years. Most of the staffs of school C are less than 40 years old, while school D shows greater dispersion. Distribution in age groups is consistent with the population of teachers in the direct environment because those schools are located in an area which welcomes fresh tenured teachers.

As shown in Fig. 2, we found in the sample 17 % of people who teach mathematics, 13.5 % literature, 11 % social studies, and 18 % foreign languages. Proportions of the disciplines represented in the sample are consistent with the students' schedule discipline. There are more women who teach literature and foreign languages than mathematics and gym. As for age groups, the gender distribution is consistent with the trends of the population from which the sample is coming from.

Respondents appear to be quite familiar with the Web: 46 % have a personal account on Facebook, and 63 % report frequently using technologies; only seven of them have a personal web page, four have a blog, and three have a *Twitter* account. Only 15 % consider themselves advanced, while 79 % feel that they have a beginner or an intermediate level. Men outnumber women to report an advanced level.

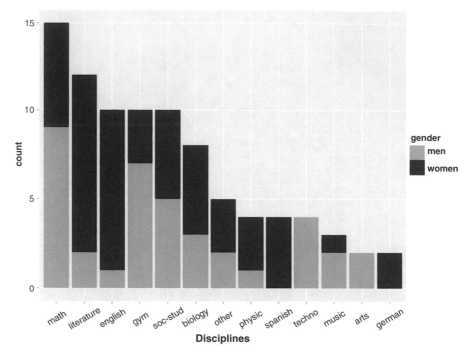

Fig. 2 Discipline distribution in regard to gender

Results

ICT in the Classrooms

As shown in Fig. 3, teachers' main activities in classrooms are *search for informa-tion*, *exercises*, *dynamic geometry*, and *screening activities*. Seventy-eight percent of the sample report that they ask their students to do information search. Among them, 57 % state that they require students to do it at home, 44 % at the school library, and 37 % in the computer lab.

However, these activities have only a relative importance for students with only 34 % who declare assessing activities with ICT, including 16 % for literature and 3 % for geometry. Usage in lesson by students is modest: only 46 % report having made one or several students use the computer. Those elements reveal that the importance of ICT in the classroom is humble in regard to teaching progressions. This does not mean that technologies are not part of the teaching system.

Seventy-two percent of teachers claim to use computers in their classroom almost every day, but the observations made in the staff room tend to show that it is prob-ably mainly for administrative purposes. Only 34 % use the computer lab once a month or a little more and 11 % once a week. As shown in Fig. 4, in the classroom the Internet is the most widely cited and then comes office suites and dynamic geometry application.

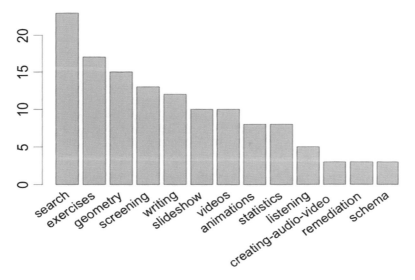

Fig. 3 Classroom activity citation occurrences

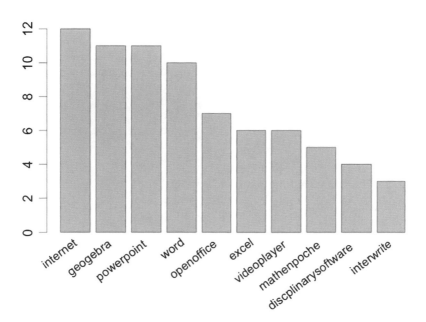

Fig. 4 Software and applications used during the classroom citation occurrences

Classroom Preparation with ICT

On the other hand, usage for classroom preparation appears large and stable. In preparing the course, technologies are particularly sought. Professional web sources are preferred when researching information for setting the course.

However, software packages are more important than disciplinary software, except for dynamic geometry application.

Eighty-three percent of the sample report seeking information frequently to prepare their classes. Most viewed websites were first institutional websites, then teachers' personal websites, and, third, professional association websites. *YouTube*, *Wikipedia*, and *Google* are much less cited. There is a significant link between the use of digital textbooks to prepare lessons and equipment reliability and availability. In sum, when the material's availability is medium or low reliable, teachers are significantly less likely to report using the digital textbooks to prepare their classes.

The preferred instrument for the preparation of courses is the word processor: 87 % reported using it more than once a week and 62 % almost every day. Thus, 43 % reported using an image-processing software more than once a month. Disciplinary software mostly used in the preparation of lessons are free dynamic geometry software: *Geogebra, Geospace, Geoplan, Cabrigeometre*, and *Sesamath*.[1] In general, there is a predominance of proprietary software. For example, *MSWord* is the most cited word processor with 24 occurrences whereas *Libre Office* and *Open Office* come with 14 occurrences. Overall, free and open-source software are present but in a secondary place.

Technologies appear mostly used professionally by teachers to communicate with each other: 76 % claim that they use ICT to write to their colleagues and 58 % with management and administrators. Seventy-four percent use the online home-work notebooks. We find the same proportions for the application counting the missing students as 74 % reported. In addition, 95 % reported using the online application for entering assessment results.

Infrastructure Issues

It is essential to enlighten some contrasts between the discourses of the administrative teams and those of the teachers, noted in the staff rooms. Administrators tend to report that things are going well or that practices with ICT are more frequent, whereas in the teachers' breakroom, a lot of claims are expressed: about delays in digital textbooks' delivery, classrooms that are not equipped with interactive whiteboards, network dysfunctions, problems related to software for managing the school life, equipment maintenance, etc. In two schools, the replacement of teachers responsible for ICT had important implications: several remarks evoke responsibilities that are going beyond the scope of the teachers responsible for ICT in terms of time, remuneration, and sometimes also skills.

---

[1] Sesamath (www.sesamath.net) is an association aiming to spread under a free and open-source license documents and educational software for mathematics.

We noted that changes had occurred in the management teams between the endowment and the 2012 study. A new head teacher had taken a position opposite to that of his predecessor and did not provide specific information about the continuity of the endowment program. Similarly, two teachers newly responsible for ICT said that everything was going well overall, thanks to a continuous handover. In contact with the ancient responsibles, they also evoked a solid foundation but they declared that it is difficult to make as well as them. They also said that they refuse certain tasks or that they are not qualified for it, such as setting up computers to access and deploy new textbooks.

The lack of technical support given by institutions appears as a source of discontent among teachers responsible for ICT. Some data from the questionnaire show this phenomenon. First, teachers responsible for ICT are sought for technical support almost exclusively: as 34 % stated, and only between 7 and 12 % indicated requesting them for a pedagogical dimension which is their main assignment. This result is probably linked to the departures of experimented teacher responsible for ICT in two schools. Secondly, to the question "Do you give help to someone using ICT in education?" 24 % responded "yes," including 21 % who stated that it is for their colleagues. Thirty-four percent of respondents indicated asking their colleagues for help and educational aspects on the technical aspects.

During interviews, infrastructure access has been highlighted as a determinant factor on practices. In these quite well-endowed schools with technological equipment, organizational and practical difficulties in the management of computer fleet appear. These problems hinder the development of ICT usage: few significant evolutions in terms of classroom practices are declared despite the tenacity of teams and the almost intact motivation to seize the means in helping their students succeed.

Access to Equipment

Nine out of ten teachers reported having a computer in their room, a projector, and a computer room in the school. Fifty-two percent indicated that the material is highly available and 39 % medium or low. Forty-five percent indicated that the equipment is very reliable, while 38 % described it as slightly or moderately reliable: it is mainly Internet connections that are not robust and computers obsolete.

Evidence shows that the equipment is not perceived as available in the same way for all teachers: gender and seniority appear as discriminating factors in the perception of this availability. By performing a chi-square test in Table 1, we found that female teachers are significantly more likely to report that the material is medium to low available whereas men teachers are significantly more likely to respond that the material is available (chi-squared $= 4.2286$, p-value $= 0.03975$).

Table 1 Equipment availability based on gender		Medium or low availability	High availability
	Women	24	21
	Men	11	25

By performing a logistic regression as described by Dalgaard (2004) we can claim that in our sample, with an equal seniority, men have 3.2 greater chance to declare equipment "very available" than women.

Seniority in the profession is also an issue to access equipment: teachers recently tenured are less likely to agree that the material is available. In three schools, interviews show a difference of treatment between old and new teachers; older teachers often have their own classrooms and significantly more equipment than new teachers. The difference among the old and the new teachers can be a source of tension within the teams.

Discussion

The purpose of our survey was to get a better understanding of the dynamics of ICT uses in the everyday teachers' professional running pattern in order to identify propitious and obstacle factors. We considered, in this research, an initial situation and the evolution of this situation of four schools that were involved in a national endowment program on digital textbook. These schools are better endowed with technology and digital resources than the other French schools. Interviews were conducted in three middle schools with eight teachers and managers, and a questionnaire was filled by 89 teachers in four schools.

According to our results, we can underline that in those relatively favorable contexts for technology uses, ICT is not a major concern for teachers. Above all, leading pupils to the exam success is the main goal, and technologies are not perceived as a reliable medium to do so. The departures of teachers locally responsible for ICT impacted the coordination and the development of ICT's uses in teachers' practices, even if this could appear as a local and punctual need. Teachers who responded to our questionnaire used technology as a vehicle for their cultural practices in consistence with their age groups (Donnat, 2009) and professional affiliation (Bourdieu, 1984).

For investigators, in order to engage in these schools, create trust, and approach a global vision, it is necessary to implement a long qualitative research based on ethnographic methods and to combine it with a questionnaire survey. Two years after the first endowment in these schools, the managers' interest was not the same as in the first investigation and, thus, access to the schools was made more difficult for collecting data. The complexity of the phenomenon we have sought to characterize only allows modest interpretations. It would be necessary to test further our results in other contexts and to investigate the field with a much more qualitative method. This study attempts to outline elements that are prominent in our methodological context, but it deserves a more ambitious continuity.

For teaching purposes, office software are cited more frequently than disciplinary software. The main activity with the technologies is information search, but it is mainly requested to be done outside the classroom. This result concurs with Wikan and Molster (2011), who report that the use of ICT is mainly for sustaining motivation and for resources. Uses of a computer with a projector in the classroom remain as one of the most important elements in the practice. We can't identify an important use of technology for assessment. The use of technologies by teachers in the classroom seems to be determined by the infrastructure's quality and the equipment reliability. Gender and seniority are discriminating factors in the availability perception of technologies. This element is convergent with what Jimoyiannis and Komis (2007) have reported on gender.

On the other hand, usage for classroom preparation is important. Training and educational support are essentially made by peers, and institutional support is almost exclusively sought for technical reasons. As Erixon (2009) shows, insufficient access to computers is one of the most important reasons for teachers not using ICT in their teaching. We can presume that teachers did not have an equal access to computers. In our context, it is highly possible that technology is one of the "apanage" of individuals with a good legitimacy and a significant weight in their establishments. Thus, a male teacher with seniority in his school will probably have a better access to the equipment than a new young female teacher. To confirm this trend, it would be necessary to examine the possible interaction between the taught discipline and the availability of equipment which is not permitted at this time with our number (89) of respondents.

Leader postures on ICT and animation are a key feature pointed by Drent and Meelissen (2008). As in a one-to-one project, teachers' use of ICT is revealing a major issue of the general professional context. In all professional fields, seniority is an indicator of legitimacy (Bourdieu, 1999). Moreover, disciplines do not have the same prestige or importance. Other factors such as gender, diploma, and institutional status are a source of disparity. Depending on the school history and traditions, the ambience may be created in several ways. In other words, institutions can promote achievement against archaism such as gender equity vigilance and generational diversity program. From those impulses, a general organization of the day-to-day work is collectively made and supported by the chief administrator. This could be an extension of this work to characterize these elements in a long temporality and to link those evolutions with changes in the use of ICT.

Acknowledgement We would like to thank Pr. Georges-Louis Baron and Pr. Éric Bruillard for the time they spend on rereading this document.

Appendix: Teacher's Questionnaire

TIC & éducation - Questionnaire enseignants

Date : ___/___/___

Ce questionnaire a pour objectif de mieux comprendre les activités réalisées avec les Technologies de l'Information et de la Communication (TIC) en éducation.

Collège _____

Ce questionnaire est anonyme. Les données fournies ne serviront que dans un but scientifique. Nous vous remercions de bien vouloir consacrer du temps pour y répondre.

Pour toute information, contactez _____

A- Données personnelles

Votre année de naissance : 19 _____   **2. Votre genre :** ○ H   ○ F

3. Nombre d'années d'expérience professionnelle: ____ **dont dans le présent établissement:** ____

Êtes-vous titulaire de votre poste ?   ○ Non   ○ Oui   **depuis** ____ **an(s).**

Votre grade : _____

Votre discipline : _____

Vos classes de l'année en cours :

☐ 6ᵉ   ☐ 5ᵉ   ☐ 4ᵉ   ☐ 3ᵉ   ☐ 2ᵈᵉ   ☐ 1ᵉʳᵉ   ☐ Terminale ☐BTS

☐ 6ᵉ SEGPA ☐ 5ᵉ SEGPA ☐ 4ᵉ SEGPA ☐ 3ᵉ SEGPA ☐ CAP ☐ BEP ☐Autre :____

Êtes-vous membre d'une association ou d'un groupe d'enseignants (hors syndicat) ? ○ Oui   ○ Non

   Si oui, laquelle ? _____

B- Votre préparation de cours

Pour préparer vos cours, quels logiciels utilisez-vous ? et à quelle fréquence ?

Logiciel	Lequel ?	Tous les jours ou presque	Au moins une fois par semaine	Au moins une fois par mois	Plus rarement
Tableur		○	○	○	○
Traitement de texte		○	○	○	○
Présentation diaporama		○	○	○	○
Logiciel de Tableau Numérique Interactif (TNI)		○	○	○	○
Traitement de l'image		○	○	○	○
Traitement du son		○	○	○	○
Traitement de la vidéo		○	○	○	○
Logiciel(s) disciplinaire(s)		○	○	○	○
		○	○	○	○
Autre		○	○	○	○

Pour préparer vos cours, réalisez-vous des recherches sur Internet ?

○ À chaque fois ○ Souvent   ○ Rarement ○ Jamais

Pour préparer vos cours, utilisez-vous un manuel numérique ? ○ Oui   ○ Non

   Si oui, lequel ? _____

   À quelle fréquence ? ○ À chaque fois   ○ Souvent   ○ Rarement

Pour préparer vos cours, quels sites utilisez-vous fréquemment ?

☐   Sites   Précisez : _____
   Internet personnels
☐   Sites   Précisez : _____
   Internet institutionnels
☐   Sites   Précisez : _____
   d'associations de profs
☐   Sites avec   Précisez : _____
   abonnement
          Précisez : _____
☐   Autres   _____

C- Votre activité en classe

Disposez-vous d'une salle de classe attitrée ○ Oui   ○ Non

Vous arrive-t-il d'utiliser votre ordinateur personnel en classe ?   ○ Oui   ○ Non

   Pourquoi ? _____

Dans votre établissement, quel équipement	...est disponible	...et à quelle fréquence l'utilisez-vous ?			
		Tous les jours ou presque	*Au moins une fois pas semaine*	*Au moins une fois par mois*	*Plus rarement*
Un ordinateur du professeur en classe	○ Oui ○ Non	○	○	○	○
Un ordinateur du professeur dans l'établissement	○ Oui ○ Non	○	○	○	○
Des ordinateurs dans votre classe. Combien ? ___	○ Oui ○ Non	○	○	○	○
Une salle informatique	○ Oui ○ Non	○	○	○	○
Une classe nomade (chariot de portables)	○ Oui ○ Non	○	○	○	○
Un TNI (Tableau Numérique Interactif)	○ Oui ○ Non	○	○	○	○
Un vidéo projecteur	○ Oui ○ Non	○	○	○	○
Des tablettes	○ Oui ○ Non	○	○	○	○
Des boîtiers de votes (clickers)	○ Oui ○ Non	○	○	○	○
Autre :	○ Oui ○ Non	○	○	○	○

Selon vous, l'équipement collectif de votre établissement est :

a) ○ Très disponible   ○ Moyennement disponible   ○ Peu disponible ○ Non
disponible. Précisez:

b) ○ Très fiable   ○ Moyennement fiable   ○ Peu fiable   ○ Non
fiable. Précisez:

Décrivez quelques-unes des activités faites en classe en utilisant les TIC :

Activité	Matériel / Logiciel	*avec* manipulation		*sans* manipulation par les élèves
		par *les* élèves	par *un* élève	
		☐	☐	☐
		☐	☐	☐
		☐	☐	☐

Selon vous, quels sont les objectifs *majeurs* de l'utilisation des TIC dans une activité ?

Pour l'enseignant	*Pour l'apprenant*

D- Activités et évaluation des élèves

Demandez-vous à vos élèves de faire des recherches d'informations ?   ○ Oui ○ Non

Si oui, où ?   ☐ En salle informatique ☐ Au CDI ☐ En classe ☐ Chez eux

Comment ? ☐ En recherche libre ☐ À partir d'une liste de sites ou de pages

À des fins d'évaluation, quelles activités proposez-vous aux élèves avec les TIC ? _____

_____

_____

Est-ce que votre établissement a une application pour saisir les notes des élèves ? ○ Oui ○ Non

Si oui, laquelle ? _____ L'utilisez-vous ? ○ Oui ○ Non

Que pensez-vous de la gestion automatisée des notes ? _____

E- Autres activités scolaires

Parmi les activités de communication suivantes, que faites-vous *régulièrement* avec les TIC?

Communiquer avec :	Oui	Non	Pour quoi faire ?
- les élèves	O	O	
- les parents	O	O	
- la direction de votre établissement	O	O	
- la Personne Ressource Informatique ou le référent TICE de votre établissement	O	O	
- des enseignants du même établissement	O	O	
- des enseignants d'autres établissements	O	O	
Faire communiquer les élèves entre eux	O	O	
Autre :			

Utilisez-vous le cahier de texte numérique ?   O Oui   O Non

Selon vous, qu'est-ce que l'utilisation du cahier de texte numérique change ?
- dans les pratiques des enseignants ? _____
- dans le travail avec les élèves ? _____
- dans le rapport aux parents ? _____

Utilisez-vous une application institutionnelle pour saisir les absences des élèves ?   O Oui

O Non

Si oui, la(es)quelle(s) ? _____

Que pensez-vous de la gestion informatisée des absences ? _____
_____

Est-ce que votre établissement a un Environnement Numérique de Travail (ENT) ?   O Oui

O Non

Si oui, l'utilisez-vous ?   O Oui   O Non

Selon vous, qu'est-ce que l'utilisation de l'ENT change ?
- dans les pratiques des enseignants ? _____
- dans le travail avec les élèves ? _____
- dans le rapport aux parents ? _____

F- Les TIC et vous

Avez-vous un diplôme, certificat ou attestation en lien avec les TIC ou l'informatique ?
O Oui O Non

Si oui, le(s) quel(s) ? _____

À votre domicile, de quels équipements informatiques disposez-vous ? _____
_____

Avez-vous ?	Pour un usage personnel	Pour des activités scolaires
□ Un site web	□	□
□ Un blog	□	□
□ Une page Facebook	□	□
□ Un compte Twitter	□	□
□ Autre :	□	□

Apportez-vous de l'aide à quelqu'un pour son utilisation des TIC en éducation ?   ○ Oui

○ Non

Si oui, à qui ? _____

En quoi ? _____

À qui demandez-vous de l'aide pour votre utilisation des TIC ?	Pour des aspects techniques	Pour des aspects pédagogiques
□ Une Personne Ressource Informatique (PRI)	□	□
□ Un référent TICE	□	□
□ Un autre collègue	□	□
□ Une personne de votre entourage : Qui ?	□	□
□ Autre :	□	□
□ Personne	□	□

En tant qu'utilisateur des TIC, dans quelle catégorie vous classeriez-vous ?

    ○ Avancé   ○ Intermédiaire   ○ Débutant   ○
Inexpérimenté

En général, vous jugez votre utilisation des TIC comme étant :

    ○ Très fréquente   ○ Assez fréquente   ○ Modérée   ○ Rare

Que proposez-vous pour faciliter l'utilisation des TIC dans votre métier ? Pourquoi ? Comment ?

_____

_____

_____

References

Baron, G.-L., & Bruillard, É. (1996). *L'informatique et ses usagers dans l'éducation*. Paris: Presse Universitaire de France.

Beauné, A., Khaneboubi, M., Tort, F., & Bruillard, É. (2013). *Collèges numériques de l'académie de Créteil*. Seconde étude. Rapport final.

Bebell, D. & Kay, R. (2010). One to one computing: A summary of the quantitative results from the Berkshire Wireless Learning Initiative. *The Journal of Technology, Learning, and Assesment, 9*(2).

Bourdieu, P. (1984). *Distinction: A social critique of the judgement of taste*. Cambridge, MA: Harvard University Press.

Bourdieu, P. (1999). Une révolution conservatrice dans l'édition. *Actes de la recherche en sciences sociales, 126*(1), 3–28.

Bruillard, É., Blondel, F.-M., Denis, M., Khaneboubi, M., Laghzal, B., Lamoure, J., et al. (2011). *Collèges numériques de l'académie de Créteil*. Rapport final. Laboratoire STEF - ENS Cachan.

Cavallo, D., Papert, S., & Stager, G. (2004). Climbing to understanding: Lessons from an experimental learning environment for adjudicated youth. In *Proceedings of the 6th International Conference on Learning Sciences* (pp. 113–120). Santa Monica, CA: International Society of the Learning Sciences.

Dalgaard, P. (2004). *Introductory statistics with R*. New York, NY: Springer.

Donnat, O. (2009). Les pratiques culturelles des Français à l'ère numérique. *Culture études, 5*(5), 1–12.

Drent, M., & Meelissen, M. (2008). Which factors obstruct or stimulate teacher educators to use ICT innovatively? *Computers & Education, 51*(1), 187–199.

Dwyer, D. C., Ringstaff, C., Haymore, J., & Sandholtz, P. D. (1994). Apple classrooms of tomorrow. *Educational Leadership, 51*(7), 4–10.

Erixon, P.-O. (2010). School subject paradigms and teaching practice in lower secondary Swedish schools influenced by ICT and media. *Computers & Education, 54*(4), 1212–1221.

Fulton, K., Glenn, A., & Valdez, G. (2003). *Three preservice programs preparing tomorrow's teachers to use technology: A study in partnerships.* Naperville, IL: Learning Point Associates.

Fulton, K., Glenn, A. D., & Valdez, G. (2004). *Teacher education and technology planning guide.* Naperville, IL: North Central Regional Educational Laboratory, Learning Point Associates.

Grimes, D., & Warschauer, M. (2008). Learning with laptops: A multi-method case study. *Journal of Educational Computing Research, 38*(3), 305–332.

Hennessy, S., Ruthven, K., & Brindley, S. (2005). Teacher perspectives on integrating ICT into subject teaching: commitment, constraints, caution, and change. *Journal of Curriculum Studies, 37*(2), 155–192.

Jaillet, A. (2004). What is happening with portable computers in schools? *Journal of Science Education and Technology, 13*(1), 115–128.

Jimoyiannis, A., & Komis, V. (2007). Examining teachers' beliefs about ICT in education: Implications of a teacher preparation programme. *Teacher Development, 11*(2), 149–173.

Karsenti, T., & Colin, S. (2011). Une étude sur les apports des ordinateurs portables au primaire et au secondaire. In G.-L. Baron, E. Bruillard, & V. Komis (Eds.), *Didapro 4—Dida&STIC. Sciences et technologies de l'information et de la communication (STIC) en milieu éducatif. Analyse de pratiques et enjeux didactiques.* Patras, Grèce: Université de Patras.

Khaneboubi, M. (2007). *Usages de l'informatique au collège et habitus professionnels des enseignants: exemple de l'opération « un collégien, un ordinateur portable » dans le département des Landes.* PhD Thesis, Université Victor Segalen Bordeaux 2.

Khaneboubi, M. (2010). *Description de quelques caractéristiques communes aux opérations de dotations massives en ordinateurs portables en France.* Rubrique Revue STICEF, 16.

R Development Core Team. (2011). *R: A language and environment for statistical computing.* Vienna, Austria. http://www.R-project.org

Rinaudo, J.-L., Turban, J.-M., Delalande, P., & Ohana, D. (2008). *Des ordinateurs portables, des collégiens, des professeurs, des parents: rapport de recherche sur le dispositif Ordi 35 2005–2007.*

Silvernail, D. (2005). *Does Maine's middle school laptop program improve learning? A review of evidence to date. Occasional brief.* Portland, ME: Center for Education Policy, Applied Research, and Evaluation. University of Southern Maine.

Warschauer, M., & Ames, M. (2010). Can one laptop per child save the world's poor? *Journal of International Affairs, 64*(1), 33–51.

Wikan, G., & Molster, T. (2011). Norwegian secondary school teachers and ICT. *European Journal of Teacher Education, 34*(2), 209–218.

Windschitl, M., & Sahl, K. (2002). Tracing teachers' use of technology in a laptop computer school: The interplay of teacher beliefs, social dynamics, and institutional culture. *American Educational Research Journal, 39*(1), 165–205.

Woods, P. (1996). *Researching the art of teaching: Ethnography for educational use.* London: Routledge.

Zucker, A. A., & Light, D. (2009). Laptop programs for students. *Science, 323*(5910), 82–85.

Teacher Preparation for Educational Technology

Ioanna Vekiri

Introduction

The Internet provides quick and easy access to a large variety of information resources and tools and therefore has the potential to support instructional approaches that are consistent with current learning theories and educational reform efforts, such as inquiry-oriented learning (Schofield, 2006). A typical characteristic of these approaches is that learning activities evolve around open-ended questions and ill-structured problems that are relevant to the real world. Activities also involve student interaction and collaboration and require the use of, as well as promote the development of, high-level cognitive and self-regulatory learning strategies. Research has shown, however, that web-based learning, and online inquiry in particular, is very demanding and challenging both for the students and for the teachers. Typically, students do not have sufficient prior knowledge and fully developed cognitive skills to grapple with new subject matter while carrying out online inquiry tasks (Kupier, Volman, & Terwel, 2005; Quintana, Zhang, & Krajcik, 2005; Zhang & Quintana, 2012). Also, teachers need to be able to design learning activities that engage students in meaningful learning, to select and provide appropriate resources, and to possess a large repertoire of pedagogical techniques so as to effectively support their students (Wallace, 2004).

What do teachers need to know in order to design and implement web-based instruction that utilizes the wealth of information resources available on the web in ways that enhance student learning? The present study addresses this question through an analysis of the lesson plans submitted by preservice teachers after attending an introductory course on the educational applications of ICTs. The study aims

I. Vekiri (✉)
Independent Researcher, PO BOX 20103, Kalamaria, 55101 Thessaloniki, Greece
e-mail: ivekiri@otenet.gr

C. Karagiannidis et al. (eds.), *Research on e-Learning and ICT
in Education: Technological, Pedagogical and Instructional Perspectives*,
DOI 10.1007/978-1-4614-6501-0_16, © Springer Science+Business Media New York 2014

at examining preservice teachers' understandings of Internet use in the classroom, so as to identify needs that should be addressed in teacher preparation for ICT educational integration.

Literature Review

The Internet provides teachers with access to a wealth of information and a variety of representation tools which they can use to improve teaching and learning. When using it as an information source learners can find content represented in multiple visual formats, including photos, diagrams, graphs, videos, and animations, having thus more opportunities to connect ideas and to construct rich mental models of the concepts and phenomena they study (Moreno & Mayer, 2007; Osborne & Hennessy, 2003). In addition, the Internet can enable learning experiences that otherwise would not be feasible inside the classroom. Interactive representations of content such as interactive models and simulations enable students to test hypotheses, observe patterns and relationships in data, and draw their own conclusions (Osborne & Hennessy, 2003). Students can explore questions of personal interest and importance by accessing authentic sources (e.g., data archives of governmental organizations, museum collections, news archives of TV and radio stations) and real-time data (e.g., satellite maps, reports on recent earthquakes) (Schofield, 2006).

The above make the Internet an ideal information resource for inquiry-oriented approaches to learning (Schofield, 2006). Inquiry learning is hard to define because there are many conceptualizations and approaches to inquiry instruction, even within the literature of the same field such as science education. However, all of these approaches share three critical elements: they evolve around authentic, complex questions, require student active engagement, and include at least some part of the investigation cycle (question generation, study design, data collection, drawing conclusions, and communicating findings) (Anderson, 2002; Minner, Levy, & Century, 2010). The Internet can support student inquiry in multiple ways. Students can utilize the wealth of internet resources to ask open-ended questions about real-world issues that are more interesting and meaningful to them. They can collect real-time and authentic data as well as design and carry out virtual experiments to test theories and predictions. They can engage actively in knowledge construction because they have to interpret, organize, compare, and integrate all this information to draw their own conclusions from their investigations.

While the Internet is an incredibly valuable resource that can support teaching and learning in diverse ways, its use yields many challenges for both teachers and students. Information on the Internet is unstructured and unfiltered. Inexperienced users can get lost or distracted while navigating their way through hypertext and may come across content that is not credible, relevant, or age and task appropriate. Users need to know how to perform productive searches, to identify and select the right sources, to evaluate and make sense of content that is presented in multimedia formats, and to coordinate different information sources. Research shows that finding relevant and credible information online is a time-consuming and difficult task for young students, who have several misconceptions about the nature of the Internet, do not understand fully how search engines work, and lack sufficient prior knowledge to come up with good keywords and to select relevant websites from the list of their search results (Julien & Barker, 2009; Kupier et al., 2005; Wallace, Kupperman, Krajcik, & Soloway, 2000). As a result, in online inquiry-oriented activities students tend to spend much of their time searching for information than engaging deeply with content (Wallace et al., 2000; Walraven, Brand-Gruwel, & Boshuizen, 2009; Zhang & Quintana, 2012). Also, not only elementary students but also adolescents and many adults are not able to discriminate between reliable and unreliable information, and they often use insufficient and superficial criteria to judge the trustworthiness of information, such as the appearance of a website, the amount of content, and the presence of pictures (Kupier et al., 2005; Walraven et al., 2009; Wiley et al., 2009).

In addition to the challenges regarding information search and evaluation, students face several difficulties in their efforts to process the information they find, especially when they have to coordinate facts and data from multiple sources (Rouet, 2006). Due to the hypertext structure of web documents, comprehending Internet text is a cognitively demanding activity that requires prior knowledge on website structures and a range of self-regulation strategies, because readers in a sense compose their own texts through the choices they make on what to read and which links to follow (Coiro & Dobler, 2007). Another challenge is the multimodal nature of most online texts. Students often lack "visual literacy" skills to interpret and extract important information from graphs, diagrams, and other complex visual displays as well as to synthesize information from verbal and pictorial presentations of content (Hannus & Hyönä, 1999; McTigue, 2009). Finally, integrating information from multiple sources requires readers to evaluate the trustworthiness and the nature of each source (e.g., first-hand data vs. a report), corroborate information across sources, and combine information from all sources to create a coherent whole (Rouet, 2006). Young students tend to follow the easy way to get answers to open-ended questions. They hope to find a website that provides "the right answer" and do not spontaneously engage in evaluation, selection, and synthesis of information from multiple sources to draw their own conclusion (Wallace et al., 2000; Walraven et al., 2009). In general, students are good at well-structured tasks, requiring the retrieval of specific pieces of information from given websites, but not as successful at ill-structured tasks that involve navigation, collection, and synthesis of information across multiple sites (OECD, 2011).

Web-based instruction is very demanding for the teachers because most websites are not designed for teaching and learning purposes. Leaving aside the textbook, which provides some structure for instruction, and working with the Internet require extensive planning on teachers' part. Teachers need to search and select online resources that meet the needs of their students, to transform them into instructional materials, to design learning activities that are aligned with the curriculum, and to build curricular coherence so that students "experience a reasonable progression of ideas" from one activity or website to another (Wallace, 2004). Giving students open-ended research assignments may require less preparation but places excessive demands on teachers during lesson enactment in the classroom. They need to monitor the work of their students, whose research activities typically develop into completely different directions as each group or individual comes across different content, and to provide them with extensive scaffolding due to the difficulties they face with the search, evaluation, and critical synthesis of the information they find (Wallace, 2004; Zhang & Quintana, 2012).

Although school access to the Internet has become widespread in many countries, research shows that the Internet is underused in the classroom or it is used in ways that do not utilize its full potential to enrich student learning (Schofield, 2006). This is in line with research on ICT educational integration in general, showing that, not only in Greece but also in other developed countries with higher ICT educational adoption rates, many teachers have not embraced ICTs, while most of those who have integrated technology into their teaching have not employed it in ways that support critical and active learning (Jimoyiannis & Komis, 2007; Osborne & Hennessy, 2003; Webb & Cox, 2004). According to relevant empirical studies and literature reviews, the problem is not so much teachers' lack of ICT skills but mostly their lack of knowledge about how to teach with ICTs (Jimoyiannis & Komis, 2007; Osborne & Hennessy, 2003; Webb & Cox, 2004).

Scholars have drawn on Schulman's idea of pedagogical content knowledge (PCK) and proposed the notion of PCK of educational technology (Margerum-Leys & Marx, 2002) or technological pedagogical content knowledge (TPCK) (Angeli & Valanides, 2009; Mishra & Koehler, 2006) to describe the knowledge sources that teachers need in order to successfully integrate technology into their teaching. According to the various conceptualizations of TPCK (for a review see Voogt, Fisser, Pareja Roblin, Tondeur, & van Braak, 2012), teaching with ICTs requires not only technological knowledge, content knowledge, and pedagogical knowledge, but also new, complex forms of knowledge that develop from the integration of knowledge about technology, pedagogy, and content. These other forms involve knowledge of the role of particular technologies in teaching and learning (technological pedagogical knowledge), effective pedagogies for teaching specific content (PCK), affordances of certain technologies for representing specific content (technological content knowledge), and how to teach specific content with technology in a specific context (TPCK). TPCK is a unique body of situated knowledge that develops when teachers have to transform content, pedagogical, and technological knowledge so as to solve problems regarding the use of technology as a teaching and learning tool in various contexts (Angeli & Valanides, 2009; Benson & Ward, 2013; Mouza & Karchmer-Klein, 2013).

Studies on the instructional use of the Internet as an information resource show that both in-service and preservice teachers feel ill prepared to teach with the Internet and express the need for web-related pedagogy, particularly for selecting appropriate resources and tools, for designing activities in which these resources are used creatively by the students to promote deep learning, and for techniques to scaffold the students (Childs, Twidle, Sorensen, & Godwin, 2007; Lee & Tsai, 2010; Wallace, 2004) However, there is little research about what it takes for teachers to teach effectively with the Internet and what they need to be taught to inform teacher education practice. The present study looked at preservice elementary school teachers' first attempts to design a web-based lesson, in which the Internet was used as an information resource, in order to identify challenges, misunderstandings, and learning needs that should be addressed in teacher preparation for educational technology integration. Lesson plan analysis addressed the following questions:

1. What learning activities did preservice teachers include in their lesson plans?
2. In case when they selected and provided specific Internet resources to their students, what were the characteristics of these resources?
3. What guidance and support did they consider providing to the students, through both the materials they designed (e.g., student worksheets) and the specific techniques they were planning to employ in the classroom during instruction?

Method

Participants and Context

Participants were 30 preservice teachers who were enrolled in a 4-year undergraduate teacher education program in Greece during the spring term of 2009. At the time of the study all students were attending an introductory course in educational technology that was offered in the third year of the program. The purpose of the course was to familiarize students with educational software programs that were approved by the Ministry of Education and were available in public schools for the teaching of elementary school subjects. More specifically, students were expected to develop knowledge and skills for evaluating and selecting educational software as well as for designing learning activities that involved the use of educational software.

All course sections were led by the author. Instruction took place in a computer lab and involved lectures, group work, and discussions. Students explored a variety of software programs that differed in their pedagogical design, ranging from multimedia encyclopedias, tutorials, and behaviorist drill and practice programs to constructivist software designed to support open problem solving and inquiry-oriented learning in various subject areas. Typically students collaborated in small groups to examine an educational scenario involving the use of a particular software program and were guided with worksheets to complete specific learning activities by undertaking the role of elementary school students. These scenarios and worksheets were either part of the software packages or were developed by the author. Educational scenarios employed a variety of student-centered, constructivist approaches to learning, such as problem solving of open geometry problems, a science teaching sequence designed to promote conceptual change through hypotheses testing and experimentation with a simulation, and inquiry-oriented learning in history and geography where students had to investigate open-ended questions by organizing, interpreting, and synthesizing information presented in verbal and various visual formats. The worksheets that were used in the context of these scenarios modeled a wide range of student scaffolding techniques that have been discussed in the literature (Puntambekar, Stylianou, & Goldstein, 2007; Quintana et al., 2005; van de Pol, Volman, & Beishuizen, 2010), such as simple illustrated instructions on how to use particular software features; prompts that recommended specific steps or requested students to provide hypotheses, predictions, observations, and conclusions; as well as prompts and tables for organizing information and drawing conclusions. Lectures and discussions focused on the pedagogical design of each software program, its affordances and the instructional approaches it could support, the potential difficulties that elementary students might encounter while learning with it, and the scaffolding they would need to successfully meet the learning goals of the lesson. Also, through discussions focusing on the analysis of each educational scenario, students were encouraged to make connections between curriculum learning goals, pedagogy, and characteristics of the software.

One of the 3-h course sessions, which was structured in a similar manner, focused on web learning. After an introductory lecture that addressed the challenges of web learning for elementary students as well as the areas in which they need pedagogical support, preservice teachers examined two educational scenarios (one designed by the author and one found online) that introduced them to a variety of online information resources and some of the ways these resources could be utilized in instruction. In these scenarios students explored specific research questions using pre-selected web resources, guided with worksheets. However, the scenarios differed in their pedagogical approach. The first modeled an inquiry-oriented approach, as it requested students to draw their own conclusions by organizing and comparing information from multiple sources, including authentic data, while the other scenario requested students to answer a series of factual questions using a variety of sites that provided predominantly encyclopedic knowledge. Preservice teachers then compared the two scenarios focusing on the types of learning they promoted, the affordances of the information resources, potential challenges for elementary school students, and the types of support that was provided through the student worksheets.

One of the course requirements, to be fulfilled at the end of the course, was the design of a 2-h lesson involving the use of ICTs. Students were provided with five options (i.e., using a specific software program to teach a specific curriculum topic), one of which involved teaching an earth science topic using information resources from the Internet. The topic, which was included in the sixth-grade geography curriculum, was entitled "Natural disasters and their impact in human lives" and addressed the causes and the impact of earthquakes and volcanoes as well as the phenomena of erosion, weathering, and deposition. Preservice teachers were provided with detailed instructions on what to consider in designing their lesson plans (see section "Data" below) and were expected to use pedagogical approaches and techniques that were modeled through the scenarios that they had explored in class during the semester. Of the 116 undergraduate students who completed this requirement 30 designed a lesson that involved teaching earth science with the Internet.

Data

The data of the present study consist of the lesson plans submitted by the 30 preservice teachers who chose to design a hypothetical lesson in which sixth-grade students were going to use learning and informational materials on the web. Following the instructions that were provided, in these lesson plans preservice teachers had to present the learning goals of the lesson; discuss the knowledge and skills as well as the misunderstandings and difficulties that sixth-grade students might have relative to the content and the use of online materials based on the literature (i.e., relevant articles and lecture slides that were included in course materials); explain in detail how they would carry out the lesson and which teaching methods and techniques they would use to support their students so as to attain the goals of the lesson; describe how they would assess their students; and, finally, provide all the materials they would use (e.g., worksheets, slides, tests, pre-selected websites) and explain the rationale for their selection or design.

Analysis of instructional practice artifacts, such as lesson plans and learning materials designed by prospective or in-service teachers, has been used successfully in teacher education research for the study of teacher thought processes and practices (e.g., Mouza & Karchmer-Klein, 2013; Silver, Mesa, Morris, Star, & Benken, 2009), either as an alternative to or in combination with classroom observations and survey methods. Although artifact analysis is a less direct method of teaching effectiveness research compared to observations of actual teaching, relevant studies show that it enables researchers to accurately characterize classroom practice and to draw valid inferences about teacher knowledge and beliefs (Borko, Stecher, & Kuffner, 2007; Matsumura, Garnier, Pascal, & Valdés, 2002). In the present study preservice teachers' lesson plans were analyzed so as to identify knowledge gaps and possible misunderstandings regarding the use of the Internet as an information resource in teaching and learning.

Data Analysis

Guided by the research questions of the study, data analysis attended to three issues: the activities that preservice teachers had designed, the characteristics of the web materials they had selected, and the guidance and support they had considered providing to their students.

The unit of analysis was the activity. Activities, which involved tasks assigned to the students and instructional sequences carried out by the teacher, were identified based on preservice teachers' lesson plan descriptions and student worksheets. Specifically, transition from one activity to the other was recognized through changes in at least one of the following: the learning goal, the content, and the teaching–learning approach. Activities that did not involve or were not directly relevant to the use of Internet resources (e.g., teacher-led question answering in the beginning of the lesson to elicit student knowledge and experiences relevant to the topic) were not included in the analysis.

Activities. Instructional activities were classified based on (a) whether they were teacher directed or student centered and (b) the complexity of the online research task that was assigned to the students (e.g., well-defined query to answer a factual question vs. ill-structured research).

Websites. Websites that had been selected by preservice teachers, to be used in teacher-led instruction or student-centered activities, were analyzed in terms of their level of *multimodality* and *interactivity*. Multimodality refers to the range of modes (verbal and nonverbal) that were used to present information (Moreno & Mayer, 2007). Each selected webpage was examined for the types of nonverbal representations (e.g., diagram, map, photo, animation) that were present besides printed words or narration. Then a multimodality score was calculated to characterize the range of pictorial representations that were utilized in the entire lesson plan. Specifically, each lesson received 1 point for each type of visual representation that was utilized.

Two levels were used to code interactivity based on the classification system proposed by Moreno and Mayer (2007). A website provided low interactivity if it allowed the user to perform simple navigation and search actions, such as click on a link or button to move, select an option, or enter a simple query. High interactivity was enabled when users could manipulate a simulation, control the pace and order of a presentation, and receive feedback to their input.

Support. The coding scheme for analyzing teacher support, as reflected in preservice teachers' activity descriptions and student worksheets, was developed through multiple readings of the materials. I looked for scaffolding techniques that have been recommended in the literature (e.g., Kupier et al., 2005; Li & Lim, 2008; Quintana et al., 2005; Segers & Verhoeven, 2009; Wallace, 2004; Zhang & Quintana, 2012), which were modeled or explained to preservice teachers during the course, as effective or needed to guide students with three aspects of web learning: searching for information, evaluating information, and processing of information. Examples of relevant techniques involve explaining how particular search engines work, modeling or recommending specific steps and actions, providing keyword lists, navigation instructions and criteria for evaluating the trustworthiness of information on websites, and asking questions or providing prompts that help students retrieve, compare, organize, and interpret information. The final coding scheme for the techniques that were identified during this iterative process is presented in Table 1.

When the development of the final coding scheme for activity type and teacher support was completed, one-third of the lesson plans were coded by an independent examiner. Inter-rater agreement was 94 % for activity type and 89.5 % for teacher support.

Results

Analysis of the teaching and learning activities that preservice teachers designed shows that they utilized the Internet in four ways: (a) they used visual web resources to enrich *teacher-directed instruction*, that is, teacher presentations and class

Table 1 Types of support for information search, evaluation, and processing by activity type

| | Student activities | | |
	Information search ($n=8$)	Information retrieval ($n=37$)	Information research ($n=17$)
Types of support			
Information search			
Shows how to search with a search engine	1	1	4
Provides URL/keywords and site selection guidance	5	29	9
Shows how to navigate a site and what to select		13	
Total	6	43	13
Evaluation of information			
Shows how URLs can be used in source evaluation			1
Uses author as a criterion to evaluate content			1
Total	0	0	2
Processing of information			
Asks questions to help focus on important ideas	2	23	2
Asks reflection questions			1
Asks students to make a hypothesis		3	
Asks students to interpret information			1
Provides a table to organize information			1
Asks summarization questions		1	
Provides background information		6	
Provides concept map to organize information		1	
Total	2	34	5

Note: Numbers in columns show the presence of each type of support in each learning activity

discussions; (b) they included *search activities* requiring students to perform an open-search web query; (c) they designed *information retrieval activities* in which students would explore the content of one particular website to obtain factual information; and (d) they designed *open-ended research activities* requiring students to search for, retrieve, and synthesize information about a particular topic from multiple web sources. *Web-search activities* involved searching for images and/or videos relevant to lesson topics. *Information retrieval activities* included viewing images, animations, and videos or reading a webpage with the purpose of obtaining factual information, running a simulation (e.g., build a volcano and watch it explode), and locating geographical information using Google Earth. Although the last two activities involved learning through interaction with a system, they were categorized as information retrieval activities because students were asked to either make a simple observation or answer a factual question (i.e., use Google Earth to find the location of particular volcanos). Often in information retrieval activities students were guided with questions, to be provided orally by the teacher or through worksheets, that aimed at helping them focus on and retrieve specific pieces of information. Finally, in *open-ended research activities* students were asked to gather and present information about a topic (e.g., the volcano of the Greek island Santorini, the most disastrous earthquakes, or the most important volcanos on earth). These activities were open ended in some sense because they required gathering information from multiple sources (although it was likely that someone might locate a single webpage containing enough information to cover the topic). However, none of these activities involved the investigation of a complex, authentic question, requiring students to come up with their own answers by interpreting, comparing, and integrating information, which is an essential element of inquiry-oriented learning.

None of the participants designed a "traditional" lesson where ICTs would be used exclusively by the teacher to explain content or stimulate discussions. Most preservice teachers ($n=17$) used a combination of teacher-directed instruction and activities to be carried out by the students, while the remaining 13 based their lesson solely on information search, retrieval, and/or research activities. Overall, 15 participants included information retrieval activities, 15 designed open research activities, and 8 used web-search activities. Typically, students did not combine information retrieval with open research activities. It seems that they either adopted a "structured" approach, involving information retrieval activities, which in some cases were combined with teacher-directed instruction and/or search activities, or an "open" approach involving open research activities that were often combined with teacher-directed instruction and/or search activities.

Twenty-seven preservice teachers selected webpages or materials found online, such as photos and videos, to be used either in teacher-directed instruction or in student activities. These websites or materials were analyzed for their level of multimodality, and a score was calculated for each lesson. Participants used five types of representations: photos, maps, diagrams, animations, and videos. The mean multimodality score for their group was relatively low ($M=2.55$), indicating that on average preservice teachers had utilized a small range of visual resources in their lesson plans. A closer inspection of the data showed that while half of the participants ($n=14$) had selected at least three types of representations, many participants ($n=10$) had used only photos. Typically, teacher presentations and discussions were enriched with static visual displays, which were primarily photos and to a lesser extent maps and explanatory diagrams, although some participants also included videos and animations. In addition, preservice teachers tended to select sites that enabled little interactivity. Only five participants selected interactive representations of content (e.g., simulations, Google Earth) to be utilized in the context of information retrieval activities.

An incidental finding from the analysis of the websites was that about half of the participants had selected at least one resource that was inappropriate relevant to the activity for which it was used. Specifically, some preservice teachers ($n=7$) had included content from unreliable sources such as commercial sites and personal blogs, treating them uncritically as authoritative sources, although some of them provided scientifically inaccurate information. In addition, about half of the participants used texts from sites that were designed for adults to provide students with background encyclopedic information on lesson topics. However, these texts could not be easily accessible to elementary students due to text length and excessive use of scientific terms and sophisticated explanations. Also, some of the selected resources provided affordances not clearly tight to lesson learning goals, such as a simulation that enabled students to create different types of volcanos by manipulating gas and viscosity levels. Finally, many preservice teachers selected images and videos that did not communicate information clearly and effectively due to poor quality (e.g., low resolution) or the provision of many unnecessary and irrelevant details.

An examination of the techniques that preservice teachers had considered using so as to support their students, either orally or in the form of prompts and questions in student worksheets, showed several interesting patterns. First of all, as Table 1 shows, most participants included a small range of techniques which focused mostly on the search process and to a lesser extent on information processing. Regarding the latter, the majority of the participants who planned to provide support on information processing used questions to help students retrieve specific pieces of information. Also, only one preservice teacher thought to provide students with support on how to evaluate the trustworthiness of web content.

Another interesting pattern is that students were more likely to provide support for the information retrieval activities than for the research activities. Typically, in information retrieval activities preservice teachers guided students to locate specific pages, by providing them with keywords or specific URLs, and gave navigation instructions for websites that offered many options. This guidance was expected because elementary students were going to use pre-selected sites. On the other hand, participants who designed open research activities provided minimal or no guidance on how students should search for, evaluate, and choose appropriate sites for their projects. In addition, in information retrieval activities most preservice teachers provided students with questions to help them focus on important information when exploring the content of websites. On the other hand, the vast majority of participants who included open research activities in their lesson plans did not consider providing support to help their students retrieve, comprehend, organize, compare, and integrate information that was relevant to their topics. Finally, students who included web-search activities were likely to provide some support for the search process, but only two of them thought to give students some instructions on what to do with the results of their query.

Discussion

The data of this study represent preservice teachers' first attempts to design a lesson that involved teaching using Internet information resources. This particular group of undergraduate students had one more year of study in their teacher preparation program, involving more coursework on teaching methods in the subject areas as well as field experience in local public schools and, therefore, more opportunities to further develop their knowledge and skills about teaching and learning. So, it is likely that their instructional materials would have been more sophisticated if they had been asked to design a similar lesson near the end of their fourth year in the program. Also, in the present study preservice teachers designed hypothetical lessons which were not going to be implemented in a real classroom with real students and real technologies. This suggests that their ideas were not fully developed because preservice teachers did not have to think through all the details of an actual lesson enactment, and their lesson plans were based on a hypothetical, abstract classroom context.

Despite the above limitations, the patterns that emerged from the analysis of the data provide useful insights into the possible misunderstandings and knowledge gaps that preservice teachers may have about teaching with the Internet and about online inquiry. Therefore, the conclusions of the present study can guide the design of future teacher education and professional development courses and seminars focusing on teaching with ICTs and, more specifically, on teaching with the use of Internet information resources.

It is encouraging that all participants included in their lesson plans instructional activities that involved the use of ICTs by their students, as opposed to the use of technology exclusively as a demonstration tool in teacher-directed instruction. Two distinct patterns emerged in their approaches. About half of preservice teachers used a "structured" approach that involved information retrieval activities or some combination of information retrieval activities, teacher-directed instruction, and search activities, while the other half used an "open" approach, involving open research activities or some combination of open research activities, teacher-directed instruction, and search activities. Participants adopting a structured approach appeared to be aware of the difficulties that their students might have with the information search process, with website evaluation and navigation, and with the extraction and comprehension of relevant content. So they provided guidance by directing students to pre-selected sites and by helping them locate and focus on important information through navigation instructions and factual questions. However, this approach was over-structured because it limited independent learning and focused on the acquisition of fragmented factual knowledge. Students were not encouraged to engage actively with content by exploring hypotheses, organizing and comparing information, and making new connections among ideas. On the other hand, preservice teachers who adopted an open approach seemed to have unrealistic expectations about elementary students' abilities to learn via open online research with minimal guidance (Kirschner, Sweller, & Clark, 2006; Quintana et al., 2005). These participants provided some support for the search process but no guidance on how students were going to evaluate, select, and utilize the resources they would find online in order to achieve the learning goals of the lesson. Also, none of the preservice teachers designed an activity addressing an authentic inquiry question. Elementary students were given some general topics or questions that required the collection of factual information (e.g., "The volcano of Santorini," "What were some of the most disastrous volcanic eruptions?"), as opposed to questions requiring them to draw conclusions through the corroboration and integration of information from multiple sources. It would be quite hard even for experienced teachers to design an inquiry project that could be realized within two periods. However, it was expected that preservice teachers would have included in the design of their lesson plans more opportunities for deep and meaningful learning, utilizing some of the pedagogical techniques that were modeled throughout their educational technology course. It was also interesting that a large number of preservice teachers designed open research activities, although this approach was not modeled during the educational technology course. On the contrary, both through the lecture and the discussion of the educational scenarios that focused on web learning, it was stressed that open research learning is an ineffective approach when implemented without extensive teacher scaffolding due to the many challenges that young students face with the search, selection, evaluation, and processing of information.

The analysis of the types of support that preservice teachers had considered for elementary students showed that most of the techniques they described concerned the information search process. This indicates that preservice teachers were generally aware of some of the difficulties that elementary students might have with online search and could also come up with specific techniques to make this process more manageable. However, preservice teachers demonstrated a limited repertoire of techniques to scaffold elementary students with web learning beyond the level of factual information extraction. Very few participants considered assisting students with the evaluation, selection, organization, critical analysis, and integration of information or with the preparation of their project presentations. And none of the participants considered it necessary to provide specific suggestions to help students comprehend and think critically about the visual resources.

Overall, preservice teachers made extensive use of videos and static visual displays (i.e., photos, diagrams, and maps), but about half of them did not utilize the full range of content representations that were available online. Specifically, ten preservice teachers used only photos and only five participants selected interactive representations of content, which have the potential to engage students more actively in learning. However, even these five participants did not take full advantage of the representations' affordances because their proposed use by the students was limited to making simple observations and to retrieving factual information as opposed to asking questions, testing predictions, or observing patterns. Also, those who chose the "build-a-volcano" simulation were possibly attracted by the interactivity it provided, but they used it in a way that was not clearly relevant to their lesson goals. In addition, according to the analysis of preservice teachers' website selections, many of the participants did not know how to select appropriate sites for young students in terms of the quality, trustworthiness, and age appropriateness of their content.

The findings of the present study point out several issues that should be addressed in teacher preparation programs regarding web-based instruction. In line with the TPCK framework (Angeli & Valanides, 2009; Benson & Ward, 2013; Mouza & Karchmer-Klein, 2013), they highlight that, in order to use the Internet productively and creatively as an information resource, teachers need to develop complex forms of knowledge that require the integration of knowledge about technology, pedagogy, and content.

First of all, as previous studies have shown (e.g., Childs et al., 2007; Wallace, 2004) it is clear that preservice teachers are in great need for instruction on how to select appropriate web content. Selecting Internet resources involves several complex criteria that require the consideration of the technological characteristics of the resources, their affordances for learning and their credibility, the subject matter, the learning goals and the teaching approach, as well as students' prior knowledge and digital skills. Based on the findings of this study, preservice teachers need to learn how to evaluate websites for:

(a) Their general quality as learning resources using established, research-based text-design and multimedia-design principles (Hartley, 2004; Mayer, 2005).
(b) The nature and credibility of their source.
(c) Their appropriateness for students of particular age relative to their prior knowledge and navigation abilities.
(d) Their relevance relative to lesson content and learning goals.
(e) Their affordances regarding the types of learning they can support.

In addition, preservice teachers need to develop technological pedagogical knowledge about inquiry-oriented approaches to web-based instruction as well as about students' potential difficulties with web-based learning, which concern not only the process of information search and evaluation but also the comprehension of multimodal documents and the critical analysis and synthesis of information from multiple texts and data sources. Teachers need to also develop TPCK about techniques for scaffolding students to engage successfully and productively both with the processes and with the content of online inquiry.

All the above are complex forms of knowledge which develop progressively and require extensive teacher involvement in critical reasoning and problem solving regarding authentic instructional situations (Angeli & Valanides, 2009; Margerum-Leys & Marx, 2002; Mouza & Karchmer-Klein, 2013). In order to help preservice teachers integrate knowledge of content, pedagogy, and technology, teacher preparation programs should provide student teachers with opportunities to analyze, plan, enact, and reflect on web-based instruction in the content areas. This in turn may require that, at some level in the teacher preparation program, educational technology courses are integrated with field practicum and teaching method courses, so that preservice teachers are supported to transform and integrate theoretical knowledge obtained through separate courses into practical forms of technological pedagogical and technological pedagogical content knowledge.

In agreement with what research has shown about experienced in-service teachers (Osborne & Hennessy, 2003; Schofield, 2006; Wallace, 2004), the participants of this study could not find an alternative or a balance between two extreme approaches to Internet use in the classroom: the open research and the over-structured approach, both of which, for different reasons, do not enable learners to engage actively with content. In the open research approach students are likely to encounter many inappropriate sites and to spend most of their time and effort searching for relevant information, which severely reduces the cognitive resources they can allocate to the comprehension, evaluation, and synthesis of the information (Segers & Verhoeven, 2009; Zhang & Quintana, 2012). Without enough guidance and scaffolding, students typically gain only superficial understandings of their research topics. Poor learning outcomes may also be observed with the over-structured approach. The latter offers security and direction, but, by focusing on factual learning and by constraining students' independence, it limits their opportunities to develop deep content understandings and critical skills. The fact that these two extreme approaches have been observed not only in the preservice teachers of this study but also among experienced in-service teachers is related to the nature of the Internet itself and reflects teachers' confusion regarding how to both capitalize on its potential to support independent, student-centered learning and set boundaries so as to ensure that students learn something while using it (Schofield, 2006; Wallace, 2004). Although several scholars (e.g., Li & Lim, 2008; Segers & Verhoeven, 2009; Zhang & Quintana, 2012) have been exploring the effectiveness of particular approaches (e.g., web quests), scaffolding techniques, and technological tools that aim at maximizing the benefits of web-based instruction and online inquiry for students, there is clearly a need for more research in this area to provide productive suggestions for teachers regarding alternatives to these two typical extremes.

References

Anderson, R. D. (2002). Reforming science teaching: What research says about inquiry? *Journal of Science Teacher Education, 13*(1), 1–12.

Angeli, C., & Valanides, N. (2009). Epistemological and methodological issues for the conceptualization, development, and assessment of ICT-PCK: Advances in technological pedagogical content knowledge. *Computers and Education, 52*(1), 154–168.

Benson, S. N. K., & Ward, C. L. (2013). Teaching with technology: Using TPACK to understand teaching expertise in online higher education. *Journal of Educational Computing Research, 48*(2), 153–172.

Borko, H., Stecher, B., & Kuffner, K. (2007). *Using artifacts to characterize reform-oriented instruction: The scoop notebook and rating guide (CSE Tech. Rep. No. 707).* Los Angeles: Center for the Study of Evaluation, National Center for Research on Evaluation, Standards, and Student Testing (CRESST). Accessed November 12, 2010, from http://www.cse.ucla.edu/products/reports/R707.pdf

Childs, A., Twidle, J., Sorensen, P., & Godwin, J. (2007). Trainee teachers' use of the Internet—opportunities and challenges for initial teacher education. *Research in Science and Technological Education, 25*(1), 77–97.

Coiro, J., & Dobler, E. (2007). Exploring the online reading comprehension strategies used by sixth-grade skilled readers to search for and locate information on the internet. *Reading Research Quarterly, 42*(2), 214–257.

Hannus, M., & Hyönä, J. (1999). Utilization of illustrations during learning of science textbook passages among low- and high-ability children. *Contemporary Educational Psychology, 24*, 95–123.

Hartley, J. (2004). Designing instructional and informational text. In D. H. Jonassen (Ed.), *Handbook of research for educational communications and technology* (2nd ed., pp. 917–945). Mahwah, NJ: Lawrence Erlbaum Associates.

Jimoyiannis, A., & Komis, V. (2007). Examining teachers' beliefs about ICT in education: Implications of a teacher preparation programme. *Teacher Development, 11*, 149–173.

Julien, H., & Barker, S. (2009). How high-school students find and evaluate scientific information: A basis for information literacy skills development. *Library & Information Science Research, 31*(1), 12–17.

Kirschner, P. A., Sweller, J., & Clark, R. E. (2006). Why minimal guidance during instruction does not work: An analysis of the failure of constructivist, discovery, problem-based, experiential, and inquiry-based teaching. *Educational Psychologist, 41*(2), 75–86.

Kupier, E., Volman, M., & Terwel, J. (2005). The web as an information resource in K-12 education: Strategies for supporting students in searching and processing information. *Review of Educational Research, 75*(3), 285–328.

Lee, M.-H., & Tsai, C.-C. (2010). Exploring teachers' perceived self-efficacy and technological pedagogical content knowledge with respect to educational use of the World Wide Web. *Instructional Science, 38*(1), 1–21.

Li, D. D., & Lim, C. P. (2008). Scaffolding online historical inquiry tasks: A case study of two secondary school classrooms. *Computers and Education, 50*, 1394–1410.

Margerum-Leys, J., & Marx, R. W. (2002). Teacher knowledge of educational technology: A case study of student teacher/mentor teacher pairs. *Journal of Educational Computing Research, 26*(4), 427–462.

Matsumura, L. C., Garnier, H., Pascal, J., & Valdés, R. (2002). Measuring instructional quality in accountability systems: Classroom assignments and student achievement. *Educational Assessment, 8*, 207–229.

Mayer, R. E. (2005). *The Cambridge handbook of multimedia learning*. New York, NY: Cambridge University Press.

McTigue, E. M. (2009). Does multimedia learning theory extend to middle-school students? *Contemporary Educational Psychology, 34*, 143–153.

Minner, D. D., Levy, A. J., & Century, J. (2010). Inquiry-based science instruction—what is it and does it matter? Results from a research synthesis years 1984–2002. *Journal of Research in Science Teaching, 47*(4), 474–496.

Mishra, P., & Koehler, M. J. (2006). Technological pedagogical content knowledge: A framework for teacher knowledge. *Teachers College Record, 108*(6), 1017–1054.

Moreno, R., & Mayer, R. (2007). Interactive multimodal learning environments. *Educational Psychology Review, 19*(3), 309–326.

Mouza, C., & Karchmer-Klein, R. (2013). Promoting and assessing pre-service teachers' technological pedagogical content knowledge (TPACK) in the context of case development. *Journal of Educational Computing Research, 48*(2), 127–152.

OECD. (2011). *PISA 2009 results: Students on line: Digital technologies and performance* (Volume VI). Accessed December 18, 2012, from http://dx.doi.org/10.1787/9789264112995-en

Osborne, J., & Hennessy, S. (2003). *Literature review in science education and the role of ICT: Promise, problems and future directions*. Bristol: Futurelab. Accessed September 24, 2011, from http://www.nfcr.ac.uk/publications/FUTL74

Puntambekar, S., Stylianou, A., & Goldstein, J. (2007). Comparing classroom enactments of an inquiry curriculum: Lessons learned from two teachers. *The Journal of the Learning Sciences, 16*(1), 81–130.

Quintana, C., Zhang, M., & Krajcik, J. (2005). A framework for supporting metacognitive aspects of online inquiry through software-based scaffolding. *Educational Psychologist, 40*(4), 235–244.

Rouet, J.-F. (2006). *The skills of document use: From text comprehension to Web-based learning*. Mahwah, NJ: Lawrence Erlbaum Associates.

Schofield, J. W. (2006). Internet use in schools: Promise and problems. In R. K. Sawyer (Ed.), *The Cambridge handbook of the learning sciences* (pp. 521–534). New York, NY: Cambridge University Press.

Segers, E., & Verhoeven, L. (2009). Learning in a sheltered Internet environment: The use of WebQuests. *Learning and Instruction, 19*, 423–432.

Silver, E. A., Mesa, V. M., Morris, K. A., Star, J. R., & Benken, B. M. (2009). Teaching mathematics for understanding: An analysis of lessons submitted by teachers seeking NBPTS certification. *American Educational Research Journal, 46*(2), 501–531.

van de Pol, J., Volman, M., & Beishuizen, J. (2010). Scaffolding in teacher-student interaction: A decade of research. *Review of Educational Research, 22*, 271–296.

Voogt, J., Fisser, P., Pareja Roblin, N., Tondeur, J., & van Braak, J. (2012). Technological pedagogical content knowledge—a review of the literature. *Journal of Computer Assisted Learning, 29*, 109–121.

Wallace, R. M. (2004). A framework for understanding teaching with the internet. *American Educational Research Journal, 41*(2), 447–488.

Wallace, R. M., Kupperman, J., Krajcik, J., & Soloway, E. (2000). Science on the Web: Students on-line in a sixth-grade classroom. *Journal of the Learning Sciences, 9*(1), 75–104.

Walraven, A., Brand-Gruwel, S., & Boshuizen, H. P. A. (2009). How students evaluate information and sources when searching the World Wide Web for information. *Computers in Education, 25*, 234–246.

Webb, M., & Cox, M. (2004). A review of pedagogy related to information and communications technology. *Technology, Pedagogy and Education, 13*, 235–286.

Wiley, J., Goldman, S. R., Graeser, A. C., Sanchez, C. A., Ash, I. K., & Hemmerich, J. A. (2009). Source evaluation, comprehension, and learning in internet science inquiry tasks. *American Educational Research Journal, 46*(4), 1016–1106.

Zhang, M., & Quintana, C. (2012). Scaffolding strategies for supporting middle school students' online inquiry processes. *Computers and Education, 58*, 181–196.

Part VII
ICT for Specialized Uses

Conversational Agents for Learning: How the Agent Role Affects Student Communication

Stergios Tegos, Anastasios Karakostas, and Stavros Demetriadis

Introducing Conversational Agents

In the field of artificial intelligence, the terms "agent" or "intelligent system" refer to any entity that perceives its environment through sensors and acts upon it using effectors (Franklin & Graesser, 1997). However, through the prism of e-learning, a "pedagogical agent" refers to a computer-generated character typically employed to fulfill a series of pedagogical aims in an educational system (Gulz, Haake, Silvervarg, Sjödén, & Veletsianos, 2011).

In our work, we focus on "conversational agents," a subgroup of pedagogical agents that engage in a conversation with the learners using natural language. The type of communication occurring between a conversational agent and a learner can be text based, oral, or even nonverbal, including body language movements and facial expressions (Kerly, Ellis, & Bull, 2009).

Moreover, the graphical representation of conversational agents may also vary, ranging from a two-dimensional cartoonish appearance to a three-dimensional photo-realistic character (Veletsianos, 2010). Conversational agents that have a visual representation are frequently mentioned as "embodied" conversational agents (Cassell, Sullivan, Prevost, & Churchill, 2000). Research has repeatedly identified the agent visual appearance as an important design element, which affects learners' stereotypes or expectations of the agent intelligence (e.g., Haake & Gulz, 2008; Veletsianos, 2010). Indeed, the agent embodiment had a major impact on the evolution of conversational agents from the impersonal characters found in the intelligent tutoring systems (ITSs) of the past to the tangible personalized pedagogical agents of today (Gulz et al., 2011).

S. Tegos (✉) • A. Karakostas • S. Demetriadis
Department of Informatics, Aristotle University of Thessaloniki,
University Campus, 54124 Thessaloniki, Greece
e-mail: stegos@csd.auth.gr; akarakos@csd.auth.gr; sdemetri@csd.auth.gr

C. Karagiannidis et al. (eds.), *Research on e-Learning and ICT in Education: Technological, Pedagogical and Instructional Perspectives*, DOI 10.1007/978-1-4614-6501-0_17, © Springer Science+Business Media New York 2014

Another important factor regarding the agent design is the role of the agent in the learning environment. Conversational agents have been developed to serve multiple pedagogical roles including—but not limited to—coaches, tutors, motivators, or learning partners (Haake & Gulz, 2009). Many studies have been conducted to explore the various roles and uses of conversational agents in individual learning settings, where the agent has engaged in one-to-one interactions with the learner (Kerly et al., 2009). Agents acting as peer learners have been shown to lower students' anxiety and promote students' empathy (Chase, Chin, Oppezzo, & Schwartz, 2009). Additionally, it was reported that such agents tend to be less intrusive than agents acting as instructors (Sklar & Richards, 2010).

More recently, taking into account the pedagogical benefits of computer-supported collaborative learning (CSCL) (Dillenbourg, 1999), researchers have expressed their interest in assessing the use of conversational agents in providing dynamic collaborative learning support (e.g., Chaudhuri, Kumar, Howley, & Rosé, 2009; Walker, Rummel, & Koedinger, 2011). A study revealed that conversational agents can efficiently utilize both social and task-oriented intervention strategies to support students' collaboration (Kumar, Ai, Beuth, & Rosé, 2010). Furthermore, other studies explored the positive impact of conversational agents on collaborative learning settings by emphasizing on discourse scaffolding (Stahl, Rosé, O'Hara, & Powell, 2010), reflective prompting (Walker et al., 2011), or reasoning elicitation (Kumar, Rosé, Wang, Joshi, & Robinson, 2007).

Encouraging as such findings may be, several key questions have emerged. For instance, what types of collaborative problems are best suited for such conversational agent systems? (Harrer, McLaren, Walker, Bollen, & Sewall, 2006) Should the supportive prompts provided by the agent be solicited or unsolicited? (Chaudhuri et al., 2009) How can the different roles of the agent (e.g., tutor, peer, motivator) affect peer dialogue? What is the impact of the agent presence ("persona effect") on the behavior of students working together? (Veletsianos & Russell, 2014)

Following this potentially promising research direction, we have argued that conversational agents for collaborative learning can be designed by focusing on the role of the teacher as well as the peers' interactions occurring while students work together (Tegos, Demetriadis, & Tsiatsos, 2012). Based on this rationale, we have developed a prototype conversational agent system, named MentorChat (Tegos, Demetriadis, & Tsiatsos, 2014). In the following sections, we present an overview of the MentorChat system and an evaluation study exploring how the students' perceptions of the agent and their conversational behavior may be affected by the different roles (peer or tutor) of a conversational agent.

MentorChat System Overview

MentorChat is a cloud-based multimodal dialogue system that utilizes an embodied conversational agent to scaffold learners' discussions (Tegos et al., 2014). We have developed MentorChat as a domain-independent dialogue system that (a) promotes

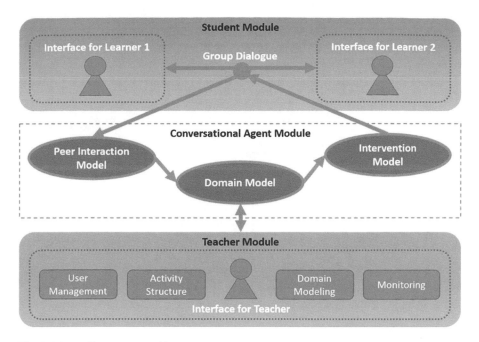

Fig. 1 MentorChat system architecture

constructive peer interactions using facilitative agent interventions (prompts) and (b) enables the teacher to configure the support provided by the conversational agent.

MentorChat can support discussions in English or Greek and was implemented using modern web technologies, such as HTML5, CSS3, and AJAX. The system infrastructure is based on a client–server model, which allocates workloads between the server and the clients. Its architecture comprises three main modules: the student, the teacher, and the conversational agent module (Fig. 1).

The conversational agent of MentorChat is based upon the following three models:

- The peer interaction model, which records and stores the students' interactions in a computational format
- The domain model, which utilizes the teacher's domain knowledge representation in conjunction with the pattern-matching algorithms to determine whether an agent intervention would be appropriate
- The intervention model, which examines a series of various micro-parameters (e.g., the time passed since the last agent intervention) to determine if an intervention will eventually be displayed

A teacher can use MentorChat to design, deploy, and monitor an online dialogue-based learning activity. These can be accomplished using the MentorChat administration panels, which are available in the teacher's interface. More specifically, the teacher may set up the discussion topics/phases of the collaborative

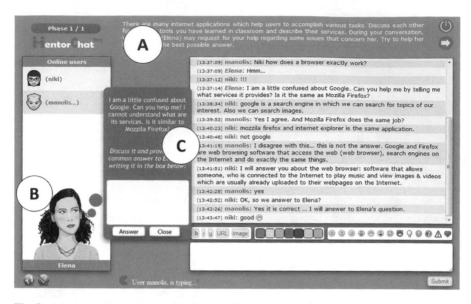

Fig. 2 A (translated) screenshot of the MentorChat student interface

activity (activity structure panel), manage the participating users and groups (user management panel), monitor groups' discussions (monitoring panel), or configure the agent domain model for the activity by inserting a set of rules or creating a concept map (domain modeling panel).

Students entering MentorChat are asked to collaborate with their partner(s) on a given task (Fig. 2, A) using text-based synchronous communication. During the students' dialogue, an animated humanlike conversational agent (Fig. 2, B) analyzes their discussion providing supportive interventions that trigger fruitful peer interactions on key domain concepts. Each agent intervention is dynamically displayed in a pop-up frame, next to the peers' chat frame (Fig. 2, C), allowing learners to complete their ongoing conversational interaction before answering the agent question.

Method

MentorChat was used in an experimental activity, which was conducted in the context of a computer science course offered by the Second Chance School of Thessaloniki in Greece. The aim of the study was to explore the impact of two different agent roles (peer vs. tutor) on students' perceptions and behavior. The total participants of the study were 24 Second Chance School students (13 males and 11 females), who were not able to attend mainstream secondary education for various socioeconomic reasons. Students were adults whose age ranged from 19 to 67 years ($N=24$, $M=37.4$, SD $=13.36$). Although their nationality also varied (e.g., Albanians, Bulgarians, Greeks), all of them spoke Greek in class.

Procedure

In the course lectures, the students were introduced to the concepts of the Internet and the web-based applications. The classroom sessions involved many discussions around synchronous and asynchronous communication tools, micro-blogging, blogging, and social networking. The MentorChat environment was also presented to the students as an example of an online collaborative learning environment.

After a 3-week period, an experimental activity was carried out in the computer lab of the Second Chance School for 2 teaching hours (90 min). The participating students were asked to use MentorChat to discuss the web applications they had learned and used in class. They were also informed that during their conversation a virtual peer or tutor would raise some questions, which they should discuss within their group in order to provide a joint answer.

The agent was configured by the two classroom teachers to raise issues regarding social networking, search engines, and modern communication tools. In particular, the teachers used the MentorChat domain authoring panel to form the agent domain model by entering a set of rules. Each rule consisted of a domain concept (a key word or phrase—e.g., "Mozilla Firefox") along with a particular intervention. The interventions were reflective questions that asked students to elaborate on the subject and provide a thoughtful joint response (e.g., "If you want to create a webpage featuring articles in a chronological order, should you use a blog or a wiki? Why?").

During the students' discourse, the conversational agent displayed the teacher-defined intervention whenever the associated domain concept (keyword or phrase) was identified. Subsequently, the students were encouraged to discuss with each other and provide a joint response, typing their answer into the agent answer box (Fig. 2, C). In addition to this intervention method, which was active throughout the students' discussion, a final intervention was also made by the agent at the end of the activity. More specifically, before exiting the activity, the agent reminded students all the teacher-defined domain concepts that had not mentioned during their discussion, providing them with the option to continue their conversations on the suggested topics (e.g., "It seems that you have not discussed wikis. Do you want to continue your discussion or finish the activity?"). If students' discussion included all the teacher-defined domain concepts, the agent did not display any intervention.

Compared Conditions

The teachers assigned the students into small groups consisting of two or three members (six dyads and four triads). Each student was given a score, which indicated students' expertise in computer science (based on the course grades and in-class performance), and the final groups emerged in such a way as to be slightly heterogeneous. According to Rovai (2007), the above method constitutes an effective strategy for creating an educational context that facilitates peers' online discussions and promotes equal participation.

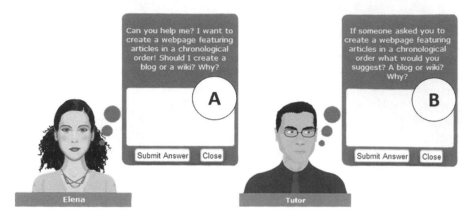

Fig. 3 The agents acting as peer (A) and tutor (B) in the P and T conditions, respectively

Furthermore, a combined score was also calculated for each group based on the average of the individual students' scores. Taking this score into account, instructors stratified the student groups by their domain knowledge and assigned them to two conditions so that both conditions were balanced in terms of the overall scores of the groups.

Our two-condition experimental design involved (a) six groups (four dyads and two triads) interacting with a conversational agent that enacted the role of a peer (P condition) displaying the interventions in an informal manner (Fig. 3, A) and (b) five groups (two dyads and three triads) interacting with an agent that enacted the role of a tutor (T condition) employing a more formal appearance and communication style (Fig. 3, B). Each of the teacher-defined agent interventions was tailored according to the different agent communication styles in the two conditions (Fig. 3).

Data Collection and Analysis

Post-task Questionnaires

After the activity, students were asked to fill in a post-task questionnaire, which aimed to explore students' opinions about the MentorChat interface and the agent interventions. The questionnaire included three multiple-choice questions, two open-ended questions, and ten Likert-scaled questions. Measures of central tendency were computed for all questionnaire items. Additionally, a series of Pearson product-moment correlation coefficients was calculated to examine the relationships among the questionnaire variables.

Interviews

Interviews were conducted in order to record details of how the students worked or perceived the learning activity. The interviews were semi-structured and lasted for about 10 min each. They focused on students' opinions about (a) the collaborative dialogue-based activity as a whole, (b) the usability of the MentorChat tool, and (c) the pedagogical efficacy of the conversational agent interventions. Students were interviewed individually. All interviews were transcribed verbatim and analyzed in search of common themes using the open-coding process of the constant comparative method (Corbin & Strauss, 1990).

Discourse Data Observations

Following the completion of the activity, the authors examined the text files of all group discussions. In particular, the authors acted as independent raters assessing the degree of formality/informality of users' responses to the agent. A scoring rubric, deriving from Moskal's study (2000), was used to measure the formality of students' utterances on a simple 2-point scale (0 for formal and 1 for informal). The inter-rater reliability for the scoring process was found to be high (Kappa=0.82; ICC=0.83). Following this asynchronous process, raters participated in a roundtable discussion elaborating on each group dialogue to draw joint inferences.

It should be noted that the individual student constituted the unit of analysis for the post-task questionnaires and the interviews, whereas the discourse data observations involved both individual- and group-level analyses.

Results

Post-task Questionnaire Analysis

The post-task questionnaire results revealed that most students were familiar with instant messaging applications ($F=70.83\%$), while only some of them used them on a daily basis ($F=41.2\%$). They also rated their typing speed as slightly below average ($N=24$, $M=2.38$, $SD=1.27$) on a 5-point scale ranging from 1 (slow) to 5 (fast).

Table 1 presents the descriptive statistics computed for the Likert-scale questions that measured the user acceptance of the MentorChat tool. Likewise, Table 2 presents a selection of the results relating to the agent behavior.

Furthermore, a Spearman's product-moment correlation analysis revealed two significant correlations among the questionnaire variables. First, there was a negative correlation between the "learners' age" and the "system ease of use" ($r=-0.51$, $p=0.01$). Second, the "learners' typing skill" was found to be positively correlated

Table 1 The questionnaire results concerning the MentorChat tool

Question (translated)	Mean (*M*)	Standard deviation (SD)
The texts displayed on MentorChat are easy to read and comprehensible.	4.21	1.25
The options available in the environment are easily understandable.	4.08	1.10
The icons and symbols used are familiar to me.	3.96	1.36
I believe that MentorChat is an easy-to-use application.	4.42	1.06

Table 2 The questionnaire results concerning the interventions of the agent

Question (translated)	Mean (*M*)	Standard deviation (SD)
The agent interventions, which appeared during the discussion, were simple and comprehensible.	4.50	1.14
The agent interventions made the discussion more interesting.	4.63	0.65
The agent interventions that appeared during the discussion helped me to recall/find out valuable information about the topics under discussion.	4.63	0.65
The agent interventions that appeared at the end of my discussion helped me to recall/find out valuable task-related information.	4.62	0.59
The agent interventions distracted me, and I would prefer they did not appear.	1.31	0.48
I understood the subject better through answering the agent questions.	4.25	1.07

with the "comprehensiveness of the interface options" ($r=0.48$, $p=0.02$). These correlations were anticipated since younger students are typically more familiar and experienced with the interface and functionality of instant messaging applications.

Given that the normality and the homogeneity of variance criteria were satisfied, we proceeded to apply parametric statistics to our individual-level questionnaire data. More specifically, a series of independent samples T-tests was performed comparing the scores of the questionnaire variables in the P and T conditions. The analysis did not reveal any significant difference in the scores for the two conditions. Nevertheless, although nonsignificant ($t[22]=4.76$, $p=0.07$), worth mentioning is the difference in how students in the two conditions perceived the content of the agent interventions. In respect to the agent interventions appearing during students' discussions, the students who interacted with the peer-agent (P condition) considered its interventions as more comprehensible ($M=4.00$, SD$=0.35$) than the students who interacted with the tutor-agent (T condition) ($M=4.92$, SD$=0.05$).

Interview Analysis

The qualitative data that derived from the analysis of the interview transcripts indicated five common themes, as presented in Table 3.

Table 3 Common themes identified

No.	Theme
1	Agent voice usefulness (e.g., "the agent voice drew my attention to the agent intervention")
2	Spelling auto-correction suggested (e.g., "it would be nice to have a spelling auto-correction feature activated while composing new messages")
3	Directed agent interventions suggested (e.g., "each agent intervention should address only one group member and explicitly state who is being addressed")
4	Interdisciplinary use of agent suggested (e.g., "besides computer science, agent interventions could also be helpful in other learning contexts such as language learning")
5	Agent for educational purposes only (e.g., "the use of an agent, which monitors peers' discussions, would not be appropriate when chatting with friends out of educational settings")

Discourse Data Observations

The examination of the groups' discussions revealed a series of patterns regarding the students' interaction and conversational behavior. First of all, we observed that when participants entered their group discussions, they posted a number of messages ($N=10$ groups, $M=7.10$, $SD=4.15$) that played a purely social function and were not related to the task. Although a lot of students (10 out of 24) initiated their discussion typing in "Greeklish" (i.e., writing in Greek but using Latin characters), all of them altered their typing to Greek when at the beginning of the activity they saw the agent prompt urging them to use Greek characters.

Furthermore, the agent interventions displayed, especially at an early stage of the activity, seemed to have caused some confusion in half of the groups (5 out of 10). More specifically, a relatively high number of task coordination contributions was identified in students' utterances after the first agent intervention occurred. Taking a closer look at the students' dialogues we found that, despite the agent explicit instructions (Fig. 2, C), some peers (8 out of 24) could not understand at first if they should individually answer to the agent or provide a joint response. In fact, in some occasions, some of these students rushed to provide a response without reaching an agreement with their partner.

It should also be noted that even though all students communicated with each other in a friendly manner, we observed a considerable difference in the way the learners interacted with the agent in the P and T conditions. Specifically, the descriptive statistical analysis of the rubric scores indicated that the student groups ($N=5$) in the P condition responded to the agent questions in a far more informal way ($M=0.84$, $SD=0.21$) as compared to the student groups ($N=5$) in the T condition ($M=0.18$, $SD=0.16$). In particular, the students in condition P responded to the agent as they would respond to a question of their human partner(s) (e.g., "Hi Elena! I can help you with the webpage ...") while the students in condition T engaged in a more formal communication with the agent (e.g., "From my point of view, the webpage should be developed ..."), as a student would answer the question of a human tutor in class.

Moreover, an examination of the agent interventions made revealed that most of the groups (seven out of ten) did not discuss all the teacher-proposed topics and, hence, triggered an agent intervention at the end of the activity. Although these agent interventions reminded these groups of the domain topics not discussed, only some of them (four out of seven) decided to resume their discussion on the topics proposed. Nevertheless, we consider that this happened mainly due to the limited duration of the learning activity.

Discussion and Conclusions

The main goal of the study is to investigate whether the different roles (peer or tutor) of the conversational agent may affect students' perceptions of the agent and their utterances. The study results indicate that the different appearance and communication styles of the agent affected the formal/informal style of the students' responses to it (discourse data observations) but did not conclude in any significant difference in students' opinions about the agent (post-task questionnaires).

More specifically, all students had a favorable opinion regarding the user interface and the usability of MentorChat (Table 1). Moreover, students believed that the agent interventions were simple and comprehensible and made the discussion more interesting. They also stated that the agent interventions helped them recall and identify valuable points of the topics being discussed (Table 2, rows 3 and 4) or understand the domain subject better through answering the agent questions (Table 2, row 6).

Furthermore, all the students seemed to appreciate the agent interventions and the analysis did not reveal any significant difference between P and T conditions. The students in both conditions perceived the agent as a valuable discussion facilitator whether acting as a tutor or a peer (Table 2). Students' perceptions were not adversely affected by the different appearance or communication styles of the agent.

However, although no statistically significant differences were reported in the post-task questionnaires, there is some evidence to suggest that students in the P condition considered the agent interventions as more comprehensible than the students in the T condition. Based on our findings, we argue that the friendlier interventions of the peer agent had a more positive impact on students, making them feel as if they were engaged in human-to-human conversation, and eventually more willing to focus on prompt information.

This result seems to support the "personalization principle" of multimedia learning theory as described by Clark and Mayer (2011). This principle suggests that instructional designers should use a conversational rather than formal communication style so that learners interact with the interface in a way that resembles human-to-human conversations. Indeed, although the students interviewed reported being aware that the virtual character was not in an actual conversation with them, they seemed more likely to act as if the agent was their conversation partner in the P condition.

Moreover, the discourse data revealed that students in the P condition responded to the agent questions in a more friendly/informal way as compared to students in the T condition. This result shows that the appearance of the agent or the conversational style of the agent interventions may influence students' conversational behavior. Hence, the different role of the agent in a collaborative learning activity can impact on specific social characteristics of students' utterances.

This finding appears to be consistent with the outcomes of other studies exploring how the different roles and appearances of contextually relevant conversational agents can affect learners' impressions, stereotypes, or engagement (Veletsianos, 2010). For instance, Rosenberg-Kima et al.'s study (2010) indicates that the strategic use of pedagogical agents of various races and genders can provide learners with social models that are similar to them, thus increasing their interest towards the agent.

Furthermore, Gulz et al. (2011) highlight that a key challenge for the agent design is to manage students' expectations about the social profile of the conversational agent. Students have expectations of both what the agent may be able to say to them and how it will address them. Thus, a good match between the students' expectations of the agent's social profile can alter how the students perceive the agent's general personal features (e.g., a humorous or a serious character, a figure of authority, or a peer) as well as enhance the pedagogical objective of making the conversation engaging and motivating.

In spite of the various study limitations, such as the small number of participants and the limited duration of the activity, we consider that this study provides preliminary evidence and valuable insights into the potential effect of the conversational agent roles (peer or tutor) and their subsequent appearance and communication styles in collaborative learning settings. We consider that teacher-configurable conversational agents have a pedagogically beneficial role to play in the e-learning systems of the future. We expect this study to contribute towards exploring various agent roles or interventions that can improve collaboration in everyday instructional situations.

Acknowledgments The authors would like to thank Kleoniki Agrafiotou and Normperta Magkitouka for their continued support in this project. We are also grateful to the students and teachers of the participating school for their valuable comments and suggestions.

References

Cassell, J., Sullivan, J., Prevost, S., & Churchill, E. F. (Eds.). (2000). *Embodied conversational agents*. Cambridge, MA: MIT Press.

Chase, C., Chin, D., Oppezzo, M., & Schwartz, D. (2009). Teachable agents and the protégé effect: Increasing the effort towards learning. *Journal of Science Education and Technology, 18*, 334–352.

Chaudhuri, S., Kumar, R., Howley, I., & Rosé, C. P. (2009). Engaging collaborative learners with helping agents. In Proceedings of the 14th Intl. Conf. on Artificial Intelligence in Education (AIED 2009) (pp. 365–372). Amsterdam: Ios Press.

Clark, R. C., & Mayer, R. E. (2011). *E-learning and the science of instruction: Proven guidelines for consumers and designers of multimedia learning* (3rd ed.). San Francisco, CA: Pfeiffer.

Corbin, J. M., & Strauss, A. (1990). Grounded theory research: Procedures, canons, and evaluative criteria. *Qualitative Sociology, 13*(1), 3–21.

Dillenbourg, P. (1999). What do you mean by collaborative learning? In P. Dillenbourg (Ed.), *Collaborative-learning: Cognitive and computational approaches* (pp. 1–19). Oxford: Elsevier.

Franklin, S., & Graesser, A. (1997). Is it an Agent, or just a Program? A taxonomy for autonomous agents. In *Intelligent agents III agent theories, architectures, and languages* (pp. 21–35). Berlin: Springer.

Gulz, A., Haake, M., Silvervarg, A., Sjödén, B., & Veletsianos, G. (2011). Building a social conversational pedagogical agent-design challenges and methodological approaches. In D. Perez-Marin & I. Pascual-Nieto (Eds.), *Conversational agents and natural language interaction: Techniques and effective practices* (pp. 128–155). Hershey, PA: IGI Global.

Haake, M., & Gulz, A. (2008). Visual stereotypes and virtual pedagogical agents. *Educational Technology & Society, 11*(4), 1–15.

Haake, M., & Gulz, A. (2009). A look at the roles of look & roles in embodied pedagogical agents—a user preference perspective. *International Journal of Artificial Intelligence in Education, 19*(1), 39–71. IOS Press. Retrieved January 13, 2012.

Harrer, A., McLaren, B. M., Walker, E., Bollen, L., & Sewall, J. (2006). Creating cognitive tutors for collaborative learning: Steps toward realization. *User Modeling and User-Adapted Interaction, 16*(3–4), 175–209.

Kerly, A., Ellis, R., & Bull, S. (2009). Conversational agents in E-Learning. In Applications and Innovations in Intelligent Systems XVI - Proceedings of AI (pp. 169–182). London, UK: Springer.

Kumar, R., Ai, H., Beuth, J. L., & Rosé, C. P. (2010). Socially capable conversational tutors can be effective in collaborative learning situations. In *Intelligent tutoring systems* (pp. 156–164). Berlin: Springer.

Kumar, R., Rosé, C. P., Wang, Y. C., Joshi, M., & Robinson, A. (2007). Tutorial dialogue as adaptive collaborative learning support. In R. Luckin, K. R. Koedinger, & J. Greer (Eds.), *Proceedings of the 13th International Conference on Artificial Intelligence in Education* (pp. 383–390). Amsterdam: Ios Press.

Moskal, B. M. (2000). Scoring rubrics: what, when and how? *Practical Assessment, Research & Evaluation, 7*(3). Retrieved February 17, 2014, from http://PAREonline.net/getvn.asp?v=7&n=3

Rosenberg Kima, R. B., Plant, E. A., Doerr, C. E., & Baylor, A. L. (2010). The influence of computer-based model's race and gender on female students' attitudes and beliefs towards engineering. *Journal of Engineering Education, 99*(1), 35–44.

Rovai, A. P. (2007). Facilitating online discussions effectively. *Internet and Higher Education, 10*, 77–88.

Sklar, E., & Richards, D. (2010). Agent-based systems for human learners. *The Knowledge Engineering Review, 25*(2), 111–135.

Stahl, G., Rosé, C. P., O'Hara, K., & Powell, A. B. (2010). Supporting group math cognition in virtual math teams with software conversational agents. In *First North American GeoGebra Conference*. Ithaca, NY.

Tegos, S., Demetriadis, S., & Tsiatsos, T. (2012). Using a conversational agent for promoting collaborative language learning. In *Proceedings of the 4th International Conference on Intelligent Networking and Collaborative Systems (INCoS)* (pp. 162–165). IEEE.

Tegos, S., Demetriadis, S., & Tsiatsos, T. (2014). A configurable conversational agent to trigger students' productive dialogue: A pilot study in the CALL domain. *International Journal of Artificial Intelligence in Education, 24*(1), 62–91.

Veletsianos, G. (2010). Contextually relevant pedagogical agents: Visual appearance, stereotypes, and first impressions and their impact on learning. *Computers & Education, 55*(2), 576–585.

Veletsianos, G., & Russell, G. S. (2014). Pedagogical agents. In *Handbook of research on educational communications and technology* (pp. 759–769). New York, NY: Springer.

Walker, E., Rummel, N., & Koedinger, K. R. (2011). Designing automated adaptive support to improve student helping behaviors in a peer tutoring activity. *International Journal of Computer-Supported Collaborative Learning, 6*(2), 279–306.

Anxiety Awareness in Education: A Prototype Biofeedback Device

Hippokratis Apostolidis, Panagiotis Stylianidis, and Thrasyvoulos Tsiatsos

Introduction

Biofeedback is a means for gaining control of our body processes to increase relaxation, relieve pain, and develop healthier, more comfortable life patterns (Wall, 2004). Biofeedback gives us information about ourselves by means of external instruments. Biofeedback training familiarizes the person with the activity in his/her various body systems, and therefore he/she may learn to control this activity to relieve stress and improve health.

Educational activities in complex learning contexts produce negative or positive emotions. Stress is such an emotion that might have an impact on the educational activity and learning outcome. Therefore, student's stress-level self-awareness and self-regulation can be a major issue in the educational process. Furthermore, student's stress-level awareness by the tutor could help the tutor to adapt the educational approach in order to promote the student's positive emotions.

The recent interest in the link between emotions and learning is based on the assumption that deep learning is not entirely limited to cognition, discourse, action, and the environment, because emotions or affective states are inextricably bound to the learning process (D'Mello, Craig, & Graesser, 2009; Lepper & Henderlong, 2000; Linnenbrink & Pintrich, 2002; Meyer & Turner, 2006; Stein & Hernandez, 2007).

A very important feature of learning environments is the support provided to students and to the instructor. The emotion recognition in many cases can be considered as students' motivation in order to regulate their emotional state or trying to relax their teammates in cases of high anxiety during collaborative learning activities.

This chapter aims to (a) identify whether anxiety awareness can motivate the students to regulate their emotions; (b) explore if a well-known biofeedback

H. Apostolidis (✉) • P. Stylianidis • T. Tsiatsos
Department of Informatics, Aristotle University of Thessaloniki,
University Campus, 54124 Thessaloniki, Greece
e-mail: aposti@csd.auth.gr; pastylia@csd.auth.gr; tsiatsos@csd.auth.gr

C. Karagiannidis et al. (eds.), *Research on e-Learning and ICT in Education: Technological, Pedagogical and Instructional Perspectives*, DOI 10.1007/978-1-4614-6501-0_18, © Springer Science+Business Media New York 2014

technique (i.e., diaphragmatic breathing) supports the students supported to regulate their stress lever; (c) evaluate students' acceptance of biofeedback device and sensors during a learning activity; and (d) examine the usefulness of student's anxiety awareness for the teacher.

The chapter is structured as follows: The next section is devoted to student academic emotions and adaptive learners' support. Then, the biofeedback device for anxiety awareness is described. Section "Pilot Study" presents a pilot study that has taken place in order to evaluate the usefulness of the biofeedback device for the educational activities. The last section presents the concluding remarks and our vision for the next steps.

Student Emotions and Adaptive Learners' Support

Emotions are very important functions that affect students' academic motivation, behavior, performance, health, and development of their personality. Research from 1950s (Zeidner, 1998) investigated students' anxiety and produced sufficient knowledge in order to support the educational practice. The impact of emotions during problem solving as well as during the participation in educational activities seems to be very important. More specifically, emotions can affect positively or negatively the learning process (Allen & Carifio, 1995). Efforts to study difficult subjects at deeper levels of comprehension involve a complex coordination of cognitive processes and affective states (D'Mello, 2012). In the academic context, the treatment focused on the problem seems to be the most appropriate adjustment. The emotion-oriented treatment may also be an adaptive solution. The following factors seem to be important to students' motivation and can be controlled by the teachers in order to stimulate positive emotions for the educational process:

- *Teaching quality and motivation*: Factors, such as lack of structure, lack of clarity, and excessive demands, are known to enhance the students' anxiety during the test (Pekrun, 2006; Zeidner, 1998, 2007). Also if the learning environment meets the students' needs, then students' engagement is encouraged (Hatfield, Cacioppo, & Rapson, 1994; Pekrun, 2006; Zeidner, 1998, 2007).
- *Collaboration*: Collaborative activities and structures in the classroom (Johnson & Johnson, 1974) in many cases promote positive academic emotions (Pekrun, 2006; Zeidner, 1998, 2007).
- *Management of students' mistakes*: Managing mistakes as learning opportunities rather than as a personal failure, and linking benefits to achievements, might help students develop adaptive emotions (Pekrun, 2006; Zeidner, 1998, 2007).
- *Challenging and deep inquiry*: The authors of the model of dynamic affective conclude that the main pedagogical strategy that yields in deep learning is the challenging which can inspire deep inquiry instead of comfortable learning environments (D'Mello & Graesser, 2012).

Our proposed approach to challenging and deep inquiry would systematically scaffold the student out of the confused state which can cause frustration and high anxiety. This approach would presumably work better for less experienced learners with lower domain knowledge and lower ability to self-regulate their learning activities and their emotional states. Moreover, our approach might be systematically used as adaptive support to the learning activity. This approach is a biofeedback-based approach that aims to keep the student on the qui vive and active but not stressed. More specifically, this method aims to (a) wake the student if he/she is very relaxed or bored trying to avoid deactivation and (b) support the student to relax applying a biofeedback technique called diaphragmatic breathing if the student is stressed.

The synthesis and analysis of emotions is an interdisciplinary scientific field consisting from the combination of computer science, psychology, and cognitive science (Allen & Carifio, 1995). In order to apply this proposed approach we have implemented a biofeedback device for anxiety awareness. Next section presents this device.

Description of Biofeedback Device for Anxiety Awareness

The biofeedback device for anxiety awareness is based on two physiological techniques in order to collect bio-signals from students who are engaged in a learning activity. The techniques used are the following:

- Galvanic skin response (GSR): This is a test of the sweat function, which measures the change in conductivity of the skin during the flow of low-voltage current after a stimulus. The recording of the conductivity (or the inverse of conductivity, i.e., resistance) is based on the application of external constant voltage to the skin (Lykken & Venables, 1971).
- Photoplethysmography (PPG): PPG is a simple and low-cost optical technique that can be used to detect blood volume changes (BVP) in the microvascular tissue (Challoner, 1979).

The biofeedback device (Fig. 1a) collects, identifies, and utilizes bio-signals resulted by physiological reactions to stressful situations, such as epidermal ephidrosis (GSR, Fig. 1b) and heart rate (HR, Fig. 1c). The device is connected to a computer and collaborates with dedicated software in order to convert bio-signals into a stress level (relaxed, waking, or anxious) on the screen as well as to advise the user to regulate stress through relaxation techniques.

The software (Fig. 2) has the following functionality for each person:

- Displays the student code (Fig. 2a).
- Displays the emotional state progress bar and color (green for relaxed, orange for waking, or red for anxious) as depicted in Fig. 2b.
- Recommend the user to apply a biofeedback technique in order to relax in case of high anxiety level (Fig. 2c).

The tutor can monitor the students' stress level in real time as depicted in Fig. 3.

The next section presents a pilot study that has taken place in order to evaluate the usefulness of the biofeedback device for the educational activities.

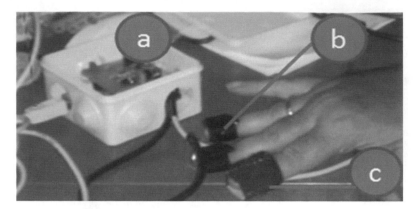

Fig. 1 Biofeedback device for stress-level awareness

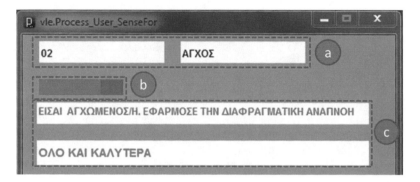

Fig. 2 User interface of biofeedback device software for personal stress-level awareness

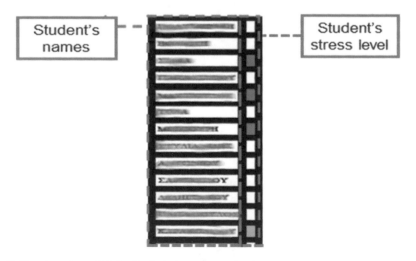

Fig. 3 User interface of biofeedback device software for the tutor

Pilot Study

As referred before this chapter aims to (a) identify whether anxiety awareness can motivate the students to regulate their emotions; (b) explore if a well-known bio-feedback technique (i.e., diaphragmatic breathing) supports the students in order to regulate their stress level; (c) evaluate the students' acceptance of biofeedback device and sensors during a learning activity; and (d) examine the usefulness of student's anxiety awareness for the teacher.

A pilot study has taken place in the postgraduate course "Educational Virtual Environments" of the Postgraduate Studies Program of the Informatics Department at the Aristotle University of Thessaloniki, Greece. Four educational activities were taken place. Two of them were synchronous in the same place, and the other two were synchronous from distance.

The activities were applied on 13 students, 4 males and 9 females, and each of them concerns oral examination. In each session each group has been examined by presenting its project and answering to tutor's questions. Every member of a group has presented his/her contribution. The schedule of activities and the deliverables of each activity were clearly stated at the beginning of the semester.

Method

The students were divided into four groups, one consisting of four people and the others of three. Each group had identical assignments. The collaborative technique used in educational test activities was fishbowl (Leonard, Dufresne, Gerace, & Mestre, 1999).

For the evaluation of the activities the students answered to 23 questions. The questions were divided into two groups. The first group included questions about the evaluation of anxiety recognition support to the educational activity and biofeedback-relaxing technique. The second group followed the Unified Theory of Acceptance and Use of Technology framework (UTAUT) (Venkatesh, Morris, Davis, & Davis, 2003).

In addition an unstructured interview was taken by each student separately and by the professor who was teaching the course in which the activities occurred. The professor (tutor) was watching the students' anxiety measurements from the monitor application.

Materials

In all activities the students were connected to the biofeedback device for measuring their stress level (Fig. 1). The tutor was aware about every student stress level using the stress level-monitoring application depicted in Fig. 3.

The first oral examination activity and stress-level measurement took place at the classroom. It could be considered as the familiarization activity, since extra care was taken to practical matters on using the implemented device. For example most of the students had trouble to get connected properly to the GSR and HR sensors.

The second and third oral examination activities have taken place from distance, and they were supported by an open-source videoconferencing tool called the Big Blue Button (http://www.BigBlueButton.org/). The students presented the basic technical characteristics and architecture of the systems they were implementing.

Finally the fourth activity that was the final examination took place at the same time within the classroom. Each group presented the implemented system and its evaluation.

Instruments

Two questionnaires have been filled by the students. For the needs of the first questionnaire the participants were separated to control and test group with identical questions.

In both kinds of questionnaires the first question was a nominal scaled about student's gender and the others were interval-scaled questions following the five-level Likert scale (Likert, 1932) (from 1 = strongly disagree to 5 = strongly agree).

Evaluation Procedure

An important issue of this work was to identify whether anxiety awareness can motivate the students to regulate their emotions and to explore if a well-known bio-feedback technique (i.e., diaphragmatic breathing) supports the students to regulate their stress level. In order to evaluate this issue a two-step evaluation process has been followed. In the first step of this process the students filled a psychometric questionnaire (Spielberger, Gorush, & Lushene, 1970) in order to collect data about their emotional mentality. In the second step and according to the results of this questionnaire the students have been separated into two groups (control and test) consisting of equivalent number of stressful and relaxant members. The control group was consisting of two males and five females, and the test group was consisting of two males and four females. The difference between these groups was that the students belonging in the control group were not aware about their stress level and they didn't receive any biofeedback messages.

Evaluation Results, Discussion, and Conclusions

Investigating if students' stress-level awareness can augment to educational and leaning activities, the majority of the students (61.2 %) answered that they "strongly agree" that this information would be useful in examination activities. Also, most of

Fig. 4 The applied UTAUT framework (Venkatesh et al., 2003)

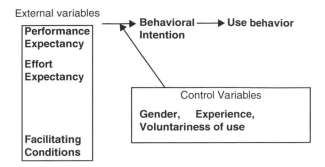

the students (53.8 %) agreed that stress-level awareness would be useful to workshops. However, most of the students do not think that students' stress-level awareness can augment distance-learning teleconferences and individual studying.

Furthermore, independent sample t-test was applied to identify whether anxiety awareness can motivate the students to regulate their emotions with confidential interval of 95 % and assuming equal variances. The significance for equal variances was $0.290 > 0.05$ satisfying the homogeneity assumption. The mean of the test group was significantly greater than the mean of the control group, and the effect size was greater than 1. This could be interpreted that the test group having the representation of the measurements was more motivated than the control group.

Concerning the support of the diaphragmatic breathing technique to the students to regulate their stress-level question, most of the students answered (38.5 % of them agree and 30.8 % strongly agree) that they believe it helped them to be more relaxed. However, there was no significant statistical difference between control and test group.

Concerning users' acceptance of biofeedback device and sensors during a learning activity, the UTAUT model (Fig. 4) has been applied to all students with common questions.

In order to examine the reliability of the question groups, Cronbach's alpha reliability test has been applied. For the performance expectancy group of six questions the reliability was 0.73, for the expectancy effort (three questions) was 0.712, and for the behavioral intension (four questions) was 0.745. So the three question groups approved reliable. Concerning the difficulty of connecting to the sensors of the developed device most of the participants (46.2 %) answered that they strongly agree that it is difficult and 30.8 % of the participants found little inconvenience. Also about the difficulty of using this device in parallel with the main activity, a strong majority (69.2 %) found it a little inconvenient. So the majority of the participants had a little difficulty with the device without any serious problem. Then Spearman's correlation significant at the 0.05 level was applied to performance expectancy, effort expectancy, facilitating conditions, gender, experience, voluntariness of use, and behavioral intension. Significant correlation approved between (a) performance expectancy and facilitating conditions (0.610*), (b) performance expectancy and behavior intension (0.573*), and (c) experience and behavior intension (0.586*). Also significant correlation approved between expectancy effort and voluntariness of use (0.630*).

According to the teacher the screen of the monitor application, where he could have a representation of his students' emotional state, was very useful especially at the distance activities and supported him in regulating his behavior when he was noticing that there were stressful conditions. The professor who was responsible for the evaluation activities was interviewed. He mentioned two significant benefits from using the biofeedback device in an educational activity: (a) *Awareness of the class emotional state for both distance and onsite activities*: In distance-education activities class anxiety awareness appears to be quite helpful for the teacher. It is a factor that reduces academic distance between the teacher and the students. In addition, the prototype device enables the teacher to better understand students' anxiety level. Furthermore, he/she had a more comprehensive awareness about his/her class during the examinations. (b) *Teacher's self-regulation during oral examinations*: As the professor reported, the awareness about students' anxiety helped him to support the students to relax during the oral examinations. This resulted to establish a better academic context during the examination.

After completing the questionnaires the students were interviewed separately. All students suggested that the anxiety measurement may be useful to learning activities such as examinations and workshops.

In summary, all the participants were willing to reuse these sensors in other academic activities. All students admitted that stress-level awareness can motivate the students to regulate themselves. From the teacher's point of view students' stress-level awareness support him to realize his students' emotions and to adapt his approach, rhythm, and pace of oral examination. Our future plans involve (a) repeating learning activities with bio-signal measurements on a larger scale with more students, (b) examining more bio-signal measurement techniques in addition to GSR and HR, and (c) applying these measurements in collaborative distance-learning activities.

References

Allen, B., & Carifio, J. (1995). *Methodology for the analysis of emotion experiences during mathematical problem solving*. Annual Conference of the New England Educational Research Organization, Portsmouth.

Challoner A. V. J. (1979). *Photoelectric plethysmography for estimating cutaneous blood flow Non-Invasive Physiological Measurements* vol 1 ed P Rolfe (London: Academic) pp 125–51.

D'Mello, S. K. (2012). Affect trajectories during complex learning. In N. Seel et al. (Eds.), *Encyclopedia of the sciences of learning*. New York, NY: Springer.

D'Mello, S., Craig, S., & Graesser, A. (2009). Multi-method assessment of affective experience and expression during deep learning. *International Journal of Learning Technology, 4*(3/4), 165–187.

D'Mello, S. K., & Graesser, A. C. (2012). Dynamics of affective states during complex learning. *Learning and Instruction, 22*, 145–157.

Hatfield, E., Cacioppo, J. T., & Rapson, R. L. (1994). *Emotional contagion*. New York, NY: Cambridge University Press.

Johnson, D. W., & Johnson, R. T. (1974). Instructional goal structure: Cooperative, competitive or individualistic. *Review of Educational Research, 4*, 213–240.

Leonard W. J., Dufresne R. J., Gerace W. J., & Mestre J. P. (1999). Collaborative Group Techniques. A discussion of teaching via small-group cooperative learning work.

Lepper, M. R., & Henderlong, J. (2000). Turning ——play into ——work and ——work into ——play: 25 years of research on intrinsic versus extrinsic motivation. In C. Sansone & J. M. Harackiewicz (Eds.), *Intrinsic and extrinsic motivation: The search for optimal motivation and performance* (pp. 257–307). San Diego, CA: Academic.

Likert, R. (1932). A technique for the measurement of attitudes. *Archives of Psychology, 140*(1), 44–53.

Linnenbrink, E. A., & Pintrich, P. R. (2002). The role of motivational beliefs in conceptual change. In M. Limon & L. Mason (Eds.), *Reconsidering conceptual change: Issues in theory and practice* (pp. 115–135). Dordretch, Netherlands: Kluwer Academic Publishers.

Lykken, D. T., & Venables, P. (1971). Direct measurement of skin conductance: A proposal for standardization. *Psychophysiology, 8*, 656–672. Designated a Citation Classic, Institute for Scientific Information.

Meyer, D. K., & Turner, J. C. (2006). Re-conceptualizing emotion and motivation to learn in classroom contexts. *Educational Psychology Review, 18*, 377–390.

Pekrun, R. (2006). The control-value theory of achievement emotions: Assumptions, corollaries, and implications for educational research and practice. *Educational Psychology Review, 18*, 315–341.

Spielberger, C. D., Gorush, R. L., & Lushene, R. E. (1970). *The State-Trait Anxiety Inventory*. Palo Alto, CA: Consulting Psychologists Press.

Stein, N. L., & Hernandez, M. W. (2007). Assessing understanding and appraisals during emotional experience: The development and use of the Narcoder. In J. A. Coan & J. J. Allen (Eds.), *Handbook of emotion elicitation and assessment*. New York, NY: Oxford University Press.

Venkatesh, V., Morris, M. G., Davis, G. B., & Davis, F. D. (2003). User acceptance of information technology: Toward a unified view. *MIS Quarterly, 27*(3), 425–478.

Wall, S. (2004). *What is Biofeedback?* Available at http://www.7hz.com/what.html.

Zeidner, M. (1998). *Test anxiety: The state of the art*. New York, NY: Plenum Press.

Zeidner, M. (2007). Test anxiety in educational contexts: What I have learned so far. In P. A. Schutz & R. Pekrun (Eds.), *Emotion in education* (pp. 165–184). San Diego, CA: Academic.

Digital Storytelling for Children with Autism: Software Development and Pilot Application

Konstantina Chatzara, Charalampos Karagiannidis, Sofia Mavropoulou, and Dimos Stamatis

Digital Storytelling: Definition and Benefits

As narration is the symbolic presentation of a sequence of events (Scholes, 1981), storytelling might be defined as a form of narrative (Lathem, 2005; More, 2008). Narrative is defined as a sequence of events which refer to a unifying subject represented in a perspicuous order in time (Carroll, 2001; Worth, 2005). The terms "narrative" or "story" are used interchangeably in the literature (Velleman, 2003; Worth, 2005). It is well known that children begin to write their stories through images that often entail a symbolic function. They use pictures to create a sequence with a plot, which tells a story (Gershon & Page, 2001). Children's stories may be short and serve different aims such as telling a personal tale, recounting a historical event, or making a presentation aimed to give information or instructions on a particular topic of interest (Robin, 2006). This process, reflecting an old concept, has been defined as storytelling and has been used extensively in different levels of education (Lathem, 2005; Robin, 2006; Valkanova & Watts, 2007; Yuksel, Robin, & McNeil, 2011). It refers to

K. Chatzara (✉)
NOUS Institute of Digital Learning & Communication, 7, Filikis Etaireias, 54621 Thessaloniki, Greece

Department of Special Education, University of Thessaly, Argonafton & Filellinon, 38221 Volos, Greece
e-mail: synthe@otenet.gr

C. Karagiannidis • S. Mavropoulou
Department of Special Education, University of Thessaly, Argonafton & Filellinon, 38221 Volos, Greece
e-mail: karagian@uth.gr; smavrop@uth.gr

D. Stamatis
Department of Informatics, Alexander T.E.I. of Thessaloniki,
P.O. BOX 141, 57400 Thessaloniki, Greece
e-mail: demos@it.teithe.gr

C. Karagiannidis et al. (eds.), *Research on e-Learning and ICT in Education: Technological, Pedagogical and Instructional Perspectives*, DOI 10.1007/978-1-4614-6501-0_19, © Springer Science+Business Media New York 2014

a linear narration of a story with a starting point, a middle point (climax), and an ending point (Gershon & Page, 2001). Storytelling may include text as well as other forms of media such as images, sounds, animation, and videos (Lathem, 2005). Following the expanding use of digital media, it has been developed into a different form of creation and presentation. Digital storytelling (DS) is based on digital images, videos, text, and sounds to form a genre in order to present a story to readers, viewers, and listeners via a computer system (Li, 2007; More, 2008; Robin, 2006). In educational terms, new instructional methods, based on the use of technology, have been developed for facilitating learning. As Levin (2003) argues, known concepts are adjusted in a new pedagogical setting and enhanced with the use of technology.

There is a range of DS software such as PhotoStory3, Animoto, ComicLife StoryBird, Digital Vaults, VoiceThread, and Glogster, Kerpoof that offer the tools to create a story with images and text through a computer system. Users can freely place images in a sequence in order to create their own story, since there is no correct or wrong order. Digital storytelling offers several benefits to the educational process in variable domains and for different learning groups (Heo, 2009; Kulla-Abbott & Polman, 2008; Li, 2007; Meadows, 2003; More, 2008; Robin, 2006; Yuksel et al., 2011). In particular, Kulla-Abbott and Polman (2008) suggested that a digital storytelling program can assist students in improving their writing skills because learners need to create and organize a sequence of images in correspondence to their ideas for making a story. They also concluded that DS can make students more engaged and creative, by helping them to discover different ways to express their own ideas. Other researchers, such as Valkanova and Watts (2007), asked children to make sound "voice over" in a narrative form for their own videos. They reported that this procedure enabled children to express themselves verbally and visually in an artistic, productive, and inspiring way. The same conclusion was reached by Burgess (2006), whose research offered evidence for the positive effect of DS for creative thinking. Sadik (2008) explored teaching and learning through the application of digital storytelling with Microsoft Photo Story 3 and found that it increased their comprehension and learning. Meadows (2003) observed that when students used multimedia software to visualize their thoughts, they were more active and engaged with the subject matter. Li (2007) evaluated the integration of multimedia technologies into higher education and concluded that through DS students improved their learning. Furthermore, DS has been used as an educational tool for learners with special needs. O'Neill and Dalton (2002) used successfully digital story books for teaching literacy to students with learning difficulties.

Overall, researchers agree that DS is an effective approach that engages learners and supports teachers to effectively integrate technology into learning. Its application with special learning groups has been examined in a few research projects (Daigle & Sulentic Dowell, 2010; Daigle and Free, 2007; Gal et al., 2005; Tartaro, 2005). Researchers have also examined the implementation of DS to students with ASD regarding activity schedules via computer applications (Stromer & Kimball, 2004; Stromer, Kimball, Kinney, & Taylor, 2006). Activity schedules are defined as a set of pictures or words that cues someone to engage in a sequence of activities (McClannahan & Krantz, 1997; Stromer & Kimball, 2004). They can be considered as a form of storytelling, as they are often used to display a sequence of steps for the completion of an activity and this could also form a story constructed with a sequence of images and text. Moreover, the potential benefits of activity schedules presented with computer support have been well documented (Stromer et al., 2006).

The Education of Students with Autism

Autism spectrum disorders (ASD) have been identified as pervasive developmental disorders with neurobiological background, causing impairments and delays in social communication and imagination (Barry & Burlew, 2004; Welton et al., 2004). Consequently, children with ASD prefer to get engaged in solitary repetitive activities, avoiding social interaction. Moreover, they have a cognitive bias to local processing, that is, they pay special attention to details which prevents them from grasping the purpose or the steps of an activity (Carnahan, Musti-Rao, & Bailey, 2009; Odom, Collet-Klingenberg, Rogers, & Hatton, 2010; Rajendran & Mitchell, 2007). Also, persons with ASD present major difficulties in executive functioning (Carlson, Mandell, & Williams, 2004; Pellicano, 2007), which involves organizing and following sequences of steps. Therefore, educating people with ASD can be challenging and it is necessary to adopt appropriate educational methods matching closely the needs of these individuals. A range of educational interventions utilizing visual methods have been successfully applied to children with ASD for overcoming the aforementioned difficulties. Structured teaching has been found to be an effective educational method for increasing on-task behavior and independence of children and adults with ASD (Ganz, 2007; Hume & Reynolds, 2010; Mesibov, Shea, & Schopler, 2005). The main component of Structured Teaching is the application of visual structure in the physical environment, in daily schedules and tasks, so that individuals with ASD can follow predictable routines and visual instructions for executing tasks and participating in activities.

On the other hand persons with ASD seem to have a strong motivation to use computers for both learning and leisure (Heo, 2009; Moore et al., 2000; O'Neill & Dalton, 2002; Valkanova & Watts, 2007). The use of computers offers the opportunity to the learner with ASD to interact in a controlled environment, which is predictable and with minimal social stimuli. Besides, it has been found to be effective for students with ASD by increasing their attention span and their performance in a range of academic tasks as well as by developing a repertoire of social skills and behaviors (Bernard-Opitz et al., 1994; Moore et al., 2000; Tanaka et al., 2010; Williams, Wright, Callaghan, & Coughlan, 2002). There is considerable evidence showing that the main characteristics of people with ASD related with their learning are the following: (a) they have a different way of communication, (b) they prefer a predictable environment, (c) they find it difficult to understand emotional cues, (d) in general, they prefer images to text or oral information, (e) they concentrate better in structured environments, with clear expectations and visual instructions, (f) they learn by repetition of learning tasks, (g) they need frequent breaks in their schedule, and (h) they take pleasure using computers for learning and leisure (Bernard-Opitz et al., 1994; Hume & Reynolds, 2010; Moore, McGrath, & Thorpe, 2000).

Therefore the use of computers may entail several benefits associated with the special characteristics of persons with ASD (Golan & Baron-Cohen, 2006; Mineo, Ziegler, Gill, & Salkin, 2008; Moore et al., 2007; O'Neill & Dalton, 2002; Williams et al., 2002). In particular, computers:

- Are predictable and thus they are controllable devices. They do not display emotional behavior which can often be confusing for persons with ASD.
- Enable nonverbal or verbal expression.
- Present a less threatening environment compared to an adult or a peer.
- Can be used repetitively.
- Provide positive reinforcement.
- Are easy to use.
- Can be tailored to the individual needs of each learner.
- Are based on special hardware solutions designed to help persons with special needs.
- Are versatile, since they use software which can be adaptive and adaptable to users' needs and special interests.

Digital Storytelling and Students with ASD

In the field of ASD, DS has been used to achieve student involvement as it relies heavily on visual information; a suitable way of presenting stimuli to this special group of learner (Daigle & Sulentic Dowell, 2010; Flippin et al., 2010; Stromer et al., 2006; Stromer & Kimball, 2004). It also provides a framework integrating images and text to form a story that narrates useful information. In addition, this method could be viewed as an alternative means of instruction in an inclusive classroom.

Social Stories describe social situations aimed to share social information (Gray, 1998; Gray & Garand, 1993). Sansosti, Powell-Smith, and Kincaid (2004) presented Social Stories through DS to children with ASD and reported positive effects of the intervention recommending further research on the use of DS for effective learning. In addition, Heo's recent research (2010) indicated that DS increases children's involvement in the learning of subject matter. His research was conducted over a period of 6 weeks with 17 fifth graders and his analysis showed evidence that DS can offer a motivating and effective learning experience. It is commonly agreed that the creation of a story through digital media engages children's interest and increases their creativity and involvement in a subject matter being taught (Meadows, 2003; Robin, 2006; Valkanova & Watts, 2007; Yuksel et al., 2011). However, their use, in special learning groups, has not been thoroughly examined (Daigle & Sulentic Dowell, 2010; Gal et al., 2005; Tartaro, 2005).

In Daigle and Sulentic-Dowell's initial study (2008) on the use of DS as an intervention to improve the academic performance and social interactions of a sixth grade student with high-functioning autism, positive findings were reported. Similar findings were documented by Gal and his colleagues (2005) and Tartaro (2007) who combined DS with virtual peers for children with ASD. Also, Lindsey-Glenn and Gentry (2008) reported promising results following the use of DS to improve vocabulary skills of students with ASD.

It is notable that the software tools that have been used in the aforementioned studies have not been designed specifically to cater for the special needs of this group of learners. Subsequently the software does not accommodate the components of structured teaching suitable for persons with ASD. Educators use the existing software by modifying its scope and operation in order to teach social skills to children. Special education teachers need to organize the learning material and the way information is presented in order to maximize the achievement of their instructional goals.

The Di.S.S.A. Environment

The present chapter presents a software system of DS targeting children with special needs. The software created is called Di.S.S.A., which stands for Digital Structured Storytelling for Autism. The software is designed and developed purely for this research work and is programmed in action script 3 in Adobe Flash authoring environment. It is an online application. This is the first time such software, based on combining visual supports with elements of structured teaching, is developed to cater specifically for persons with ASD. To our knowledge, similar software development has not been published.

The system is aimed to help people with ASD learn social skills through storytelling with the use of images, as sole text is, often, not the preferred way of presenting information. It evaluates user's performance and presents information about user's progress. Its design is imposed by the need for a structured way of presentation, which has been proposed as appropriate for this group of learners (Mesibov et al., 2005). Persons with ASD need to be aware of the meaning of an activity and clear guidelines on how it will be done, how long it will be, and when it will be finished. If this information is missing, they get confused and cannot perform tasks independently. The development of Di.S.S.A. accommodates the above components and users always know where they are in the application, what the purpose of their actions is, and what the desired outcome is.

The design of the system (Di.S.S.A.) is based on the A.D.D.I.E. (Analysis, Design, Development, Implementation, Evaluation) model. A.D.D.I.E is a framework that lists generic process for instructional design software (Dick & Carey, 1996; Leshin, Pollock, & Reigeluth, 1992). The content is adapted to the individual's capabilities by providing different levels of access (users have different capabilities depending on the severity of ASD), then the content is presented accordingly to the adaptation module, the user creates the story, the system evaluates user's performance, and a story with different actors but with the same concept is presented so that the users can interpret in a conceptual way the given task (children with ASD have difficulties *generalizing* what they learn in one setting to another setting) (Stromer et al., 2006).

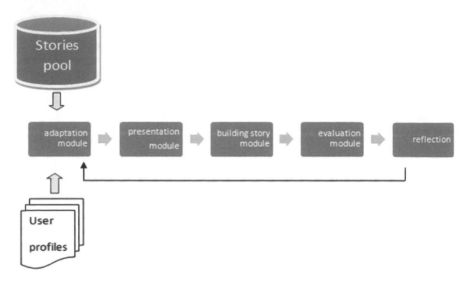

Fig. 1 The design of Di.S.S.A.

Stages of the Application

The system is adaptive to cater for different levels of ASD and evaluates user's tasks in order to provide feedback for user's performance. The architecture is based on experiential learning (Kolb, 1984) and follows the basic steps of experiential learning; namely, experience—reflective observation—conceptualization, and active experimentation.

When the application launches for the first time, a questionnaire is presented that is filled by an adult, such as the parent or the special education teacher. The questions of this instrument refer to the student's skills and preferences, the level of ASD, the use of text, movements, sound, or text messages, the number of pictures used and the visibility of the evaluation model. The relevant story is picked up from the stories pool (Figs. 1 and 2). The story is adapted to suit user's special characteristics and preferences. The system decides how information is presented to users (adaptive approach) with respect to the adaptivity dimensions of user and content. This is not an intelligent system as the system follows a series of production rules (if …then).

The user logs into the system by inserting his/her name. The system "remembers" him/her next time he or she logs in and automatically starts from the last point he or she left the application. This function is accommodated, considering that students with ASD might give up trying while using the application. As repetition helps them comprehend the task, the system "remembers" them so that they can continue their trials from the point they stopped last time. Users (teachers, parents, or students with ASD) choose a social skill to learn.

open a present   ride the bus   brushing teeth   cross the road   throw rubish

Fig. 2 Screenshot from Di.S.S.A. showing how the user can pick up a story

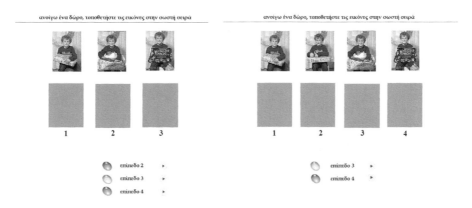

Fig. 3 Screenshot of the Di.S.S.A. showing the selection of level of difficulty for users

The user is presented with four levels of graduated difficulty for constructing a story (Fig. 3). That is, he or she can choose the length of the story by selecting either three, four, six, or eight images as breaking an activity into distinct steps has been proved to be an effective method for achieving task mastery and independence in special education (Swanson & Hoskyn, 1998). In the case of the system being used by the student without supervision he or she can choose the desired level independently. In all other cases, a professional or a parent will select the appropriate level of difficulty for the student with ASD, considering the student's ability level and the severity of autism.

Next, a sequence of images making a story is presented (Fig. 4a). Following this presentation, the images are placed randomly in the screen (Fig. 4b) and users are asked to rearrange the pictures in the correct order to create the story. An example of a story (i.e., "opening up a present") is presented in Fig. 4. For a realistic representation, the images used are photographs. A step-by-step procedure is followed. At this point, Di.S.S.A. has been designed following structured teaching which

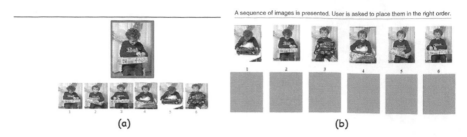

Fig. 4 Screenshot of the Di.S.S.A. for making a sequence of images for the story

places a strong emphasis on the execution of a sequence visually presented (Mesibov et al., 2005; Stromer et al., 2006). Therefore, the user can move to the next step only if he or she is correct in selecting the first picture of the sequence.

Feedback/Evaluation

The system provides sound messages to reflect user's actions such as messages that inform the user for the correct or false completion of tasks. The messages "lead" users to the right direction in order to make the correct decision. The system tells the users orally and through text messages what they have to do and what the outcome will be at all stages of performance. Text messages are presented too, in order to build a relationship between images and words. For the evaluation of use, their performance is recorded, stored, and compared with past trials for the same story by the same user. Depending on the outcome of the evaluation, the system executes a reflective function by selecting the same story theme, but with different images. This is necessary given the need for skill generalization. Therefore, a new story is presented to make sure the learner has acquired the social skill being practiced independently of the particular sequence of images.

A "present" is given every time the user places an image in the correct place. Persons with ASD are very fond of animals (O'Haire, McKenzie, Beck, & Slaughter, 2013). So the system is designed to include an animated animal that places itself in a different area in the screen other than the user's working space, to prevent any distractions (Fig. 5). The user is given a different present for every story to avoid boredom. In the end of the session the user can save a collection of all animated animals in the system.

Following task completion, a result log is presented that contains the number of errors of the user and the duration of engagement in each task. This is a useful tool for comparing data to check for improvements between different trials of the same user (Fig. 6).

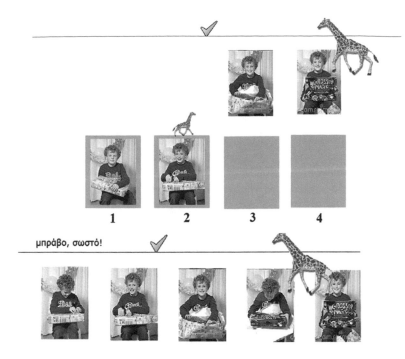

Fig. 5 A "present" is given every time user puts an image

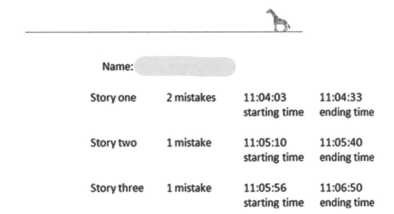

Fig. 6 Sample evaluation log with data about task performance

Pilot Application of Di.S.S.A.

A pilot application of Di.S.S.A. was carried out with four pupils (7–11 years) with a formal diagnosis of mild autism. Two aspects of the application were evaluated: user's satisfaction and user's task accomplishment. The evaluation was conducted in collaboration with the parents of the children and took place in their homes.

The researcher met with the parents to demonstrate the application and explain to them how to operate it. Each child used the system on their own with instructions and supervision by their parents, who had chosen the level of difficulty that was suitable for their own child. Each child learned three social skills by using DiSSA and three social skills with DS software for typically developing children. The software used is Photo Story by Microsoft that doesn't use steps when operated and its interface design is "busy" as it is addressing typically developing children. It is used to create a story but it does not accommodate features as correct sequence of images and subsequently a module of informing the user for the correct completion of tasks. The stories were aimed to teach them: (a) to cross a road, (b) to open a present, and (c) to wash their teeth.

Interviews with the parents were carried out by the first author of this chapter. In general, the findings were positive for both aspects of the application and all children with ASD reported that they enjoyed using the application. Their parents emphasized that their child had learned the sequence—stressing that story was easier than using printed images or other educational tools. They mentioned that their children showed a strong motivation to operate the application and seemed highly concentrated on the tasks. Also, they repeated patiently the whole procedure as often as it was required. In contrast, when they were asked to repeat the task with the DS software not specific for ASD, their parents had to spend more time to convince them to practice the repetition. Parents reported that their children appeared to view Di.S.S.A. much more like a game than as a learning tool. They particularly liked the animated "presents" and this function (to collect as many animals) motivated their engagement with the application.

One of the parents described user's experience as an enjoyable activity: "My son didn't want to leave the application. He liked using it."

The same parent added: "My son wanted to use it even after he did all three stories. He asked for more stories. I think he thought it is a game, maybe because he was getting the animated animal as presents when he was finishing a task and he wanted to get more presents."

Another parent reported that his son learned the sequence of images very easily comparing tasks with printed images that he had tried before. Also, he reported that his son considered the application as a game and not as a lesson. He said: "I think that my son wanted to get as many more animals as possible, I am not sure but I think that this is one of the reason he liked using DiSSA."

Another comment was the following: "My son got confused with the other software and I needed to stand by him all the time he was operating it. I needed to tell him every time he was placing an image if he used the right one. When I left him alone for a while he got upset."

In summary, the main findings of the pilot application were the following: (a) children with ASD liked more using Di.S.S.A. than the DS software nonspecific for ASD, (b) the structured style of presentation helped them maintain their attention on the task, (c) they could operate Di.S.S.A. almost independently, and (d) they learned the tasks given faster using Di.S.S.A comparing to the DS software nonspecific for ASD. The above are important findings for children with ASD as they address crucial elements in their learning process as these children have different learning characteristics than their typical peers. The special needs that complicate their learning are difficulties with verbal expression, difficulties with remembering verbal instructions, their short attention span, the lack of organizational skills, the difficulties to generalize the skills taught and to make transitions from one task to the other. Since Di.SS.A. utilizes greatly visual processing and presents information in a structured way through computer systems it carries the potential to be an appropriate method for teaching social skills to this special group of learners.

Following the positive outcomes of the pilot application, an intervention with more participants has been scheduled to take place, including persons with differing levels of autism severity.

Conclusions

Despite the changes of the format of narrative storytelling over the years, its purpose remains the same. Digital storytelling serves the same principles as the inclusion of new media using computer technology. The number of available DS systems is indicative of their importance for teaching academic and leisure skills. Their use, for learners in the autistic spectrum, has been introduced in the last decade and systems appropriate for this special group of learners need to be designed and evaluated.

Di.S.S.A is our first attempt to design DS software specifically for users with ASD. It utilizes components of Structured Teaching, such as minimal use of written messages and extensive use of images, for the instruction of social skills to persons with ASD which have been recommended as appropriate for students with ASD. Another useful feature for professionals and parents is the continuous evaluation which allows them to record user's competence in the learning task.

It is anticipated that the use of DS is a promising method for making learning more appealing, raising students' productivity and positive affect during individual or collaborative activities. Future work includes testing the application to a large number of people with AS, in different settings, targeting not only social skills but other skills too such as safety and hygiene skills and other learning subjects such as mathematics and history.

References

Barry, L., & Burlew, S. (2004). Using social stories to teach choice and play skills to children with autism. *Focus on Autism and Other Developmental Disabilities, 19*, 45–51.

Bernard-Opitz, V., Sriram, N., & Nakhoda-Sapuan, S. (1994). Enhancing social problem solving in children with autism and normal children through computer-assisted instruction. *Journal of Autism and Developmental Disorders, 31*, 377–384.

Burgess, J. E. (2006). Hearing ordinary voices: Cultural studies, vernacular creativity and digital storytelling. *Continuum: Journal of Media and Cultural Studies, 20*, 201–214.

Carlson, S., Mandell, D. J., & Williams, L. (2004). Executive function and theory of mind: Stability and prediction from ages 2 to 3. *Developmental Psychology, 40*, 1105–1122.

Carnahan, C., Musti-Rao, S., & Bailey, J. (2009, February). promoting active engagement in small group learning experiences for students with autism and significant learning needs. *Education and Treatment of Children, 32*(1), 37–61.

Carroll, N. (2001). On the narrative connection. In W. van Peer & S. Chatman (Eds.), *New perspectives on narrative perspective*. Albany, NY: SUNY Press.

Daigle, B., & Free, J. (2007). *Digital storytelling for students with Autism*. Invited presentation at the Annual Georgia Council For Exceptional Children Conference, Athens, GA. http://www.gacec.org/conference09.htm

Daigle, B., & Sulentic Dowell, M.-M. (2010). Can digital storytelling improve outcomes for students with autism? *Georgia Journal of Reading, 33*(1), 25–34.

Dick, W., & Carey, L. (1996). *The systematic design of instruction* (4th ed.). New York, NY: Haper Collins College Publishers.

Flippin, M., Reszka, S., & Watson, L. (2010, May). Effectiveness of the picture exchange communication system (PECS) on communication and speech for children with autism spectrum disorders: A meta-analysis. *American Journal of Speech-Language Pathology, 19*, 178–195. doi:10.1044/1058-0360(2010/09-002)

Gal, E., Goren-Bar, D., Gazit, E., Bauminger, N., Cappelletti, A., Pianesi, F., et al. (2005). Social communication through story-telling among high-functioning children with autism, intelligent technologies for interactive entertainment. *Lecture Notes in Computer Science, 3814*, 320–323.

Ganz, J. (2007). Classroom structuring methods and strategies for children and youth with autism spectrum disorders. *Exceptionality, 15*, 249–260.

Gershon, N., & Page, W. (2001). What storytelling can do for information visualization. *Communications of the ACM (CACM), 44*(8), 31–37.

Golan, O., & Baron-Cohen, S. (2006). Systemizing empathy: Teaching adults with Asperger syndrome or high-functioning autism to recognize complex emotions using interactive multimedia. *Development and Psychopathology, 18*, 591–617.

Gray, C. A. (1998). Social stories and comic strip conversations with students with Asperger syndrome and high functioning autism'. In E. Schopler, G. B. Mesibov, & L. J. Kunce (Eds.), *Asperger's syndrome or high-functioning autism?* (pp. 167–198). New York, NY: Plenum Press.

Gray, C. A., & Garand, J. D. (1993). Social stories: Improving responses of students with autism with accurate social information. *Focus on Autistic Behavior, 8*, 1–10.

Heo, M. (2009). Digital storytelling: An empirical study of the impact of digital storytelling on pre-service teachers' self efficacy and dispositions towards educational technology. *Journal of Educational Multimedia and Hypermedia, 18*(4), 405–428.

Hume, K., & Reynolds, B. (2010). Implementing work systems across the school day: Increasing engagement in students with autism spectrum disorders. *Preventing School Failure, 54*, 228–237.

Kolb, D. A. (1984). *Experiential learning: Experience as the source of learning and development*. Englewood Cliffs, NJ: Prentice-Hall.

Kulla-Abbott, T., & Polman, J. (2008). Engaging student voice and fulfilling curriculum goals with digital stories. *Technology, Humanities, Education & Narrative, 5*, 38–60.

Lathem, S. A. (2005). Learning communities and digital storytelling: New media for ancient tradition. In C. Crawford et al. (Eds.), *Proceedings of Society for Information Technology & Teacher Education International Conference 2005* (pp. 2286–2291). Chesapeake, VA: AACE.

Leshin, C. B., Pollock, J., & Reigeluth, C. M. (1992). *Instructional design strategies and tactics*. Englewood Cliffs, NJ: Education Technology Publications.

Levin, B. B. (2003). *Case studies of teacher development: An in-depth look at how thinking about pedagogy develops over time*. Mahwah, NJ: L. Erlbaum Associates.

Li, L. (2007). Digital storytelling: Bridging traditional and digital literacies. In T. Bastiaens & S. Carliner (Eds.), *Proceedings of World Conference on E-Learning in Corporate, Government, Healthcare, and Higher Education 2007* (pp. 6201–6206). Chesapeake, VA: AACE.

Lindsey-Glenn, P. F., & Gentry, J. E. (2008). Improving vocabulary skills through assistive technology: Rick's story. *TEACHING Exceptional Children Plus, 5*(2) Article 1. Retrieved November 19, 2013, from http://escholarship.bc.edu/education/tecplus/vol5/iss2/art1

McClannahan, L., & Krantz, P. (1997). In search of solutions to prompt dependence: Teaching children with autism to use photographic activity schedules. In E. M. Pinkston & D. M. Baer (Eds.), *Environment and behavior* (pp. 271–278). Boulder, CO: Westview Press.

Meadows, D. (2003). Digital storytelling: Research-based practice in new media. *Visual Communication, 2*, 189–193.

Mesibov, G. B., Shea, V., & Schopler, E. (2005). *The TEACCH approach to autism spectrum disorders*. New York, NY: Kluwer.

Mineo, B. A., Ziegler, W., Gill, S., & Salkin, D. (2008). Engagement with electronic screen media among students with autism spectrum disorders. *Journal of Autism and Developmental Disorders, 39*, 172–187.

Moore, D. J., McGrath, P., & Thorpe, J. (2000). Computer aided learning for people with autism—a framework for research and development. *Innovations in Education and Training International, 37*, 218–228.

More, C. (2008, January). Digital stories targeting social skills for children with disabilities multidimensional learning. *Intervention in School and Clinic, 43*(3), 168–177.

O'Haire, M., McKenzie, S., Beck, A., & Slaughter, V. (2013). Social behaviors increase in children with autism in the presence of animals compared to toys. *PLoS One, 8*(2), e57010. doi:10.1371/journal.pone.0057010.

O'Neill, L. M., & Dalton, B. (2002). Thinking readers, Part II: Supporting beginning reading in students with cognitive disabilities through technology. *The Exceptional Parent, 32*, 40–43.

Odom, S., Collet-Klingenberg, L., Rogers, S. J., & Hatton, D. (2010). Evidence-based practices in interventions for children and youth with autism spectrum disorders. *Preventing School Failure, 54*(4), 275–282.

Pellicano, E. (2007). Links between theory of mind and executive function in young children with autism: Clues to developmental primacy. *Developmental Psychology, 43*, 974–990.

Rajendran, G., & Mitchell, P. (2007). Cognitive theories of autism. *Developmental Review, 27*, 224–260.

Robin, B. (2006). The educational uses of digital storytelling. In C. Crawford et al. (Eds.), *Proceedings of Society for Information Technology and Teacher Education International Conference 2006* (pp. 709–716). Chesapeake, VA: AACE.

Sadik, A. (2008). Digital storytelling: A meaningful technology-integrated approach for engaged students learning. *Educational Technology Research and Development, 56*(4), 487–506.

Sansosti, F. J., Powell-Smith, K. A., & Kincaid, D. (2004). A research synthesis of social story interventions for children with autism spectrum disorders. *Focus on Autism and Other Developmental Disabilities, 19*, 194–204.

Scholes, R. (1981). Language, narrative, and anti-narrative. In W. J. T. Mitchell (Ed.), *On narrative* (pp. 200–208). Chicago, IL: University of Chicago Press.

Stromer, R., & Kimball, J. W. (2004). Translating behavioral research into improved educational services for children with autism. In J. E. Burgos & E. Ribes (Eds.), *Theory, basic and applied research, and technological applications in behavior science: Conceptual and methodological issues* (Proceedings of the Eighth Biannual Guadalajara Symposium on the Science of Behavior, pp. 179–208). Guadalajara, Mexico: University of Guadalajara.

Stromer, R., Kimball, J. W., Kinney, E., & Taylor, B. (2006). Activity schedules, computer technology, and teaching children with autism spectrum disorders. *Focus on Autism and Other Developmental Disabilities, 21*, 14.

Swanson, H. L., & Hoskyn, M. (1998). Experimental intervention research on students with learning disabilities: A meta-analysis of treatment outcomes. *Review of Educational Research, 68*, 277–321.

Tanaka, J. W., Wolf, J. M., Klaiman, C., Koenig, K., Cockburn, J., Herlihy, L., et al. (2010). Using computerized games to teach face recognition skills to children with autism spectrum disorder: The Let's Face It! Program. *The Journal of Child Psychology and Psychiatry, 51*, 944–952.

Tartaro, A. (2005). Storytelling with a virtual peer as an intervention for children with autism. In *Proceedings: ASSETS 2005* (pp. 42–44). ACM Press.

Valkanova, Y., & Watts, M. (2007). Digital story telling in a science classroom: reflective self-learning (RSL) in action. *Early Child Development and Care, 177*(6–7), 793–807.

Velleman, D. (2003). Narrative explanation. *Philosophical Review, 112*, 1–25.

Welton, E., Vakil, S., & Carasea, C. (2004). Strategies for increasing positive social interactions in children with autism: A case study. *Teaching Exceptional Children, 37*, 40–46.

Williams, C., Wright, B., Callaghan, G., & Coughlan, B. (2002). Do children with autism learn to read more readily by computer assisted instruction or traditional book methods? A pilot study. *Autism, 6*, 71–91.

Worth, S. (2005). Narrative knowledge: Knowing through storytelling. In *Proceedings of the Fourth Media in Transition Conference*. Cambridge, MA: MIT Press.

Yuksel, P., Robin, B., & McNeil, S. (2011). Educational uses of digital storytelling around the world. In M. Koehler & P. Mishra (Eds.), *Proceedings of Society for Information Technology & Teacher Education International Conference 2011* (pp. 1264–1271). Chesapeake, VA: AACE.

Index

C. Karagiannidis et al. (eds.), *Research on e-Learning and ICT*   301
in Education: Technological, Pedagogical and Instructional Perspectives,
DOI 10.1007/978-1-4614-6501-0, © Springer Science+Business Media New York 2014

Printed by Printforce, the Netherlands